AIR CASTLE OF THE SOUTH

WSM and the Making of Music City

CRAIG HAVIGHURST

University of Illinois Press

Urbana and Chicago

Library of Congress Cataloging-in-Publication Data
Havighurst, Craig.
Air castle of the South : WSM and the making of
Music City / Craig Havighurst.
p.   cm. — (Music in American life)
Includes bibliographical references (p.) and index.
ISBN-13 978-0-252-03257-8 (cloth : alk. paper)
ISBN-10 0-252-03257-8 (cloth : alk. paper)
1. WSM (Radio station : Nashville, Tenn.)
2. Radio broadcasting—Tennessee—Nashville—History.
I. Title.
PN1991.3.U6H38   2007
791.4409768'55—dc22   2007011425

FOR MOM, DAD, AND TAYLOR

It seems to me the radio's like drink;
it just gets a hold on you.

—Margery Allingham

It was not the city we once knew.

—Jesse Wills

Contents

Illustrations follow page 120

Acknowledgments

This book began to take shape thanks to the kindness of Wade Jessen and Kyle Cantrell, both of whom shared time and information with me many years ago when I had nothing to offer them but questions about country music, radio, and Nashville. They offered me an overview of WSM's remarkable story, encouraged me to dig deeper, and offered dozens of potential sources.

Space doesn't allow such specific reasons for my appreciation toward the rest of the people who put their faith in me and this project, but for support of one kind or another I offer my sincerest thanks to: Eddie Stubbs, Bud Wendell, Neil Craig, Debbie Craig, Margaret Ann Robinson, Elizabeth Proctor, Ward DeWitt, Sykes DeWitt, Cary Allyn, Ralph Emery, Charlie Lamb, Allen Reynolds, Paul Corbin, Paul Kingsbury, Don Cusic, Ronnie Pugh, Richard Peterson, Brenda Colladay, Pam Matthews, Robert K. Oermann, Ridley Wills II, D and Mary Jane Kilpatrick, Tom and Billie Perryman, Les and Dot Leverett, Howard and Ruth White, Leroy Troy and family, Margaret Parker, Donia Craig Dickerson, Liz Ferrell, Jo Walker-Meador, Jud Collins, John Rumble, Watt Hairston, Harold Bradley, Frances Preston, Bill Berry, Mac Wiseman, John and Delores Seigenthaler, Ken Paulson, Jerry Strobel, Bill Cody, Gary and Peggy Walker, Chet Flippo, Robert Ikard, Liz Thiels, Jay Orr, Ellen Pryor, Jack Hurst, Clay Bradley, Connie Bradley, Jerry Bradley, Patsy Bradley, Bill Carey, Micki Estes, Carl Kornmeyer, Bill Denny, Beegie Adair, Cal Young, Beverly LeCroy, David Hall, Dick Frank Jr., Don Cook, Eddie Jones, Elmer Alley, George Reynolds Jr., Harrianne Condra, Joe Layne, John Hartford, Matt Combs, Larry Munson, Teddy Bart, Tom Adkinson, Dr. Reavis Mitchell, Dr. Paul Kwami, Mike Armistead, Marty Stuart, Dick Hill, William D. Jackson, Doug Seroff, Dave Black, James Foust, Michelle Hilmes, Peter Guralnick, Trudy Stamper, Walt Trott, Karen Hicks, Liz Norris, Caroline Davis, Jerry Bailey, Bob Tubert, Kevin Lamb, Jim Foglesong, Tandy Rice, Mary Ann McCready, Paul Wells, Bruce Nemerov, Beth Curley, Christina Melton, Bart Herbison, and Ed Salamon.

Fellow scribes and editors who have offered knowledge and friendship and have helped this project along include Tim Ghianni, Peter Cooper, Linda Zettler, Bill Choyke, Brad Schmitt, Jeanne Naujeck, Brad Schrade, Michael Gray, Craig Shelburne, Alanna Nash, Steve Betts, Michael McCall, Bill Friskics-Warren, Barry Mazor, Lucas Hendrickson, Jack Silverman, and Jon Weisberger.

Several key contributors passed away during the work on the book, and they are dearly missed: Dr. Charles K. Wolfe, Irving Waugh, Aaron Shelton, Buddy Killen, Marge Kirby, and Marjorie Cooney.

For a careful reading of and invaluable feedback on the manuscript, I must thank my old friend and mentor Barry Yeoman and my father Clark Havighurst, who did his best to teach me how to write in the first place. I am forever grateful.

I offer special thanks to the staff of the Nashville Room at the Nashville Public Library, where I was granted an invaluable writer's room and where everybody let me take advantage of them in my search for the heart of Music City.

And finally, very special thanks to Tamara Saviano, the über-believer.

Introduction

THE MUSE OF MUSIC CITY

On the bitter cold morning of January 8, 2002, a grassy berm at the sprawling interchange of Briley Parkway and McGavock Pike in Nashville, Tennessee, became an impromptu grandstand for protesters. More than one hundred citizens waved signs, clapped their mittens, and urged passing motorists to honk in support of traditional country music. "Keep country alive!" they chanted. "Keep country alive!" Singing legend George Jones drove up to voice support from behind the wheel of his SUV. Local honky-tonk glam character Melba Toast shouted in the wind from beneath her outlandish, platinum bouffant wig.

The rally pitched its message toward the seven-lane street and the depressed motel, fast food, and outlet mall development across it. But the protesters' ire was directed over their shoulders, at a huge tourism and shopping complex encompassing the Gaylord Opryland Resort and Convention Center (formerly the Opryland Hotel), the Grand Ole Opry House, Opry Mills shopping mall, and, immediately behind them, the offices and studios of 650 AM WSM, the most influential and exceptional radio station in the history of country music.

They were angry because Gaylord Entertainment, the Nashville company that owned WSM and the Grand Ole Opry itself, had decided internally to drop the station's classic country music format for an all sports/talk diet. The sounds of Johnny Cash, Tammy Wynette, Loretta Lynn, Buck Owens, and Patsy Cline were to be replaced with call-in shows about NASCAR and the city's new professional football team, the Tennessee Titans. The Grand Ole

Opry, the longest-running show in broadcasting history, was to move off WSM-AM for the first time in seventy-five years and join the Saturday night lineup of WSM-FM, a station that played only new country hits.

Gaylord was making significant investments in the Opry, and it had successfully renovated the Ryman Auditorium downtown, but in this third American institution, the company's new CEO saw a radio station with ratings and profits that were less impressive than its history. Many in the city weren't ready for such cold calculus. News of the planned format change, which had leaked to the local newspaper around Christmas, riled traditional country music fans and historically minded Nashvillians. They felt they'd seen too many icons of the city's country music past shuttered, sold, or torn down in recent years, including Opryland USA, the wooded music and amusement park Gaylord had razed in 1998 to build the enormous Opry Mills mall. Nine thousand people from around the world signed an Internet petition to "keep WSM country." Opry stars like Vince Gill and Marty Stuart publicly and personally implored Gaylord executives not to unplug country music and bluegrass from WSM, the very origin of the music's successes in Nashville. The daily newspaper editorialized that to do so would "seriously alter the sound and identity of Music City."

The protesters weren't in front of WSM to harangue it. They were there to protect it, the way a family rallies around a loved one in trouble. WSM's staff was under orders to stay inside and not talk to the media. Somebody from the Opry's corporate office did, however, send out hot coffee for everyone.

"Music City USA," Nashville's world-famous nickname, was coined at WSM. And country music defines Nashville to the world. But when announcer David Cobb ad-libbed the slogan on the air in 1950, he wasn't talking about country music per se or the country music business, because there scarcely was such a thing in Nashville at the time. Instead, from his fifth-floor perch at this Southern radio powerhouse, Cobb surveyed a remarkable music scene. It was diverse, sophisticated, and commercially viable—underdeveloped perhaps, but rich in local talent and nationally relevant at the same time. To be sure, country music was enjoying its first great nationwide heyday, with an astonishing cast of legends and would-be legends at work, including Hank Williams at the top of his game. And a new, jazz-influenced offshoot of country that would come to be known as bluegrass was in full blaze. But Cobb would have also told you about WSM maestro Francis Craig, whose "Near You" had been the top pop record of 1947, or about Pee Wee King, a Polish American Grand Ole Opry star from Milwaukee, whose song "Tennessee Waltz" would soon become a national smash for pop singer Patti Page. Cobb was even pals with the song publishers about to make a small fortune from it.

Cobb's friends and colleagues had left marks on Broadway and at the Metropolitan Opera. Dinah Shore, a WSM alum, had been a major star for a decade, and fellow singer Snooky Lanson was poised to join the highly visible radio/television show *Your Hit Parade*. Owen Bradley conducted superb bands, on the air and in local night clubs, years before he would produce smash records by Patsy Cline and Brenda Lee. Nashville was home to important black gospel groups, such as the Fisk Jubilee Singers and the Fairfield Four; the renowned Ryman Auditorium; the War Memorial Auditorium; and a fine symphony orchestra. Depending on what time of the week it was, David Cobb himself was a classical disc jockey, a pop music show host, and an announcer on the Grand Ole Opry.

WSM, "The Air Castle of the South," embraced, cultivated, and evangelized on behalf of all of these disparate styles and artists. In its most influential years, when a modern music industry was maturing in Nashville between the 1940s and the 1960s, WSM was, in the words of music journalist/promoter Charlie Lamb, "the emperor of all." The station's leaders and employees were no mere bystanders in the development of Nashville as a music center. They instigated the revolution, nurturing a talent-rich Middle Tennessee town into a show-business phenomenon—a city with the soul of a singer, songwriter, and entertainer. WSM did more than merely give Music City its name; it nurtured Nashville's pioneering music entrepreneurs. Its employees and alumni launched the city's first recording studios, its first successful independent record company, its first music publishing companies, and its first independent talent agency. Owen Bradley, Nashville's legendary producer, said his many years at WSM were his "college," preparing him for all he achieved on Music Row. "The influence of WSM on the city of Nashville is unique in the annals of broadcasting," wrote the show business trade magazine *Variety* in 1969. "Over a period of forty-four years, dating from the first broadcast of 'Grand Ole Opry,' the radio station has had a profound effect on the character and international image of the city it serves." That city didn't easily welcome or adapt to its new image and industry. But therein lies a tale.

WSM was first turned on in October of 1925, thanks to the efforts of Edwin Craig, a vice president of the National Life and Accident Insurance Company. A genteel and conservative man, Craig was heir apparent to a genteel and conservative firm, built and owned by a partnership involving five Tennessee families.

The company came to broadcasting reluctantly, intending only to promote a slogan—"We Shield Millions"—and generate good will in its community and among its potential customer base. But National Life and Accident lived up to its oddly providential name and spawned a chain of happy accidents for American culture. As the century unfolded, WSM more than met its stated goals of broadcasting professionalism, corporate promotion, and community service, while its unintended consequences proved historic. It gave voice to a city already brimming with musical talent and cultural ambitions. It nurtured and attracted a still larger pool of artists, writers, and entrepreneurs, many of whom were drawn to Nashville by WSM's electromagnetic force. As the enterprise grew, the station and its owners embraced and shaped a series of platforms during the slow dawning of the media age: radio, television, syndication, cable, the Internet, satellite radio, and more.

WSM is most famous—and justifiably so—as a promoter of country music and as a midwife to the modern country music industry. In 2001, *Radio & Records* magazine, a leading trade publication, named WSM country music's "Radio Station of the Twentieth Century." And historians have ably documented the Grand Ole Opry's rise from a local, unpretentious Saturday night radio show to its pinnacle of star-making power. But the Grand Ole Opry may well have lived and died like so many on-air "barn dances" of the 1920s through the 1960s had WSM not been a remarkable broadcaster in its own right. WSM's investment in talent discovery and development across many types of music built a sturdy foundation on which country music could build its permanent home in the otherwise inhospitable terrain of Nashville, Tennessee.

"A city of schools and churches," is how a character in a novel by Tennessee writer Peter Taylor described Nashville of the 1920s. It was a place, she said, "where phrases like 'well bred' and 'well born' were always ringing in one's ears and where distinctions between 'genteel people' and 'plain people' were made and where there was almost constant talk about who was a gentleman and who wasn't a gentleman." In 1927 Donald Davidson, a Vanderbilt-based writer and critic, called on Nashvillians to cultivate "a provincialism of the high-minded sort, which made Athens great."

Davidson may have been alluding to Athens of classical antiquity, but he was talking about Nashville, the self-described "Athens of the South." At a time when outsiders like the acerbic H. L. Mencken dismissed the South as a benighted "Sahara of the Bozart," Nashville saw itself as an oasis of learning and culture. The city's main park was graced with a full-scale replica of the Greek Parthenon. Downtown, a new Athenian memorial to honor war heroes included a concert hall for a burgeoning symphony orchestra. Next to that was the 1859 state capitol, whose cupola was designed after the choragic monument to Lysicrates, a site in ancient Athens where awards were given for dancing and singing. "Rival cities like Memphis, Birmingham, or Atlanta may have overshadowed Nashville in their commercial and industrial might," wrote city historian Don Doyle, "but perhaps for that reason, none cultivated the arts and letters that Nashville boasted."

At the same time, Nashvillians believed what they believed. That summer of 1925, Clarence Darrow and William Jennings Bryan squared off just down the road in Dayton, Tennessee, over John Thomas Scopes's right to teach Charles Darwin's theory of evolution. The trial became a national spectacle, a larger-than-life drama that magnified and focused America's deep ideological struggle between traditionalism and modernism. The outcome was ambiguous. Schools and churches indeed.

That is to say that when WSM first went on the air, nobody outside of Nashville could have predicted, and few inside of Nashville would have wished, that the city would become a haven for show business, something that until then was only on big city résumés. Songs were written and published in New York and Chicago. Movies came from Hollywood. If the nation had a country music business center, it was arguably Atlanta, a town nearly twice the size of Nashville. Yet by 1950, Nashville's first music entrepreneurs had taken root. One explosive decade later, Nashville was the second busiest recording center in America. By 2000 Music City had launched some of the best-selling solo artists in history. Today it claims a heritage worthy of a major museum, big-time press coverage, and regular scholarly symposia. WSM, and its direct broadcasting progeny, The Nashville Network (TNN), can claim a mighty share of inspiring, imagining, and supporting that success.

This transition from religious and academic bastion to show town took place over eight decades, in a dance between station and city that moved in tempo with the times, even if (this being the South) they sometimes lagged a bit behind the beat. Nashville encountered the Depression, World War II, the fifties boom, the Civil Rights Movement, and every other large social movement of the twentieth century in ways unique to its geography and its society. Much of that dramatic history played out over the WSM airwaves, sometimes vividly, sometimes with blinders on. As the property of white, wealthy owners, WSM reflected its segregated southern surroundings, internally and on-air. African

American music, so crucial to the roots of country, was marginalized at WSM, almost certainly making country whiter than it might have been. Moreover, though WSM was a news station with a small army of reporters in the 1950s and 1960s, it downplayed the Civil Rights Movement, even as critical early developments took place blocks from National Life's WSM headquarters.

Yet in later years, WSM's essential, ingrained conservatism may have preserved its best qualities, helping it survive buffeting changes in broadcasting and the music business, as they evolved from cottage industries to global, intertwined oligopolies. WSM-AM, despite the high winds kicked up by the world rushing past it, remains locally owned and music driven, making it exceptional among the first big American radio stations.

Broadcasting, reminds historian Michele Hilmes, "brought together some of the most powerful agents in the transformation of American culture in the twentieth century—technology, advertising, big business, the federal government, mass audiences, home, and family—and combined them in ways that had never before been possible." That is just as true locally as nationally. Nashville and WSM shaped each other profoundly, as they traded information, values, money, power and—most seductively—music. It's curious that Hilmes doesn't include music in her list, because through the long reign of radio and even through the television era, music over the air changed American life, sparking social movements and political upheavals. It has given us vocabulary, perspective, and fashion, and it has provoked millions of us to dream, to dance, to write, and to perform. Only when we consider the power of music, with its pervasive, shape-shifting claim on our emotions, can we begin to understand why a city would rally to the defense of an AM radio station on the verge of something as ordinary in the modern media age as a format change.

I first became fascinated with WSM when I moved to Nashville in 1996 and began asking questions about country music, which I had recently fallen in love with, and the country music business, which was then coming down from its highest of all highs, the blockbuster global success of Garth Brooks and Shania Twain. For many, the genre of country had never been healthier or cooler in the public eye. For others, country music had been co-opted by pop music sounds, mainstream fads, and unrealistic industry expectations. This schism over the heart and soul of country music seemed packed with insight into American culture, art, and enterprise. Both interpretations could be reasonably defended, but the distance between the two sides was perplexing. Most of my questions about what exactly had happened here led to the music's relationship with radio, and questions about country radio in Nashville led inevitably to WSM.

Great, I thought, there must be a book. And yet for all the writing about country music's past, no single work drew a line from WSM's origins to Nashville's golden age, let alone to that winter morning's protest against one more act of collective forgetting. Thus the impulse for this book. The inspiration to follow through came when I began talking to the elder statesmen and stateswomen of the industry, for it was clear that they believed WSM should be remembered as well. I was deluged with affection, passion, and memories. I have tried to sift and sort their stories into a narrative that strolls through the twentieth century, inviting the reader to decide whether an AM radio station can be a sacred thing, whether the folk art of country music is alive and well, and whether Nashville gets the attention and respect it deserves in conversations about American entertainment culture.

Nashville's quest for its own destiny is a great American story that feels like biography. So heeding Ralph Waldo Emerson's observation that "there is properly no history, only biography," that's how I've approached the subject. WSM is now a character to me, a life made of its composite influences, its accomplishments, and history's grander sweep. At more than eighty years of age, WSM feels sometimes like a shrinking light that may or may not revive for another act. For now, it asks only that we acknowledge its accumulated wisdom and listen to its story.

ONE ⚡ *On the Very Air We Breathe*

Dr. Clayton E. Crosland, associate vice president of one of the Southeast's finest finishing schools, wasn't precisely sure what to say, but he did not wish to be misunderstood.

"*This is Ward-Belmont, Nashville,*" he said, a bit too loudly, into his "microphone."

The contraption wasn't entirely foreign—quite like a telephone without the ear-piece—but it was *most* modern. After a pause, Crosland spelled out the name of the school, as if to make sure: "*W-A-R-D—B-E-L-M-O-N-T.*"

He continued, "*We have today installed a radio sending station and will tonight broadcast the concert by Mr. Philip Gordon, the distinguished American pianist.*"

Crosland may have been on the air, but he was also on a stage. In the auditorium before him, a large gathering of poised young ladies in ruffles and bows, some attended by their even more put together mothers and fathers, canted forward in hushed curiosity, taking it on faith that Dr. Crosland's voice was, in fact, spiriting out through the open air and reaching somebody—up to two hundred miles away, they'd been led to understand. Center stage, beneath a grand piano, sat two more microphones. Black cables converged at stage left, where a rolltop desk held glowing vacuum tubes and black machinery, all connected to a wire that ran out into a hallway and up to the roof.

The assembler of this electrical conduit, a sixteen-year-old with a severe haircut and a long jaw, stood off to the side. He was listening through hard plastic headphones plugged into a warm monitoring amplifier of his own construction. John H. DeWitt Jr., "Jack" as he was called, was well known to Crosland and the other school officials. He lived just a block away, in the shady green bower of Belmont Heights, a brow of hill capped by the wedding-cake splendor of Ward-Belmont's campus with its fountains and statues. By this evening, in the spring of 1922, he was well established as the local radio boy. The broadcasting antenna he built in his back yard was a neighborhood landmark. He rode around on a bicycle rigged with electrical gear and a spiderweb antenna, listening to his friends transmit from his homebuilt sending station. Jack had already visited the Ward-Belmont campus two years before, when he demonstrated his wireless telegraph to the girls of the Agora Club. He had tuned in and decoded odd, buzzing dots and dashes from as far away as the Great Lakes, which the young ladies had found "novel and unusual."

Moreover, as Dr. Crosland well knew, Jack's family meant a great deal to the school itself. His mother was Rebekah Williams Ward, whose father William was the *Ward* in *Ward-Belmont*. He had founded Ward Seminary, a finishing school that merged in 1913 with Belmont School. Hailed as one of the finest academies for Southern women, Ward-Belmont rarely trafficked in things futuristic, yet here it was making local history. WDAA, as it was called, was the third radio station licensed in Tennessee and the first in Nashville.

The recital by Mr. Gordon was enthusiastically received, and before it was over four or five messages came in through the school's telephone switchboard from people who were picking up the program clearly and with great satisfaction.

The news sent a flush of surprise and wonder through the auditorium. Invisible waves really were spreading out from the school's roof like ripples in an ethereal pond— racing north right through the walls of the sturdy homes on Sixteenth and Seventeenth Avenues and over the noisy automobile and trolley traffic of downtown. They rippled east, across Centennial Park with its mute, majestic Parthenon; west, across the Civil War battlements of Fort Negley; and south, to Franklin, Brentwood, and dozens of surrounding burgs.

The waves radiated out to and over the city's hilly perimeter and across vast acreages of the farms, verdant forests, and meandering creeks of Middle Tennessee. They crackled against the bell towers of the city's mighty universities—all-white Vanderbilt and all-black Fisk. They outran the steam locomotives that pulled passengers and freight out of the city toward Cincinnati,

Louisville, St. Louis, Atlanta, and points beyond. They pierced the miasma of oily smog that roiled up out of the railroad gulch and cloaked the clock tower of Union Station. They ricocheted off the broad shingle roof of the Ryman Auditorium. They raced up and down the serpentine Cumberland River, which churned with paddle wheelers, packet boats, and cargo barges. They went unnoticed by the evangelists and anarchists who bellowed and proselytized where Broadway, the city's aortal artery, terminated at First Avenue and the river. They overpassed the shacks and flophouses of Black Bottom, the African American ghetto south of Broadway, which rang with blues music and violence. They moved at the speed of light, carrying a message of unstoppable change.

"I think my interest in radio broadcasting first came about when I heard my first voice over the air," wrote Jack DeWitt, years after he retired as president of WSM, Inc. "I believe that was 1920. Dr. Frank Conrad, who was chief engineer of the Westinghouse Company, had a ham radio station in Pittsburgh, 8XK, which later became the famous KDKA." From Nashville, DeWitt could listen as Conrad talked with other broadcasting pioneers, just as radio was evolving from talk among hobbyists or "hams" to broadcasting stations aimed at the general public, of which KDKA was one of the first. Radio was a magic thing for DeWitt, a mixture of romance and science that captured him early, and he soon discovered he wasn't alone.

DeWitt was born February 20, 1906, to a Vanderbilt-educated lawyer, some six years into his practice. Household passions included history and music. They had an Edison cylinder phonograph and later a gramophone record player, along with a record collection that reflected the era's best sellers—Enrico Caruso, Antonio Scotti, and John McCormack. These tenors had voices that could cut through the limited fidelity of the early 78-rpm records, and they stirred in Jack a lifelong love of opera. "I really don't see how anyone can live properly and comfortably without some music around part of the time," DeWitt wrote years later. Although he was very much expected to make something of himself, he felt no pressure to follow his father into law. "I would have been no good as a lawyer," he said. "I was interested in radio from the beginning, and my mother and father helped me."

Jack wanted to know how things worked, especially things electrical. At age seven, he fixed the doorbell of a neighbor, who wrote him a check for a dollar. When he was twelve, Jack earned a Boy Scout merit badge for wireless telegraphy, constructing his first crystal receiver with a wire coiled around the family rolling pin. (The cook had to roll out biscuit dough with a syrup bottle for a time.) By 1921, DeWitt was transmitting in Morse code over a homebuilt transmitter, reaching people in Oklahoma, Louisiana, and Illinois. He confirmed the reach of his set as part of a trial conducted by the American Radio Relay League, which dispatched a man to Scotland to see how many U.S. stations he could pick up. There, in the records of the test, were DeWitt's call letters, 5FV. In the Dewitt backyard, Jack and a friend built a tower that he recalled being sixty or seventy feet high. It supported a wire antenna strung to a pole on the roof of the house, and it worked until the day a mule being used to dig a swimming pool in the yard next door tripped over one of the guy wires and sent the whole thing crashing to the ground. Easily rebuilt, it served for many months as DeWitt's chief antenna, while he delved further into transmitters that could send voices through a microphone. He taught himself higher-order mathematics and electrical engineering. He kept notes of his contacts in Tennessee and well beyond. He made friends over the wireless and then had them over for long nights of sending and receiving. Mrs. DeWitt would call upstairs in the morning to ask how many for breakfast.

DeWitt and his friends were part of a national movement, fueled by "the genius of the American boy," as then Secretary of Commerce Herbert Hoover famously put it. All over the nation, wrote Erik Barnouw, "amateur-made transmitters were suddenly leaving garages, attics, and chicken coops, and some of them were turning up on the roofs of newspapers, department stores, hotels, factories." KDKA's debut in late 1920 broadcast election returns, ushering in the era of instant news. In the middle of 1921, the nation marveled at blow-by-blow coverage of a Jack Dempsey fight from Jersey City. In 1922, WEAF, a New York station owned and operated by RCA, broadcast the first commercially sponsored show, a pitch for apartments from real estate brokers in Queens.

Soon the air overflowed with signals. When DeWitt became chairman of the electrical committee of the local radio club, he participated in contentious meetings about who could broadcast at what hours. "Civil war almost broke out in Nashville with the advent of the early commercial radio sets," wrote one early magazine profiler of DeWitt. "An enthusiast would have his earphones clamped on listening to the latest jazz or an obscure newscast when his ears would be assaulted by the powerful dot and dash signals of the local short wave operators." Cities began implementing weekly "quiet nights" when local stations had to remain off so enthusiasts could receive distant stations with less interference. Yet interference was part of the price of listening in.

As fast as the air filled with broadcasts, it filled with utopian predictions. *Radio Broadcast* magazine speculated that "elected representatives will not be able to evade their responsibilities to those who put them in office" and that a "people's University of the Air will have a greater student body than all of our universities put together." When opening one of the many new college-based stations that sparked on during the fall of 1922, North Carolina statesman and future newspaper publisher Josephus Daniels predicted that with radio, "nobody now fears that a Japanese fleet could deal an unexpected blow to our Pacific possessions. . . . Radio makes surprises impossible." Naive but optimistic, pundits portrayed radio to Nashvillians as a new wonder of the world. "What a day for dreamers!" declared syndicated columnist William Ellis in the *Banner*. "The radiophone has outrun prophesy; already we see that it holds possibilities of transforming almost the entire organization of human life upon this planet. . . . The whole earth is made one neighborhood."

Ward-Belmont's WDAA "broadcast on an irregular basis" for about six months, DeWitt recounted later. "When some prominent speaker or artist appeared at the school, a microphone was placed in front of him and the proceedings could be heard over a fairly wide area around Nashville." The school's voice teacher, Gaetano de Luca, took pleasure in playing Caruso records over the air from his Victrola. It was a modest legacy to be sure, but with stations coming and going like lightning bugs on a summer's evening, it wasn't long before further opportunities presented themselves, including one with a young man whom Jack would know, not always cordially, for decades.

His name was Harry Stone, a polished and ambitious man in his early twenties who had recently moved with his family from North Carolina, where his father had owned a Coca-Cola bottling plant. In Nashville, Harry and his younger brother David worked in their father's machine shop, but they were drawn to entertainment. Whereas David branched out with jobs in local theater companies, Harry began to forge a career in radio in a town virtually without radio by teaming up with the right people and by launching his own stations. He approached Jack about starting a radio station for a men's organization called the American Business Club.

Jack obtained a license for the call letters WABV, giving him permission to convert his ham radio rig into a full-service broadcaster. His ever-supportive parents bore most of the costs of Nashville's second radio station. Mrs. DeWitt sold her Dominicker hens and let Jack convert the family chicken coop into a transmitter house. The boys nudged furniture aside and set up microphones in the drawing room. A family diary noted the first broadcast on December 7, 1923. Mack Rowe, owner of a phonograph shop, played violin, accompanied by a friend on the DeWitt's upright piano. They played contemporary popular songs ("My Sweetie Went Away," "End of a Perfect Day," and "My Buddy") and light opera numbers from *Cavalleria Rusticana*. Jack's friend from radio overnights, George Reynolds, acted as assistant engineer. And Jack's brother Ward stepped up as announcer for the broadcasts. Before long, Stone recruited two of the town's young orchestra leaders—Francis Craig and Beasley Smith—to set up their groups in the cramped quarters. A prize of $5 for the furthest reception of the 50-watt station was claimed by a listener in Pennsylvania.

Jack DeWitt, George Reynolds, Harry Stone, Francis Craig, and Beasley Smith would soon form the core of a far more professional and permanent radio station. But there would be a few more stops along the way for DeWitt. He was approached by one W. A. Marks, who, like many others then and since, was inspired to spread the word of God over the air. Marks, a member of the Business Men's Sunday School Class at the First Baptist Church in downtown Nashville, secured volunteers from his class and put up $1,500 to launch a station, which Jack built. It debuted with a Sunday morning service on April 6, 1924. Its call letters stood for the Baptists' penchant for evangelizing: WCBQ—"We Can't Be Quiet."

That spring DeWitt graduated with honors from Duncan School and set out on his first worldly adventure. He applied to the United Fruit Company for a job as second radio operator on a ship. He was assigned to the S.S. *Ellis* out of Tela, Honduras, a cargo boat with a Norwegian crew, which mainly hauled bananas from Central America to New Orleans. On his maiden voyage, which lasted just two or three weeks, the eighteen-year-old witnessed his rum-buzzed commanders slipping upstairs with Jamaican prostitutes, turned down a proposition from a woman who wanted to give Jack a pet monkey in exchange for sex, and became violently seasick after eating green bananas on the trip home. "I decided sea was not for me," he wrote later.

When he entered Vanderbilt that fall, DeWitt wasn't ready to set aside his passion for radio to apply himself to courses in trigonometry, French, and history. There was no electrical engineering for freshmen, and what there was looked irrelevant—civil engineering, street car electrical systems, and other tedium. He continued to build radios and improve the ones he'd built, and in his second term, he was suspended for academic indolence. He completed some make-up courses in the summer, but after a floundering fall in his sophomore year, he dropped out.

From father DeWitt's point of view, there was only one, depressing recourse: Jack would have to enroll at the University of Tennessee in Knoxville, 180 miles east. It would be a minor embarrassment to the family, but perhaps no worse than Jack's leaving school altogether. "It was almost expected for local boys growing up in Nashville in the early part of the twentieth century to go to Vanderbilt," says Jack's nephew Ward DeWitt Jr., a Vanderbilt alumnus, whose grandfather and great-uncle also attended the school. "There was a great chasm between Vanderbilt and the U of T in those days. I remember my daddy saying, 'Son we don't just dislike the University of Tennessee. We *hate* 'em.' It was a big thing."

Jack fared no better at UT. "I became interested in a broadcasting station which was owned by a local telephone company and spent my time at it rather than in studying," he recalled. And yet he had been studying, not only radios and how they worked but how to design them, how to improve them, and how to communicate in the hieroglyphics of electrical circuit diagrams. He came home for the summer of 1925, through with college forever—at least as a student. But he wasn't idle. Another local project attracted him. An insurance company—a big one with lots of money—was assembling what would be Nashville's most powerful radio station. He found his way there through a friendship with a man who had sought out his radio expertise some years earlier, a businessman with a peculiar dream—Edwin Craig.

Edwin Wilson Craig spent his early years in a prosperous, comfortable home in the countryside community of Pulaski, Tennessee, about seventy-five miles south of Nashville. As a boy he was dressed in satin Buster Brown outfits and taken to boating parties. At boarding school, he knew a future surgeon general of the United States. At Vanderbilt, his fraternity brothers included Prentice Cooper, a future governor. Edwin could have gone any number of directions, but he wanted to join the family business, the National Life and Accident Insurance Company, and though his obituaries said he graduated, he left Vanderbilt early to do so. He was, in fact, the son of the company's senior founder, but nobody could say Edwin didn't work his way up the ladder. He "walked the debit," the same door-to-door circuit of sales and account management made every day by the other two thousand National Life agents. In small towns all across the South, on dirt streets, in mud, cold, and miserable heat, properly dressed "Shield Men" fanned out in a highly regimented, year-in-year-out campaign. By his midtwenties, Craig was an exemplary Shield Man, so named for the National Life blue shield logo, and he seemed destined for leadership, over sales and probably much more.

When Edwin was born in 1893, his father, Cornelius Abernathy Craig, ran a drug store in a partnership with his older brother Edward and another brother who practiced law. Edward had been successful in banking and business in Giles County, Tennessee. That same year, 1893, Governor Peter Turney invited Edward to Nashville to become treasurer of the state. Brother Cornelius followed, liquidating his holdings in the drug store and moving his family to Nashville to climb up a rung. Soon he was working for Edward as deputy commissioner of insurance and gaining experience which he parlayed into the acquisition, at a 1901 auction, of a young and shaky company called National Sick and Accident Association. The following year, Craig and his partners changed the name to the more upbeat National Life and Accident Insurance Company.

The new business forged a bond that would last for decades among its five foundational families. Asked how they related to one another initially, Ridley Wills II, grandson of a founder, described the group with a Bible Belt-dweller's frame of reference. "Dr. Fort was a Baptist from Robertson County who had married a sophisticated woman from Boston," he said. "Runcie Clements [president of National Sick and Accident when it was sold] was a Roman Catholic. The Craigs were members of the West End United Methodist Church. The Wills were Presbyterians. The Tynes were Catholics too. So it was a wonderful mix. And they all got along beautifully—respected each other. It's interesting to me how well they got along with those different backgrounds. But all of them were from small towns."

Cornelius, by virtue of his leadership in the origins and organization of the company, was president and later chairman of National Life between 1902 and 1943. A bookish man with sandy hair parted severely in the middle and round, horn-rimmed glasses, C. A. was known improbably as "Neely" by his colleagues and family. As upright a businessman as one could hope to meet and a self-styled business philosopher, C. A. made his presence known with solemn, didactic letters to his field sales force, issued regularly for decades through *The Shield* newsletter. One early version of his guide for agents noted characteristically that "moral excellence and business honesty are not the fruits of regulation. They are inborn and of higher source but more to be desired than the most rigid adherence to fixed statues."

About his company's core product, the elder Craig said, "National Life . . . felt . . . that the industrial classes needed, above all other forms of insurance, a policy providing benefits that would replace the pay envelope when they were sick or disabled by accident, and would also carry sufficient life insurance to provide a Christian burial." Shield Men collected premiums door-to-door, sometimes a mere quarter at a time. And although National Life's policies have often been criticized in retrospect as paltry "burial insurance," they may have been a modest advance in thrift for a largely hand-to-mouth population.

When Edwin Craig left Vanderbilt in 1913 and went to work for National Life, he did so not in the Nashville headquarters but in Dallas, as a regular Shield Man. His father had admonished the Dallas officials to "forget [his] name and require of [him] a full day's work every day, showing no consideration not extended to every other man in the district." Craig arrived by train from Memphis with Eldon Stevenson Jr., a fraternity brother from Vanderbilt. The young men settled into the YMCA and hit the dusty streets in tumbledown neighborhoods where the company was utterly unknown and began knocking on doors one-by-one. The early client base of National Life was almost entirely black or Mexican, a point that goes unmentioned in official company histories. "He didn't have a white policy holder in Dallas," his son Neil has said.

Craig advanced through strata of positions and titles as scintillating as only the insurance industry could conjure: from superintendent to district office cashier, to district manager, to field supervisor, to auditor. In 1916 he married Elizabeth Wade from Tennessee's Giles County. Two years later the couple moved to Nashville and had a daughter. During World War I Craig organized and managed the company's new "ordinary life" department. By 1924 Craig was a vice president and manager of the much larger industrial department. *The Shield* called him "extremely popular, not only at home in both a business and social way, but [he] is considered by the National Field Force as a friend and counselor." During those years, perhaps as early as 1921, Craig began to bother his father and the National Life board about a company radio station.

Craig could see businesses spawning radio stations by the score, from local concerns to national giants like Sears, Roebuck and Co. whose Chicago-based WLS stood for "World's Largest Store." Craig could have tuned in early Tennessee broadcaster WMC, launched by the Memphis *Commercial Appeal* newspaper, beginning in January 1923. Newspapers, radio equipment makers, churches, and telephone companies were starting radio stations, with varied agendas and uncertain prospects. There weren't any standout examples of insurance companies or similarly conservative financial services firms taking to the airwaves, and Edwin Craig began asking himself why not.

About this time, probably early 1922, Craig sought out young radio guru Jack DeWitt. Neither left a record of their first meeting, but it marked the beginning of a lengthy and prolific friendship. Craig was not interested in building homemade sending sets. He wanted to hear the revolution on the air, so he consulted DeWitt in setting up a receiver before they were easily available in stores. Daughter Elizabeth remembered it as a long, boxlike contraption: "The radio sat up on feet, and the battery boxes slipped under it," she said. "People that we didn't even know would call up and say, 'Could we just come by and hear the radio for just a few minutes?' So there was a stream of people up to the sleeping porch." Craig was especially fond of the spirited programs coming from WWJ in Detroit, WSB in Atlanta, and WBAP in Fort Worth. He sent telegrams of appreciation to some of the popular radio personalities of the day: George D. Hay, "The Solemn Old Judge" from WLS in Chicago; Leo Fitzpatrick in Kansas City, who called himself "The Merry Old Chief"; and "Little Colonel" Lambdin Kay, director of WSB. Craig even visited Fitzpatrick on several occasions when his business took him to Kansas City, and one account says those meetings inspired Craig to imagine broadcasting himself.

Edwin Craig's growing passion for radio reflected forward-thinking enthusiasm shot through with corporate pragmatism. He'd been swept up by the national mania for broadcasting. And he knew what the National Life sales force—by then 2,500 men in twenty-one states—confronted day to day as they walked the streets. "The company didn't have enough money to buy advertising" town by town, said Neil Craig. "So he conceived the idea of a radio station that would support our agents. That's what that station went on the air to do." DeWitt wrote that Craig "saw the possibilities in radio for the nationwide advertisement of" National Life. And company historian Powell Stamper wrote that the station was to earn its keep by "extending company identity, service to the community, the influence of public relations, and supporting the company's field men in their relations with both prospects and policyholders."

National Life president Ridley Wills once wrote that "Mr. Craig faced serious resistance in selling the idea to the older executives, but kept hammering away for some three years." Accounts surfaced that Craig almost quit National Life over the matter, but Neil disputes that, saying that Craig's identity and family were tied too closely to the business. The more likely scenario is that the elders of the company, although initially skeptical about radio's potential to be both effective and dignified, were brought around to a point where at least they thought it couldn't hurt. The station's so-called old guard are said to have patronized the idea, calling it Edwin's "toy" or his "plaything." Daughter Elizabeth Proctor says with confidence that her grandfather C. A., Edwin's own father, was one of the hardest to convince. "And finally, in a board meeting, Daddy brought it up again, the need for the company to have a radio station," she recounted. "And the other men said, 'Oh, Neely, let the young man have his radio station. It's not important. We don't want it. But it won't do any harm. Let him have it.' So Grandfather heaved a sigh maybe of relief, and said, 'All right. Go ahead and investigate as best you can about what you want.'"

Craig seems to have won his permission by February 1923, the date of an official announcement that National Life was about to lay the cornerstone of a new headquarters building. Vice President W. R. Wills described the planned new office to the sales force as "the South's most beautiful insurance home"—60,000 square feet rising five elegant stories above the corner of Seventh Avenue North and Union Street. Craig's idea was at least on the drawing board. "The fifth floor," wrote Wills, "is for a recreation room, emergency hospital, and assembly room. The roof is a playground, and perhaps a broadcasting station."

Craig faced other obstacles, however. Easy access to radio licenses was over. The airwaves were crowded, and the government was rationing signals. In a telegram to the New Orleans–based Radio Supervisor's Office of the Department of Commerce in April 1924, Craig requested an available wavelength (a channel on the radio spectrum) so engineers could start construction of a 500-watt station by that August. Mr. D. B. Carson, commissioner of navigation in Washington, arbiter of broadcast licenses, replied that there were no more wavelengths available. He suggested that National Life work out a signal-sharing arrangement with the Memphis *Commercial Appeal* newspaper's WMC, but that was a far-fetched solution. WMC was, by this time, a veteran in Tennessee broadcasting and highly unlikely to give up its prime-time hours.

Broadcast licenses were, however, transferable. Craig discovered that James D. Vaughan, owner of a music school and a gospel songbook publisher in Lawrenceburg, Tennessee, eighty miles south of Nashville, had been running 250-watt WOAN since November 1922 at 282.8 meters, an attractive wavelength. With the slogan, "Wake Up America!" WOAN broadcast only an hour each night, mixing live gospel music with pitches for Vaughan's songbooks. On April 7, 1925, National Life reached an agreement with Vaughan, in which the company would take over Vaughan's signal with its own, much stronger transmitter, and

Vaughan could supply the programming between 9:00 and 10:00 on weeknights and 9:15 to 10:15 on Sunday nights. It wasn't an ideal solution for Craig, but it was all he had to work with. By April 10, the deal was in Carson's hands, along with a cordial letter from National Life general counsel Thomas Tyne, asking for permission to go ahead with the time-sharing plan.

Now things moved forward rapidly. Craig, doubling his initial power requirements, ordered a 1,000-watt transmitter from Western Electric, promising to make his the only station in the South equal to Atlanta's WSB. Early plans were to transmit from the roof of National Life's headquarters at Seventh and Union, over a horizontal wire antenna, strung like a laundry line between two towers. In May an amusing illustration ran on the cover of *The Shield,* imagining the elegant building topped out with two ungainly radio towers, each taller than the building itself. Completion was scheduled for August.

Also by this point, National Life was more willing to take credit for the idea. "The erection of this mammoth broadcasting station by The National has been on the program of the Shield Company's plan of progress for more than two years," the company announced. "And after much thought and earnest consideration the executives of the Company have succeeded in giving to the radio world one of its greatest broadcasting stations." Programming, the company said, will be "varied and of an outstanding nature. Lectures, sermons, music, sports and many other attractions for which Nashville is noted will be given to radio fans all over the country."

When they said "all over the country," they meant it. As Jack DeWitt found out firsthand with his homebuilt transmitter, radio signals in the early twentieth century carried vast distances, in part because the airwaves were relatively uncluttered by other broadcast media. There is also a physical phenomenon called a "skywave," in which nighttime radio signals bounce between the earth and a charged layer of the atmosphere, over thousands of miles. National Life officials predicted that under the right weather conditions, its station could reach Canada, Mexico, Cuba, and (inaccurately, it turned out) Europe.

Moreover, the purpose of the station became clearly defined within the company well before it went on the air. In a May 19, 1924, newsletter, a cartoon pictured a Shield Man sitting on top of the world while the Home Office floated in the clouds. The rooftop antenna flashed out lightning bolts and the messages: "Musical Programs," "Insurance Talks," and "Publicity Helps." Then, on May 26, another cartoon cut to the bottom line. This time the Home Office had a radio horn coming out the top, and the Shield Man had his hat out. Flying out of the horn and wafting down like pieces of confetti were papers that said: "New Business," "Opportunity," "Service," "Prestige," and a big money bag marked "PROFITS."

In July 1925, Edwin Craig received clearence fron the Federal Bureau of Navigation to use the call letters WSM. He seems to have had a clear preference for the name, as he reportedly negotiated with the Navy to have the letters reassigned from a ship. All that remainied was a slight refocusing of the company's slogan, so that as with Sears and most other radio owners of the day, the call letters could reinforce a brand. Ever since the company had adopted a blue shield as its trademark in October 1922, the logo had often been accompanied in advertising by the slogans "The National Life and Accident Insurance Company, Incorporated, Shields You" or "Shielding Millions—Are We Shielding You?" After the inauguration of the station, "We Shield Millions" became the de facto motto of Nashville's fastest-growing insurance company and its newest, most prestigious broadcaster.

By August the idea of using towers on the roof had been abandoned in favor of a transmitter on a hill two miles away and just a few blocks from Ward-Belmont. Each of its two towers was 165 feet tall, with a flat-top antenna strung between them. A lead ran down into a tidy clapboard-sided broadcast house, which doubled as a home for the station's chief engineer. Half of the house was occupied by generators, transformers, radio tubes, and cooling pipes; the other half comprised a cottage with two bedrooms, a kitchen, and a small dinette. Its first occupant, Vanderbilt graduate Thomas L. Parkes, could claim radio experience that predated World War I. In 1913 he'd been noted in Nashville as a ham telegrapher. Then he'd been around the world on steam ships, surviving a ferocious North Atlantic storm. He'd seen his ship's boiler explode in Greece, killing an engineer. Now twenty-three years old, he'd been married for just four months. His job was to be on call twenty-four hours to maintain the new Western Electric behemoth. The property was surrounded with a five-foot-high cyclone fence topped with barbed wire. One can only imagine how the young Mrs. Parkes felt in 1925, setting up the couple's first long-term home at Fifteenth Avenue South and Weston Street, with her husband in the next room, tending to large, humming machines.

On the fifth floor of National Life's headquarters on Seventh and Union, WSM's lone studio was small but luxuriously appointed. Though the company described the room to be "as perfect in acoustics as inventive genius can make it," it was deadened with carpet, oriental rugs, and pleated burgundy velvet drapes that lined the walls and hung from a central point in the ceiling, like the interior of an Arabian tent. It was a typical approach for the day. Radio stations discovered that bright, reflective rooms produced an unbearable echo effect over the air. Lacking the panels that would soon come along to absorb sound, stations commonly draped their studios or put bands outdoors. WSM's room was furnished like a parlor, with an ebony Steinway grand piano, wingback chairs, frilly floor lamps, a rococo desk, and a crystal chandelier. The studio abutted a small control room whose console resembled a manual telephone switchboard. Master control was connected to the transmitter house on the hill through three private phone lines, one for the regular broadcast signal, one for emergencies, and one for regular communication between the studio engineer and the chief engineer at the transmitter.

Having sunk about $40,000 into the station's physical plant (more than $400,000 in today's dollars), National Life went to great lengths to promote its broadcast debut as a major community watershed. The company crafted a supplement to the *Tennessean* and the *Banner,* offering a wealth of information about the station's capabilities and possibilities. Both newspapers independently acknowledged the historic proportions of the event and offered inexpensive crystal radio sets as a premium for new subscribers. Many Nashville homes had well-used radios by this point; picking up Atlanta, Cincinnati, or Louisville was by then routine entertainment. Newspaper ads touted receivers from $10 table sets to $130 floor-standing models. Thousands of homes acquired radios from furniture dealers and hobby shops in the weeks running up to WSM's launch.

Everything was ready by the first of October. The country was anticipating the World Series. Nashville had its traditional "moving day," a peculiar occasion when most of the city's leases expired and thousands of people simultaneously moved. The economy was heady, and speakeasies flourished. The chamber of commerce unveiled a stilted "Sell Nashville To Itself" campaign, a nine-month display of boosterism that featured facts about Nashville's business prowess on streetcar placards, movie screens, and elevators. That first week of October, Nashvillians learned that the city roasted over 100 million pounds of coffee every year, anchored by hometown company Maxwell House. It was amid this ordinary activity that Edwin Craig received approval of his license by telegram on Sunday, October 4, with but one day to spare before opening night, October 5, 1925.

Engraved invitations for the gala inauguration featured the WSM call letters etched as lightning bolts. Among those accepting were Nashville mayor Hillary Howse and Tennessee governor Austin Peay. The men who'd helped get WSM licensed were there, too. Commissioner of Navigation Carson traveled from Washington, and Major Walter Van Nostrand, regional director, came from Atlanta. Perhaps the greatest acknowledgement of WSM's instant prestige, however, was the presence of three giants of the airwaves: Lambdin Kay, Leo Fitzpatrick, and George D. Hay. The newspaper supplement bragged on them as "the three most popular announcers and radio executives in the world today." Kay is said to have invented musical station identification, including the three-note chime that would be famously adopted by NBC. Fitzpatrick, Craig's friend, reached a national late-night audience as a jovial emcee and leader of a band called the Nighthawks, first from Kansas City, then Detroit. And Hay was a major personality at WLS in Chicago, with a rustic, old-time variety show—*The National Barn Dance*—that was putting "hillbilly music" on the American map.

The VIPs were accommodated in the studio and in the hall just outside the studio window, where they could listen over loudspeakers. Police minded hundreds of onlookers who gathered at dusk in the streets outside the Seventh and Union headquarters of National Life. Larger loudspeakers had been mounted outside of the building (almost certainly by Jack DeWitt) to relay the signal that would be going out over the air. A band from the Tennessee Industrial School assembled on the building's roof, taking in a view that included the capitol spire two blocks away. The Al Menah Shrine Band, resplendent in fezzes and billowing pantaloons, gathered on the street outside.

National Life arranged with Western Union for a special wire to handle a flood of telegrams. Across the city, in private homes and in radio stores, restaurants, and cigar stores, Nashvillians twiddled knobs in anticipation. A few young people put battery-powered radios on the backs of automobiles and drove around during the broadcast. Shield Man W. A. Scott placed a gold leaf lettered message on the rear window of his car encouraging people to "Tune in on WSM." A New Orleans–based agent named T. E. Brenan set up a radio on the front steps of his home, and dozens listened from his leafy lawn. In Chattanooga, National Life sales superintendents helped assemble a crowd to listen in from a fire hall, and before the night was over, they sold a policy to an enthusiastic fan.

A wide range of other artists assembled for the broadcast: the Knights of Columbus Quartet, a male vocal group; the Fisk Jubilee Singers, a celebrated local black ensemble that sang formal spiritual music; and various duos and trios of local instrumentalists and vocalists. Two remote broadcast hook-ups were in place at the nearby Hermitage and Andrew Jackson hotels, where Francis Craig and Beasley Smith, respectively, stood by with their orchestras, and with considerably more room than had been available during the early broadcast sessions from Jack DeWitt's living room. DeWitt, nineteen years old, manned master control just off the studio, where the signals converged and were dispatched to chief engineer Parkes, two miles away at the transmitter site.

Shortly after 7:00 p.m., DeWitt, from behind the control room glass, gave Edwin Craig the cue to begin. Craig stepped to the microphone and let his voice pierce the airwaves: "*This is station WSM—We Shield Millions—owned and operated by the National Life and Accident Insurance Company, Nashville, Tennessee,*" he said. There followed a prayer, the national anthem performed by the Shriners' band, and an hour of congratulatory speeches, announcements, and music. C. A. Craig officially dedicated the station "to the public service" and rhapsodized about radio, the very invention he'd sniffed at two years before, recognizing it as "the greatest agency we have for communion over our vast country, and that such communion tends to make us a homogeneous people."

The first vocalist to perform on the station was Joseph MacPherson, a local baritone. The mayor and governor spoke of the station's potential for public service and for spreading awareness of Tennessee. Major Van Nostrand observed that WSM would cover rural areas not previously served well by radio. The rest of the long evening was devoted to music. The Fisk Jubilee Singers got a full half an hour, performing songs like "Shout All Over God's Heaven" and "Swing Low, Sweet Chariot." Beasley Smith's orchestra introduced its swinging sound, and the guest announcers took turns on the microphone. George D. Hay blew his signature wooden whistle for emphasis. Francis Craig's orchestra didn't even start playing from the ornate ballroom at the Hermitage Hotel until midnight, and National Life employees and friends held an impromptu dance party on the building's fourth floor. A little before 1:00 a.m., Craig and his band packed up and headed for the studios two blocks away. There, a free-form jamboree had ensued with Smith's boys and others, emceed by local entertainer and polymath Jack Keefe. He and WSM's first program director, young Bonnie Barnhardt, led an on-air party that lasted until after 2:00 a.m.

Congratulations poured in. Mr. W. E. Ward of the Baird-Ward Printing Company wrote, giddy that he'd received a signal over a two-dollar receiver aided by a water pipe, a bedspring, and wire screen. Messages came from Ithaca, New York; New Orleans; Houston; Parkersburg, West Virginia; and all over Tennessee. The staff of Memphis radio station WMC, which took the night off the air to listen to its new Nashville colleagues, wrote, "you are leaping the mudholes to Memphis as no automobile has yet done." The *Banner* declared the city had "radiolitis" and editorialized with foresight: "Doubtless the radio station will prove a splendid advertisement for the company which is sponsoring it, but it will be no less so for Nashville." National Life joined happily in the hype. *The Shield*'s story about the dedication of "the Voice of the Athens of the South" reported in all modesty: "the most pretentious and elaborate array of superlative talent ever assembled at one time in Tennessee . . . WSM's debut into the world of broadcasters was by far the most brilliant ever achieved by any station in America." Ridley Wills proved more accurate and more poetic when he announced that thanks to WSM "the name of the National is now on the very air we breathe."

TWO

The Ears Are Eyes

WSM took Tuesday off and switched on again Wednesday afternoon. Opening-night announcer Jack Keefe sat before a microphone in the velvet opulence of the WSM studio and described game one of the World Series, based on a steady stream of balls, strikes, hits, and outs from a news wire. A few blocks away, police had shut down Commerce Street for a promotion sponsored and hyped by the *Banner*. Men in boater hats and boys in knee britches listened to Keefe's broadcast over loudspeakers and watched the game unfold on a mechanical Playograph scoreboard. Animated players cycled about the bases as hits and home runs were announced. The Washington Senators took the first game from the Pittsburgh Pirates. As the series went to seven games, throngs listened and watched as the shadows grew long on cool autumn evenings and trolley cars clanked up and down Third Avenue. They cheered when Kiki Cuyler—a former Nashville minor league star—broke a 7–7 tie in the eighth inning of the final game with a ground rule double. The Pirates upset the Senators after trailing three games to one.

Ball games had been narrated at a distance since 1922, and legendary Nashville sportswriter Grantland Rice had called the nation's first live on-the-scene baseball game that same year. Though Keefe had heard such broadcasts, he'd never announced one, so the forty-year-old attorney relied on his knowledge of baseball (he'd lettered in the sport at Harvard) and his savvy as an entertainer to make it up as he went along. His improvisation kept with his life story, that of a renaissance man inclined to try anything once.

Born in Boston, Keefe graduated from a leading music conservatory at seventeen. Then, with a degree from Harvard's education program, he uprooted and became superintendent of schools in Pendleton, Oregon. There, he cultivated his skills as an entertainer and helped organize the Pendleton Roundup, a famous Western rodeo. He obtained a one-year leave to tour with a musical production troupe and "never returned after playing an engagement in Nashville," the *Banner* wrote years later, for he seems to have fallen in love. Keefe married in Nashville in 1915, then took a completely new turn as a chemist and professor of bacteriology at Vanderbilt's medical school. Meanwhile, he sang about town in theatrical productions and with a glee club. He could reel off hundreds of popular songs and novelties at the keyboard. Apparently not feeling his time was full enough, he entered Vanderbilt law school, graduating in 1925 with the school's highest academic honors. Although he went immediately into practice, he also spent many evenings at WSM, where his voice became an aural signature of the new station.

"He had a very unusual voice," recalled early WSM announcer David Stone. "It was just like a Gatling gun, [with] a strange gargle in his throat. People called up frequently to find out who he was and what he was." When Keefe moved out of the studio and began doing live play-by-play from local football games, he became a sensation. "I get quite a kick out of your details and enthusiasm," wrote Virginia Garrott, a shut-in at the Watauga Sanitarium in the hilly country north of Nashville. "I've actually learned more football from listening to your details than I ever did in watching the game played." *Tennessean* sports writer Blinkey Horn, laid up in a hospital during a Vanderbilt versus Georgia game a year later, rhapsodized about Keefe's announcing.

"Across my mental vision, Jack Keefe—over WSM—guided me through the gridiron epic in Dudley Stadium," he wrote. "With painstaking attention to every detail, with rare grasp of the intricacies of play, through my ears, he 'showed' me that moleskin masterpiece." When Peck Owen caught a pass and scored the winning touchdown after a seesaw game, Horn felt "a typhoon of emotion." Vanderbilt beat the Bulldogs 14–13, and Horn almost believed he'd been there. "[Keefe] showed me that the ears are eyes, and I am very grateful to him."

Besides Keefe and two engineers, WSM employed a program director and "radio editor" named Bonnie Barnhardt. Known on-air as "The Lady o' The Radio," she had come to Nashville with a following as a musician and storyteller from Atlanta's WSB, where she had been program director under Lambdin Kay. Twenty-three years old, plain but for her deep blue eyes, and not much of a typist, she set about building a schedule of local volunteer artists and rebuilding her fan base of "kiddies" who tuned in by the thousands for her 7:00 p.m. bedtime stories.

For a time in the 1920s, before male radio station owners fully understood the gravity or potential profitability of their enterprise, women were frequently assigned to manage what was seen as an administrative role. Although several important female broadcasting pioneers emerged from that short-lived window of semi-opportunity, Barnhardt was unfortunately not one of them. Craig seems to have wanted an anchoring announcer and manager with national prestige, and around the time WSM went on the air, he recruited George D. Hay of WLS in Chicago.

Craig, an avid hunter, could have gone after no better prey. Hay had already been with two powerful stations (WLS and WMC in Memphis), and in 1924 he had earned the *Radio Digest* cup as America's favorite announcer. Born in Attica, Indiana, in 1895, Hay may have inherited some of his showmanship from his father, a jeweler who staged publicity stunts. When his father died, George was moved as a third grader to Chicago. But as an adult, he took to newspaper work and moved to Memphis, where he covered municipal courts for the *Commercial Appeal.* When the paper launched WMC in 1922, a reluctant Hay was recruited into radio. Once committed, he followed the fashion of the day for announcers by taking on a nickname, adapted from his comic serial newspaper column "Howdy Judge." He proved good at radio, matching an original style with substantial accomplishments, including breaking the news over the air that Warren G. Harding had died in 1923. He developed a low, mantralike style, heavy with aural punctuation, and he highlighted his broadcasts with the dark tones of a wooden riverboat sound effect whistle he bought at a music store. Hay had never much cared for Chicago, but he moved back in 1924 when WLS offered him a job. The riverboat whistle became a train whistle, and he coined the on-air idea of the "WLS Unlimited" coursing along "the trackless paths of the air."

Hay once said that Craig approached him two weeks after the October opening of WSM at a broadcasting convention in Texas to offer him the top job at WSM. Hay accepted on November 2 and drove his family to Nashville about a week later. The *Banner* heralded his arrival, noting that Hay was "neither solemn nor old . . . his personality radiates the sunshine of youth . . . He is planning to make Nashville his permanent home and to give to the local station that part of his personality which has made other radio stations famous throughout the land." He took the title "radio director in charge." Barnhardt continued her bedtime-story slot through the end of the month, but then slipped away, from WSM and apparently from radio altogether.

Hay found a station in step with national trends in broadcasting. The signal was strong, the talent was decent, and all the programming was live. Prestige broadcasters of the day disdained the idea of playing Victrola discs into a microphone, and once the musicians, announcers, and engineers were set in motion (most evenings that happened at 6:00 p.m.), they were "on," just as surely as if they'd been on stage in a theater, until about 11:00 p.m.

Musically, WSM featured what some have called "potted palm" music—light orchestral and operatic fare played by efficiently small and sufficiently cultivated ensembles. One of Nashville's early exemplars was a swarthy young man with hooded eyes and coarse black hair combed back to reveal a grand widow's peak. Vito Pellettieri looked as Italian as a Neapolitan fisherman, but he'd been born in Nashville to an Italian father and a Swiss mother. He attended Hume-Fogg High School, a prominent landmark on Broadway, and studied violin. In his teens he thought about a law degree but "drifted into music." As early as 1906, he assembled a locally innovative combo of violin, piano, and drums. For years, he found regular work in hotels, including the Andrew Jackson. He was also tapped to entertain over the Baptist-sponsored WCBQ, but now Hay sought him out for regular WSM broadcasts. Pellettieri's "Radio Five" (or Three or Seven) could play Vivaldi, popular songs, or a polite simulation of the blues, including such staple tunes as "Sitting on Top of the World," in a stiff and formal style.

Music schools provided armies of early radio entertainers, and Nashville had a particularly good talent pool. Gaetano de Luca, who had played his opera records over Jack DeWitt's first radio station at Ward-Belmont School, directed music studies there for nine successful years. In 1927 he left to direct the new Nashville Conservatory of Music, which was launched by a group of musicians and business leaders, including Joel Cheek, the Maxwell House coffee baron, and Luke Lea and James G. Stahlman, the publishers of the *Tennessean* and *Banner*. They raised a quarter of a million dollars and told de Luca to do what it took to make "Nashville the musical center of the South." Before and after the move, de Luca's pupils streamed through WSM, offering swooning art songs and gentle classics.

Still, with no records allowed and no network to draw from, filling the hours could be a challenge. Craig's daughter Elizabeth remembers Miss Daisy

Hoffman, her piano instructor and a WSM prime-time regular, taking her up to the fifth floor of National Life's headquarters at Seventh and Union. "When they couldn't fill it up any other way, they would call my piano teacher," she said. "She always insisted that I go. And I was scared to death ... [An announcer] always said what our names were, how old we were, and how many years of music we had had with Miss Daisy. I remember that one of the pieces I played was MacDowell's 'To a Wild Rose.'"

The new station made its microphones and studios available to Vanderbilt chancellor James Kirkland so he could invite alumni to the school's upcoming, four-day, fiftieth-birthday campus reunion. An entire show was built around promotion of the event, with music and a substantial speech by Kirkland, who was fully aware that he suddenly had a platform from which he could reach across the entire South, calling his graduates home. The *Banner* editorialized with enthusiasm about the National Life's "vision, courage and civic enterprise" and pointed to Kirkland's talk as the kind of public service it appreciated and expected from its new local tribune. Millions, it anticipated, will tune in and "be reminded anew and in an agreeable manner of Nashville."

Other groups embraced WSM as a promotional tool. The Nashville Shriners offered a live, on-air preview of their minstrel show to attract people to an upcoming three-night run at the Orpheum Theater. When a hurricane hit Miami in 1926, WSM made appeals for American Red Cross donations and helped with emergency communications in the faraway disaster. Closer to home and on a smaller scale, WSM was able to act like a community bulletin board and emergency response service. In one case, when attempts to reach a Nashville traveling salesman by telegram failed, Keefe put word out over the air that he was needed at home. The salesman heard of the plea and called from High Point, North Carolina, to learn that his daughter had died in an accident.

Ultimately, however, it was music that best showcased WSM's highbrow aims, and few WSM artists got more early airtime than another of Edwin's relatives, first cousin Francis Craig. When he was eight years old, Francis passed by a pool hall in Clarksville and heard ragtime piano for the first time. Family lore has it that he headed home, ascended the piano bench, and so convincingly played a facsimile of what he'd heard that his strict Methodist parents were torn between admiration of his gift and concern that he'd been irredeemably corrupted. Heeding a biblical admonition in the book of Matthew to nurture talent, the Craigs offered Francis piano lesson and heavy doses of formal church music. Then at an early recital for the Ladies Missionary Society, Francis whipped his mother's favorite hymn "Brighten the Corner" into a ragtime tune. The ladies loved it. "Mother Craig," wrote Craig's biographer Robert Ikard, "was crushed."

When Francis Craig started at Vanderbilt in 1919, he joined Phi Delta Theta, where he was briefly a fraternity brother of Jesse Wills and Allen Tate. Both Wills and Tate were well-known poets, and Wills was also a future president of National Life. But Craig was a terrible student, who was in and out of Vanderbilt over the next two years. During this time, he organized his first band, matching three students with five local professionals to play a Sigma Nu dance for forty-five dollars. James Kirkland, the larger-than-life chancellor of Vanderbilt, welcomed Craig into the Jazz Age by dressing him down over his group's name, the Vanderbilt Jazz Band. At the time, the very word *jazz* evoked sex and licentiousness to men like Kirkland. He ordered Craig to change the name or leave the school.

Craig did both in 1922, ditching campus life for good and changing his group's name to Francis Craig and His Orchestra. The new name better suited the music Craig would conduct over the coming years anyway, for it was not jazz, but popular tunes pitched for polite social dancing or atmosphere in hotels and dining rooms throughout the South. It was convivial, conservative, and at least somewhat lucrative, so Craig spent most of the next decades of his professional life in a tuxedo or dinner jacket, working a good deal harder than he had as a student. Francis Craig's groups showed up on time, and he paid his players reliably. They jobbed in ever-widening circles beyond Vanderbilt, including the prestigious Belle Meade Country Club, where most of the senior National Life brass were members. The group also traveled to North Carolina, Georgia, and Birmingham, Alabama, where it found steady work at the Cascade Plunge Pool, a dinner club with swimming.

Robert Craig, Francis's father, had grown increasingly critical of his son's chosen profession. It was simply beneath the family's stature, and "jazz" (he could not see the difference) was a wastrel's music. Uncle C. A. joined in the campaign, offering wayward Francis a post at National Life. But the young bandleader proved as willful in the pursuit of his passion as Edwin Craig ("Cud'n Edwin," as he would have said it) had been in his. In October of 1924, Francis married Elizabeth Gewin and moved to Birmingham. Her family managed to talk him out of music briefly, connecting him to a job in sales with a marble company. But he was "ill fitted and miserable," Ikard wrote, and he "persuaded Elizabeth to return to Nashville."

Francis Craig may have surprised his families—and himself—when he was offered a regular job at the Grill Room at the luxurious Hermitage Hotel, one block from the capitol and National Life. The Hermitage had opened in 1910 to great acclaim as the city's jewel. Craig's band played lunch and dinner in a warmly lit downstairs restaurant, where white-jacketed waiters served the city's business and political elite. Though the band included reeds, piano, drums, banjo, and tuba, it swung lightly without getting too hot. The job earned Francis legitimacy in his own heart, in Elizabeth's eyes, and even in his father's estimation. And when Robert heard his son's music coming over the remarkable new radio, he began to understand the choices his son had made.

If jazz constituted the opposite of civilized music in the eyes of chancellors and ministers, Tennessee old-time music was only marginally more respectable, and yet fiddles and banjos found a place on WSM almost from the start. Back in the summer of 1925, a National Life employee had informed a musician friend about his company's new radio station. The friend, Dr. Humphrey Bate, was a part-time bandleader and a full-time country doctor who made house calls, often in exchange for produce, poultry, ham, and molasses. A distinguished, well-dressed man some fifty years old, he held medical credentials from the University of Nashville and fighting credentials from the Spanish-American War. Besides his work and his family, Bate loved fishing and his band. The six-piece group featured a fiddle and banjo core, complimented with cello or string bass and his own harmonica.

Bate's local renown earned an invitation to play WDAD, another local radio start-up, as soon as it went on the air in the late summer of 1925. After checking with National Life to make sure the engagement wouldn't preclude appearances on WSM, he led his group forty miles to the city to play. Then, during the first month of WSM's life, Bate was given his own hour-long slot there as well. Historian Jack Hurst quoted Bate's daughter Alcyone, then the band's pianist: "We played [at WSM] before Mr. Hay came. We would drive to Nashville and perform on WDAD in the afternoon, then we would walk up the hill and play WSM later in the evening."

During the first week of November, Bate and other WSM regulars were part of a gala evening at the Ryman Auditorium—a fund-raiser for the Policeman's Benefit Association. The eclectic slate of local talent looked like a match for WSM's ambitions, so its newest engineer, Jack Montgomery, hired in late October from WCBQ, was charged with setting up the microphones and telephone lines that would connect the studios to the city's venerable concert hall. On a Thursday, one night after Will Rogers had played the Ryman to standing ovations, WSM's Jack Keefe presided as master of ceremonies. After Mayor Howse greeted the thousands of policemen, families, and guests crushed in the hall's pews, Keefe sat down at a piano to accompany a soprano. Beasley Smith's Andrew Jackson Hotel orchestra followed, as did another WSM regular, the Knights of Columbus Quartet.

Then the program took a hillbilly turn. Bate led his band on his harmonica, followed by a character whom Charles Dickens might have invented, had be been a Southerner instead of a Londoner. Uncle Dave Macon, billed as "the struttinest strutter that ever strutted a strut," had a mouthful of gold teeth, a portly carriage, and a vaudevillian's whoop-de-do. Like Bate, he had for years been a professional man with a music habit, but his Macon Midway Mule and Wagon Transportation Company of Murfreesboro, Tennessee, had been wiped out a couple of years back by things called "trucks," and he'd more or less retired into a life of professional entertaining. In 1925 he was fifty-five years old and a star of the Lowe's theater circuit. He'd even made a record a year before in New York. And he'd already enjoyed radio exposure on WDAD. Uncle Dave's frequent partner, fiddling Sidney Harkreader, also played with Bate. When Uncle Dave took the stage, seated as if on a bouncing chair, with a banjo tilt-a-whirling in his lap, Sidney cut away on "Sugar Walks Down the Street" and "Turkey in the Straw" to enthusiastic whoops and applause.

It was this broadcast, aired just as George Hay was making his move to Nashville, that most directly anticipated the birth of the Grand Ole Opry. The oft-repeated story goes that a few weeks after Hay's arrival, on November 28, 1925, he invited country fiddler Uncle Jimmy Thompson to play for an hour on a Saturday night. The crotchety seventy-eight-year-old had come to Hay's attention through the fiddler's niece, Eva Thompson Jones, a regular WSM pianist. His old-time fiddling struck a chord. Telegrams, calls, and letters poured in from rural Tennessee and beyond, cheering and begging for more of the same.

"The Barn Dance program was not formally established on that night, though Uncle Jimmy returned the next week to play again," wrote Opry historian Charles Wolfe. "In neither case did Hay bill it, through the newspapers, as any sort of special old-time program. Probably during December the idea for such a program was taking shape in Hay's head." About that time, Hay reportedly told a local old-time musician that "he was going to start something like the National Barn Dance in Chicago and expected to do better because the people were real and genuine and the people really were playing what they were raised on."

Edwin Craig appears to have endorsed the old-time turn early on. "We were looking for something which would give us national identification," he once said. "Hay had become acquainted with string bands when he worked in Memphis, and he thought there was a great future for folk music . . . He met with us, and we decided to feature a Saturday night folk music program." Hay also would have learned that Craig had been a mandolin player in a string band during his prep school days. "He liked the music played by rural people," wrote Opry historian Jack Hurst. "He knew its heritage." Neil Craig agreed that all that is true, but he noted another motivation: "The Grand Ole Opry was put on the air to try to get into the white [insurance] business."

Bundles of mail and telegrams proved an audience was out there. Saturday night was the best time to reach working people (the "industrial" class targeted by National Life's Shield Men) at their most relaxed, as they hovered in a carefree limbo between six days of toil and Sabbath-day propriety. In late December a story in the *Tennessean* said that "because of this recent revival in the popularity of the old familiar tunes, WSM has arranged to have an hour or two every Saturday night, starting December 26."

Nashville's tiny radio community had to coexist with the suddenly powerful WSM. Initially, cooperation was the rule. Stations shared talent and observed "silent" nights in deference to one another. Jack DeWitt's former collaborator Harry Stone continued to build a broadcasting career quite literally out of thin air. Working part-time at WCBQ and part-time at a radio store, he impressed potential customers by calling the station and having the operator there play a record over the air at the customers' request. He reportedly arranged Nashville's first sponsored radio show, a Maxwell House Coffee program with the Fisk Jubilee Singers and a small Beasley Smith–led combo.

In the spring of 1926, WCBQ changed hands, from the unquiet First Baptist Church to a joint venture of the Braid Electric Company and Waldrum Drug Company. Around that time, Stone became station manager. With new call letters WBAW to reflect the new ownership, Stone set up studios in an old theater at the corner of Sixth Avenue and Church Street, a block from National Life. The station, Jack DeWitt recalled, "eked out a living by transmitting commercial messages along with musical selections from recordings or from live talent." When a department store hired Uncle Dave Macon do to a series of daily programs from one of its show windows, Stone ran a microphone line across the street and broadcast until the police came to break up the crowd that gathered. When an expensive radio tube blew out, Stone had to stay off the air several weeks to raise money to replace it and improvise a cooling system for the tubes with a garden hose. When some drapes caught fire and destroyed the broadcasting gear, WSM helped him rebuild.

Another Nashville station that would shape WSM took to the air just days before National Life. WDAD belonged to charismatic Fred "Pop" Exum, who ran Dad's Auto Accessories, which also sold radios and radio parts. WDAD immediately began playing music that was more down-home and low-down than its local competition. Dr. Bate and Uncle Dave were early regulars. And on at least one occasion, Bessie Smith, the Empress of the Blues, two years into her wildly successful recording career on Columbia Records, visited the city and played with her orchestra over WDAD. The event was previewed with some acclaim in the *Banner,* promising listeners "one of the most wonderful treats they have ever listened to over radio." The coverage marked a rare instance of mainstream Nashville celebrating black blues, which locally was as segregated as the record bins delineating "hillbilly" and "race" or "sepia" music.

More propitious for the future of country music and WSM were the WDAD origins of another black performer, the Harmonica Wizard, DeFord Bailey. Pop Exum first knew Bailey as an odd-jobs fellow who traveled chiefly by bicycle and acquired parts at his store. Besides being an agreeable young man, he was the best harmonica player Pop had ever heard. Bailey's family was steeped in old-time and folk music, including songs like "Lost John" and "Old Joe Clark," which would have been popular among rural whites. His grandfather, Lewis Bailey, who had been a slave until 1863 and who served in the Union Army, was renown as a fiddler. One of Bailey's aunts played guitar. An uncle played harmonica. The Bailey family band became an annual highlight at the Wilson County Fair, and area barn dances relied on them.

Bailey had been born into a new century, on December 14, 1899. Instead of a baby rattle, he was given a harmonica. At age three, he contracted polio. Stuck in bed, he plunked a banjo his father made out of a groundhog skin stretched over a hoop from a cheese box. Bailey survived the ordeal, but grew to scarcely five feet tall. He also recalled making fiddles out of corn stalks, whistles from cane, and percussive bones from cow's ribs dried in the sun. But the harmonica became an extension of his hand and voice box. When he at last began to play beyond the boundaries of his family, word spread fast. In a county loaded with harmonica players Bailey became famous quickly.

Nineteen-year-old Bailey became a house servant for J. C. Bradford, a pioneering Nashville investment banker. Mrs. Bradford discovered his harmonica talent and had him play, in white coat, black tie, and white hat, for high society company. After that, Bailey worked a variety of jobs—helping in the kitchen of the Maxwell House Hotel, working at a motion-picture house, shining shoes at a barber shop on Third Avenue, and running an elevator in the Hitchcock Building. Everywhere he could, including the elevator, he'd play his mouth harp. One day a secretary to Runcie Clements, the new vice president and comptroller of National Life, heard Bailey and invited him to play at a formal dinner at the company's new headquarters. He made five dollars.

Bailey was invited to be one of the first entertainers on WDAD. Besides his regular spots, he was coaxed into entering an on-air harmonica contest. Nobody objected to a black man in an otherwise all-white competition, until he outplayed everyone. Exum, against his own best instincts, named Bailey runner-up to avoid trouble. Despite such obstacles, fellow WDAD entertainer Humphrey Bate prodded Bailey to come along with him to WSM, and convinced Hay to let Bailey play one Saturday night without an audition. It didn't take much for a delighted Hay to realize he had a spectacular musician on his hands. "We're going to use you," he told Bailey.

At one year old, WSM could point to a competent record as a new broadcaster in the South. It had showcased local talent, brought the Nashville Symphony and Vanderbilt football into thousands of homes, and spotlighted local businesses, hotels, and civic organizations. It had opened up local concert halls, like the Ryman Auditorium and the new War Memorial Auditorium, to new audiences. It had made a regional star out of James I. Vance, pastor at the First Presbyterian Church, whose sermons were broadcast every Sunday and who announced that he was convinced the radio was saving souls and boosting church attendance. Station publicity noted that WSM had broadcast music "ranging from the most austere of the operas to the popular songs of the day, including musical comedy numbers and operettas." It even touted its barn dance, "which has received a large amount of applause from the radio listeners throughout the country."

A birthday show called on some 130 entertainers who had been a part of the station's first year. The studios filled with gifts from well-wishers: fruit baskets, sweets from the Union Ice Cream Company, and scads of flowers, including an arrangement made to look like a broadcast station with two tiny aerials. Radio stars Leo Fitzpatrick and Lambdin Kay returned, as did political ally Major Van Nostrand. Local radio mover and shaker Harry Stone was also on hand.

Edwin Craig thanked the city and its musical talent for a year of support and entertainment. He noted that the station, now with three full-time engineers, was growing. He thanked Martha Rowland Brown, who had taken over the bedtime story slot and its large fan club. And he gave special kudos to George Hay and Jack Keefe for holding down the announcing duties during more than 1,200 hours of broadcasts. "WSM has demonstrated two things," he said. "First, that Nashville is in the very forefront of all cities of America of like population in the number of its artists, in the merit of its artists, and in the versatility of its artists. Second, that its artists, without exception, gladly and graciously give of their talent to the great radio public." The commemorative broadcast ran until well after 3:00 in the morning.

WSM spawned the sincerest form of flattery when National Life's most formidable competitor, Life & Casualty Insurance Company, launched its own 1,000-watt radio station in November 1926. Despite their business rivalry, WSM stayed off the air for WLAC's debut and shared many of its regular talents. Coincidentally, WLAC also had its studios on the fifth floor of its company headquarters, on Fourth Avenue, and it was run by a company vice president, one J. Truman Ward.

Meanwhile at Seventh and Union, Edwin Craig and Runcie Clements, appointed as the elder overseer of the radio service, were thinking about ways to further develop WSM's profile and prestige. Though Clements was also the company's comptroller, there seems to have been little concern about cost. After spending about $40,000 to get WSM on the air, the company dropped $50,000 more in 1926 and more than that in 1927 with nary a dime in commercial revenue, for it did not run advertisements. But to grow, besides solving persistent interference problems, WSM would need to be part of the emerging radio networks being built among the cities of the East. At the hub of the most important network was New York's WEAF, the station that had pioneered sponsored shows. Owned and operated by AT&T, it's not surprising that WEAF also pioneered shared programming among stations tied by telephone lines. By 1925, AT&T had networked twenty-six stations. Because the company's maps connected the stations with red pencil lines, the web became known as the Red Network.

The other key corporate players in early radio—General Electric, Westinghouse, and RCA—were at war with AT&T over access to those lines and the use of certain disputed patents. Huge projected fortunes in a brand-new medium were in the balance; they'd even begun to contemplate the inevitability of television at that point. This so-called radio group made a stab at a chain, building its own Blue Network centered around New York's WJZ. But because they were forced to lease antiquated telegraph wires, the sound quality couldn't compete with AT&T's tube-amplified lines. Finally, after years of acrimony, peace was made possible when AT&T decided the controversial new field of "toll" broadcasting was too uncertain and full of potential pitfalls for them to continue as a radio network. AT&T sold WEAF and its web of connections to the radio group for $1 million in early 1926. The networks were bundled together under a new corporate entity, creating the first of many acronyms that would populate the mediascape over the next century: NBC, the National Broadcasting Company.

Craig wasted no time. He and Runcie Clements took the train to New York that winter and came back with, evidently, an oral agreement making WSM the first NBC station in the South. The first feed to WSM, at 6:20 on a Sunday night in early January 1927, brought a live variety show from the Capitol Theater in New York, followed by the *Atwater-Kent Hour*, a showcase of grand opera and other vocal stars sponsored by a prominent manufacturer of radio sets. Initially, WSM broadcast NBC programs only on Sunday and Tuesday nights, but before long the network became part of every broadcast day.

New York and Nashville drew closer in other ways. Between 1926 and 1928, WSM saw its first homegrown talents graduate to the big time. Obed "Dad" Pickard of nearby Ashland City performed a one-man-band novelty act on the Opry and soon added his family members to the show. An audition in Detroit led to an NBC contract for a show called *The Cabin Door*. The Pickard Family would occupy a national stage for years after getting its start at WSM. A very different talent, bass-baritone Joseph MacPherson, was invited to join the Metropolitan Opera early in 1926. By the summer, he'd been slated for a series of roles and was in New York being coached in various languages.

Nashville fussed over and adored none of its hometown heroes, however, so much as James Melton, a singer who worked the boundary between popular and classical music. He had approached Francis Craig in about 1923 at an engagement at the University of Georgia, where Melton, a student, asked about a saxophone slot. Craig didn't need another reed, but when he found out how well Melton sang, he made the kid the band's featured vocalist. Melton moved to Nashville, where he struggled at Vanderbilt but thrived studying voice with Ward-Belmont's Gaetano de Luca. He grew into an operatic-quality tenor who could sing an aria or a romantic ballad with equal aplomb. When he struck out for the Great White Way in late 1927, Francis Craig went with him for support. A seemingly fruitless week ended in discovery. After being repeatedly denied an audition by the prestigious Samuel Lionel "Roxy" Roth-afel, Melton burst into song in the impresario's lobby. Roxy reconsidered, and Melton was hired at $250 per week to sing on NBC's popular variety show *Roxy and His Gang*. Before long, Melton was voted America's favorite radio tenor. Nashvillians bragged on him for decades. WSM carried Roxy locally, further stoking community pride. It earned WSM a surplus of local goodwill, which a certain Saturday night show was starting to tax.

George D. Hay's Saturday-night radio hootenannies lacked a name or a consistent identity. During its first year and a half, it was listed variously in the newspapers as "the Saturday night program," "the popular and barn dance program," and "general good times and barn dance party," and the show ebbed and flowed in length. At various times it featured Hawaiian music, barbershop and gospel quartets, popular tenor singers, Dixieland, and the Castle Heights Military Orchestra. Even announcer Jack Keefe's piano playing made it on several times. Uncle Jimmy Thompson, Dr. Humphrey Bate, and DeFord Bailey made up its core, playing generally half-hour-long sets. But as Wolfe described it, the show initially was a "rather confused, locally aimed, and informally structured radio presentation."

During these early months, WSM's country music leanings first attracted local controversy. In mid-1926, the station held an informal referendum over whether to keep fiddlers and other rustic sounds on Saturday night. The results were published in the *Tennessean* on May 9. "While some listeners seem to prefer the so-called popular tunes . . . they have not indicated their wishes in the mail to any extent," the station announced. Indeed a follow-up story in *The Shield* said that mail ran "about fifty to one" in favor of keeping the barn dance on the air. Despite that lopsided ratio, WSM compromised, most likely because it had to balance enthusiasm coming from out of town with *local* objections to having the Athens of the South represented by hillbillies. "Several letters have been received from Nashville expressing a decided opinion against the barn-dance programs," it explained. "In an effort to please as many people as possible, WSM will continue the barn-dance programs on Saturday night; but the time allotted to the old-time music will be cut down considerably, and a program of so-called popular music will be given during the later hours of the evening." Some loyal listeners felt snubbed. Thomas Martin wrote from Toronto: "I think you would make a mistake to change your Saturday-night program to any other class of music than old-time barn dance, as it is the best program that is broadcast by any other station on the map, and I have listened to a great many."

In any event, the barn dance wouldn't begin to have a genuine impact until it had a name. And as it turns out, its famous title was forged out of the very highbrow/common folks dichotomy that had begun to define WSM's unique personality. NBC piped in a show called the *Music Appreciation Hour* hosted by Walter Damrosch, one of the radio era's first great music popularizers and educators, the very personification of refined taste. As his show wound down one Saturday in 1927, Hay had the studio monitors on and could hear the host introduce a novel piece: "While most artists realize that there is no place in the classics for realism, nevertheless I am going to break one of my rules and present a composition by a young composer from 'Ioway' who sent us his latest number, which depicts the onrush of a locomotive . . ."

At that point, Hay wrote, "the good doctor directed his symphony orchestra through the number which carried many 'whooses' depicting an engine trying to come to a full stop. Then he closed his programme with his usual sign-off. Our control operator gave us the signal which indicated that we were on the air. We paid our respects to Dr. Damrosch and said on the air something like this: 'Friends, the programme which just came to a close was devoted to the classics. Dr. Damrosch told us that it was generally agreed that there is no place in the classics for realism. However, from here on out for the next three hours we will present nothing but realism. It will be down to earth for the 'earthy.' In respect-ful contrast to Dr. Damrosch's presentation of the number which depicts the onrush of the locomotive we will call on one of our performers, Deford Bailey, with his harmonica, to give us the country version of his 'Pan American Blues.' Whereupon, Deford Bailey, a wizard with the harmonica, played the number. At the close of it, your reporter said: 'For the past hour we have been listening to music taken largely from Grand Opera, but from now on, we will present 'The Grand Ole Opry.'"

Hay's famous account probably embellishes the truth and elides events to some degree. Broadcasting histories, for example, say that the *Music Ap-preciation Hour* launched on Fridays in 1928 rather than Saturdays in 1927. Accuracy aside, as the story has echoed down through the years, it has perhaps overshadowed the fact that WSM was a general-interest radio station whose leaders identified more with Damrosch than with their local radio barn dance. Indeed, Hay wrote that, "The members of our radio audience who loved Dr. Damrosch and his Symphony Orchestra thought we should be shot at sunrise and did not hesitate to tell us so." So he knew what he was up against, but at the end of the day he had the support of Edwin Craig, who believed in the worth of folk music. His endorsement alone was enough to keep the old-time show on the air. Hay seems to have seen himself in the role of a prairie populist ready to elevate the music of common people to a place of respect among the fine arts. The piquant contrast between the classical and the rustic, between opera and Opry, he said, "is part of America—fine lace and homespun cloth, our show being covered entirely by the latter."

Just as country musicians had no idea of the import of the newly named Opry, Nashvillians didn't hear the so-called Big Bang of the country music business, though history records that it happened a mere two hundred miles away in Bristol, Tennessee, in the summer of 1927. A few record companies had been flirting with old-time music for a decade or so when Ralph Peer, an executive with the pop and folk Okeh label, made a savvy deal with the much larger Victor Talking Machine Company. He'd scout for southern folk talent and let the company own the recordings if he could keep the publishing rights to the songs he committed to disc. Never mind that many of the songs he "discovered" were ages old; Peer staked copyright claims on a catalog of American folk songs that rapidly made him rich and made Peer Music one of the world's largest music companies. In so doing, Peer took his portable disc-cutting equipment to numerous southern towns. One was Bristol, a city that straddles the Tennessee/Virginia border, where his newspaper advertisements attracted unknowns Jimmie Rodgers and the Carter Family. The records made at those sessions sold in large numbers, launching two of the seminal acts of what would come to be called country music.

One year later, Peer's traveling operation made its first stop in Nashville. He found an eager WSM talent pool, grateful to record close to home. Uncle Dave Macon, Sidney Harkreader, Obed Pickard, DeFord Bailey, and others had already made records, but chiefly in Atlanta or New York. Nashville was home to exactly zero serious recording studios. Peer's studio was a room draped with blankets in the YMCA building just next door to National Life. Ten acts, including talent from WSM, WLAC, and WBAW, cut more than fifty songs over seven working days. And as a result, a couple dozen sides were issued for the Victor label encompassing string bands, DeFord's blues, and the gospel harmonizing of the Vaughan Quartet. Though the Victor operation packed up and moved back to Atlanta, the sessions marked Nashville's debut as a recording town.

Perhaps Edwin Craig's most vexing problem during WSM's first years on the air was interference. Though he badly wanted his station to meet the highest standards of broadcasting, he couldn't control the airwaves, which were an overcrowded, unregulated cacophony of signals. Craig heard as much complaint about poor reception as he did praise for the high quality of the programming. Listeners got to know the technical term *heterodynes,* the squalls and whistles that resulted when two signals of nearly the same frequency crashed into and disrupted one another. When Craig got word that three different radio outfits—including one in Cincinnati—had been issued licenses to broadcast on exactly WSM's frequency, he sent an urgent protest to radio official D. B. Carson: "We will suffer serious interference," he pleaded. "We hope this report is incorrect."

During his negotiations with federal radio officials, Craig had forged a particularly close relationship with Carson's regional subordinate Major Walter Van Nostrand. In January 1926, Major Van Nostrand came to the station's defense, arranging a three-way meeting in Nashville with Commissioner Carson. But half a year of meetings, memos, and waiting produced no solutions, and in July 1926, Craig blew his stack: "If it were not for the fact that my stenographer is a nice young lady I would be able to express myself in terms which would more nearly do justice to my feelings," he vented to Van Nostrand. "It seems to me a disgrace to our form of government that an industry of so great value to the citizenship of this country would be laid open to the destructive will of any who wish to abuse it." Craig said he'd just returned from a long trip through the South, up the Pacific coast and to Canada and found "reception greatly impaired and in places utterly destroyed by exactly those same stations which have always been responsible for our trouble." He promised WSM would continue to abide by the law, stick to its assigned frequency, and hope for the best. "We hope very much that you will not altogether abandon in disgust the Field of Broadcasting but that you will pay us a little visit at some early date. With best wishes and kindest personal regards, I am yours very truly, E. W. Craig."

The problem persisted into 1927, and WSM's only consolation was that it was suffering along with the entire radio industry. About the same time Edwin Craig was writing his angry letter, Commerce Secretary Herbert Hoover was notified by the courts that under the current law he had no authority to regulate who was using what frequency or signal strength, even though he'd been doing so, to a point, for several years. Hoover's preferred solution was to get the radio business to come together and draw up its own scheme for the assignment and regulation of signals, but the industry's proposals remained only theories without an act of Congress and an enforcement body. Stations began to pop on without licenses and jump around on the dial to find their own best frequency. Or they'd bump up their power without asking anybody's permission. By 1927, the number of stations had grown from five hundred to seven hundred (scores of others simply failed), and chaos reigned in the ether. Hoover told an interviewer in mid-1926 that radio was acting like a "spoiled child . . . acting up before company."

At last, the convoluted world of broadcasting rose to the level of presidential attention. Hoover's boss, President Coolidge, asked in his December 7, 1926 address to Congress for a new legislative framework for broadcasting. "Congress," wrote radio historian Daniel Garvey, "which had failed eight times in six years to enact such legislation, pushed through the Radio Act of 1927 in little more than a month." The law created the Federal Radio Commission (FRC), a body with the power to assign or allocate stations to certain frequencies in a way that would minimize interference nationally. Intended to be a one-year transitional body that would issue broadcast licenses until the Department of Commerce took over radio, the FRC was in fact recast as the Federal Communications Commission in 1934, and the Department of Commerce never directly regulated broadcasting again.

During the radio conferences of the early 1920s, the major broadcasting and radio companies had proposed a system in which a limited number of stations would have exclusive rights to a specific frequency and higher power than others. The first cap imagined was 5,000 watts, but some eagerly wanted to proceed to 50,000 watts or even more. Tension between small stations and deep-pocketed broadcasting companies spawned debates about how much power should be concentrated in how few stations' hands. A General Electric representative said at one conference that small stations should "learn to keep out of it," and a Westinghouse representative proposed there should only be twelve to fifteen stations nationwide at very high power.

In the midst of these power plays, congressman Ewin Davis, a Tennessee Democrat with whom Craig had cultivated a relationship, was looking out for WSM. Also a Vanderbilt graduate, he and the National Life families ran in the same circles, and he was a good friend to have. He attached an amendment to the Radio Act that divided the country geographically into five radio zones, with the understanding that the FRC would allocate signals equitably within those zones. This critical break prevented WSM from having to compete for special designation with longer-standing northeastern stations. Against its regional brethren, WSM looked like and indeed was a leader, even if it was a latecomer. Several times in 1928, Representative Davis directly defended WSM against a proposed power reduction and campaigned for the station's freedom to move on the dial. He complained at one hearing that he wasn't able to get the station even in his home in Tullahoma, just sixty-nine miles from Nashville.

At last, WSM acted unilaterally to obtain a stronger, clearer signal. The station went off the air in early December 1926 and came back on January 7, 1927, with a new 5000-watt transmitter. Craig and Clements also appear to have jumped to a more advantageous point on the radio dial. By April, however, WSM was back to its original wavelength and power of 282 meters at 1,000 watts. Then in mid-June, a government order granted WSM official permission to move on the dial and boost its power back to 5,000 watts, which quickly improved its reach. But the final solution to the interference problem came in November 1928, when the FRC ordered a sweeping reallocation of the broadcast spectrum. WSM was placed at 650 kilohertz (expressed as a frequency, not a wavelength), where it would remain evermore. By virtue of its political connections through Representative Davis, Craig's growing profile in the broadcasting world, his expenditure on WSM, and the station's obvious position of influence in its federally set zone, WSM was one of only forty stations in the country to be given its frequency exclusively. It was a huge victory, giving WSM a national monopoly on the 650 signal. Reports of dramatically better reception poured in from all over the United States. A term was soon coined for these privileged signals; they were America's *clear channel stations.*

The year 1928 was auspicious for WSM in other ways. In February, the station hired on Harry Stone from WBAW. Just thirty, Stone was now a well-known local radio voice who could manage any aspect of a station, from basic engineering and announcing to promotion and ad sales. His move merited a picture on the *Banner*'s Sunday radio page showing a confident, handsome man with dark hair slicked back in a sharp center part. George Hay remained director, and while Keefe divided his time between lawyering and appearing on WSM, Stone became the station's first full-time staff announcer. About the same time, WSM made the leap into commercial broadcasting with "a limited number of sponsored musical programmes, representing several of the outstanding business houses of the city," according to station publicity.

Sponsors initially included investment bankers Caldwell & Company, Standard Candy, and Loveman's department store.

In September, according to Clements, "we realized that in order to maintain the high standard of our studio programs it was necessary to compensate our artists and engage a staff of performers." A local orchestra leader named Orin Gaston was asked to assemble and direct a studio group that could play anything from "opera to the 'St. Louis Blues.'" He had appeared on WSM a number of times as leader of the Loew's Theater Vendome Orchestra. When he arrived at WSM, he brought his library of sheet music, a vital resource for a growing station. Most ambitiously, WSM occupied more of National Life's fifth floor, more than doubling in space. In a 1928 *Radio Digest* article, WSM was said to have "proved its real value to the community," and a new Studio B "has been deemed in order."

NBC feeds had allowed programming to grow from ten hours per week in 1925 to about fifty hours per week in 1928. Weekdays began about 11:00 a.m. with the *Farm and Home Program* followed by a luncheon concert by Vito Pellettieri's Andrew Jackson Hotel Orchestra. Dusk on weeknights marked the juxtaposition of the closing market quotations and business news followed immediately by a bedtime story. NBC opened up the world to Nashville with a vividness it had never known in the newspapers. In 1927 Nashvillians listened with rapture to the arrival of Charles Lindbergh in Paris. Later, local man Bill Hart praised the station for its broadcast of Commander Richard Byrd's address on his polar and transatlantic flights. "It was thrilling and inspiring to hear from the very lips of the man whose daring accomplished them, an account of these two adventures, and I thank you for it," he said. The Republican and Democratic national conventions were carried in full that summer. "We had a large crowd with us the entire time and assure you that the courtesy of WSM is appreciated very much by all of us," wrote C. L. Ferguson from his Pikeville, Tennessee, drugstore about the Republican event in June. Other NBC programs included the *General Motors Family Party*, the National Grand Opera Ensemble, the *Philco Hour*, and the Cliquot Club Eskimos, a sextet of very tan young men who played banjos while wearing huge fur coats (to believe their publicity pictures), all to bolster their sponsor, a ginger ale.

Locally, WSM looked for ways to grow more integrated into its community, largely with live remote broadcasts, a common practice at prestige stations around the country. Junior engineer Aaron Shelton worked his first remote "pickup" from a series of motor-boat races late that summer, which turned into something more illuminating. He took a rudimentary mixer and three microphones down to the Cumberland River wharf at the bottom of Broadway just after lunch on a Saturday and set up the gear on a viewing platform, hooking into the telephone system to send his signal back to the studios at Seventh and Union. George Hay arrived at a quarter to three to announce the event and found he had time to kill between races. "He described our location, the other adjacent buildings, the weather, the wind direction, the temperature and any other thing he could see across the river," Shelton remembered. Eventually, "something upstream on our side of the river caught Judge Hay's attention. One of the large Negro churches had brought what seemed to be the entire congregation down to the river for a Saturday afternoon baptizing ceremony." He remembered Hay's midtempo, midrange monotone: "*The pastor has his flock all lined up on the river bank, and he and one of the brethren lead one of the sisters out into the river. The sister gives vent to several impassioned 'Hallelujahs' and 'Praise the Lords.' Those remaining upon the bank, awaiting their turn, answer back with equal enthusiasm. And now the pastor, holding the sister's nose, dips her completely beneath the surface. He raises her back quickly and the whole congregation gives forth more 'Hallelujahs' but now at a much greater volume.*" And so it went, as Hay transformed a broadcast from a regatta into an on-air sketch of Nashville life.

About this time, National Life reiterated to its sales force that "WSM is more than a radio station. It is a part of The Shield Company in ideals and aims, and it represents to a high degree all that the institution stands for as a benefactor of the people." This commitment grew deeper and more expensive, with costs approaching $100,000 in 1929. For one thing, WSM took on its first staff "orchestra" (as distinguished from Orin Gaston's all-purpose group) under NBC veteran Oliver Riehl to play light classical and popular tunes. Fortunately, joining a network was more than just convenient. It was a source of revenue. When NBC sent out commercial shows, it ensured the wide coverage it promised its sponsors by paying its affiliates to carry it. WSM ran $31,000 worth of NBC programming in 1929. Without it, that year's net loss of $34,000 would have been almost twice as great.

Nashville was not only living with, but was also celebrating its thriving station. When Kappa Sigma, a so-called business fraternity, held its gala "advertising dance," a Home Office Shield Girl named Elizabeth Kinney and her date, Vanderbilt student Joe Neuhoff, earned applause and long looks for their WSM costumes. "Miss Kinney was dressed to represent the microphone," reported the company newsletter. "Her dress was of red, white and blue satin, trimmed in cut-out Shields. Her turban was fashioned in imitation of a microphone . . .

and she carried on her arm a beautiful floral shield. Mr. Neuhoff impersonated the announcers, wearing a sash bearing our Company's slogan, and on his hat an improvised radio antennae. He carried and blew 'Old Hickory,' the 'Solemn Ol' Judge's' famous whistle, which has been heard around the radio world."

Meanwhile, WSM publicity started calling the Opry a "national institution." The waterfalls of letters that came in from fans suggested that wasn't overstating the case. They spoke in many voices, from scarcely literate to highly nuanced. Many shared common themes of home, nostalgia, and dancing. "Would you please send one of your agents down here to insure my carpets, floors, shoes, and everything in connection with the household?" wrote George Britting of Angola, New York. "Your Saturday-night 'shindig' has got my floors down to the second plank, and I am afraid someone will drop [through] on my barrel of preserves." The Casey family from Spiro, Oklahoma, spoke of how the Opry attracted company. "We had a house full Saturday night past, two large cars full," they wrote. "All enjoyed the program very heartily and said for us to look for them back again." The writer added that "I have my two babies insured with your Company." Many writers praised DeFord Bailey, and several indicated that the simulated dog yelps in his tour de force "Fox Chase" whipped their dogs into frenzies. Overturned pipe stands and busted back door screens were reported in all earnestness. And from New York City, Don Forrest reported the Opry helped his homesickness for Carroll County, Tennessee. "Our place of business is located at the very top of the bright-light district of Broadway, but I would leave the Metropolitan Opera any night for a good program from WSM. Those three letters spell home to me."

In the fall of 1928, Jack DeWitt found himself deeply in love with Ann Elise Martin, who lived across the street. But by now he'd dropped out of two different colleges and didn't have more than part-time engineering work at Nashville's various radio stations. Without a proper career, his prospects, for Elise or anything else, looked dim. Salvation arrived in the person of R. E. J. Poole of Bell Telephone Laboratories, who visited Nashville to tour WSM. Jack's father seems to have been paving a path for his son when he invited Poole over for dinner. Poole found himself impressed with Jack and wound up offering him a job in radio transmitter design at Bell Labs, starting in February 1929. For a young engineer, an invitation to work at Bell Labs was like winning a Rhodes scholarship. The institute had been founded in 1925 by AT&T and Westinghouse as a hive for basic and applied research across a series of campuses in New Jersey and New York, near where Alexander Graham Bell, Thomas Edison, and others had done historic and inspiring work.

Jack successfully proposed to Elise then moved to New York. He spent the winter berthed at the Fraternities Club at Thirty-eighth Street and Madison Avenue. He walked through biting winds to work on West Street on the Hudson River, stopping in drugstores along the way to stave off frostbite. He worked on a new design for using quartz crystals to stabilize the broadcast frequency of a station, in much the same way that they control the timing of watches. He heard Yankee colleagues disparage the South, but he fell in love with the city anyway. A new mechanic friend at Bell Labs, whose cousin worked backstage at the Met, gave him access to two-dollar opera seats, and Jack became especially enamored of Wagner. Another colleague introduced him to astronomy, a passion that would play a large role in his life. In late April he and Elise were married, and they set up housekeeping in Whippany, New Jersey. Meanwhile, the deeper mysteries of waves and fields were opening up, and the world seemed full of possibility. He was getting a real education at last.

THREE   *A Pleasing Spectacle*

The skywave, bouncing between the atmosphere and the earth, carried WSM's 5,000-watt, clear channel signal remarkable distances. In the early 1930s, the station received letters from Honolulu, New Zealand, and Northern Ontario. Margaret Joyce, the ten-year-old daughter of a Royal Canadian Mounted Policeman stationed near the Arctic Circle, wrote a letter that traveled seven hundred miles by Eskimo-driven dogsled to a railway, and ultimately to WSM. All to say, "We have a dandy radio set, and have been listening to your music. We enjoy it very much." Gustavo Barros of Havana, Cuba, wrote to alert WSM that he'd been translating its program schedules and promoting it over his own local radio station. "I hear your station WSM every day, and believe me, it's perfect clear and strong," he wrote. "Your station is well known in Havana because I tell them that your programs are some of the best in the United States."

But even before WSM's first power boost, Edwin Craig hoped for more. There had been inklings during the radio conferences of the early 1920s that 50,000-watt stations might come to pass. And even by the time WSM went on the air, some prestige stations like WJZ and WEAF, both out of New York, had been granted selective permission to venture above the legal limit of 5,000 watts, with excellent results for reception. By 1929, four stations in the country were reaching the nation with 50,000 watts. In June 1930 the Federal Radio

Commission (FRC) announced hearings that fall, where each clear channel station could vie to be one of twenty granted 50,000-watt or "superpower" status. They would be competing against one another based on their proposals to maintain gold-standard programming, cutting-edge technology, and—most important—service to rural America.

Craig needed insider firepower in Washington, so he retained the services of an attorney there named Louis Caldwell, who, as former chief counsel for the FRC, was in a potent position to lobby the agency. Caldwell, along with Runcie Clements, Harry Stone, and National Life lawyer Thomas Tyne, took WSM's case to the FRC on a Monday morning in late September in the National Press Building between the White House and Capitol Hill. And they were met there by a younger man from the North. Craig had called on Jack DeWitt, twenty-four years old, his mind charged with all he'd seen at Bell Labs, to vouch for WSM's technical leadership.

After Caldwell fended off a last-minute bid by Memphis station WMC to join in the competition for full power with the five other applicants, Clements offered an overview of National Life, now with $26 million in total assets, $310 million of life insurance in force, and three thousand agents. He said the company had so far invested $330,000 in WSM and that it was prepared to spend another $250,000 to achieve 50,000 watts. Sponsored shows brought in $250 per hour in the evening, but he said that revenues didn't come close to covering costs and that WSM "is not and never has been, in the strictest sense of the word, a commercial station." It refused to air ads that included prices or claims of superiority. It routinely turned away quack doctors and patent medicines. It did not advertise National Life itself, save for station identification. "We are content," he said, "with the good will which we believe the station has established and is maintaining for us among listeners." He did concede under questioning that National Life was funding WSM in part with money that would otherwise have been directed toward advertising and marketing.

Stone's testimony focused on the station's content. WSM now ran most days from about 6:30 a.m. to 11:30 p.m., totaling about one hundred hours of programming per week, evenly divided between local features and network shows, he said. It employed eighty-one musicians, full or part time, including seven in a concert orchestra, ten in a dance orchestra, five pianists, ten vocal soloists, and thirty-three other regular entertainers. Stone spoke of "the most complete music library in the South" and a full-time musical director. The station broadcast football games from Birmingham, Atlanta, and Knoxville, and had, he claimed, arranged to bring the Kentucky Derby to the NBC network for the first time. Via NBC, he said, WSM had broadcast a presidential inauguration, a King George address from England, and the landing of the Graf Zeppelin. Local affairs included daily stock and farm market reports, church services from First Presbyterian and Vine Street Christian, and educators from Vanderbilt, Peabody, and other local schools. Stone even noted that for about an hour per day, WSM broadcast phonograph records or shows via transcription disc, but at no time did Stone mention a Saturday show called the Grand Ole Opry.

DeWitt's testimony showed he'd mastered the technology of radio. He traded talk on signal attenuation and absorption factors with station representatives from Tulsa and Memphis. He was asked repeatedly about the population around Nashville and if the rural areas had grown and what kind of rock was underneath the ground (he knew it was limestone). His questioners wanted to discuss adequate minimum signal strength per meter at nighttime in the South. Ten millivolts, said an unfazed DeWitt—over and over again. At one point he made a bold prediction: that 50,000 watts over the new tower he and WSM were contemplating would more than double its local footprint to sixty-five miles in all directions, bringing in about 400,000 additional local listeners. What kind of people are they, an official from WMC wanted to know. DeWitt's answer was both factual and politically savvy: "Small towns and farms." To supplement their oral testimony and bolster their case, the WSM officials presented the FRC with a bound portfolio of financial statements, photographs, floor plans, and other supporting documents. It was all they could do besides wait and trust in Caldwell.

By 1931 WSM was literally wired into the city, with permanent pickup connections at the War Memorial Auditorium, two churches, two hotels, the Ward-Belmont Conservatory, and the Tennessee Division of Markets for stock news. Astute Nashvillians began to notice that WSM wasn't merely enhancing the airwaves; it was having an economic impact on a city that had long taken pride in its music. A letter from a listener to Edwin Craig praised the "excellent" Orin Gaston orchestra and WSM's "well-balanced and splendidly rendered" programming. He also remarked on WSM's important benefits for moonlighting musicians. "But for your enterprise, many of these players would have found it necessary to leave Nashville for lack of employment," he wrote. "The Nashville Symphony Orchestra would have felt the loss of these players keenly."

Whereas Orin Gaston and Oliver Riehl defined the WSM sound in the 1920s, the next decade would belong to Francis Craig and Beasley Smith. The bandleaders had known each other since their days at Hume-Fogg High School, where they had a piano duo. And they were roommates at Vanderbilt, about the time each decided to form his own band. They'd shadowed each other from WABV in the DeWitt family living room through the opening day of WSM, and they held some of the same hotel jobs. Then in the early 1930s, Craig, after a fight for his life with tuberculosis, took his Nashville band out on tour, while Smith came home from years on the road to settle in at WSM for good. Despite their shared backgrounds, each brought a distinctive flavor and style to the burgeoning station.

In 1930 Craig left the Hermitage Hotel for its nearby rival the Andrew Jackson, which gave him a two-year contract and announced that it had secured "the best all-around orchestra in the South." Craig's time on the air only increased. He often played both a lunch and dinner concert, and in April 1930, readers of the *Banner* voted him the most popular radio feature in town. (The Grand Ole Opry was sixth.) Then Craig, twenty-nine years old and a new father, was diagnosed with tuberculosis, the fourth leading cause of death in the United States. His father-in-law had died of TB one year prior, and there was no medicinal therapy. The best doctors could offer was quarantine, prolonged exposure to clean, cold air, and a diet of five thousand calories per day to combat wasting. Craig spent most of a year at an elegant sanatorium in Denver and beat the odds. By the end of 1931, the maestro was back on his Nashville podium, and his Rhythm Symphony made what appears to be WSM's first feed to NBC, a late night soiree from 12:30 to 1:00 a.m.

After high school, Beasley Smith spent a year in the Fifth U.S. Cavalry, patrolling the Mexican border for incursions by Pancho Villa. He returned to Nashville and entered Vanderbilt with premed ambitions, but music won him over. By 1925, Beasley and His Orchestra were playing the Andrew Jackson Hotel, the Knickerbocker Theater, and society dances. "We seldom even removed our tuxedoes to sleep," he recalled. Smith had appeared several times on WSM during its first year or two, but in the late 1920s, his group toured a circuit from Texas to New York, including the Garden Pier in Atlantic City, the Pla-Mor in Kansas City, and the Playland Casino in Rye, New York. In the era of speakeasies and mob-controlled nightclubs, Smith was, as Nashville music historians Broome and Tucker wrote, "a band leader who traveled to where the work was." During that time, Smith also become a familiar presence on both NBC and CBS, through one-off broadcasts from various venues. But in the early 1930s he found himself battling failing eyesight, and he returned to his hometown for an operation and to settle down from life on the road. WSM welcomed him back as a solo pianist as well as an accomplished arranger. His band stepped to the fore when Craig took a sabbatical out West. Musicians loved Smith for his laid-back style and the respect he afforded them. Soon, WSM made him the station's music director.

Musically, the contrasts between Smith and Craig were unmistakable. Smith's band swung with a touch of Memphis spice. Craig's orchestra swayed and swooned with, in the parlance of the day, a "sweet" rather than a "hot" sound. Smith's downbeat was a casual flop of the baton. Craig was crisp and buttoned up; he rarely used a baton, and while his right hand chopped in a clean, regimented count, his left generally reposed in the pocket of his tuxedo jacket. Biographer Ikard called Francis Craig's style "reserved, almost aloof," though Craig's daughter Donia Craig Dickerson bristles at that description, calling him, with boundless respect, "a quiet southern gentleman, just filled with rhythm, and a very dignified conductor."

Clay Tucker, a well-traveled trumpet player who cowrote the best history of Nashville's dance and pop bands, remembered an encounter that illuminated the difference between Craig and Smith. "I was in high school playing in the Pulaski Municipal Band's dance band unit—a group of high school kids plus two or three older musicians—somebody arranged for Craig to hear me play. I made my way to Nashville and up to WSM where I met Beasley Smith, who, as it turned out, was to accompany me on the piano. Craig came in, picked several tunes, and I played a chorus of each with Beasley. When I finished, Craig gave me a brief critique that went something like this: 'It's good but your tone sounds too much like a jazzy black musician's.' On the way out Beasley took me to one side and said, 'Don't let it bother you. And don't try to change that tone.'"

If Smith and Craig defined WSM's dance and dinner orchestra vibe, singers like John Lewis sustained its fine arts agenda. He'd been a soloist with the National Symphony and was Gaetano de Luca's assistant in his early days running the Nashville Conservatory. He also had experience in local radio, having managed programming at Life & Casualty's WLAC for three years. WSM promotional rhetoric about him suggested the kind of musical values the station was going for: "Mr. Lewis has a remarkable range, excellent sustained tones and operatic resonance, combined with a real stage presence." In the studio, he sang with one hand cupped to his ear.

Somewhat more daring was Johnny Payne, "King of the Novelty Pianists." Only twenty-four years old, the Nashville native was already established on the RKO-Publix theater circuit and had played a vaudeville mecca, the Palace Theater in New York. He'd also been a hit as an opening act for the great Rudy Vallee. In a studio darkened but for a dim, shaded lamp, Payne played in an extravagant ragtime and blues style on a grand piano, and he drew mail begging for his slots to be expanded.

Velma Dean, by contrast, needed an audience in the studio when she sang. Whoever was available, from engineers to fellow artists, was called on to sit and listen to her shows. "Sparkling and vivacious," WSM's early fan magazine *Broadcast News* said of the "former RKO and radio headliner." Dean had started her career in Fort Worth, when WBAP went on the air there, then sang on stations in San Antonio, Chicago, St. Louis, and elsewhere. She recorded for Brunswick and Gennett. Known as "the Southern Crooner" or "the Girl Tenor" depending on time and place, Dean was seen by WSM as a "blues singer." She joined the station in 1931 and sang on *Sleepy Town Express,* a soothing half hour sponsored by Anchor Spring and Bedding.

A trio of young men regularly around the studios after August 1931 brought a new level of professionalism to the station's music business and a new degree of polish to the Grand Ole Opry. The Vagabonds—Dean Upson, Curt Poulton, and Herald Goodman—had been touring and performing together since early 1929, when a long stint at KMOX in St. Louis became their platform for network syndication. They formed their own production company and rounded up their own sponsors, including a year-long deal with Anheuser-Busch as "The Vagabond Club," which put them on as many as fifty-six stations. Musically, they blended folk, hillbilly, and barbershop into a mass-appeal pop/country hybrid. Harry Stone hired them as staff musicians, thinking their heart songs and hymns would lend a bit of panache to the otherwise rustic Opry while being acceptable during other program slots. Once on board, the Vagabonds launched what appears to have been WSM's first morning show by Opry artists and sold songbooks that included their signature hits "Ninety-nine Years" and "When It's Lamp Lighting Time in the Valley." They formed the Old Cabin Company, Nashville's first folk song publishing concern, headquartered initially at WSM. They organized the first traveling unit of Grand Ole Opry talent, taking Uncle Dave, Sam McGee, and the Fruit Jar Drinkers on the road. And they sent free promotional records to radio stations in 1933, before that became an accepted marketing idea.

Numerous other musicians made up WSM's fifteen-person office staff, playing roles on both sides of the microphone. Margaret Rich Ackerman, a former voice student at Ward-Belmont, a soloist, and a member of WSM's ever-so-proper Sacred Quartet, also ran the programming department, with her hard-back ledger book schedule always near at hand. Christine Lamb, an admired contralto, was the music librarian. The station's very first clerical employee, stenographer and chief clerk Zena Jones, was still on staff five years later. She played piano somewhat more delicately than she typed.

Young Aaron Shelton doubled as an engineer and a radio sound effects man. He remembered the early 1930s as "a period of experimentation, [when] almost any and every idea for a program was given some air time." Telegrams and mail generally determined how long a show survived. Programs developed and funded by WSM (or the network) that had no commercial sponsor were called "sustaining" shows, and the ratio of sustaining shows to commercial shows was one important measure of public service commitment whenever stations went before the FRC and FCC to defend their licenses. More and more, however, acts simply paid WSM its commercial rate for fifteen-minute spots, during which musicians or ministers could entertain, edify, and sell a product or a songbook. The *Easy Way Piano Course* ran for a time in the late afternoon, Shelton remembered. One mid-morning flop featured a red-headed kid named Rod Dinwiddie, who gave tap-dancing lessons over the air with a microphone on the floor near his feet.

Another self-sponsoring act proved far more popular and marked one of the early music business synergies to take place under WSM's roof. Asher Sizemore, a coal mine bookkeeper turned radio singer, bought a fifteen-minute block of time on weekday afternoons. Little Jimmy Sizemore, his cherubic son, wore a satin cowboy outfit and a big white hat and sang sentimental songs in a choirboy voice. Asher would kick off the segment with some father-son banter then launch a solo tune. A quick duet with Jimmy would follow, and then a Jimmy solo tune, and a closing prayer. In between, Asher pitched souvenir songbooks for a buck and photos "suitable for framing" for a quarter. Thousands of letters flooded in with their quarters and dollars. A National Life porter called Clifford was tipped a quarter per day for hauling large boxes full of cash down to Asher's waiting car.

The station's management consisted ostensibly of George D. Hay, director, and Harry Stone, associate director, though in truth, Stone carried most of the burden. Hay, it turned out, was a depressive man—probably bipolar, according to Opry historian Wolfe. In early 1931, Hay suffered the first of several spells that made it impossible for him to work, and he more or less vanished for the rest of the year.

Jack Keefe moved on too, late in 1931, though an accepted story that he was fired for an on-air gaffe probably isn't entirely true. Preparing to introduce a speech by President Hoover and, unaware that he was on the air, Keefe said something like: "Who the hell wants to listen to Hoover?" Keefe's daughter confirms the incident happened, but she says Keefe stayed on a good many months afterward, quitting on his own terms to practice law.

Although WSM's personality was shaped mainly by local shows and artists, half or more of every program day came from NBC. The network became a vital, energizing presence on the air, and in the studio. The signature three-toned station break marked time on the fifth floor of National Life, sometimes jolting a slacking announcer to his feet and into a steeplechase over chairs and down the hall to do a live station identification. The telephone pipeline to New York brought news and special events, including fifty-eight hours of wall-to-wall coverage of both political parties' nominating conventions in the summer of 1932. Day to day, NBC introduced Nashville to many of the era's national hit shows, including *Roxy and His Gang*, with its huge symphony orchestra; variety shows like the *Palmolive Hour;* and stars like Rudy Vallee, a sophisticate of stage, screen, and radio who crooned through a megaphone and paved the way for Bing Crosby.

No network show was bigger in that era than *Amos 'n' Andy*, written and played by two white men about two black cab drivers scuffling in Chicago. Former vaudevillians Freeman Fisher Gosden (Amos) and Charles J. Correll (Andy) worked up a blackface act after meeting in a touring company. Their radio career began as "Sam 'n' Henry" on Chicago's WGN, but they adopted their famous label upon moving to nearby WMAQ. *Amos 'n' Andy* truly exploded in 1929 when they went on NBC, sponsored by Pepsodent toothpaste. They wrote the whole show together and played multiple characters in a brisk, ten-minute nightly drama, every night but Sunday. Funny and topical, *Amos 'n' Andy* proved that serial drama could be even more addictive on the air than it had been in newspapers. The nation virtually came to a standstill when it was on; President Hoover was a devoted fan. Even the Grand Ole Opry broke away every Saturday night for years, making it the only show the Opry ever worked around.

WSM had its own blackface comedy team in the early 1930s. The duo "Lasses & Honey" was part of a vaudevillian extravaganza called the *Lasses*

White All-Star Minstrels Show. Lee Roy "Lasses" White, a Texan, had understudied for George "Honeyboy" Edwards, one of the pioneers of blackface minstrelsy and cowriter of "In the Good Ole Summertime." It had been quite a few years since White had started working with sidekick Lee Davis "Honey" Wilds; George Hay had been impressed with them in Memphis in the early 1920s. By the time Lasses White accepted an invitation by WSM to adapt his own minstrel show to radio in about 1931 or 1932, the entire format was something of a holdover or revival of a format popular before the turn of the century. WSM publicity referred to White as the "dean of the burnt cork artists." He and partner Honey Wilds performed in blackface, tuxedos, and white gloves when they were before a live audience. He mingled some of his own cast of entertainers with staff artists from WSM, like the Vagabonds, Beasley Smith's groups, baritones John Lewis and Priestly Miller, and tenor Claude Sharpe. The All-Star Minstrels featured ten singers and ten musicians, who were as ready to turn a joke as perform a satiric or novelty song. A new WSM production manager and writer from Dallas named Arthur Stowe (called "Tiny" for his 250-pound frame) played the critical role of "interlocutor," the announcer and comic foil for minstrel humor. The Minstrels represented the largest WSM production to date, and they became identifiers for WSM in the larger radio industry. When the station took out its first full page ad in the relatively new *Broadcasting* magazine in November 1932, it featured Lasses White.

More faux African American comedy came from Ed McConnell, who broke into radio with Lambdin Kay at WSB before coming to Nashville. WSM hired him to handle commercial accounts, but he also took to the air as a character named "Uncle Wash" described in promotional material as "an old colored man who was loyal to his master." The Uncle Wash character opened the Grand Ole Opry for a time in 1929 "and proved to be very popular." As early as 1929, WSM was getting mail calling McConnell "the greatest broadcaster of them all." One said "his laugh is the best medicine for the blues we ever had." He played off Hay in a feature called "Uncle Wash and the Judge," and he was a fair singer too. *Our Shield* (previously *The Shield*) published a letter from S. D. Winn, who said that since he was "born and raised in Georgia," he felt qualified to say "that 'Uncle Wash's' 'nigger' talk is perfect."

As a station owned by Depression-era southern aristocrats and pitched to conservative white society, it should come as no surprise that WSM's relationship to blacks and black music mixed guarded respect with commercial pragmatism and a strong dose of patronizing paternalism. WSM's leaders, including Hay and Craig, knew how good many of Nashville's black musicians were, yet it would have been beyond their experience and beyond their audience's comprehension to present those artists as equals on their stage of the air. Perhaps the most telling case from the era is Pee Wee Marquette, a three-foot-nine-inch African American performer, who for about ten years, acted as the personality in front of Francis Craig's orchestra. First hired in 1934, when he was sixteen, Marquette told Craig he'd been the "mascot" of the University of Alabama football team, and he became the "mascot" of the band. In his red bellhop uniform, he was an integral part of nearly every Craig performance, trading banter with the band, strumming a ukulele or a mandolin, and tap dancing. Marquette was admired as a performer and reportedly made friends throughout Nashville. He would go on to become a well-known master of ceremonies at New York's Birdland jazz club. But his WSM years were certainly made more difficult by his race. He had to stand on the opposite side of the stage from white singers who thought Pee Wee's presence demeaning—to them. Maestro Craig's family doted on him and liked him very much, but when he joined them for Sunday dinner, he had to sit at a separate, miniature table, ostensibly to avoid insult to the family maid.

Meanwhile, WSM's most prominent black performer, DeFord Bailey, made legions of white fans via the Grand Ole Opry. He also earned a place of affection and acceptance at the radio station, but at a cost. When fans began sending him cash gifts of appreciation in the mail, WSM made an official on-air announcement bidding fans not to send money to the performers and then screened his fan letters for violators. Nor did WSM pay Bailey commensurate with his popularity. When he moved to Knoxville in 1928 to triple his fee playing over WNOX for station announcer W. C. Taylor, Taylor and George Hay conspired to keep Bailey away from travel opportunities that would lead his career anywhere but back to WSM. He returned in 1929, albeit at the higher fee that he'd been earning in Knoxville. Then Hay figured out a way to garnish Bailey's income from his important Brunswick recording sessions. Bailey said that while he had genuine friends and champions in acts like Uncle Dave and the Delmore Brothers, he maintained many of his cordial relations around WSM by acting deferential. "I stayed in my place," he said. Though he wore a silver National Life shield pin on his lapel most of his life, he would say that he'd been treated like a "civilized slave."

Besides Bailey's exceptional country blues, the black music that got the most exposure on WSM in the 1920s and 1930s was of a gospel flavor. Various groups from Fisk University sang on the air regularly, sometimes from the studio, sometimes from their campus. On several occasions, the group was accompanied by John Work, the younger of a father-son line of folklorists, educators, and composers who led the Jubilee Singers and published vital scholarship on black folk and spiritual music. The Golden Echo Quartet was a similarly polished gospel vocal group that recorded in 1927 for Columbia as artists "of Station WSM, Nashville, Tenn." Black jazz and blues were largely kept at a distance, though engineer Aaron Shelton related that on at least one occasion, King Oliver, the New Orleans mentor of Louis Armstrong, performed from Studio A.

How WSM positioned itself to black audiences is a harder question. WSM didn't go out of its way to court a black audience on the air, though in years to come, once the Opry evolved into a stage show, Edwin Craig would send instructions down the chain of command that any black person seeking Opry admission should be let in. DeFord Bailey recalled Hay signing off one night saying 'colored people could come' to the Opry show. "He let them know they was welcome," he said. Hay also told Bailey that he'd been an asset to the company in securing many black policy-holders. African Americans remained a substantial part of National Life's business, said Edwin's son Neil, so substantial that the great migration from the Delta region to Chicago, Detroit, and other large northern cities was the key catalyst for National Life to expand into those territories.

Up on the hill at Ward-Belmont School, where a colonnaded white academic hall stared down Sixteenth and Seventeenth Avenues, a new class of debutantes moved into dormitories for the fall term. Sarah Ophelia Colley was plainer than most of her class and, she quickly discovered, not as wealthy either. Her father, a Centerville lumber magnate, was losing his business to the sudden economic crash. Phel, as he called his daughter, had known a life of dinner parties and romantic formal balls, but she'd faced narrowing choices for her long-awaited formal education. She wanted very much to be an actress, to go to New York and tour capitals and play serious roles, and she'd hoped to attend the American Academy of Dramatic Arts. Instead, all that could be managed was a choice between the University of Tennessee or the well-regarded drama program at Ward-Belmont, affordable because it lasted two years instead of four. Sarah chose the latter and almost immediately wondered what she had done.

Colley would later describe the campus as "aloof, untouched, an oasis of Bourbon opulence." Behind its edifice was a wooded park with life-size animal statues, gazebos, and a lily pond with a tiered fountain that burbled day and night. The inside dripped with crystal chandeliers dimly lighting Old South-meets-Old Europe décor—leaded Venetian glass, rococo curlicues, stolid antique furniture, and oriental rugs throughout. Mostly Colley noticed the quiet. "Everyone spoke in dulcet tones, just above a whisper and moved at a very precise, carefully measured ladylike pace," she wrote. "Comparing my first impression with the noisy, active household I'd come from, I felt like I'd been dropped into a funeral home." Then she met her roommate, a Texas debutante marinated in oil money. She shamed Colley as she unpacked "outfit after outfit, all coordinated with different shoes, bags and gloves, several black dresses and a half-dozen formals" and two full-length mink coats.

It was the beginning of a strange two years during which Sarah struggled through her awkwardness and into a reasonably happy student life. She did study Shakespeare, as she'd dreamed, and played Petruchio in the *Taming of the Shrew*. And she learned to take the most outlandish parts of Belmont life with a sense of humor, such as the mandatory prevacation lecture "The Conduct of Young Ladies While Traveling on Public Conveyances." For her final recital, a formal and celebratory night, she performed all the parts in an abridged version of *The Charm School*, to great acclaim. A career on stage was perhaps not so impossible after all.

WSM officials had their minds back on Washington in the spring of 1931, as they continued their campaign for 50,000 watts. A top official at the FRC had recommended WSM's approval, and when Louis Caldwell, WSM's D.C. counsel, took a seat in the FRC hearing room, he offered a rhetorical flourish that aimed to leave WSM's competition—WBT, WAPI, and KVOO—behind. "Mr. Chairman and gentlemen of the Commission," he began, "I want to take you now from the seductive climate of Charlotte and the educational walls of Birmingham and the oil of Tulsa to the quiet, historical splendor of Nashville."

Caldwell then proceeded to lay out his case for a station that had been "a pleasing spectacle of a fine American institution, cleanly run on a dignified basis, without a blemish on its record." He came with several arguments: First, lower frequency, longer-wavelength stations like WSM had longer range and should be given preferred treatment. Second, WSM had the most advantageous location—dead center of the eastern United States, whereas much of the signal of a Charlotte station would be lost at sea. Furthermore, Caldwell said, WSM should be given the nod because it was a locally owned station with an open-ended arrangement with NBC, while Charlotte's WBT was a property of CBS. WSM, he said, is as "free as any station to change its connections, or abandon any of them entirely tomorrow . . . Which is likely to best serve the interests of the community, a corporation which is owned and controlled by local people, or one which is owned and controlled by a distant organization?"

The remarks played to the prevailing biases of the FRC, toward localism and away from sponsor-centric or agenda-driven programming. One commissioner seemed concerned about the latter when he asked, "Why does an insurance company have a station? . . . Do you sell insurance policies over it?" Caldwell assured the panel "there is no promotion of the company from early morning until late at night," and that the Tennessee insurance commissioner had already approved of WSM. He added that the slogan "We Shield Millions" was uttered only at the beginning and the end of the day. National Life was putting public service above its own interests, he was saying, even though the station and its parent company were already seeing valuable synergies emerging.

The pitch worked. On October 1, 1931, the FRC gave 50,000-watt clearance to two stations in zone three: WSB in Atlanta and WSM. The commitment would require unprecedented levels of engineering expertise, so Edwin Craig called Jack DeWitt in New Jersey and asked him to return as WSM's chief engineer to oversee the installation of a new transmitter and tower. The invitation would prove a watershed for the station and the man. "It was one of the tough decisions of my life," DeWitt said later. "I thought long and hard on it, because here was the great Bell Telephone Laboratories, where I really got a good education in electronics, with all sorts of facilities and everything. And here was WSM, a radio station in Nashville, my hometown. Well, that was a great incentive, you see. I was married. Should I go back to my hometown, where I would be a big frog on a little pond, or would I stay in New York and try to make my career?" Ultimately the tug of home won out, and in March 1932 he bought a two-year-old Model A Ford sedan and drove with Elise for several days, through the rambling roads of the Shenandoah Valley of Virginia, between levees of plowed early spring snow. He arrived March 21 and started on April 1 at the typically parsimonious National Life salary of $275 per month.

DeWitt wasn't happy to find that the new transmitter building had been started and a new model 50,000-watt transmitter had already been purchased from RCA. For DeWitt, a stickler who believed in testing before proceeding, this was a question on which it was too late for input. He did however, launch a vigorous discussion about what kind of tower to erect. RCA had recommended a larger version of the kind of suspended, horizontal antenna WSM had used since the beginning: two four-hundred-foot towers with radiating wires strung between. At a meeting in the National Life legal department with C. A. and Edwin Craig, Runcie Clements, and a local architect, DeWitt argued for something bolder. He had studied a new antenna that had been designed by Bell Labs in cooperation with the new Columbia Broadcasting Service. The so-called half-wave antenna had been put into service for CBS station WABC in Wayne Township, New Jersey, and the results had been excellent. As DeWitt described it, such a tower for WSM would be an engineering feat and an electrical marvel. Instead of a suspended radiator, the Bell Labs antenna was the metal tower itself. It was to be a tapered diamond of steel standing nearly nine-hundred feet tall, weighing 300,000 pounds, and sitting on a base about the size of a dinner plate, held upright by eight guy wires. It would be the tallest structure ever built in Tennessee, the tallest radio tower in North America, and a striking symbol for National Life.

On a Friday in late April, the station took another step forward by inviting an audience up to its fifth-floor studios to watch a show in progress for the first time. Sponsored by the Union Ice Cream Company and slated for a twenty-six-week run, the show was headlined by Beasley Smith and Marjorie Cooney, a duo billed as the Piano Twins. Smith had come home from heavy roadwork that winter feeling too ill to tour and had been made an orchestra leader at WSM. Cooney was a brisk and bright young woman who'd moved to Nashville about a year before, after gaining radio experience in her native Huntsville, Alabama. She'd found Harry Stone hungry for professional talent and earned a job based on her references alone. She'd had solo slots, but her duo with Smith was earning wider recognition. The Union show found them collaborating with each other on two pianos and with "Southern Crooner" Velma Dean. Stone saw to it that tickets for the general public were distributed at Union Ice Cream counters, and two hundred ice cream vendors came to the show's premiere.

Also at the end of April, C. A. Craig, now the company's chairman, made perhaps his longest-ever address over WSM to talk about National Life's upcoming Pearl Jubilee—its thirtieth birthday. He noted that the company had "never undertaken to use [the station] to selfish ends other than to obtain the good will of those who were kind enough to tune in on the station." That night, however, he said "for the first time and for only a few moments are we deviating from this practice to tell something of the owner Company." Though Louis Caldwell had told the FRC just a year before that WSM wasn't there to plug National Life, Craig offered a history of the company, a briefing on its generous reserves, and a sermon on its tradition of paying claims, concluding with: "It has been truly said that just now Life Insurance is a great sheltering rock in a weary land." He urged Shield Men to come back to the Home Office for the celebration, and the next month, many did. Orin Gaston and Johnny Payne entertained the Jubilee revelers, attracting a swarm of Shield Men up to the WSM studios. "The Detroit delegation flocked into the studio during the 'Grand Ol' Opry' and each man had a word to say about the policyholders back home," reported the company newsletter. "Youngstown grabbed the gauntlet and marshaled their forces. They even sent back to the hotel for the boys that had turned in and got their names on the air—and a few 'cracks' about what they intended to do in the way of setting a new record for next year."

Late May saw production of WSM's first in-house dramas, with office staff as actors. Zena Jones, Christine Lamb, and Margaret Ackerman portrayed the Strawberry Point Ladies' Aid in a gossipy skit directed by matronly Madge West of the Nashville Little Theater. West had acted since childhood and worked in New York and San Francisco before moving to Nashville. Her next production several weeks later was a thirteen-week series of true police dramas, beginning with *The Murder of the Count* with Dick Swint, Nashville Legion Commander, as a traffic cop. Tiny Stowe played tough-guy roles. Harry Stone declined to be in the drama; he had too many parts to play already, he said. Aaron Shelton, besides getting everybody properly miked, secured a real police siren and hauled off with it during a show. "Everybody in the YMCA across the street rushed to the windows looking for the fire," Stowe reported at the time. Later that summer, West produced *Does Crime Pay?* on Wednesday nights at 8:00. Shelton continued to refine his sound effects for the cop thrillers: gun shots, stealthy footsteps, breaking glass, doors opening and slamming, knife stabs, airplane and auto motors, corks popping, and a fire made from crinkled cellophane.

In June Studio A had its heavy, wine-colored drapery removed and replaced with Acoustone tiles. Suddenly, the place, painted white with light-green trim, felt brighter and much larger, and it sounded better too. Studios A and B got separate control panels for the first time. And the large, double-plated glass windows looking from the hall into the studio were replaced with small, one-foot square windows. One could see in if need be, but it kept the ever-increasing parade of artists, ad-men, and executives, on their way to

Stone's or Hay's office from the elevator lobby, from distracting the sessions. For several weeks, all programs had to come out of Studio B, and staffers reported feeling piled on top of one another.

Construction got underway on the tower that summer too. Huge concrete moorings had to be poured, and deep grounding pits had to be dug and filled with copper shavings. Trenches for underground copper leads fanned out in all directions. An elegant brick transmitter house in colonial style with a columned portico was finished in May, and the last of the transmitter gear was installed by June. Then in the first week of July, about an hour after the Grand Ole Opry concluded the evening's regular entertainment, DeWitt ran a signal from the WSM studio through his new black behemoth of a transmitter and up a temporary antenna, transmitting the sounds of Johnny Payne, the Vagabonds, and announcer Tiny Stowe at 50,000 watts for the first time. Stowe asked the listening audience for reception reports, and they came flooding in over the next twenty-four hours, from Canada, Wisconsin, Oklahoma, and all parts of the South. A second test the following Wednesday seemed even more successful, with reports from Oregon and Washington. Anticipating large future maintenance needs, Stone made plans to expand the engineering staff to ten full-timers, and he bought them their own wood-paneled truck.

In early July Stone got a wire from NBC indicating they wanted an hour of WSM's talent late on a Saturday night. Network feeds were still new for the growing station, so the staff whipped into a frenzy of rehearsals to present a curious mix of Grand Ole Opry artists, including the Vagabonds, plus Beasley Smith and Marge Cooney as the Piano Twins.

Despite the pressure to have the tower and transmitter running in harmony, Jack DeWitt took some time out in late August to indulge his newest scientific passion. While at Bell Labs, he'd met people involved in astronomy, and when he discovered that his brother Ward, back in Nashville, was similarly fascinated, they resolved, via ham radio, to build six-inch telescopes. Jack had ground his mirror by hand night after night in his apartment kitchen in New Jersey and then mounted it in a four-foot tube to make a traditional Newtonian reflector. Ward finished his the same day. On a bright August day they put both scopes into service to observe and photograph a partial eclipse of the sun. (Inspired by the results, Jack and Ward collaborated on a twelve-inch telescope in the coming months, grinding the mirror day after day at Ward's house. They hired a metalsmith to build a housing for the large scope—an eight-foot-diameter dome large enough for two people and including a sliding door. It won rave reviews from local astronomy buffs and eventually the faculty of Vanderbilt.

The brothers set up their masterwork in Ward's backyard, coincidentally on Observatory Drive.)

That October Edwin Craig found himself looking skyward as well. He would don sunglasses and sit back in a camp chair at the new transmitter site to watch his tower grow by some fifty feet per day. By month's end it was a rhomboid spire of iron, 878 feet tall, spreading from two feet wide at its base to almost forty feet at the middle and then back to a tapered nose topped with a 120-foot telescoped pole. It touched the earth and yet remained insulated from it. At the bottom of the slender needle, two ceramic cones capped with hoods of steel kissed each other on their pointed ends, invisibly held together by a single arm-thick bolt. This giant pivot point allowed the tower to sway or twist ever so slightly in the wind, its verticality supported by eight guy wires bolted to the earth nearby, each bearing 55,000 pounds of tension. The bolts that anchored them to their fifty-four-ton concrete piers were as long as a man was tall.

The transmitter apparatus took up three walls of the largest room in the white building, about two-hundred yards from the tower. Somewhere behind its black phalanx of dials and gauges, in a chamber held at a consistent sixty degrees, a shard of quartz some two millimeters thick and nudged by a tiny pulse of electricity oscillated exactly 650,000 times per second, generating one watt of carefully calibrated energy. Four radio tubes amplified that delicate stream to a 200-watt river, which was then imprinted with the WSM signal, coming by phone line from Seventh and Union. Then it hit two more banks of radio tubes. The second set, water-cooled monsters some five feet high, boiled the signal up to 50,000 watts in an incredibly inefficient system that spent twice that much energy to obtain the legal limit of power. Thus primed, the signal raced over fat cables to a house at the base of the tower and hit a transformer that adjusted it for maximum effectiveness in flowing through the tower's iron.

In many radio towers, that would be it, but DeWitt's tower had a hidden component that vastly increased its effectiveness. Underground, an array of 120 copper wires spread out in all directions from the tower's base like spokes in a wheel. These maintained a stable electrostatic field perpendicular to the tower's huge electromagnetic field. Like a man cracking a bullwhip 1,500 feet long (WSM's wavelength), the tower and the copper radial ground field snapped back and forth in rapid succession. The final result was something violent but invisible: the shock excitement of the Earth's enveloping, omnipresent magnetic field. It was this vast field—not the legendary "ether" or the air we breathe—that rippled away at the speed of light north to Nashville, south to the Gulf of Mexico, and up into space.

Craig likely asked DeWitt about the thick prongs of steel sticking out of the tower and base that nearly touched each other but for tennis ball sized knobs at the end of each. Or maybe he knew intuitively. It was the biggest lightning rod he'd ever seen—two conductors with just enough space between them to invite atmospheric charges to run down the tower, leap across the spark gap, and dive harmlessly into the earth. It was a sobering reminder that this tower would have to weather any wind, rain, and lightning that swept across Middle Tennessee for as many years as it stood. Ten years before, Edwin had been pleased to have a rudimentary radio receiving set on the sleeping porch. Now, he was looking at the largest transmitting device in the United States, aware of his blessings and responsibilities in equal measure.

Alton Delmore, one of the many musicians who made the pilgrimage to Nashville to audition for the Grand Ole Opry, wrote one of the only accounts of seeing the tower when it was still very new. He and his brother Rabon— they were a duo—drove the two-lane country highway out of Alabama, which rambled mile after mile past hedgerows, forests, farmers' fields, barns, and livestock. They passed through the town square of Franklin with its Confederate war memorial and courthouse and knew they were close to Nashville, hot with anticipation after a long drive. Before long, they hit a clear spot and saw the tower ahead of them. Alton was about twenty-five, his brother only in his late teens. They'd seen small town radio stations around the country, little shacks with laundry line antennas where you could drop in and meet the owner/operator and be on the air in ten minutes if you were both pleasant to each other. But the sight of a nine-hundred-foot skyscraper was a jolt as sure as the electricity that ran through it. Alton, years later, reached beautifully for what it meant:

> It gave off a seeming challenge to anyone who wanted to go far and do things. There it was, blinking and flashing its facility out to some little person or persons, who thought they deserved the plaudits of the great Grand Ole Opry audience . . . It is a strange thing for me to say, but the manager of the station and the others there who heard our audition didn't add up to anything like the challenge that tall tower did. It was a tall tower, and it takes a lot to stay tall like it does. But we tried it. Our listeners thought we were tall, like the tower, but we never felt we quite made it to our own way of thinking and judging. And I, personally, don't think anyone had ever made it and I don't believe they ever will. That old tower is a gigantic and magnificent object to

live up to. To me, a former Grand Ole Opry entertainer, it represents the Bible of radio achievement.

The tower quickly became the station's iconic image. It was issued on postcards, sometimes by itself and sometimes paired with an image of an Opry artist. Its picture was ubiquitous in company publications and eventually it would make its way onto WSM's letterhead in many configurations. A Nashville company packaged a brand of flour with the WSM tower on its bags. For some WSM artists who lived in town, the tower was a reminder of their reach and influence. And sometimes it was a destination. "We used to drive out Franklin Pike and look at the tower and say, 'Just think, our voice goes out of that tower,'" recalled pianist Marjorie Cooney late in her life. "We were living in an unreal world. We couldn't believe that that was what was happening. We'd go out to the tower to see our words go out, which of course was impossible."

In the first week of November 1932, Franklin Roosevelt was elected president of the United States and Harry Stone was named to the newly created post of station manager of WSM. Hay had given Edwin Craig much of what the station needed in its early days—enthusiasm, personality, and warmth. But he'd missed over a year due to health problems, and though he was a dedicated office man, answering mail as fast as it came in, it was now clear he lacked the mental or fiscal discipline to make WSM a self-supporting venture. Hay would focus on the two things he did best: coaching the Opry and station publicity. He revived his "Howdy Judge" column from his Memphis days, which started running in *Our Shield*. Symbolic of his role as minister of whimsy, one early column proposed cutting through a bitter partisan standoff in Washington by electing Lasses White president and Honey Wilds vice president on the "Laugh Party" ticket. In his "inaugural address," White proposed that "all meetings of the Senate and House be accompanied by music in syncopated time."

November 12, a chilly Saturday, was selected as dedication day for WSM's new 50,000-watt transmitter and its record-breaking tower. Nashville was swarming with football fans, who saw (or heard) bitter rivals Vanderbilt and Tennessee, both ranked among the nation's elite, battle to a scoreless tie. WSM's big night proved equally frustrating.

Celebrated station alumni arrived, including Dad Pickard, Smilin' Ed

McConnell, and—in white tie and tails—celebrity singer James Melton. Two vice presidents from NBC arrived by train, as did Harold LaFount, acting chairman of the FRC. The station's women—Marjorie Cooney, Madge West, Christine Lamb, and the others—wore gowns of chiffon and velvet. At 8:00 p.m., the station's local programming began, with offerings from John Lewis, Alven Masten's concert orchestra, Beasley Smith's group, and the Fisk Jubilee Singers. At 10:15 p.m., the show was scheduled to link up with NBC, to be carried live over thirty-five stations, with real-time tributes from a half dozen stations around the nation, including Francis Craig from Denver.

But as the time grew near, word came from New York that President Hoover—America's newly lame-duck president—was preparing to address the nation. "Speculation, in view of his recent defeat in the presidential election, ran rife as to what national emergency was the occasion of his sudden decision to have both broadcasting networks stand by," wrote a *Nashville Banner* reporter. WSM's national show was suspended as the hours ticked by, and the cast made the best of it with more performances by the luminaries on hand. Ed McConnell filled some of the latter minutes of tedious waiting with the song "Holding My Breath, Scared to Death of You." Then at 12:15 p.m., Hoover came on the air and delivered a short and entirely anticlimactic address about the importance of the Boulder Dam project.

The NBC officials apologized profusely for the unnecessary hang-up and arranged to broadcast the WSM dedication one week later. On November 19, WSM offered a variety show from 10:00 to 11:15 p.m. over about forty stations. Musical tributes from other NBC stations in New York, Cleveland, Chicago, and San Francisco came off fine. A proud Francis Craig broadcast from Denver. And Edwin Craig offered a short but heartfelt dedicatory address. "As we join the ranks of America's radio giants, we realize not only our increased opportunities, but also our heavily increased obligation to the public service," he said, as he presented "the new WSM."

FOUR ⚡ *Air Castle of the South*

Late in the fall of 1933, WSM transmitter engineer Jack Montgomery stirred himself at about ten minutes to five in the afternoon and left the white transmitter house in the meadow in Brentwood. The sun was setting early now, heralding the nightly coming of the skywave that would amplify WSM's signal over thousands of miles. The tower soared above his head, poised as if for take off, caught in the sunset like a tall flame against a darkening sky. Gravel crunched beneath Montgomery's feet as he walked out the gate and down Calendar Road toward the road cut. A half mile away he arrived at a white shed with a shingle roof, adjacent to the tracks of the Louisville & Nashville Railroad, an iron artery running south to New Orleans and north to Cincinnati. He unlocked the shed and found the microphone, uncoiled its cord, switched on its amplifier, and hung it on a hook outside the shed next to the tracks.

From a field telephone in the shed, Montgomery called the WSM studios at Seventh and Union. Aaron Shelton took the call and checked the line to the amplifier in the shed and confirmed the connection. A few minutes later another expected call came. An engineer from the L&N at a switching house six miles south of Nashville confirmed that the locomotive Pan American was on time, heading south under full steam. Six minutes later the train tripped a switch on the track that rang a bell in the shed. Montgomery informed Shelton in the studio. He gave a visual cue to the announcer on duty, David Stone, and he signaled Marjorie Cooney to wrap up her piano interlude. It was 5:07.

"*Ladies and gentlemen,*" Stone said, "*we now take you to a point twelve miles south of Nashville where the L&N's crack passenger train, the Pan American, is about to pass the 878-foot tower of station WSM on its journey south from Cincinnati, Ohio, to New Orleans, Louisiana.*"

Listeners with very good radios might have heard the engines against the background white noise, but most first heard the bell, then the whistle letting go a regulation grade-crossing signal of two long blasts, one short, and a final long blast. A rhythmic click of iron wheels against the track seams grew along with the churning of the steam engine. Montgomery watched the eye of the locomotive get brighter and its belching, steaming iron bulk grow like a charging dinosaur. Then it passed, with a blast of wind, shaking the broadcast house and forcing a roar through the microphone that pushed radio sets around the nation past their distortion point. The whistle hovered on top and suddenly dropped in pitch in a Doppler-effect downshift that marked the passing of the locomotive, followed in a swoosh by the coal tender, six passenger cars, a Pullman car, a dining car, and the caboose, chattering away toward its southern vanishing point.

Montgomery recoiled the mike cable, switched off the amplifier and locked the shed while an engineer mixed Stone back in over the fading rumble: "*And there goes the Pan American, L&N's crack passenger train speeding south to the Crescent City.*"

For more than ten years, beginning in 1933, the passing of the Pan American was a daily feature on WSM and indeed one of its signature programs. The idea may have grown out of a friendship between C. A. Craig and L&N Railroad executive J. B. Hill. Conceived as a special promotion, it proved—like the Grand Ole Opry—too popular to cancel. Though it took three audio engineers and at least that many train employees some effort every day, the Pan American resonated with listeners from farms, factories, and fine homes. Trains were the era's most potent symbol of progress and adventure, the fastest ticket to points elsewhere, besides radio signals on their "trackless paths of air." The lonesome sound of a whistle drifting across open country inspired countless country songs. And the Pan American itself had already been musically enshrined by DeFord Bailey, who still dazzled listeners with his harmonica impression of the locomotive in "Pan American Blues" most weeks on the Opry.

Over the years, WSM listeners came to know the Pan American's engineers—oily-fingered veterans of the waning steam locomotive era. Tom Burns had entered railroading in 1880 and had been an engineer for forty-eight years. Jack Hayes joined L&N in 1887. Bill McMurry had been a railroader fifty-three years and an engineer for seven. They received bags of fan mail and requests for pictures, care of WSM. Some listeners could identify the engineers merely by the way they blew their whistle and rang their bell. The train earned a cult following as far away Cuba, and a mining crew of two hundred in Pennsylvania reported using the Pan American broadcast as their signal for dinner time, over a radio speaker run down into their mine.

The broadcasts proved to be an appropriate tip of the cap to the L&N itself, for the railroad had helped shape Nashville as surely as the Cumberland River. Late in the nineteenth century, Major Eugene Castner Lewis, the eccentric president of the L&N company, found himself and his railroad in poor standing with Nashville, after years of fighting over service. In a stroke of public relations enthusiasm and generosity, he proposed and built Nashville's Parthenon, the inspiration for and centerpiece of Nashville's Centennial Exposition of 1897. As part of this elaborate undertaking, Lewis acquired detailed plans from the British Museum and specific approval for the construction from the king of Greece. Lewis, restored to public acclaim, further served the city and his own interests by building Union Station at the top of Broadway. It was a tabernacle of travel, built of stone and Tiffany glass in high Romanesque opulence. Lewis built in several eccentric features that did not survive long, including an enormous digital clock that never really worked and a pool stocked with live alligators. But he also lent the depot, which opened October 9, 1900, a grandeur that helped the city earn its place in the twentieth century.

The train shed—a vast arc of ornamental steel and glass—held the curious distinction of being the largest single-span roof in America. Topped with Greek architectural ornament, it echoed the roof of the nearby Parthenon, and ten locomotives could sit side by side beneath it. Every day, it accommodated two dozen long-distance passenger trains, several dozen freight trains, and numerous locals. When Franklin Roosevelt arrived for a famous four-hour visit to pitch his New Deal on November 11, 1934, he arrived at Union Station on the Presidential Special. That same fall, Huey Long disembarked amid throngs to attend the LSU/Vanderbilt football game and to campaign for the Democratic presidential nomination. Vanderbilt students swarmed the shed with seasonal regularity. The depot and its trains were as central to Nashville's relationship with the world as WSM itself, and the marriage of broadcasting and steam moved Hank Williams a few years later to capture the train and its place on radio with his plainspoken poetry.

She leaves Cincinnati headin' down that Dixie line
When she passes that Nashville tower you can hear that whistle whine
Stick your head out the window and feel that southern breeze
you're on that Pan American on her way to New Or-leans.

For younger radio fans like Les Leverett, the daily Pan American broadcasts blended seamlessly and spiritually with the sounds of DeFord Bailey's musical Pan American, with the Grand Ole Opry itself and with the rapidly changing world he inhabited. Leverett, who became staff photographer for National Life and the Opry in the 1960s, remembers hearing the Pan American on the radio and then, hours later, outside his window as it howled through his hometown of Perdido, Alabama. It made Nashville seem a bit less far away, but no less mystical. In this, Leverett was typical of thousands of small-town southerners of the era for whom a simple appliance opened up a manifest destiny. WSM and electricity arrived in his life at the same time, when he was seven years old.

> My daddy somehow came up with the money to buy a Stewart-Warner radio. And he had electricity put in the house and we got rid of the lanterns. They came in and put a little white wire and a little black wire across the ceiling with those little cast ceramic insulators. You could pull a string in each room and get a light. And they brought a wire down with a plug for the radio.
> On Saturday nights certain neighbors that he really liked would come up and listen to the Opry. And in the summertime Daddy would make homemade ice cream. And we'd sit around and eat ice cream listening to the Opry. My momma put a palette on the floor for my kid sister and I. We thought we were staying up all night. I know that she put us to bed by 9:30, because we had to be in Sunday school the next morning. But I remember listening to all those old guys—Sam and Kirk McGee, Louie Buck, and David Cobb, never having any idea I would come to dreamland and get to know those people.

A similar ritual played out in the home of another young dreamer destined to arrive at WSM in the coming years. Skinny young Roy Acuff from East Tennessee, although he wanted to play baseball, was poised, against all intuition, to become a Grand Ole Opry star and the King of Country Music. "I don't care how poor you were, you found some way to own a radio," he said in his autobiography. "When the 'wish books' came—the Sears and Roebuck or the Montgomery Ward catalogs—the pages with the radio were the ones everybody turned to first." And the Opry was the show they'd tune to first. "People started getting ready for Saturday night when they got up on Saturday morning. They swept and dusted their parlors, made sure there were clean and freshly starched doilies on the arms of the mohair sofas—everybody had a mohair sofa—and they got the chairs all set in a semicircle around the radio; then they took baths, and the men slicked down their hair while the women curled theirs. The parlor was the most important room of the house on Saturday night, because that's where the radio was. You see, nobody, I mean nobody had more than one radio, and it usually was such a big thing that the furniture was arranged around it, or, at least, so that everybody had a good place to sit. We all gathered around it like people do today with television, since it was always better, for some reason, if you were looking at it . . . You went to *listen.*"

WSM's listeners needed escapism like the Pan American and the Grand Ole Opry because when the Depression hit, it hit like a locomotive. The bellwether in Nashville came when local financial powerhouse Caldwell & Company declared bankruptcy on November 14, 1930, as part of a chain of southern bank failures. National Life's record of sustained and rapid growth ground to a halt. Sales fell and lapses on policies blossomed. Business bottomed out in 1932, giving National Life executives plenty of excuses to think about canceling its commitment to higher power and an expensive new transmitter for WSM. Instead, they embraced the station, asking if they were doing all they could with WSM to sell insurance.

In March 1932 company vice president Eldon Stevenson wrote to President Ridley Wills: "For some time we have been of the opinion that more efficiency is needed in sales promotion work for our Company." He laid out the beginnings of a coordinated plan to use territorial managers, the company newsletter and WSM to "carry our message to the people." Edwin Craig, thinking along the same lines, set about reinventing the recruitment, training, and deployment of the National Life sales force. Radio had been an indirect identifier and brand management tool for the Shield company up to that point. It could do more, and to get there Craig hired a dashing twenty-five-year-old advertising man named Edward Montague Kirby in March 1933.

Kirby grew up in New York and Harpers Ferry, West Virginia, before graduating from officer training at Virginia Military Institute in 1926. After the service he became a reporter for *The Sun* in Baltimore, where he briefly befriended H. L. Mencken after splattering him at a bar while cracking a steamed crab. He pursued marketing, advertising, and statistical analysis work in Detroit and then in Nashville, where he was named account executive for the General Shoe Corporation. There, in the face of early radio's codes of conduct, he demonstrated cleverness under pressure. Stations that aspired to network stature in those days refused to mention prices in on-air advertising. But General's "Friendly Five" shoe stores built their identity around selling five-dollar shoes, and they wanted to make that clear. Since Kirby couldn't say they cost five dollars, he cooked up a jingle around the line, "I've *got* five dollars." This passed muster, and the ad ran on 120 network radio stations.

Once hired by National Life, Kirby made quick use of the *Shield* newsletter. Distributed to the sales force weekly, it was full of inspirational rhetoric about company values, letters from company leaders, and detailed tabulations of individual sales accomplishments. Top Shield Men were spotlighted in the "Go-Getters" column. To underscore that the company paid claims promptly, it regularly ran pictures of checks made out to families of unfortunate victims—a man electrocuted or drowned when an electric fan fell in his bathtub, a nineteen-year-old whose boat sank on the Cumberland River, a gun-cleaning accident in Los Angeles. Juxtaposed against that, children born to salesmen—the "New Shield Babies"—were pictured regularly, and features like "What Can I Do to Sell More Ordinary?" were ubiquitous. There were even articles commending the virtues of a good "shield wife." She didn't, for example, honk the horn while waiting for her husband to close a sale.

Only a month into Kirby's tenure, *Our Shield* began to preview new WSM shows he was developing "to help the 2,500 Shield Men." The first was simply called the *National Life Variety Show,* a potpourri of WSM stalwarts like the Piano Twins, the Vagabonds, Francis Craig, Johnny Payne, John Lewis, Christine Lamb, Madge West, and the WSM Players. The announcer was Harry Stone's brother David, now an integral part of the staff. Even before the variety show had a chance to prove itself, National Life brass announced how pleased they were. President Wills wrote in an open letter to the sales force that "I am being made happier than in a long time by the fine way in which our Radio Station WSM is being tied in with the work of the Shield Man . . . It appears to me that Mr. Kirby, under the direction of Mr. E. W. Craig mainly, has begun a fine work."

The New Year's Day issue of *Our Shield* for 1934 proved that any hesitation about using the radio as a ramrod through doors across America was now history. National Life announced a new weekly half-hour show about the company itself. The *Third Century of Progress Program* began January 3. Shield Men were urged to "invite every policyholder to tune in . . . invite every prospect . . . it will tell them the story of The National . . . it will help you place the business." The same issue reported in detail on the company's first-ever *Shield Family Christmas Radio Party,* a two-and-a-half-hour show from Studio B featuring the company top brass, calls from field agents, Francis Craig's orchestra, and Judge Hay. On Christmas Eve at 9:30, Harry Stone said "Ladies and Gentlemen of the general radio audience, three hundred and sixty-five days of the year, the facilities of WSM's 50,000 watts and the tallest radio tower of the world have been devoted to your entertainment and pleasure. But tonight, on this Christmas Eve, we are asking your indulgence." He explained the show would be "dedicated exclusively to our Shield Family." Nearly all of the company leaders took turns on the microphone. Edwin Craig marveled at the fact that he likely had more field agents listening to his voice at once than ever before. Agents were encouraged to call or send telegrams, which they of course did by the hundreds, paralyzing the company switchboards.

One week later, Kirby's vision for WSM was set forth in detail. In a *Shield* column, he announced that the sales and promotions department was widening its functions to apply "to all things which might be of help to you in gaining entrance into new homes" including pamphlets, prospect lists, standardized canvas talks, and publicity distributed to local papers. WSM, Kirby said, "has a very definite position in this aggressive promotion. The coverage of WSM is available to ninety-five percent of the Field . . . The Company programs, heard in an ever-increasing number of homes, spread the name and the fame of your Company before you call." He continued, emphasizing the synergistic tie between the content of the station and the message of the sales force. "Any given radio program of the Company is built to do a job for the Company *in itself.* But, *in addition* to this, every Company program is also built to be a *provocative* agent for you on your Debit [door-to-door circuit]—to cause attention to be directed to the Company and to you *before* the program goes on the air, *when* the program is on the air, and *after* the program has been on the air."

Kirby had ushered in two new facets of WSM's mission and means: large, ensemble radio productions and vigorous cross-marketing. His late 1933 series about collegiate life involved fifty radio performers, an augmented orchestra, and a male chorus. It featured a different southeastern school each week, giving "immediate access to one million graduates, former students, students, and their parents—who had a direct sentimental interest in the program." Kirby tied specific broadcasts to homecoming weekends at Indiana University, the University of Illinois, Texas A&M, Tulane, and others. He broadcast graduation ceremonies. And he found the schools more than happy to plug WSM's shows in their local markets. Ohio State lined up 150 alumni banquets around the country to coincide with its broadcast. Oklahoma sent out 11,000 notices to its graduates.

At the same time, *Our Shield* began running house ads to help the Shield Men tie Kirby's new shows to their insurance pitches. In one, an insurance salesman in his crisp suit and hat is about to walk down a typical suburban street, where the sounds of WSM shows are coming out of the houses like cartoon bubbles. Another pictured the radio tower, with the copy: "WSM is a tireless worker for the benefit of the Shield Company and Shield Man . . . from early morn to late at night. Make it your strong ally out on your Debit!"

What National Life didn't talk about in the *Shield*—at least not yet—was how potent the Grand Ole Opry was becoming as a promotional tool. About 1933, the company published a slim magazine called *Fiddles and Life Insurance,* which Shield Men carried for years. It supplemented other trinkets: National Life sewing kits shaped like a shield, nail files, and packets of seeds. Edwin's son Neil recalled that the methods of Shield Men were little changed when he began walking a debit in San Antonio in 1951. "We'd go knock on the door and introduce ourselves. And as often as not we'd say, 'We're from WSM.' *Fiddles and Life Insurance* had pictures of the stars of the Opry. And on the back cover it said there's another program you might be interested in. And that's how we'd make the transition from the radio to the life insurance." As the months went by, the Opry's selling power became increasingly clear to Craig, as it did to hundreds of other agents. "None of the houses had air conditioning," said Neil. "Our agents were trained to walk around the neighborhoods at night and listen to what was playing on the radio. And when they found a house playing the Grand Ole Opry they'd make a note of it and go back Monday morning. It was a godsend."

Using the Opry as a sales tool appears to have been something Shield Men adopted on their own. The company's official manuals and *The Shield* newsletter didn't mention the Opry as a likely door-opener during this period. In fact, in an early 1930s National Life training guide, salesmen were encouraged to approach farmers with a line like, "Isn't that your herd of pure-bred stock that I have heard so much about?" And while many Shield Men were using Kirby's noncountry shows and promotions on their debits in the 1930s, Neil Craig couldn't recall using any other hook twenty years later.

If the Grand Ole Opry was a sales tool to an army of Shield Men and a Saturday night mainstay for fans, it made WSM and indeed Edwin Craig himself a magnet for a growing number of hillbilly musicians. Neil Craig says that string band musicians sought out his father in the uncanniest places—on his vacations and during his precious hunting time in Cajun country near the Texas border. "When everybody in Southwest Louisiana heard Mr. Craig of the Grand Ole Opry was there, they'd all come by," Neil said. "We were just staying with a family down there. And all the pickers came out." Once during a golf game at the a North Carolina resort near Linville, Edwin hit his tee shot down a gulley. "And when he got down there," Neil said, "there was a string band standing around [the ball] just picking like hell. He had many experiences like that. They all wanted to go on the Opry. And his deal with them back in the early days was boys if you can get yourself over there, we'll put you on the Opry. He'd done it many times. He wasn't going to pay their way over there. But you'd be amazed how many of them came."

That loose and open atmosphere gave way to a more formalized audition process in the early 1930s, as Hay's benevolent overseer approach gave way to Harry Stone's tougher managerial style. Stone later wrote that hundreds would come to the station directly, and that he could not afford to be as charitable as Mr. Craig. The Opry became more structured after the early 1930s, ruling out drop-in guest artists, he said. "They felt that they could play as well, if not better, than the ones who were on the air and should be given a place. One of the biggest headaches in those days was having to tell these people to go back home."

Harry Stone knew something about headaches. Though he had nominal control over WSM, engineer Jack DeWitt and program producer Ed Kirby answered directly to Edwin Craig. This irregular chain of command did not sit well with Stone, amplifying the complexities and paradoxes of his generally stern personality. Musician Alton Delmore described him as a "tall man with a dark, serious complexion" who "looked like a lawyer." Stone, he said, was stern and "poker-faced" at his (ultimately successful) Opry audition in 1933, and he and brother Raybon clashed with Stone for a decade over pay and Opry policy. In the end, Alton said Stone was "fair" even if he wasn't kindly.

Irving Waugh, a 1940s announcer who rose to WSM's presidency in the seventies, called Stone "a very solid broadcaster" who could handle all aspects of the business, from basic engineering to sales, promotion, and production. But he also said Stone could be a perplexing man. "When I went into sales, we'd travel together. He was open, effusive, friendly," Waugh said. "The minute we were back at WSM, he might pass me in the hall and not speak." Stone's niece, Sandra McClure of Springfield, Missouri, remembered in Harry a regimented and disciplined man who "didn't suffer fools gladly." On the other hand, DeFord Bailey seems to have admired Stone a great deal. He told David Morton that he had planned to name his youngest child, born in late 1936, after him, had it been a boy. (As it happened, it was a girl, and he named her for Christine Lamb, one of WSM's earliest artist/employees and a white vocalist who worked in both formal music and a pop version of the blues.)

Marjorie Kirby, widow of Edward Kirby, remembers friction between Harry and her husband, perhaps not surprising given that Kirby had freedom to produce shows while answering to Craig and Clements. "Ed had trouble with him," she said. "He was a nice guy. But he was just . . . what shall I say . . . he played by the rules strictly. He didn't see the possibilities of being creative. You did it this way because the book says. So it was hard to deal with him." On the other hand, Ed Kirby related with admiration an anecdote about Harry Stone's steadfast adherence to principles and his broadcasting professionalism.

"A group of Jehovah's Witnesses arrived in his offices one afternoon to buy time," Kirby said in a speech in the early 1950s. "Harry explained religious time was not for sale [but] was distributed fairly through the Council of Churches to fit the desires of the community. They offered to double the card rate. Harry declined. Then they threatened that unless he gave or sold them time, they would picket his local sponsors and boycott his advertisers. Harry held firm in the face of both a bribe and a threat. Then the committee invoked their Jehovah along these lines: 'Stay your hand, oh Lord. Do not let your anger leash a bolt of lightning from the blue and strike this man's transmitter to the ground. Let nothing happen to his children. Let him but see the light so that we may broadcast our message.'

"They then turned to Harry, now ashen. 'Well, Sir, you see, it's out of our hands now.'"

He may have engendered mixed emotions, but Harry Stone shaped the Opry in ways that would last into the modern era, especially the addition of a studio audience and the changes in location and staging that followed. The tight quarters of WSM's Studios A and B made it difficult for anyone other than family and guests of the artists to be let into the studio. But once an audience had been accommodated for the Union Ice Cream shows of 1932, the idea of a first-come-first-served crowd for the Opry would have seemed like a natural evolution. And in early 1934, WSM built appropriate space with the opening of a new studio on National Life's fifth floor. Built to double as an auditorium for the Shield Men during special events and as a professional soundstage for WSM, Studio C could seat several hundred people. It had an arched ceiling to prevent clanging echoes, indirect lighting, acoustic tile walls, a black-and-white checked floor, and a control room behind glass high and to the left on the back wall. An "On The Air" sign hung over the main entrance.

Engineer Aaron Shelton remembered that the earliest Opry crowds acted more bewildered than boisterous. "These people were not the kind to respond wildly, even with [musician] Uncle Dave Macon's encouragement," he wrote. "They seemed to be in awe—almost never changing expression—exhibiting the reserve of the real Anglo-Saxon stock from which most of them came. It was almost as if they were sitting on their hands at the conclusion of a song. I am sure that they enjoyed the show to the fullest—as witness the ever increasing number that came each Saturday—but their enjoyment was tempered by their natural reserve."

Soon however, younger and more excitable crowds began arriving at Seventh and Union every Saturday, parking on the downtown streets and streaming up the stairs and elevators. To accommodate them, Stone divided the evening into two shows, at 8:00 and 10:00 p.m. "This worked reasonably well except that we had to flush out people who had hidden in closets and offices to keep from having to leave," he wrote later. It also meant one crowd had to wait outside while the first show wrapped up, and that caused trouble. One Saturday night, Runcie Clements and old C. A. Craig, whose offices were on the first floor, came to Seventh and Union about 10:00 p.m. and literally couldn't break through a rowdy crowd. "When I saw them later they looked like they had run into a tornado," said Stone. The order came down: No more audience.

A threshold had been crossed, however. Stone and Hay realized that the Opry needed a live audience as much as it needed country music, which meant it needed a new home. The Opry's first refuge in the city was the Hillsboro Theater on Belcourt Avenue, a conventional community auditorium several blocks west of Ward-Belmont School that hosted live shows and movies. Accounts of its size vary. Stone said it held about 750 people. "It was a great relief to the audience and to the performers," wrote George Hay. "We had a few dressing rooms and we acquired a staff of ushers to handle the front of the house. Because it was small, we played to two audiences from eight until midnight. There was no charge for tickets. The three thousand agents of our parent company were allowed to distribute a limited number of them."

Now Stone truly focused on professionalizing and regularizing the Opry. As an intermediary to work with Hay, Stone recruited Vito Pellettieri, who had returned to WSM in 1934 as a music librarian, working with music director Oliver Riehl. Vito's orchestra had fallen victim to the hard times, and the musician remembered Edwin Craig personally inviting him back onto the WSM staff out of Depression-era charity. Pellettieri kept sheet music organized and ready for requests from the orchestra leaders, and he took care of clearances on songs—making sure royalty payments were going to the right songwriter and publisher for performances. He'd once nearly gone to law school, and the work suited him.

Harry Stone called him "Cowboy," and in the fall of 1935, Pellettieri remembered, Stone came to him and said, "Cowboy, you've got to go to the Opry to help Mr. Hay out." Vito wasn't interested in working with hillbilly musicians, but he and Hay liked each other. They'd met while collaborating on a show called *History of American Music.* "Mr. Hay had a lot of respect for me, and I had a lot of respect for him," he said. "I don't think there will ever be a man that could handle a microphone like Mr. Hay did."

Pellettieri did go work with Hay, and he helped give the Opry its first real structure: half-hour blocks of time with scheduled performances. "I want to tell each one of the fellows when they're supposed to be here, and if they're not here, that's it," he said. In addition to his orderly stage management, he sold the Opry's first sponsorship. The client, a laxative called Crazy Water Crystals, was one of numerous companies that found great success partnering with country music acts in the 1930s.

The Opry spent about a year and a half at the Hillsboro Theater, but it also proved too small. Hay tried two shows each Saturday night, but Stone wrote that "It just didn't work. We simply didn't have ushers enough to get all of the people out of the building so the ten o'clock crowd could get in." Stone's next site was on the east side of the Cumberland River, immediately across from downtown. In the middle of 1936, just a day after original Opry star Humphrey Bate died peacefully, the Opry moved into a large shed on Fatherland Street. Built for revivals, the Dixie Tabernacle perfectly fit the early Opry's style. A stage backdrop depicting the inside of a cabin, with a stone fireplace, curtained windows, and timber walls, seemed to blend in organically with the building's rustic wooden sturdiness. Two large loudspeakers were mounted on either side of the stage. Announcer David Stone likened its atmosphere to an old-fashioned carnival, with "sawdust on the floor, wood benches, and old hinged lights along the side. You'd have to go along on a hot night and put broomsticks under them to hold them up." Conditions backstage were "miserable," he said. "We didn't have any room to do anything."

Hay began to notice a shift in the crowd. About a quarter of the cars parked outside were from out of state. Visitors would approach him before the show and tell him they were from Illinois, Florida, or Minnesota, hoping they could coax him to pass on greetings home over the air. But there were too many out-of-towners in the crowds of three thousand to do so. "A rule was made of necessity to refrain from such announcements, except in the case of Shield Men and their families," Hay said. And at the Fatherland Tabernacle, Harry Stone remembered, was where the Opry first began to comtemplate charging for admission—something like a quarter—"to help slow down the crowd." In fact the first Opry tickets were sold at its next home, War Memorial Auditorium, but that didn't slow the crowd at all; they kept coming in droves.

Success bred new concerns. Artists were becoming stars thanks to WSM's powerful signal, and Stone knew it would take more than $5 per show to keep the musicians loyal to the Opry over the long run. Stone and Hay couldn't pay more, but they realized that they could attract and retain more professional and substantial artists if they made it easy for them to make a living between mandatory Saturday night appearances. This appears to have been the central impetus behind WSM's Artist Service Bureau. Loosely organized in 1933, the name and model were likely borrowed from NBC's in-house talent booking division. The agency would prove vital in expanding the Opry brand and cementing a codependent commercial relationship between the stars and the show, because stars could only bill themselves as "Grand Ole Opry" artists if they kept their Saturday night appointment on WSM, and an Opry billing on the road was like money in the bank.

The WSM artist bureau's first show was at a black church in Nashville, but a large cross section of the Opry cast drew a disappointing crowd. A second, more ambitious road show on July 4, 1934, at a rural campground 150 miles from Nashville was better promoted and much better attended. The Gully Jumpers, Arthur Smith and the Dixieliners, and Uncle Dave Macon performed for a reported eight thousand people. Initially, Hay managed the artist bureau, arranging publicity photos into catalogs that could be presented to show promoters. He set up a system whereby the artists took home the gate receipts, minus 15 percent for WSM. Hay's health issues prevented him from developing the agency for long, however, and the job fell to David Stone, Harry's brother. The younger Stone recalled working out tours that cycled musicians around school houses, lodges, and county fairs between Saturdays, when they were required to be back in Nashville to perform on the radio.

Also around this time—perhaps even prior to the Hillsboro Theater move—Hay conceived of a new image for the show and its artists. He'd grown concerned that the Opry performers, who came in each week dressed as if for church on Sunday, didn't look the way they sounded. The pickers and fiddlers, many of whom were craftsmen and laborers from the city, saw radio as a formal affair, and the lush studio surroundings only reinforced the notion. The handful of women involved wore dresses with stockings. But Hay took a notion that an "authentic" hillbilly music show ought to feature musicians who looked like authentic hillbillies. He put them in floppy hats and overalls, loose work shirts, and bandanas about the neck. Publicity photos from the era show an almost bizarre before-and-after quality. In one, average-looking Tennesseans seem to be dressed up a bit more than they'd like, and in the next, they're in a corn field or sitting on a split-rail fence, passing a moonshine jar. Hay renamed the bands with cornball clichés, like the Fruit Jar Drinkers or the Gully Jumpers. Even the distinguished Dr. Bate was made over, his band redubbed the Possum Hunters. Only the dignified and dapper harmonica wizard DeFord Bailey ducked the wardrobe change, remaining in a black suit.

These changes in venue and style began to earn the Opry a place in the national radio pantheon and even some respect at home. In the summer of 1935, the show earned a medal from *Radio Stars* magazine, which (inaccurately) praised its "authentic hill-dwellers and dirt farmers with nary a professional among them" and said the Opry had "more fast friends than any other single air-show." Previous winners had included such distinguished network fare as the Metropolitan Opera and Jack Benny, and the Opry was the first non-network show to win the prize. Even more remarkable, perhaps, was the reaction in the morning *Tennessean*, which dedicated one of its usually weighty editorials to taking on the Opry's local detractors. "There probably are thousands of radio listeners who do not care for the type of entertainment which this feature offers," the paper said. "For them there are seven days and six nights of the week in which they can search for programs over WSM more to their liking. The Grand Ole Opry is for the other thousands . . . The steadfastness with which the officials of WSM have kept the Grand Ole Opry on its schedule in reply to the great interest shown in it and in spite of the criticism from highbrows, has been rewarded . . . It is a recognition to be proud of. For it is based not on the big name of a star or on high pretense, but on the pleasure it brings to those who listen to it. And that, after all, is the best criterion of an entertainment feature."

Out back of the Fatherland Street Tabernacle, a sturdy, streetwise young man minded the stage door. He'd first come to the attention of the Opry artists and managers because he sorted their mail back at the National Life building. He had in fact been in the mail room for three grinding years, but Jim Denny had long before proven his patience in the face of hunger. Sent to the city by destitute parents to live with an aunt when he was eleven years old, Denny arrived by train with forty cents in a tobacco sack. The aunt never showed up. "I was alone and broke and scared," Denny said years later. "Even the street cars scared me." But he became one of the ubiquitous newsboys on Union and Church Streets, selling the *Tennessean* in the morning and the *Banner* at night, delivering Western Union telegrams in between. Denny biographer Albert Cunniff wrote that "at night he often slept curled up on a warm bundle of newspapers in the corner of the *Tennessean*'s press room."

When he started working full time for Western Union for twelve dollars a week around 1924, Denny was thirteen years old, and soon he was living with his single mother and younger brother. Denny took night school accounting classes. He looked for better work out of town but found nothing. Then he began pestering one of the companies on his telegram route about a job. National Life signed on the eighteen-year-old as a mail sorter in May of 1929. Physically imposing, ambitious, hot-tempered, prompt, well-dressed, and blunt, Denny slowly climbed the ladder, to filing, then accounting, then—in 1933—the tabulating room in the actuarial department. Cunniff wrote that "it was a noisy beehive that centered around wire-driven IBM machines that operated on keypunched cards containing information on new policies, policies about to lapse, cash value checks to be written (and) payroll information."

Denny's Opry work was entirely freelance and self-motivated. Soon after the Opry moved to Fatherland Street, Denny's volunteer efforts were rewarded with two dollars per night for guarding the back door and helping with sets and staging. He also became the show's de facto bouncer. "If someone was acting up and disturbing people I would ask him very sweetly to leave," he told the *Tennessean* in 1963. "If he gave me any backtalk at all, it was *wham!* Right then! A right to the head. Usually, by the time they got over their surprise, they were outside!" The job earned him the respect and affection of the Opry musicians and staff. Whether he was taking tickets, answering the phone, or looking after patrons, it became clear to the Opry's power structure that this impoverished kid was rich in talent, willpower, and loyalty.

In early 1934, drama director Madge West assembled a cast of WSM players and prominent Nashvillians for one of the station's most ambitious radio shows yet. *The Trial of Vivienne Ware* told the story of a society beauty accused of murder. The cast included a mysterious nightclub dancer, a tremulous butler, and a medical examiner. A real judge-elect for the first circuit played the judge in the radio case. A real incoming attorney general played the district attorney. WSM acting stalwart Casper Kuhn played three parts. A new WSM hire named Jack Harris played "A Reporter."

Harris was a reporter in real life as well, a local-born overachiever who took on larger roles at the station as the 1930s progressed. A dashing young man with dark, deep-set eyes and a daytime-drama jaw, Harris started a newspaper at Hume-Fogg High School, then worked at various collegiate publications, and ultimately covered sports for the *Tennessean.* He was planning to continue in print journalism, but when he was offered jobs by both WSM and WLAC at $60 and $65 per week respectively, twice what the newspaper was offering, he went into broadcasting.

Harris, who made these recollections in 1993 as a retired radio and television mogul, says that even in 1934, he recognized WSM as "one of the really great stations in the country." He chose it over WLAC and its five extra dollars per week, he said, "because of the prestige." Once hired, Harris quickly became protégé to Ed Kirby. "My job, when I first came there, was to work in the mornings with the insurance company on sales promotion, and then I would go three stories up to the radio station and I would work from one o'clock until after the ten o'clock news at the radio station," he said. Initially, he was a sports reporter, but he expanded into reading news, and by May 1938, Harris had introduced his 10:00 p.m. news show *The World in Review.*

For newspaper publishers nationwide, radio upstarts like Jack Harris were a threat and a challenge to their news monopoly. At the *Banner,* the man who worried about this the most was Jimmy Stahlman, second generation publisher and, as it happened, president of the Southern Newspaper Publishers Association. When Harris lined up the first contract for a useful news wire to WSM, Stahlman fought back.

"He was probably the most violent antiradio news man in the country," Harris recalled. "He threatened the United Press that he would go to every publisher in the south and have them or urge them to take out United Press from their newspaper if they sold this service to our station. Stahlman was a very powerful man, and United Press buckled under and came and asked us if we would give the contract back." This wasn't an unusual battle in radio. George Hay's first radio job came when he was drafted to announce on his newspaper's radio station, but the *Commercial Appeal* couldn't put news on their WMC station because in the 1920s, the wire services themselves would have cut off the newspaper. And National Life wasn't looking for any trouble with a paper with which they'd long had good relations, so company officials (Harris doesn't say who exactly) got United Press to nullify the contract.

Some time later, another wire called International News Service (INS) approached WSM, and this time, WSM signed on. Although INS was heavier on lengthy overseas stories than he wanted, Harris built his 10:00 p.m. news around it, rewriting all the copy and delivering it live. "It was a one-man operation," he said. "You didn't have tape . . . it had to be well written and well delivered."

Then in the middle of 1935, the *Banner's* Stahlman did something Harris thought unconscionable. He bought a fifteen-minute block of time at 12:30 p.m. called the *Banner News Hawk.*

"He hired a former preacher to deliver fifteen minutes of news at noon," Harris recounted. "The newscast consisted of saying, 'There was a murder in Nashville today. For the rest of the story, read the *Nashville Banner* this afternoon.' It was a fifteen-minute commercial. As a budding journalist, it appalled me, but I was just a rookie."

Appalled though he may have been at Stahlman's brazen act of promotion, Harris also wore a publicist's hat. He wrote stories about the station and then tried to place them in all manner of publications, local and national, sometimes under his own byline, sometimes under an assumed name and sometimes anonymously. His news release about the new *Banner News Hawk,* which included the fact that Stahlman was president of the Southern Newspaper Publishers Association, piqued the interest of the leading entertainment and media trade paper *Variety.* Stahlman, the crusader against radio news backing a radio news show? It ran a story, and Harris remembered a headline that trumpeted Stahlman as having flip-flopped.

"I could feel the walls tremble when that reached Nashville," said Harris. "I waited for a summons, and I got one from Mr. C. R. Clements, who was executive vice president of National Life—this was after three or four days of rumors and whatnot. I took the press release. I thought my career at WSM was going to be short-lived, because Mr. Stahlman was a man of great power, and I had heard he was demanding whoever wrote that story had to be fired."

Clements showed him *Variety.*

"Young man, did you write this story?"

"No sir, this is the story I wrote," Harris said, and handed him his original press release.

Clements looked at it for a while, then smiled. "That's a very clever news release," he told Harris. "Well, I just wanted to tell you something. The day Jimmy Stahlman can tell this company who to hire and fire will be the last day that I'm the head of it. Go ahead and do your job and don't worry about it anymore."

In the midst of the Great Depression, National Life floated like an ark on a turbulent ocean. Even with the down year of 1932, the company's so-called insurance in force grew 30 percent between 1929 and 1934, while life insurance companies nationally lost business. Officials credited WSM. Ridley Wills, who became president of National Life in early 1931 when C. A. Craig became chairman, praised Ed Kirby's "resourcefulness" in making the Shield brand more relevant and potent to the nation and endorsing further use of the radio station in promoting National Life business. *Broadcasting* magazine wrote that while in general "life insurance institutions have been slow to use radio," National Life "led every American and Canadian life insurance" company in new business during 1933, and that "radio was the only new ingredient added to the sales kit in the past two years." A year later, Edwin Craig himself called the radio/insurance marketing synergy a "once in a lifetime" arrangement.

The company continued to pour resources into the station. By early 1935, Harry Stone was in charge of an office and artist staff of two hundred full- and part-timers. The volume of mail the station received in the wake of going to 50,000 watts was staggering. A certified report for the month of January 1934 shows 174,574 cards and letters from the United States, including 1,000 from North Dakota and 106 from Washington state. Those audiences drove lucrative sponsorships, and by 1936, even WSM itself was in the black.

Almost anything attached to radio thrived during the Depression. Maxwell House Coffee, a company started in Nashville but no longer based there, exploded when it sponsored the *Maxwell House Coffee Showboat* in 1933. Pepsodent tooth powder turned itself around with the popularity of *Amos 'n' Andy.* Once controversial, radio was now an invaluable advertising tool, especially for everyday consumer goods. Transcription discs, the oversized records used to record, reproduce, and distribute radio shows, made it possible for stations to syndicate their sponsored programs to ad hoc networks of interested stations. Ed McConnell seems to have been the first WSM entertainer to enjoy this new avenue of exposure, hosting a show for Aladdin Lamps of Nashville that was sent to and played over about twenty stations sometime before 1932.

Productions in Studio C grew out of a fast-paced, collaborative, and often combative process that called on the talents of dozens of people. A late 1934 issue of *Our Shield* offered a walk-through of the National Life building for a fictional Shield Man, including a virtual tour of the radio station. A contrived but insightful scene described Oliver Riehl and Ed Kirby talking over a production.

Rough dress rehearsal has just finished in Studio C. The corridors outside the studio are alive with musicians, vocalists, dramatists, and technicians. Some of them are smoking and chatting about various and sundry parts of the dress rehearsal which is about to take place after this brief intermission.

Up the winding stairway brings us to the control room, where the engineer and two other men are making some corrections in the music, the script, and the dialogue. Let's listen in on part of the conversation:

"Now listen, Eddie; we can speed up the show on page six if we just cut that blurb in half. Then let us put in that new squawker for a two-minute go just ahead of the heavy bromide. And why not?"

"Say, Ollie, must I go through the same gripe with you again this week? To do that means losing our objective entirely; the copy slant will be shot to pieces. And, again, those sound platters are full of bugs, and your trained seals are good all right, but they are badly miscast."

"O.K. fellow; I'll change those parts around, and I believe the crooning thugs should be told again about chewing the text."

"When George [Reynolds] gets back, I'll caution him again about smoking in the control room. This is part of the studio, you know."

At this point Mr. E. W. [Edwin Craig] walks in, checking on each program as he does, and explains that the above is typical of a daily conversation wherein Company shows are produced. It really sounds pretty much to the listener as though it might be the start of a young war, but Mr. E. W. adds that that's the way Kirby and Riehl get along in producing all the Company shows, and that therein lies the success and constant improvement characteristic of all the WSM broadcasts.

Kirby wasn't as inclined toward radio production jargon as the passage suggests, his widow says. But many of the terms did float around the station for years. "Trained seals" were the part-time dramatists paid on a per-show basis. "Chewing the text" was mumbling. "Sound platters" with "bugs" were sound effects records marred by pops and scratches. In addition, the engineers called themselves "jiggers," which could be a noun or a verb ("Are you still jiggering at WSM?"), and they called Studio C's control room the "poop deck" for its elevated overlook.

The studios thrummed daily with script meetings, typewriters, mimeograph machines, visits to Vito Pellettieri in the cozy warren of the music library, and the setting and striking of music stands and microphones. The product: sweet, dreamy, and escapist fare that took cues from prime-time NBC feeds like Paul Whiteman's smooth jazz concerts or the "Chez Paree" Orchestra. WSM's in-house extravaganzas included *The WSM Hollywood Show* with a cast of seventy, including a twenty-voice mixed chorus, three arrangers, and a full orchestra. The show premiered songs from upcoming MGM pictures, like *Reckless* with Jean Harlow and *Shadow of Doubt* with Constance Collier. WSM also sent its new show *Magnolia Blossoms* over the NBC Red Network starting November 25, 1935, promoted as "a thirty-minute program of music with a Southern flavor." It featured the Fisk Jubilee Singers, opera singers John Lewis and Christine Johnson, a "girl trio from Georgia" called the Dixianas, and many others.

On the dramatic side, Ed Kirby's brainchild *America's Flag Abroad* earned critical praise. Announced by young newsman Jack Harris, it dramatized stories of American diplomacy overseas at a time when, thanks to ominous rumblings from Adolf Hitler, international relations and statesmanship were on everybody's minds. *Radio Guide* called it "a striking broadcast, much too brilliant to be confined to a local outlet. It should be given network airing as soon as possible." Kirby followed that act in January 1936 with *The Story of the Shield,* billed as "a study of man's first and most important form of protection in all ages from the dawn of time to the present time." Researched for more than a year by a Vanderbilt professor, the show dramatized stories of heroes who carried literal or metaphorical shields, like Charlemagne, Robin Hood, Sir Galahad, Roland, Lancelot, King Arthur, and the Knights of the Round Table. It also featured a new announcer, a veteran of Alabama radio named Ottis "Ott" Devine. He was tapped because, according to National Life press, he was "one of the few radio personalities who can talk effectively to both children and grownups." And that's how *The Story of the Shield* was pitched—to adults and kids alike. "Parents may feel sure no blood and thunder 'gangsterism' will creep into these heroic stories, which form fascinating, exciting, wholesome and profitable radio listening," said the station. It ran three times each week at 5:30 p.m.

The ever-more-elaborate productions required new levels of skill and attention to the fine points of radio drama, including sound effects. In 1935

WSM hired "Count" Gaetano Cutelli, a native of Sicily and a Hollywood authority on radio sound staging. He didn't stay long, but he trained Shelton and young announcer Casper Kuhn how to make mouth sounds imitating animals and how to best use specially built sound effects equipment. Shelton wrote: "There were rectangular boxes filled with sand, gravel and rocks and with two half coconut shells to clomp up and down in these boxes, a good imitation of a horse galloping along almost any kind of road was obtained. The rubber bladder of a basketball with the proper amount of BB pellets in it could be made to sound like a steam locomotive chugging up a hill or coming to a stop at the railroad station. A large open drum head with BB pellets could sound like waves crashing against a seawall or gentle waves coming up on a sandy beach."

In late 1934 WSM offered up its most ambitious early morning program to date, a 6:30 a.m. variety show called *Rise and Shine*, hosted by Hay and packed with most of the WSM staff entertainers, including Oliver Riehl directing a fifteen-piece orchestra, a devotional by Rev. Priestly Miller, and *Banner* columnist Freddie Russell with sports news. The program of "salon music, gang songs, instrumental numbers, vocalists, humor, news and a little touch of the hillbilly" included versatile guitarist Jack Shook, the Opry's Delmore Brothers, John Lewis, Marjorie Cooney, and a new singer named Snooky Landman (soon to be known as Snooky Lanson).

Snooky, whose real name was Roy, came from Memphis and had been scuffling with determination since he began singing for tips at age twelve. Some said he approached Francis Craig on a date in Memphis; the singer said he'd been called by Craig to audition. But clearly, by 1934, Lanson was singing regularly in front of Craig's orchestra on radio and at the Hermitage Hotel, where Craig had returned as a fixture after his dalliance with the Andrew Jackson. Craig had been through a number of singers, both male and female, since James Melton's departure, and Lanson seemed to have something special—a mellifluous voice mixed with boyish charisma. It was never as easy behind the scenes, for Snooky drank hard and clashed with Craig frequently over money, workload, and personal decorum. As biographer Ikard wrote, "they needed each other but never came close to getting along."

About the same time, a Vanderbilt sophomore approached Harry Stone about part-time singing work. She had dark hair, dark eyes, and the winning disposition of a confident southern songbird. Frances Rose Shore came to town when her family moved from Winchester, Tennessee, when she was about six years old. She'd survived polio as a baby, the long-term limp that resulted, the awkwardness of being in the only Jewish family in a small Tennessee town, and the taunts of school children about her nickname: Fanny. Nevertheless, she had thrived at Hume-Fogg High School in academics and sports. She also studied voice under WSM tenor John Lewis, and she was happy to battle with him over his ultimatum to quit wrecking her voice with cheerleading. When she was fourteen, she snuck out of the house to try her hand as a torch singer. Wearing her sister's dress and makeup, she talked her way in front of a band at a nightclub called The Pines to sing "Under a Blanket of Blue." It was going well—until she saw her mother and father sitting at a corner table with their mouths agape. They weren't terribly upset, but they did insist that she continue her education. Now she was studying sociology and looking for ways to keep singing. Shore's stage name—Dinah—was still a good many years in the future.

Shore's own version of her surprise WSM audition appeared in her 1979 biography. Lewis, it said, invited Shore to WSM merely to try singing with a microphone. He'd told her it would be a help to her voice, which, though sweet, was not especially powerful. Lewis set her up in a quiet studio and put Beasley Smith in the control room, out of her sight. Smith liked what he heard and invited Shore to come twice a week to sing on a slot they called *Rhythm and Romance.* To purge herself of the shame of the school yard taunts she'd endured over the name Fanny, Shore added an *e* on the end, perhaps thinking that sounded more dignified. In any event, Fannye Rose Shore found herself on more and more programs, including a 1936 broadcast called *The Wednesday Midnighter* where she and Lewis would sing with Francis Craig's orchestra. She worked to overcome her basically thin voice with phrasing and microphone control ("You'll never hold a note the way Gracie Fields does," her father told her in a discouraging comparison to his favorite singer). She listened intently to playbacks of her shows and made adjustments; her charm came naturally.

The soft and gauzy pop music at WSM was counterbalanced with some programming that was musically rarified and spiritually sanctified. In the 1920s and 1930s, the radio station had a strong relationship with Fisk University, offering music director John Work many chances to showcase the school's singing groups. In 1936, WSM's regular weekly broadcasts of the Fisk Jubilee Singers reached an apotheosis when it broadcast Easter Sunday services from Fisk Chapel. The live half hour was not only carried on NBC, it was relayed to the BBC for worldwide, shortwave distribution. Aaron Shelton engineered, monitoring the stage inputs and the relay back to the station. The copy was written by Tom Stewart, who probably announced as well. At the stroke of 12:15, local time, he said: "*The National Broadcasting Company, in cooperation with the British Broadcasting Corporation, presents a special international Easter program, originating through the facilities of WSM, Nashville, Tennessee. We are speaking to you now in the chapel of the Negro university of Fisk in Nashville. We are to hear a program of spirituals sung by the Fisk Jubilee Singers, and the Fisk University Choir, and a reading by the greatest of all living Negro poets and writers, James Weldon Johnson.*"

Aptly introduced, Johnson began with a history of the singers. It was already one of the most venerated vocal groups in the nation, having made its fame in the nineteenth century. Fisk University was established in Civil War hospital barracks as the Fisk Free Colored School, one of many missionary institutions launched during Reconstruction by northern abolitionists. A white gentleman, a former Union army band director named George L. White, organized an ensemble and began touring in a somewhat desperate attempt to save the school from bankruptcy. And in a sense, Nashville broke its first international hit act. Henry Ward Beecher, the nation's foremost preacher, championed the Fisk singers, winning them fame nationwide and in Europe, where they performed for Queen Victoria and other notables. Fisk's Board of Trustees once bragged on them: "Wherever they have gone they have proclaimed to the hearts of men . . . the brotherhood of the race."

Starting in 1935, a decade after putting its singers on its opening night show, WSM began to support Fisk directly, totaling some $33,000 over six years. The goal, Harry Stone testified, was to "hire teachers and promote the study of Negro spiritual music." By the spring of 1936, the group consisted of seven men under the direction of Mrs. James A. Myers, legendary Fisk music teacher and mentor. That Easter, again reaching the world without leaving their leafy campus, the singers offered "Steal Away to Jesus" and "Study War No More." After a 12:30 station identification break, Johnson read the poem "Creation" from *God's Trombone*. The Fisk choir closed the program with "I Want to Die Easy When I Die" and "Swing Low Sweet Chariot" and, at 12:44 and 40 seconds, as scheduled, came the NBC network ID, with its familiar, three-toned chime.

WSM's swirl of talent, production, and ever-higher aspirations inspired one of Ed Kirby's signature flashes of promotional virtuosity. In 1935, for reasons that aren't entirely clear, he tagged WSM the "Air Castle of the South." Perhaps he was reaching for another way to expand the Shield brand, and perhaps he was, as his widow Marjorie maintains, a genuine romantic, captivated by tales of knights and derring-do. Either way, Air Castle of the South became the moniker the station would use for decades, as well as an advertising icon. An early house ad in *Our Shield* featured a fanciful pen-and-ink illustration of a castle in the clouds, hovering just behind the elegant diamond of the WSM tower. WSM postcards featured the castle and clouds well into the 1960s. Ridley Wills II, one of the last National Life executives and grandson of a company founder, said the slogan certainly made an impression on his ten-year-old mind. "I would be lying out in my front yard playing with lead soldiers and I'd have a radio out there," he said. "And I thought that the 'Air Castle of the South' was the greatest nickname I'd ever heard. I'd look up in the sky, and just think about WSM, the Air Castle of the South. Eight hundred seventy-eight feet high. I'd memorized that—how tall WSM's tower was."

In the mid-1930s, Sarah Colley, having graduated from Ward-Belmont, was on her own. She taught drama and dance briefly in Centerville but soon landed a place in the Wayne P. Sewell Production Company in Atlanta, which toured the South staging plays and variety theater. Sewell was a blend of P. T. Barnum and a small-time Dale Carnegie, whose new book *How To Win Friends and Influence People* was a favorite. Sewell's organization had about ten advance men, or promoters, who sold shows town by town, and up to 150 "coaches" who staged them. That was Sarah's job, for $10 per week. In small southern towns, she encountered the weirdness and wonder of show-business people, many of them more slovenly and raw than she'd been used to. And she had to unlearn the demure, stare-at-your-book posture of Ward-Belmont. "I learned to make eye contact and smile in every encounter," she recalled. She learned to fend off male advances with wit, to travel light, to deal with every kind of personal melodrama. And she heard all kinds of southerners talk and tell their stories. Though she spent six years with Sewell, she was never offered the roles of her dreams. So she dreamed up a role for herself.

In the deep winter of 1936, Colley was dispatched to Cullman, in northern Alabama. She had to beg for a place to stay (the company expected its directors to find their own lodgings), and a schoolmaster more or less foisted her on a poor farming couple in their seventies, who lived in a cabin in the midst of nowhere. The old lady ("I've had sixteen young'uns and never failed to make a crop") was taken by surprise but took Colley in, fed her well, and put her up in her son's room for about a dollar a day, while he moved to a lean-to outside the house. The family called the son "Brother" because he didn't like his given name, Kyle. "I'd heap druther they'd a-named me Jim," he told Colley in their first candid conversation. "Then why don't you change your name to Jim?" she asked. "Oh, I got a brother named Jim," he replied. Over about ten days, she grew fond of the family. The old lady sent her off with what Colley considered a high compliment, almost a right of passage into another society. "Lord a'mercy child, I hate to see you go. You're just like one of us," she said. The mother's name is lost to history, but her personality lived on as the character/alter ego that Sarah Colley would soon develop, a simple country maid named Minnie Pearl.

Country music reflected, soothed, and informed Depression-era America with its blues-based cathartic qualities and its identification with the common folk who were taking it on the chin. Record sales, following the double-barreled blast of radio (free music) and the economic downturn, struggled out of a hole, especially after the American division of the U.K.'s Decca Records slashed records to thirty-five cents and signed new stars like Jimmie Davis ("You Are My Sunshine"), the Delmore Brothers, Bradley Kincaid, and others.

Country music saw even greater growth through other outlets. Artists proved especially effective at selling products of all kinds over the air, from laxatives and patent medicines to work clothes, farm equipment, and live baby chicks. The Carter Family, the mountain trio from the Bristol sessions, found steady work singing of hard times and redemption over the famous Mexican border blasters, radio stations which, out of the reach of the Federal Communications Commission (FCC), reached most of the United States with a half-million watts or more. From the Southeast to California, hillbilly artists toured around their radio bases, building regional fan followings. Cowboy movies spread the music of Gene Autry and other Western artists. Bob Wills and His Texas Playboys began to build their name as western swingers at KVOO in Tulsa, starting in 1934. And while polite society wouldn't admit to enjoying hillbilly records, country songs crossed over to the mainstream as hits for pop giants like Bing Crosby, who cut "I'm an Old Cowhand" and "Empty Saddles."

The record business—emerging as the center of the music industry—had no footprint in Nashville during the 1930s. Atlanta down the road remained a hotbed of recording, along with Dallas, San Antonio, New Orleans, and even Charlotte. Jukeboxes were dominated by Western singers, not the Gully Jumpers and DeFord Bailey. Song publishing remained firmly ensconced in

New York, Chicago, and Hollywood, and the lone entity that managed the flow of royalties for those songs—the American Society of Composers, Authors, and Publishers, or ASCAP—barred musicians without formal training and Tin Pan Alley pedigree from membership, and thus from the income derived from public and radio performances. And although the Opry was growing rapidly in popularity, WSM was far from the only city with a country music variety show. The *National Barn Dance* on WLS in Chicago, sponsored over NBC by Alka-Seltzer, drew a million letters a year. Wheeling, West Virgina's WWVA launched its *Wheeling Jamboree* in 1933. WBT in Charlotte had the *Crazy Barn Dance* after 1934. The *Renfro Valley Barn Dance* originated with Louisville's WHAS, beginning in October of 1937. And there were others at KVOO in Tulsa, WRVA in Richmond, KWKH in Shreveport, and WHN in New York.

Nashville needed somebody to decide that it would and could have a music business future, and arguably the first such dreamer was one Joe Frank, a child of Giles County, Tennessee. A steel mill worker and coal miner as a young man, he cast off dangerous labor and moved to Chicago to get into the business end of show business. He booked or managed Fibber McGee & Molly, Gene Autry, and pioneering country fiddler Clayton McMichen. But by the mid-1930s, his chief act was his son-in-law, Pee Wee King. "By 1937, when I came to Nashville, it was already the capital of country music. Not many people knew that but Mr. Joe Frank did," King noted in his autobiography. One of Frank's first contributions, according to that memoir, was his suggestion to Opry management that they charge for admission. Standing on stage at the Fatherland Tabernacle, looking out over the people swarming for seats, announcer David Stone had asked why, given the national exposure the Opry was getting and the goodwill it generated. Mr. Frank said, "When you give something away, people don't value it as much as they should; but if you charge even a small amount, they know it's something special." That's not to say that Frank was greedy. He is remembered as overwhelmingly generous with money, time, and counsel for musicians struggling their way up. When Frank moved from his temporary base in Louisville to Nashville after getting Pee Wee King established on the Opry, the city had more than a barn dance; it had a champion.

King himself contributed much more than music to the Grand Ole Opry over his stellar ten-year run. Born to a working-class Polish/German family from Milwaukee, his given name was Julius Frank Anthony Kuczynski, and he grew up playing polka music on the accordion. He changed his name in high school, as soon as he formed his first bands, and over the next ten years he assembled groups that blended country, polka, pop, and jazz. He formed the Golden West Cowboys in Knoxville, married Joe Frank's stepdaughter, and moved to Nashville to audition for the Opry one year later. The Cowboys, like the Delmores and the Vagabonds, made their living exclusively through music. They were polished, rehearsed, and—highly unusual for a hillbilly act—readers of music. Their adventuresome ways with country music, including the deft use of accordion, horns, and drums, would become the subject of stylistic debates with George Hay and Edwin Craig, but an even more lasting influence came when it was learned that the Golden West Cowboys were union musicians, tied to the Louisville chapter of the American Federation of Musicians. The Nashville union, Local 257, well established but focused on the city's classical performers, didn't welcome them. "They said country musicians weren't professionals and many of them couldn't read music," King said. "But I convinced them that we were professionals and could read music. They would have had to accept us anyway because we were already members of another local . . . After that, other Opry members joined the Nashville local, and within a few years the Opry was unionized."

Because National Life's leaders had always resisted labor unions with a fervor, this was no small feat. For musical Nashville, it marked an understated turning point.

FIVE

We Must Serve These People Tonight

With two additions between 1929 and 1934, the National Life Home Office grew into a muscular, U-shaped edifice just off Nashville's Capitol Hill. Out front, Union Street dropped down a block to the Hermitage and Andrew Jackson hotels and the grand quadrangle that was War Memorial Plaza. And from WSM's fifth-floor studios, it was easy to see the cylindrical cupola of the capitol building just one block away. A visitor coming up Union Street would have seen National Life across a sunken garden, watched over by a bronze tribute to "Confederate Womanhood"—two women in Greek robes ministering to a Civil War soldier. Beyond the insurance headquarters, down the other side of the hill, lay "Hell's Half Acre," one of the city's worst slums.

National Life's front steps were wide and formal. The doors, with their iron bars and shield logo, suggested the security and permanence of a bank. Inside, one was greeted by a modest man with sandy hair and a kindly disposition—Percy Craig, one of C. A. Craig's many nephews. Though he was a Shield Man before World War I, he had, since 1925, been professionally cordial to dozens of people a day as the "Home Office host." He directed visitors toward the executive suites, which were on the first floor, where walls of figured Tennessee walnut gave off a polished glow. Glass cases near the elevator held a display promoting the Tennessee Valley Authority, the new federal program of dams, power generation, and soil conservation. Past the gated elevator was a stone hall with big arched windows bathed in sunlight.

Up marble steps, National Life's working floors were open, divided only by supporting columns, rows of filing cabinets, and desks. Surfaces were of oak, steel, and brass. The walls were amply fenestrated, and in the summer the windows remained wide open, while wide slat Venetian blinds kept the blistering sunshine at bay, shrouding National Life's floors in a dark, olive and brown gloom. When natural breezes failed, floor-standing fans kept the air moving. Waxed floors clicked beneath polished dress shoes. Big black telephones rang lustily. Royal and Underwood typewriters nattered along, their keys, bells, and whisking platens making the soundtrack of a 1930s corporate concern.

On the fifth floor, WSM had its own elevator lobby and receptionists. When the door opened, visitors faced the station's credo, set in silver block letters: "To the service and interest of the American home are dedicated the ideals and facilities of this institution and its broadcasting service, WSM." Three studios and six administrative offices took up the new wing's entire floor, and the halls were lined with photomontages of the station's many entertainers, announcers, and speakers. Musicians and technical people bustled about. Harry Stone looked smart in a close-fitting, double-breasted suit with a pocket square. The orchestra leaders and sound effects specialists wore white smocks like lab coats over their shirts and ties. The studios were in nearly constant use, for shows, rehearsals, routine station identification, and news. Busy, vibrant, and professional, there was no finer place in the South to work in radio.

One unfortunate feature of National Life's location was that it faced the back entrance of one of the city's most beautiful buildings. The War Memorial Auditorium had been finished the same year WSM went on the air, and by facing the same square as the state capitol, it described downtown's most Athenian space, a mini-Acropolis where power and high culture sat comfortably side by side. War Memorial's grand front stairs approached an open Court of Honor, home to a large bronze figure dressed as if to fight in a Roman legion or to be in one of Ed Kirby's shield-themed dramas. Inside, the auditorium itself whispered refinement and fealty to the classics.

It was, in short, the last place one would expect to find the Grand Ole Opry. But by 1939, WSM's hillbilly phenomenon had worn out its welcome at even the Dixie Tabernacle on Fatherland Street. Cars and trucks parked on every patch of ground. Overflow crowds, wrote Harry Stone, would wander the streets of East Nashville "like gypsies." Thus, he went on, "it was no great surprise when a group of East Nashville citizens called on me one day and asked in a very nice way if we would take that bunch of musicians and get lost."

Stone was running out of auditoriums. He says inquiring about War Memorial required a visit with the governor and some negotiating about the state facility's prohibition on commercial use. "I apparently convinced him that this was art and culture and he let us have it," Stone said.

The Opry's War Memorial years saw the rise to stardom of a singer and fiddler from East Tennessee who would change both the business and the music of Nashville. Roy Acuff was a poor country preacher's son who took up music after a budding baseball career flared out. Joe Frank, Pee Wee King's enterprising manager, spotted Acuff's talent and recommended him for an Opry tryout. He also suggested the young artist change the name of his band from the Crazy Tennesseans to the more dignified Smoky Mountain Boys. Acuff couldn't match the Opry's best fiddle players, but when he sang, especially the song that had earned him his debut recording session, a scripturally inspired paean called "The Great Speckled Bird," Opry audiences swooned over his undeniably emotional style. Not only was he, like King, determined to make his living as a professional musician, he represented a huge step in the transformation of the Opry from a fiddle-driven hoedown to a showcase for singers. This stylistic evolution had important economic implications as well. Singers need songs. Songs need songwriters and publishers. And from that wellspring, fortunes were about to be made. Acuff, green as he was, probably didn't immediately take notice of a nearsighted pop piano player and songwriter then working WSM in the afternoons, his future business partner, Fred Rose.

WSM further matured with the addition of a dedicated newsroom in 1937. Jack Harris and new wire editor Hamilton Noland worked at close quarters in a room stuffed with chattering news wire teletypes, typewriters, reams of paper, scissors and glue, cigarettes, and a huge dictionary on a stand between their desks. They generated reams of local news and managed the flow of more and more events coming to listeners in real time. "When the Hindenburg crashed at Lakehurst recently, WSM listeners knew of the disaster *only minutes after it had occurred,*" Harris wrote in a publication for policyholders. "When the Supreme Court upheld the Wagner Act, WSM listeners knew of that *only forty seconds after it happened.*"

WSM's ambitions in remote broadcasting also grew, as engineers took microphones to revival meetings, political rallies, flea markets, state fairs, and auctions. At Columbia, Tennessee's Mule Day—a celebration of one of the South's largest livestock markets—musician Marjorie Cooney and engineer Aaron Shelton broadcast from the back of a moving mule. Announcer Ott Devine interviewed participants and spectators at a pro golf tournament at Richland Country Club, aided by an engineer carrying a field transmitter strapped to his back. At a coon hunt near Bowling Green, Kentucky, Shelton's fellow engineer George Reynolds got to show off the station's new "shotgun" microphone, capable of picking out specific sounds at long distances, while Harris reported. The engineers would have been glad to forget one ill-conceived event in which they tried to coax a circus bear to fetch honey from a large beehive up a tree. The bear was so uncooperative the announcer had to fabricate the event, live over NBC on a slow Saturday.

The station's portable transmitters were put to use celebrating the anniversaries of the Pan American broadcasts. At two years, they had the train pull to a stop at Calendar Road and a WSM announcer talked to the train crew. By the third year, the daily passing of the train was an extremely popular feature, and there was a meeting to discuss what to do. Everybody liked Harry Stone's idea of broadcasting directly from the train as it left Nashville and sped southward toward the WSM tower. At that point it became Jack DeWitt's technical challenge. His department drew up electrical plans, had a local metal shop build a housing, and assembled a tidy little 20-watt transmitter powerful enough that it required its own call letters from the government: WBPA.

The L&N Railroad procured a railroad car with its own 110-volt generator to be a studio on wheels. Aaron Shelton mounted an antenna wire three feet above the roof, running the full length of the car. On August 12, the first test from the stationary car produced a clear signal twelve miles away at the transmitter house. The next day, they tested it from the moving car, and it worked again. On the fourteenth, they made a run all the way to Lewisburg, getting a clear signal all but the last few miles. Jack Harris was dispatched to Bowling Green where he boarded the Pan American. "When the train pulled into Union Station, about 4:30 that afternoon," Shelton recollected, "a switch engine hastily coupled our car to the last coach of the Pan American, and we were ready to go."

For the fourth anniversary in 1937, the engineers topped themselves by broadcasting live from the train all the way from Cincinnati to New Orleans, a feat that required cooperation with seven radio stations along the route. The stations would pick up signals from the train and redirect them at higher power back to WSM. DeWitt's engineers took over a dining car and set up an entire rolling studio, including a baby grand piano, which Bobby Tucker played en route. Stations such as New Orleans' WWL sent talent up the tracks to sit in and play over WSM's airwaves. And the team conceived a plan on the fly to run a microphone to the engine and the man driving the train. Shelton got to do the interview, one engineer to another. As the train entered New Orleans, it was boarded by WWL announcer Lionel Ricau, who a month later would join the WSM staff. That night, Shelton dined on pompano *en papillote*, browsed Bourbon Street, and drank gin fizz and Sazerac cocktails at the Roosevelt Bar. Some of the musicians from the hotel ballroom let them sit by the side of the stage and watch their group, Glenn Miller and his Orchestra.

In April of 1938, WSM offered a tour-de-force broadcast showing off its entire arsenal of field transmitters. David Cobb strapped on the thirty-five-pound W4XFG and broadcast from an airplane. Ott Devine got on the Corps of Engineers boat the *Warioto* and talked from the Cumberland River, via WBPA, the transmitter from the Pan American broadcasts. And Tom Stewart drove the 250-watt, 350 pound WADQ to Chickamauga Dam near Chattanooga. Jack Harris was the broadcast's "pivot announcer" in the studio. He capped it off by describing how the station's new microwave backup transmitter, W4XFN, was beaming a line-of-sight signal from the National Life roof to the top of the WSM tower in Brentwood.

This proved mere practice, however, for a defining event in the station's history. No use of the WSM remote equipment and its on-the-scene presence earned more accolades than the station's coverage of the epic winter flood of the Ohio River Valley in 1937. On a Saturday in late January, WSM sent reporters and engineers to Clarksville, which was already experiencing the worst flooding in its history. Aaron Shelton, Jack Harris, Harry Stone, and another engineer boarded the Corps of Engineers cruiser the *Lock-n-Dam*, tended by a captain and two crewmen. The wharf where Broadway runs into the Cumberland was already under several feet of water. Fortunately, that would be as bad as it would get in Nashville itself.

En route in a cold, driving rain, Shelton struggled to keep his hat on while stringing up a transmitting antenna between the small mast at the bow and the pilot house. Jack Harris gave an on-air description of speeding down the swollen river, past rooftops sticking out of the water. The team stayed on the air until their connection faded at twenty miles away. Harry Stone and the second engineer got off the boat at Clarksville, which was inundated. Harris and Shelton went further down the river, hoping to broadcast from land wire circuits somewhere. About 9:00 p.m. they heard WSM announce on the Grand Ole Opry that the studio was receiving WBPA's faint carrier signal but that it could not pick up voices. Shelton toggled the carrier signal on and off in Morse code, knowing that George Reynolds would understand. He said they were an hour from Eddyville, Kentucky and would make contact from there. Shelton heard his message acknowledged over WSM. At Eddyville, Harris witnessed prisoners wearing cuffs and leg irons being evacuated to barges in choppy water. "When I got back I reported this on the radio, and it caused quite a stir in the state of Kentucky," he said. Harris and Shelton spent the night in Eddyville then headed back to Nashville by land the next day.

Saturday night at the studio, news broke that two-thirds of Louisville's streets were covered with water. Stone called Lee Coulson, his counterpart at WHAS in Louisville, to ask if he needed help. Coulson said they were fine for the time being. But the next afternoon, WSM's teletype machine began to ring, and Coulson's message came chattering out: *"Louisville power going off at eight o'clock/ WHAS studios must stay on air for relief work/ Can you give us the entire facilities of WSM through mutual lines to carry on this work over your transmitter/ We will gladly pay all commercials you miss/ We must serve these people tonight/ Please advise rush and we will hold this line."* David Stone took the message and found Harry, who agreed. WSM would carry whatever WHAS was able to generate from emergency, battery-powered equipment, over a hastily arranged line tying a fire alarm wire to the phone company cables running south. At 7:30, WSM essentially became Louisville's local radio station, a "mechanical lung" for WHAS, as Ed Kirby later called it. Louisville officials commandeered every battery-powered radio they could find and distributed them to volunteer rescue workers. They took their cues from WSM's 50,000-watt signal, which was clearly audible across the flooded city.

WSM set up a sort of war room, coordinating telephone switchboards with National Life clerical workers, who moved distress calls to the announcers and compiled offers of volunteer aid. Marjorie Kirby became one of those extra hands. "People started calling from all over the country, and they couldn't handle it at WSM, so I got some of my friends from Vanderbilt and they put out a call for volunteers to come up and man the phones," she said. "The offices were really busy with people running up and down the hall. 'What should I tell them? They've got five nurses and a doctor—where can they land? Where can they go?'" She remembers for several days the almost mantra-like calls for emergency assistance: "Send a boat. Send a boat. Send a boat." The news and bulletins, arriving by phone line, seemed always on the verge of flickering out, but officials on the Louisville end were able to triage distress calls and use WSM's tower as a dispatch center for rescue boats. WHAS broadcast for twenty-five minutes at a stretch, then WSM would fill in the last five minutes of each half hour with information it had received by phone or telegram.

Then word came that Paducah, Kentucky, was surrounded by water and cut off from phone. Another radio mission was hastily organized. Jack DeWitt, Jack Harris, and engineer Battle Klyce boarded the steamboat *Jayhawker*, which rumbled northeast toward Paducah, while DeWitt and Klyce set about modifying yet another portable transmitter to broadcast from deep in the flood zone without a phone line.

"We were out in what looked like the Atlantic Ocean," said Harris in recollection. "You could see nothing for miles and miles, and I remember asking the pilot if he knew where we were. He said, 'Well generally speaking. But rather than being over the ship channel, we are probably over Farmer Jones' cornfield.'"

They were approached by a boat with three distraught men who turned out to be the postmaster, the head of the American Legion, and the mayor of the drowning town of Gilbertsville. They were desperate for medical supplies, blankets, and food. They also wanted heavy rope, they said, to tie their houses to trees to keep them from washing away. The *Jayhawker*'s captain said he had strict orders that all his supplies were going to Paducah and he couldn't help them. But Harris interviewed the men as part of his regular newscast. "They all were in tears telling the desperate story of Gilbertsville and begging for supplies," Harris said. "I threw it back to the studio." Then, an Army colonel came on the air and ordered the major on board Harris's boat to give the people from Gilbertsville whatever they needed. They dropped a good bit of their supplies there before proceeding on to Paducah, where three-story buildings had water nearly to their roofs.

For eighty-two straight hours, WSM broadcast virtually nothing but flood news and emergency dispatch bulletins generated by WHAS. National Life even dropped its name from WSM's station identification for the duration of the crisis. For a full week, there was no other endeavor, no other story. Two hundred other radio stations rebroadcast WSM's Louisville-originated signal, an impromptu network that gave the rest of the nation a front-row seat for the disaster and relief effort. Altogether, the flood affected eleven states. By Tuesday afternoon, some 500,000 people were homeless in the Ohio River

Valley. Children and old people perished when waters rose clear over the upper stories of their homes. Firemen fought gas-main blazes while standing chest deep in icy water. Refugees arrived by train and car in Nashville, which became a Red Cross staging area for tons of relief supplies. The *Banner* described Louisville as "a picture of destruction" and editorialized that the crisis was the region's most emotionally devastating event since the Civil War.

Once the flood crested, WSM turned to the business of missing persons. Clerks typed up many hundreds of index cards with contact information for the lost and the looking. Many were never found, but many agreed that WSM's service over those four days and periodically for several weeks thereafter saved numerous lives. The *New York Times* noted WSM's efforts, as did numerous newspapers around the country. The Tennessee legislature commended the station for "patriotic service of the very highest nature." Most grateful of all perhaps was Louisville Mayor Neville Miller, who, wearing hip waders, warmly received a small WSM delegation in his muddy office a few days after the waters receded. Among that group was Ed Kirby, who had no idea at the time he was meeting, in Miller, his future boss.

Twenty miles south of Louisville, as the water gradually subsided, workers for the Southern Bell Telephone Company came upon the corpse of a horse, whose one-ton body had become tangled in the lines carrying WHAS's signal south to WSM. Its stiff rear legs were perched on a cross tie, its rear end pointed skyward, its head well underwater. L. B. Rodenhaven, coordinator of Louisville's rescue work, saw a picture of the horse straining the wire umbilical. "I shudder to think what might have happened had the lines broken," he said. "All our rescue work for four days and nights was dependent on the WSM signal. God was on our side."

Later that spring, veteran WSM musician Marjorie Cooney got off the studio elevator and promptly ran into Jack Harris. "You're just the person I'm looking for," Harris said. "Come in here and have this audition. We're auditioning for a voice to do a Faultless Starch program."

She protested, "Jack, I never did anything like this in my life."

"It makes no difference. Read this copy."

It was news. International bulletins. Local stories. She read well, and she was the only one of the three candidates who could pronounce 'Faultless Starch' faultlessly. She was given the 3:00 p.m. weekday slot, and her show,

A Woman Looks at the News, was born. Perhaps because Cooney was well known as a pianist, she was given the pseudonym Ann Ford, though it was no secret who she really was.

It represented a play for the midday female listener, seen by the station, without much fear of contradiction, as a housewife at home with babies, a sewing basket, and a duster. Cooney remembered that her newscasts were frosted with human interest stories but that she always led with the real thing: wars in China and Spain, the abdication of King Edward the Eighth, Hitler's subjugation of Austria, and the disappearance of Amelia Earhart. News editor Howard Eskridge wrote most of the copy, though at times she wrote her own.

"I imagined myself as a busy [housewife], sitting down with the newspaper and looking through it," Cooney said. "That was the way I gave my program. I had a goodly number of men [listening too], and I could understand it because they were traveling men, and they were bored stiff." Over time, she added interviews to the show, from local politicians to star musicians visiting town. And she took her reports out in the field. "It was a great life," she said. "Nobody worried too much about making mistakes. If we did, we corrected them. The town was with us. It was wonderful."

Jack Harris left no account of his inspiration for the Ann Ford broadcasts, but a likely candidate is *News Through A Woman's Eyes,* a fifteen-minute weekday broadcast that began in late 1936 over CBS. The announcer was Kathryn Cravens, said to be the first female radio commentator. Cooney, however, whose show ran for almost fifteen years, is not even mentioned in the largest encyclopedia of women in broadcasting.

In 1937 and 1938, radio station WLW of Cincinnati, owned by radio equipment magnate Powel Crosley Jr., won back-to-back *Variety* magazine Showmanship Awards for Program Origination. Among the first stations in America to broadcast at 50,000 watts, WLW was, in 1934, granted an exclusive, experimental license by the FCC to broadcast—over the same model and style Blaw-Knox radio tower WSM owned—at a ten-fold increase of power: 500,000 watts. Stories sprang up about the transmitter's power to make barbed wire fences spout music and turn the lights on in nearby homes. The station had thirty-four musicians, six arrangers, and nine conductors, all of which must have made Edwin Craig and Jack DeWitt at least mildly envious.

Craig and DeWitt had emerged by the mid-1930s as not only important independent broadcasters but leading advocates for the interests of high-powered radio stations nationally. In May 1934, Craig invited representatives from his fellow clear channel radio stations to a meeting in Chicago. Fourteen of them, including WLW and major stations in Atlanta (WSB), Chicago (WGN and WLS), Los Angeles (KFI and KNX), Dallas/Fort Worth (WFAA and WBAP), and New Orleans (WWL), established the Clear Channel Group and elected Craig its chairman. DeWitt would become its chief engineering consultant. The CCG's campaign in Washington to make 500,000-watt stations routine was ultimately unsuccessful, but the lobby did preserve their exclusive signals over many years, in the face of constant pressure from smaller broadcasters to end the clear channel system. In 1937, Craig spearheaded a major reorganization of the much larger National Association of Broadcasters, further extending his influence inside the radio world.

Craig pursued a public relations strategy as well, including a consumer/listener magazine called *Rural Radio*. Conceived and edited by Ed Kirby and written by publicity agents from the CCG stations, the inaugural issue, in February 1938, offered itself to America's fifty million rural residents, "the backbone and breadbasket of the nation." Tailored for the whole family, it offered a bit of technical know-how, recipes, and tidbits for kids. A WSM engineer wrote about "how to get more from your radio set." Handy Annie advised homemakers to periodically wash electric light bulbs, because "clean bulbs give more light." Readers wrote back with homespun admiration. "I think it is the grandest little magazine I ever saw," raved a Kentucky woman. A Georgia reader indicated he was glad to see "not so much Hollywood stuff. Keep it that way!"

Rural Radio didn't last long, not because demand was weak, but because Kirby, the magazine's mastermind, got an offer that moved him along from Nashville. The National Association of Broadcasters, now sixteen years old and growing into a formidable force in Washington, tapped Kirby to direct its public relations department. Neville Miller had gone from the muddy mayor's office in Louisville to the head of the NAB, so he'd already made a warm bond with Kirby. For Kirby, the work was not far from what he'd been doing at National Life, except it was on a national stage, as radio continued to grow in importance. Ed and Marjorie left *Rural Radio* in the hands of its printer, where it didn't stand much of a long-term chance, and moved to Washington in the fall of 1938.

Meanwhile, Jack DeWitt was keeping WSM at the forefront of technological change. He and Harry Stone experimented for about three years with a primitive facsimile system that beamed headline news and pictures to special receiving teletype sets in businesses and homes. The station installed receivers around town and broadcast the coded content from the main radio tower in the middle of the night when WSM was off the air. The teletypes would chatter out strips of paper with headlines, stories, and primitive dot-matrix photos, but the whole project turned out to be ahead of its time.

A separate operation exploited the long-proven strengths of shortwave radio, higher-frequency, long-distance broadcasting used by amateur operators and other noncommercial users like the military. Millions of people had receivers that could tune in shortwave bands when they weren't tuned to AM stations. In the mid-1930s, DeWitt and George Reynolds, his old friend and fellow engineer, built the ultimate shortwave transmitter/receiver, with three separate antennas about a thousand yards apart on the tower/transmitter grounds of WSM. The rig served many purposes. NBC experimented with shortwave communication among its affiliate stations from a twelve-mile-high balloon in South Dakota. DeWitt picked up news and music from Europe via shortwave, sometimes for his own amusement and frequently for rebroadcast over WSM. He once had a Vanderbilt Professor translate a speech by Nazi propaganda minister Joseph Goebbels. And on Tuesday afternoons, the set was pressed into service for two-way conversations between Reynolds and his sister Lena, a Presbyterian missionary in the Congo.

A few years later, DeWitt found his own self-indulgent use for the set. He'd hired a builder for a home on a hill in a Nashville subdivision, and he had high fidelity loudspeakers built into his drawing room wall. Saturday nights were an issue for Jack, because while every other NBC station in the country was broadcasting Arturo Toscanini conducting the NBC Symphony, *his* radio station preempted the network for the Opry. So DeWitt jiggered the situation. "I would have [the symphony] sent out to my home by short-wave radio, and we would invite guests up to listen to it," he said. "After that we would get into the bootleg bourbon and have a good time dancing to Strauss waltzes, polkas and popular music. The thing became so well known around town that at one time people showed up we had never met in our lives, and we finally had to disappear for several weekends."

In early 1939 WSM institutionalized its shortwave presence with the inauguration of a 1,000-watt station. W4XA, as it was called, aired no commercials. But it did serve a purpose; to defray persistent local criticism that WSM was neglecting culture in favor of hillbilly music, the new station played classical fare. Mondays were Gilbert and Sullivan night. Fridays were opera. Saturdays, it piped in the NBC Toscanini broadcasts DeWitt had gone through such trouble to hear. WSM writer and announcer Tom Stewart sat before a little tombstone-shaped table microphone and announced the selections, aware that he could sometimes be heard in Australia if the weather was right and the sunspots weren't too active. WSM announced that it wanted the station to be informal and highly responsive to its cult audience. "Criticisms, suggestions, and requests of all listeners are given the most careful consideration," they said via *Rural Radio* magazine. "This use of short waves for local broadcasting is relatively new in the radio world, and WSM engineers feel that it offers a fertile field for development." Sometimes that development looked like creative fooling around. Occasionally, WSM set up left and right microphones in the studio and simulcast the performance from one on the AM band and the other on the shortwave band. A dedicated listener could thus set up two radios and listen to WSM in stereo, twenty years before that technology came to records.

For those who received it, W4XA sounded better than AM, and the emerging technology of FM broadcasting sounded better still. In the early 1930s, radio pioneer Edwin Howard Armstrong figured out a way to broadcast rich, wide-spectrum sound without the static that plagued AM signals. His struggles to have it adopted by the radio industry are a famous and ultimately tragic chapter of broadcast history. But long before he committed suicide, Armstrong and DeWitt got to know each other. And by the very early 1940s, when the FCC was finally in a position to issue licenses for FM broadcasting, DeWitt was ready. On a clear December day in 1940, he climbed to the top of his 878-foot AM tower, taking in a view that stretched nearly from Kentucky to Alabama, to oversee the installation of four large dipole FM transmitter antennas. Three months later, he received FCC authorization to relaunch W4XA as W47NV, which took to the air as the first commercial FM station in America.

The character of Minnie Pearl developed gradually, but the old lady from Cullman, Alabama, remained Sarah Colley's touchstone. She began using Minnie as a sort of alter ego when she introduced plays to new audiences. "Howdy," she'd say in a demure voice. "I'm proud to be here." Eventually, she got an offer to do Minnie in a paid appearance. April 1939 at the Pilots Club Convention in Aiken, South Carolina, marked the first time she did the character in costume. Colley bought ten dollars worth of resale clothes, including a flat, wide-brimmed straw hat with flowers tacked on top. It wasn't a rube's costume or a caricature, she has emphasized. She never adopted painted-on freckles or blacked-out teeth. "I dressed her as I thought a young country girl would dress to go to meetin' on Sunday or to come to town on Saturday afternoon to do a little trading and a little flirting," she wrote.

Then a call came from Harry Stone. He'd been tipped by a Nashville banker and a Colley family friend that Minnie Pearl might be Opry material. Though the Opry had been more her father's thing over the years than something she ever cared about, she jumped at Stone's invitation to audition, which she did in street clothes for Stone, new Artist Service Bureau manager Ford Rush, and George Hay. "I still wanted to be Ophelia Colley, future dramatic actress, doing a comedy character part. I wasn't ready to *be* Minnie Pearl," she explained later. Reluctantly, however, Rush offered her an Opry slot, warning her, ironically, that the station's misgivings stemmed from her well-heeled background and her Ward-Belmont days. "He was afraid the Opry audiences would find that out and suspect I was a phony," she recalled. They put her on at 11:05 p.m., late in the show, long after the network broadcast and after much of the live audience had already left or dozed off. She was quavering with stage fright as she waited in the wings of War Memorial Auditorium. And that's when Hay gave her famous, steadying advice: "Just love them, honey, and they'll love you right back." She was meek, but she struck a chord. When she arrived at the station later the next week to go over script material with Rush, receptionist Margaret Frye presented her with a bag with over three hundred pieces of mail addressed to Minnie Pearl. The response was enough for Rush to offer her a place in the Opry cast, at $10 per week. Colley was delighted; she answered every letter.

By 1940, DeFord Bailey was in a complex position. On one hand, he was one of the most popular entertainers in the Depression-era South, a bona fide Opry star with white and black fans alike. He was in fact so well loved that the young and still little-known Roy Acuff invited Bailey on the road with him to draw out bigger crowds. And Bailey remembered Acuff and most of the other musicians treating him with respect and affection. On the other hand, he was in trouble and he scarcely knew it. Just a year later, the harmonica wizard's tenure at WSM would come to a sudden and embittering end. Part of the rift was driven by long-standing racial tension, to be sure, but an even bigger cause was a twist in the evolution of the music business.

Country music had come a long way in the decade of the Depression, in part because so many Americans were relying on radio for entertainment and because radio stations found so many country musicians willing to fill airtime for next to nothing. Nevertheless, country music had a problem, and that problem was the American Society of Composers, Authors, and Publishers (ASCAP), the sole conduit through which songwriters received royalties for performances of songs. Radio stations and networks signed contracts that allowed them to play unlimited ASCAP music for a blanket annual fee. ASCAP would distribute those royalties to its member publishers and writers, according to the relative popularity of their songs.

ASCAP hindered country music coming and going. Because while the organization wouldn't accept unschooled blues, folk, or hillbilly songwriters into its guild, it was all too happy to annex copyrights on "arrangements" of traditional or folk songs that were brought to them by record companies or artists. For example, when record executive Ralph Peer recorded the Carter Family singing "Wildwood Flower," an ancient song with no discernable writer, Peer claimed the copyright for his own publishing company, which collects royalties on the song to this day.

This foretold of a bleak future for a country music industry. Without a powerful agent leveraging performance income for original songwriters, country couldn't become anything more than a sort of low-rent musical ghetto where slumlords (record executives) exploited renters (artists), rather than one that rewarded the writers of hits through the copyright system. The situation might have persisted for years but for a move by ASCAP that sparked a war with broadcasters. ASCAP argued that because radio was cutting into record and sheet music sales, its writers and publishers were entitled to a lot more from radio than it was getting. So as a major contract with radio stations was nearing expiration in the late 1930s, the society proposed a veritable take-it-or-leave-it doubling of its royalties.

The National Association of Broadcasters, with Neville Miller at its head and Edwin Craig on the board, made a radical countermove by creating its own performing rights society, Broadcast Music Incorporated (BMI). Radio stations, WSM included, bought shares in the new entity, which launched in February 1940 and began trying like mad to build its own catalog of music. BMI recruited a few disaffected ASCAP music publishers and songwriters while opening its door to new writers, without musical literacy tests or stylistic boundaries. The ASCAP/broadcasters contract expired on December 31, 1940, and the next day, to prove they were serious, broadcasters pulled all ASCAP music from the air. Entire libraries of sheet music and recordings were cordoned off. Old European classics, Stephen Foster songs, and other songs whose copyrights had lapsed surged into circulation. Vito Pellettieri had to yank many Opry performers' key tunes after he traced their licensing to ASCAP. Francis Craig dropped his theme song "Red Rose" and substituted a misspelled public domain tune: "Disallusioned."

Here's where trouble began for DeFord Bailey. It turned out that most of his signature songs had been licensed by ASCAP, and when Edwin Craig ordered all ASCAP material off the air, Bailey was mystified. For years, he had resented Hay telling him to stick to a tight repertoire of proven songs, even though Bailey wanted to add new material. Suddenly, he was being ordered to do exactly the opposite.

To make matters more difficult, NBC even banned any sort of *improvisation* on the air, lest an ASCAP melody slip in inadvertently. This was devastating for Bailey's blues-based style, which, as traditional music will, built something original and spontaneous out of something old and familiar. Hay circulated the story that "like some members of his race and other races, DeFord was lazy. He knew about a dozen numbers. . . . but he refused to learn any more." Bailey disputed this, arguing that his art wasn't as simple as just working up a few new songs. "It takes years to make a good tune," he told David Morton, alluding to the process of working a song over time until it became uniquely his. Moreover, at a more visceral level, he was just tired of being paid less than he was worth for so many years. "Hurt, puzzled, offended, he responded by continuing to perform just as he always had, bearing it all in dignified silence," Morton wrote. In late May 1941, he was fired.

"They turned me loose with a wife and kids to root hog or die," Bailey said. His resentment toward WSM lasted for decades. Vowing never to work for anybody else again, he opened a shoeshine stand in his back room, carted hot lunches to workmen, and delivered coal. He would not return to the Opry until the mid-1970s, for a pair of "old-timer's night" reunion shows, the second of which coincided with his seventy-fifth birthday. Alcyone Bate Beasley, Dr. Humphrey Bate's daughter, called him "the dangdest harmonica player who ever lived."

The cause of Bailey's unnecessary career change, however, was country music's and Nashville's gain. "No other event in the history of American music did so much to aid country music's commercial success" as the birth of BMI, wrote Bill Ivey when he was director of the Country Music Foundation. "Radio suddenly opened up to blues, jazz, and country, and BMI collected millions of dollars in performance royalties for the songwriters, with the result that country songwriting and recording gained immensely in financial and professional stature." By the time the ASCAP song ban ended in October, BMI had accumulated more than 36,000 songs from fifty-two publishers and was "well on the way to success," according to historian Bill Malone.

The same could have been said for country music, WSM, and Nashville. Improbably, an insurance company had survived the Depression with the help of a radio station, and perhaps just as surprising, that radio station had helped lift country music from a regional, class-specific folk art to the edge of national commercial viability. Unfortunately, by late 1941, it was clear that more strife was at hand, something larger and darker that shouldn't have done one bit of good for a nascent music town in the South, except that it did.

SIX   *Guts and Brass*

The night of December 15, 1939, was icy cold in Atlanta, but the thousands of people crowded on Peachtree Street scarcely noticed. They were dazzled by searchlights panning the sky and playing across the facade of the Loew's Grand Theater, which, on this gala evening, was festooned with Confederate bunting and faced with a huge replica of a colonnaded Southern plantation. Loudspeakers announced the arrivals of Clark Gable, with his wife Carol Lombard, and Vivien Leigh, with beau Laurence Olivier. The day had been declared a holiday by the mayor, and three days of pomp and celebration had preceded this climactic event: the world premiere of *Gone with the Wind*. The hotly anticipated and very expensive film, a nostalgic and unapologetic celebration of southern glory presented in awe-inspiring Technicolor, was just what its Depression-weary audience wanted. When the Confederacy declared war, the audience of two thousand stood and cheered. Hattie McDaniel, who would become the first African American to win an Academy Award (for her role as Mammy), was not invited.

In the midst of the excitement was radio reporter Jack Harris, not yet thirty, his WSM microphone in hand. For six hours, he interviewed stars and fans alike, capturing the voices and the ambience of "one of the great events of Southern history." As the long film came to its operatic, Dixie-affirming conclusion, Harris recorded the swelling theme music and the lusty applause. He transmitted a post-film speech by novelist Margaret Mitchell and interviewed audience members as they emerged from the screening. *"Opinions all the way around say that it's really a smash hit,"* he announced with staccato urgency. *"We haven't had a dissenting vote yet that it is certainly one of the super-colossal productions of all time."*

As the 1930s came to a welcomed end, WSM was something of a super-colossal production itself. The station sent three shows each week over the NBC network, including the Grand Ole Opry, and the *Nashville Times* radio column noted that "WSM is fast becoming the leading NBC center in the South." It sold far more of its airtime to national and regional sponsors than to local businesses, making a tidy profit for National Life, beyond its massive marketing presence for its insurance. The only hang-up in this steady march toward national prominence was Ed Kirby's departure for Washington, because he had brought an imaginative drive to WSM programming that wasn't general manager Harry Stone's strength. Jack Harris, by then Stone's trusted second-in-command, managed special events and sports like a dashing young champ, but he didn't seem like the man to cast shows, oversee music repertoire, and hire musicians. For some time, Edwin Craig had wondered why WSM didn't have a dedicated, full-time program director anyway. Now, he insisted, and the man who won the job brought a new level of production experience to the station. He also had the appealing attribute of being a Nashville native. His name was Jack Stapp.

He started working around radio while at a prep school in Georgia, and by the time he was nineteen years old and taking over as program director for CBS affiliate WGST in Atlanta, newspapers were calling Jack Stapp a radio "boy wonder." That was 1932, by which time he'd decided to bypass college and become a radio professional. The *Atlanta Constitution* said he'd already proven his "ability to guide programs through a maze of technical details and retain the warm approval of temperamental artists." He could have been on television, had there been such a thing, with his shoe-polish sleek hair, his dark eyes full of authority and warmth, and his full, almost feminine lips. But by 1934, Stapp was a seasoned radio announcer and personality and, according to one newspaper columnist, "a highly valued addition to the life of Atlanta and the South." The writer predicted it wouldn't be long before he was drafted into the big time.

Stapp's best friend in Atlanta was Bert Parks, and he helped Parks land his first radio job. Bert Parks, an announcer with Miss America pageants in his future, paid back the favor a few years later by helping Stapp get his first network job at CBS in New York. For the latter half of the 1930s, Parks and Stapp roomed together, working as hotshots at CBS, and living the large life of New York's Cab Calloway years. Stapp produced the *Dick Tracy Show, School of the Air,* and *Mary Pickford's Parties at Pickfair.* He worked with Kate Smith and Edward R. Murrow, and once he worked a full week without leaving the studios, backing up radio news pioneer H. V. Kaltenborn during an early tipping point of World War II.

One day in the late 1930s, Stapp was producing an episode of *Buck Rogers in the Twenty-First Century* at CBS studios in New York, when Jack Harris came in, unannounced. "I'd never met him," Stapp remembered. "The pageboy was bringing him through [with] one of the men from station relations, because CBS wanted to get WSM." Stapp, still with family ties in Nashville, was a long-distance fan of WSM. He stopped the rehearsal and said, "Folks, I want you to meet a man here from the greatest radio station in America, WSM. They have the Grand Ole Opry." He went on and on. Harris didn't forget that, and when Edwin Craig and Harry Stone began thinking seriously in 1939 about hiring a full-time program director, Harris offered Stapp's name for consideration. Stapp was streaking toward senior positions at CBS. He's said he was considering an offer to be production manager for the network when WSM came inquiring. But he surprised himself. "I never knew I'd end up in Nashville again as long as I lived, except to see relatives," he said some years later. "I made up my mind, I was coming South—back home."

Before he left, Stapp called his friend Phil Carlin at NBC—his network's chief rival—to promise him he'd be pitching shows from his new NBC base in Nashville. And upon arrival in his old hometown, he shook things up. He wasn't entirely happy with WSM's house ensembles, which were good enough for an orchestra pit, he thought, but not for regular network feeds. Recruiting new talent wasn't made easy by AFM Local 257. "The union wouldn't let me bring in musicians, because of competition naturally," Stapp told the Country Music Foundation's Doug Green. "But somebody at WSM came to me and said there are a lot of good musicians from Nashville who hold Nashville cards who would love to come back to Nashville if they had a regular job here. So we got on the phone and got hold of these guys and had an excellent orchestra."

Stapp liked what he saw in vocalist Snooky Lanson, as well as a new-to-Nashville singer named Kitty Kallen. He also had good reason to be pleased with his announcing staff. Besides Harris, WSM had a cast of names and voices intimately known in the entire region. David Cobb, Ott Devine, Louie Buck, and Lionel Ricau were all sincere, engaging, and capable of introducing an opera singer or an Opry star with equal grace. Collectively, they defined the convivial, folksy personality of WSM even more than the music. They didn't take nicknames or adopt characters like announcers from Hay's generation. Instead they came across as very much themselves—polite but genuine. One afternoon each week in the late 1930s, all participated in a free-flowing, banter-filled quiz show called *Stump the Announcer,* in which host Richard Dunn read general knowledge questions sent by listeners. A bell rang when an announcer was flummoxed, which was relatively rare, and a dollar would go to the question's sender.

Stapp's relationship with Phil Carlin at NBC seems to have paid off quickly. The show *Magnolia Blossoms* was revived from a hiatus as an NBC feed, and Francis Craig's long-running local program, *Sunday Night Serenade,* hopped to the network as well. Most auspicious, however, was the inauguration of a half hour of the Grand Ole Opry on NBC. Prince Albert Smoking Tobacco, a loose pipe and roll-your-own tobacco made by R. J. Reynolds, became the presenting sponsor of a half-hour segment of the Opry in January 1939, but only locally. On October 14, that segment went national. George Hay announced and Roy Acuff starred in the first NBC network broadcast of what would from then on be called the "Prince Albert Opry" from War Memorial Auditorium.

By 1940 NBC was a massive operation, headquartered at Rockefeller Center in New York, with a multiplex of state-of-the-art studios issuing shows to 172 stations as well as shortwave broadcasts in six languages across the world. In the age before television, NBC was rivaled only by CBS as the most influential entertainment and news organization in America, and WSM was one of NBC's star affiliates. Already, the Air Castle of the South had graduated key talent to the network, including dramatist Casper Kuhn, who became nationally known as announcer Dick Dudley. Even more prominent were "Smilin'" Ed McConnell, who got his own show, and Dinah Shore, who was named the nation's outstanding new radio star in a 1940 Scripps-Howard newspaper poll. This pipeline of artistry only bolstered what had long been a special relationship. The initial union between NBC and WSM had been a handshake deal, and Edwin Craig was a lifelong friend of NBC's Niles Trammell, who became NBC president in 1940. When CBS courted WSM in 1936, NBC fought to keep WSM in its fold. *Broadcasting* magazine called the relationship "strategically important" and said that "by re-signing the station, NBC kept for itself one of the most important outlets on its networks."

One measure of that importance was how often NBC turned to WSM for live, national entertainment. While local stations like WSM occasionally filled air time with records or transcription discs, NBC prohibited prerecorded programming until the middle of World War II. So sometimes, especially on weekend afternoons, the network would call its trusted affiliate looking for live filler, sometimes fifteen minutes, sometimes more. When such requests came in, Jack Stapp arranged a band to back up a staff vocalist or a group. An announcer typed out snappy intros to three songs on a typewriter. They'd slap a name on the show, rehearse it in Studio B to tweak the timing (if they were lucky), and then run it live when the cue came from the network.

Sometimes such requests gave birth to long-running shows. One Friday in 1940, NBC's Phil Carlin called Stapp and said, "Can you feed me a show Sunday afternoon?" It wasn't much notice, but Stapp pulled together the premiere of the readily named *Sunday Down South* in a couple of days. The show aired sporadically on the network in the latter half of the year and then became a local show at (variously) noon, 3:30, or 4:30 p.m. It was a sustaining (commercial-free) show until October 1942, when it jumped to a regional network with Lion Oil of El Dorado, Arkansas as its sponsor. *Sunday Down South* eventually settled into a 5:00 p.m. slot where it ran for years following the NBC Symphony, over fifteen and later twenty-five stations. A live audience in Studio C helped the show crackle. Pop smoothies like Snooky Lanson and Dottie Dillard fronted Beasley Smith's orchestra, while emcee Louie Buck promised "a breath of magnolia and a ray of sunshine" in his enthusiastic opening patter. Smith's arrangements were dense with saxophones and trombones and heavy on post–*Gone with the Wind* romance. Although it never made the full NBC network again, *Sunday Down South* encapsulated as well as any regular program of the 1940s and 1950s the genteel Dixieana WSM cultivated for its audiences and sponsors alike.

The Grand Ole Opry became particularly symbolic of WSM's stature within the network. Not only was having a Saturday night prime-time show on NBC an honor, WSM fought for and won the freedom to locally preempt the rest of NBC's Saturday lineup to broadcast the Opry in its entirety. Craig asserted later that WSM was the only station in the NBC chain with such permission. "We almost lost our NBC affiliation" over the issue, he said, but "we felt we were acting in the public interest by bringing good entertainment to hundreds of people in our own community, so we took a firm stand."

More and more, the Opry was at the core of WSM's self-image as well. A brochure for potential advertisers proudly noted in about 1940 that the Opry "is unique in radio, a strange slice of America—the homespun voice of America speaking to the homespun heart of America." Outsiders began to see it that way too. The *New York Times* covered the Opry on January 14, 1940, offering a respectful description of the crowds, the songs, and the artists. Just over a week later, *Time* magazine's radio column described the show as "a weekly fiesta, Southern style, for hill folk from the Great Smokies, croppers, tourists." In the middle of the year, Republic Pictures released a modestly budgeted film entitled *Grand Ole Opry* with performances by Uncle Dave Macon, Roy Acuff, and others. And even at home, the media praised the Opry and WSM's role in building it as a cultural phenomenon. The *Nashville Times* editorialized: "Now we in Nashville realize that instead of being marked as a capital of hillbillydom, we have become instead a city that knew how to develop and present one significant phase of real American music which would have been untouched, had it not been for our activity in bringing it to the rest of the nation."

Not everyone saw it that way in Nashville, where there was still a stark divide between the hillbilly musicians and the power players behind the radio station that happened to be helping them. Few people described the schism as well as Pee Wee King: "Most of the rich people, the movers and the shakers, and the university crowd didn't pay us much attention," he wrote. "They didn't go to the Opry. They had their own little cliques and circles, their golf tournaments, symphony concerts, card games and dances. People who lived in the fashionable sections of Nashville, like Belle Meade and the West End, had little to do with the early Opry stars. Sometimes we'd get the cold shoulder from people who thought we weren't worth fooling with. They seemed to be saying, 'You're not in my class. You're not educated and cultured. Why should I spend my time with you?'" It was like living, he said, in two cities: "the city of the Opry and the rest of Nashville. The attitude that country music was lowbrow spilled over to the fans. I've seen them go into record shops and buy a Frank Sinatra or a Jo Stafford record and sneak an Eddy Arnold or a Pee Wee King record in the pile. For a long time it wasn't fashionable to admit in public that you liked country music."

"They *were* two separate worlds," confirms Ridley Wills II, a third generation National Life executive. "It was never talked about in my family. My father [Jesse Wills] was a poet, about as uninterested in country music as you could get. You no more talked about country music than you did Jackie Fargo, the professional wrestler. It just didn't come up."

Jim Denny got along with hillbillies just fine. He respected the Opry musicians, and they trusted him in return. In 1941, Denny became the Opry's unofficial stage manager. War Memorial could be a volatile place because so many rowdy soldiers came to the show. Charlie Sanders, a former policeman who helped Denny in those days, said that Denny was perfectly willing to manhandle drunks who would occasionally volunteer their way up on stage. If necessary, he would clock them on the head or haul them off by the collar.

At the same time, and more constructively, Denny's entrepreneurial streak surfaced. He asked Runcie Clements for permission to sell concessions and souvenirs to the Opry audience. To Clements, this looked like pocket change, and besides, the Opry lacked souvenirs. So he said yes, and Denny got crafty. "He had a guy draw an outline of a hillbilly performer and made a rubber stamp out of it," remembers Denny's son Bill. "And at home we had a jigsaw, and we would stamp plywood sheets with that and it said, 'Grand Ole Opry, Nashville, Tennessee,' and we would take the jigsaw and cut 'em out, sand off the edges a little bit, and paint 'em with lacquer. And that became a souvenir that we sold at the Opry." Father and son Denny also made key rings with a leather fob they would stamp, one by one, with a hammer and die. A similar whacking sound emerged from the family basement as they stamped gold foil Opry logos onto the wooden ashtray bottoms. Later, along came seat cushions, artist songbooks, and, to the great relief of stifling summertime patrons, hand fans.

In 1922, Owen Bradley's father got fed up with farming a hillside in West-moreland and moved fifty miles to the north edge of Nashville. Owen was ten when WSM went on the air, and Francis Craig and Beasley Smith were among the first musicians he ever heard on his crystal radio. His first music lessons were in Hawaiian guitar, which he practiced in earnest after being laid up with an eye injury. Later his mother bought him a piano, and Owen began to imitate and emulate the big band sounds he heard emanating from Chicago, New York, and Nashville. "I liked Hawaiian music, hillbilly music, anything," he once recalled. Owen's brother Harold, about ten years younger, recalls Owen organizing a group that met in a large converted chicken house on the Bradley property. "A bus would pull up out front, and a band would get off, and they'd go out back and have jam sessions. The neighbors would be hanging over the fence."

Owen's first regular jobs were on trombone with a bandleader named Red McEwen. The boss was patient as Bradley learned to read charts and play his role in a working dance band. Bradley could recall shows at the elaborate but rustic Wilson County Fair and playing underage at the gambling houses out in Cheatham County. "Beyond the county line, first came the Pines. A little further out were the Belvedere and the Ridgeway Inn. We were kids playing out there," Owen told music writer Robert K. Oermann. It was, he said, "like a little Reno, Nevada" out on Highway 70, full of booze and burlesque and sometimes amateurs doing their best. "One night we had this dancer performing in front of the band. We couldn't read music properly, so we kept repeating the melody, over and over. This poor gal was dancing herself to death. She bent over and looked between her legs backwards and said to the band, 'Shut up! You S.O.B.'s are killing me!'"

Soon Bradley began assembling his own bands, which began to make real money playing walkathons at the Hippodrome ("the South's Largest, Finest Roller Rink"), charity events that tested the bands' endurance nearly as much as the couples who aimed to be the last one standing. Meanwhile, Bradley had become a familiar face at WSM, playing trombone with show bands and sometimes piano behind young Frances Rose Shore. At the same time, he played piano and guitar in a little band called the Blue Diamond Melody Boys at WLAC for $1 per program. In about 1940, Bradley moved his base from roadhouses in Cheatham County to upscale clubs in Brentwood. There, he worked with numerous musicians whom he would know for years thereafter. Kitty Kallen, Snooky Lanson, and a dimpled Dottie Dillard all fronted the band at one time or another. Saxophonist Charlie Grant proved himself in the reed section. Drummer Farris Coursey kept civilized time.

New WSM program director Jack Stapp noticed Bradley's talents as soon as he moved to Nashville. Initially, he had to hire Bradley under the pseudonym Roland Brown to keep WLAC in the dark. And Bradley could tell Stapp had a vision. "When he came, he started acting as though WSM was a network," Bradley said in 1988. "He started filling up different spots with local programs. This was a very important time. WSM agreed to have a band. It started off small and gradually grew. By 1940, I was asked to join as a utility player."

Bradley's boss was a fascinating character named Pietro Brescia, a former violinist from Francis Craig's orchestra who became WSM's music director in the late 1930s. Born in Chile to Italian parents, Brescia had fought for the United States in World War I, played in the San Francisco Symphony, and developed a scientific interest in snakes. Now, he was conducting the NBC network feed *Riverboat Revels*—a variety show set on a virtual river steamer. Listeners heard a sound effects man ringing a boat bell and splashing in a pool to evoke a churning paddlewheel. Ott Devine, the original host, addressed a live studio audience that was keyed up to burst into applause at the right moments. A "captain" with a gratingly sweet, old-fat-man voice presided over everything, sometimes ordering a band to play, quoting poetry, shouting orders to his Negro deck boy, and contriving dramatic excuses for his guests to burst into song. Brescia led the "River Boat Roustabouts," a ragtime orchestra that kept frantic tempos with a woodblock and a banjo. Other pieces were elaborately orchestrated suites, with difficult interplay between the tiny violin section, trombones, and piano. The group was frequently joined by original WSM cast member Joseph MacPherson, who sang songs like "Old Man River" or "River, Stay away from My Door" in a stiff, operatic baritone. When the group played a southern hoedown or fiddle tunes like "Arkansas Traveler" in orchestral style, the beats were as rigid as a drumstick and really quite painful to anyone attuned to the relaxed flow of old-time fiddling.

Far more timeless and delightful was the harmony singing of Betty and the Dixie Dons, an all-purpose group led by Alcyone Bate Beasley. Daughter of the late Humphrey Bate, she was herself a veteran WSM entertainer. As "Betty," she led a crisp and note-perfect vocal trio, backed by a tactful and swinging mix of accordion, violin and guitar. Left-handed Jack Shook, the most important Nashville guitarist of the pre–Chet Atkins era, stroked his acoustic arch-top with brio and sophistication. The band as a whole could bounce energetically or flutter romantically.

Minnie Pearl joined the riverboat cast, in what was likely her earliest non-Opry WSM appearances. David Cobb played her straight man. Her routines generally centered around the fictitious town of Grinders Switch, a mythical place like Lake Wobegon or Yoknapatawpha County, where country life played out according to Minnie's imagination. One of her frequent subjects was Brother, modeled after poor Kyle from the mountain. "Every time I bring him out, something happens," she fretted in one routine. "The first time I brung him to town he like to scared every feller to death!" Cobb asked what was the matter. Pearl replied that, "They all said he had smallpox, but he didn't. It was just where we had been learnin' him to eat with a fork."

That, in high WSM style, gave way to Kay Carlisle, a pop vocalist billed as the "sweetheart of the blue grass region," who sang "Bragging."

The World in Review with Jack Harris grew more ominous as the world spiraled out of control. Some listeners told him he slanted toward supporting U.S.

intervention in his summaries of Hitler's growing threat, and in retrospect Harris couldn't disagree. On Sunday night, September 1, 1940, WSM broadcast *The First Year,* an in-house production that summarized the gathering storm. *"Today . . . marks the first anniversary of the beginning of the Second World War,"* intoned an announcer, *"a titanic struggle between two diverse political philosophies: democracy and totalitarianism."* Recordings of Adolf Hitler, Neville Chamberlain, and King George VI were spliced into live scripted synopses of key developments, bolstered with sound effects of exploding bombs and marching soldiers. When the Germans sank the cruise ship *Athenia,* the radio audience heard explosions and screams. The show concluded and cut to Jack Harris with the latest war news.

When men began to leave WSM for the service, Harris was one of the first to go, hired away by his old mentor, Ed Kirby. Kirby's colleagues at the National Association of Broadcasters were afraid the War Department would box radio reporters out of the biggest story of the twentieth century. The nation hadn't fought a war in the broadcasting era, and it was all too plausible that the government could simply commandeer radio itself. NAB's preemptive plan had Kirby at its center. They offered his services to the War Department for one dollar per year as a liaison between the military and the broadcasters, a publicity agent willing to work with and negotiate censorship policy. A graduate of Virginia Military Institute, Kirby got back in uniform and accepted the rank of lieutenant colonel. Harris answered an invitation to join him in Washington.

"On the last broadcast that I made before I went to the War Department in 1941, I called it *The World in Preview* and tried to predict what was going to happen in the world," Harris said. He wasn't right about everything, but years later he would give himself a passing grade. Over the next four calamitous years, he and Kirby produced radio programming for troops, crafted and implemented War Department policy about journalist access, and helped stitch together a web of wired and wireless broadcasting—the Armed Forces Radio Service—such as the world had never known.

The War Department worked out how to coordinate media coverage of the war even as it practiced for the war itself. When the Second Army held maneuvers in nearby Manchester in 1941, the war games became a perfect opportunity to pursue Jack Stapp's ethic of covering big stories out in the field. WSM engineers and reporters followed the exercises for two weeks via portable shortwave transmitter. As a base of operations, WSM rented a private dining railroad car, where at one point, station brass shared a white tablecloth dinner with three American generals, including the soon-to-be-famous George Patton. "I remember standing out on the railroad tracks on a hot summer evening, drinking Scotch whiskey with General Patton, and conversing with him about the upcoming war," said Jack DeWitt. He could recall the general's ivory-handled revolvers and the high pitch of his voice.

Later that summer, the War Department staged some of the biggest maneuvers ever held in the United States. The station sent new announcer Jud Collins with Aaron Shelton and George Reynolds to engineer coverage of a momentous event that was set to sprawl across much of the state of Louisiana. They loaded a backpack relay transmitter, acetate disc recorder, AC generators, spare tubes, batteries, extra-long microphone cables, headphones, microphones, and power cables in a trailer behind a used DeSoto purchased for the trip and a company Chrysler station wagon with "WSM—650 k.c.—Nashville, Tenn." emblazoned on the side. They headed for Winnfield, Louisiana, headquarters of the "Red Army," where they found rows of tents, hordes of mosquitoes, a big mess hall, and a massive contingent of national media, including CBS's Eric Sevareid and NBC's top special-events announcers Bob Stanton and Dave Garroway.

Jack Harris was there, in his new job as liaison between the radio correspondents and the virtual combatants—the "Red Army" and the "Blue Army." The Blue Army's chief of staff was a lieutenant colonel named Dwight Eisenhower. WSM listeners heard a pontoon bridge being built in the middle of the night, the metallic rumbling of tanks, and the thud of artillery fire. Collins, Shelton, and Reynolds kept on the move as the Blue Army seemed to push the Red Army all over the northern part of Louisiana. After a final exercise involving precision bombing runs at Barksdale Air Force Base near Shreveport, Harry Stone hosted some of the generals back at his hotel room for before-dinner drinks. Young reporter Jud Collins was tasked with buying the liquor, though nobody told him to excise any references to alcohol on his National Life expense report. When the document reached the third-floor treasury department, Shelton related, "The whole building fairly shook and Jud had to endure a lecture on expense reporting. After redoing his expense account and listing two fictitious meals instead of two real bottles of booze, Jud's 'swindle sheet' sailed through without question."

Radio had already changed life in the United States, but the coming war made the medium indescribably important. Beyond reporting the news and offering home-front diversion, radio companies took a direct and aggressive role in supporting the war effort. As its first official morale booster, WSM teamed with its loyal sponsor R. J. Reynolds to develop the Camel Caravan, a touring revue of Opry stars aimed at supporting the troops, widening exposure of WSM and country music, and selling cigarettes. Its formation paralleled the development of the United Service Organization (USO), making the Caravan one of the earliest free traveling shows ever organized for American soldiers.

"We had held auditions on a flatbed truck in [Nashville's] Shelby Park and put the show together in late summer of 1941," remembered Pee Wee King. "Then we brought it up to Fort Knox to try it out to see how it would go over with the servicemen and with the Camel cigarette people." Four long red touring cars were painted with a Camel Caravan logo. One pulled a house trailer used as a dressing room, and the lead car had electric bullhorns on top that blurted out: "*The Camels are coming. Da DA, Da DA.*" The instruments followed in a truck whose fold-down sides converted into a stage. The first cast featured twenty-one different entertainers. The Golden West Cowboys anchored the show. King's band member Eddy Arnold was stepping forward as a solo act. He crooned a seductive early hybrid of traditional country and silky pop. Lithe redhead Dollie Dearman danced, and Kay Carlisle brought confectionary pop singing to the mix. A versatile entertainer and businessman named Ford Rush became the Camel Caravan emcee. He'd known George Hay since their days on the WLS Barn Dance and had been running the Artist Service Bureau since David Stone left for a radio station in St. Paul, Minnesota.

The Caravan, working almost every day to captive audiences of scared new recruits, forced Sarah Colley to further develop Minnie Pearl. "You had to be quick and punchy to get through to them, and that gave me the guts and brass to let Minnie kick up her heels and have fun," she wrote. Besides getting $50 per week for the shows, Minnie got $50 more from the advertising agency for chaperoning the Camelettes, a small team of girls who danced in majorette outfits and strolled through the crowd handing out free cigarettes. That fall, the Caravan traveled in loops around Nashville, hitting four or five bases each week. "As we passed, people would wave and blow their horns at us," remembered Pee Wee King. "People came up to thank us in hotels and restaurants. We tried to do two complete shows a day, a matinee in a sports field outdoors, and an evening performance in a base theater or auditorium."

On the morning of December 7, 1941, the Camel Caravan pulled into San Antonio, set for a day off. Minnie was with Dollie Dearman when news of the Japanese attack on Pearl Harbor reached them. "We thought the Camel

Caravan would end instantly," she related. "We didn't realize there would be more need for it than ever." The next day President Roosevelt declared war on Japan, but the Caravan had shows to play at air fields Randolph and Kelly. They mustered all the spirit they could and headed for the first base. Whereas their vehicles had zoomed straight into their bases, this day they were stopped, searched, and ID checked. Minnie made jokes about seeing her initials on the arms of all the MPs. They visited hospitals, where morale was low. Eddy Arnold dropped his standard opening number "I'll Be Back in a Year, Little Darlin'" out of respect for soldiers who now didn't know when or whether they'd be going home.

When word of the attacks reached WSM's studios, some of the newsmen and announcers had to look up Pearl Harbor on a map. Among them were two new hires. Jud Collins had been discovered when he broadcast a track meet over WSM from his first broadcasting home, WSGN in Birmingham. Harry Stone had heard him and coaxed him up to Nashville with a job offer doubling his salary to $35 per week. Collins remembered that Stone painted a picture of National Life as a good employer; people who come to work for us stay with us, he'd said.

The other was a severe-looking fellow with swept-back hair, a Roman nose, and an unnerving, imperious gaze. Irving Waugh of Norfolk, Virginia, had been a small-time newscaster, a seaman on a tramp steamer, and a poor college student who sailed on the Chesapeake when he should have been studying. From his job at a CBS affiliate in Roanoke, he sent a résumé and an acetate try-out disc to Jack Stapp at WSM. Stapp referred him to WLAC, likely to get him nearby so he could study this intriguing young man. After a few months at WLAC, Waugh was hired away by an NBC station in Cleveland. "I stayed there about four or five months," he said. "I had a row with the music director. He took out his penis and tried to lead the orchestra. We had a woman vocalist and I was highly indignant at my age. I didn't think that was proper conduct and I slammed him into the wall. He was close to the manager, so I thought I better get another job." After some calls to Stapp, Waugh was hired as a part-timer a week before Pearl Harbor. Stapp and Waugh began to see qualities in each other they admired. They discovered they had been born on the same day. Early in 1942, Waugh became the newest full-time member of the announcing staff and took over for Jud Collins on the 6:00 a.m. sign-on.

Collins, acutely aware of what a break he'd been given, was on his best behavior. "This was a unique radio station," he remembered thinking. "Not many stations throughout the United States had a studio orchestra or studios where they could welcome a crowd of people." A bachelor, he moved into the YMCA just across the street from the studios, where he could be easily reached. Jud was ready to do whatever was asked of him, even giving up his Saturday nights to announce the chaotic and exhausting Grand Ole Opry, though he didn't much care for the show.

Waugh, by contrast, pushed his luck. He got in a couple of fights, including one with country star Zeke Clements that he remembers losing. And he started "taking liberties" with the editorial side of his news announcing. "I finally got into trouble—deep trouble," he said. "Tennessee was contemplating a sales tax. I grew up in Virginia where there were state controlled liquor stores. I took the trouble of calling Richmond and found out what their (revenue) was from their liquor stores. It just happened to be very close to the figure Tennessee was hoping to derive from a sales tax. So I then started pushing for state controlled liquor stores in Tennessee and not a sales tax. And my life was threatened."

But for the most part, Waugh offered color commentary at Vanderbilt football games and announced news. He also hosted some of WSM's wartime pop shows. In a 1944 episode of a Beasley Smith vehicle called *Mr. Smith Goes to Town*, Waugh's crisp diction, seasoned with the long *R*s of a Tidewater Virginia accent, introduced the NBC feed with a dense, literary flair. He set up his subject, singer Danny Ryan, by observing that the crooner was usually an up-and-at-'em kind of guy: "*As a rule, to temporize just isn't in the boy's vocabulary,*" Waugh said. "*But for some unbeknowing reason, here he is, waggishly wagging his way through a song of 'Waiting.'*" Waugh made puns and slathered on alliteration. He used words no average person should know. He made words up. It was all a bit rococo even for WSM. He almost sounded restless, like a man in need of an adventure. He'd soon have one.

A day or two after the Pearl Harbor attack, C. A. Craig sent an open letter to his employees urging them to take part in the war effort in whatever way they could. "As one man and one woman, may we who wear the Shield pledge ourselves to do gladly and freely whatever may be our part in the great tragedy faced by the land we love!" he exhorted. National Life guaranteed that employees who joined the service would have their jobs back when they returned, and many took the offer. Jud Collins volunteered for the Air Force and flew navigators out of Hondo, Texas. Owen Bradley managed to turn his Merchant Marine stint in a musical direction, leading an orchestra at officers' clubs, while his brother, WSM guitarist Harold Bradley, became a radio man intercepting Japanese code from a base in Hawaii. Aaron Shelton applied to be a communications officer but couldn't pass the physical, because he couldn't get his weight up over 124 pounds.

Jack DeWitt was called to duty immediately after Pearl Harbor, invited back to his old employer Bell Labs to work on a secret war technology that he would come to know as RADAR. A year later, he went to work at the newly completed Pentagon and then, upon being commissioned a major with orders signed by President Roosevelt, he was stationed at Belmar, New Jersey. There he spent most of the war, in charge of Evans Signal Laboratory, overseeing seventy-three officers and fourteen hundred civilians in a well-guarded research and development campus.

Jack Stapp finagled his way into an enviable job in the military's division of propaganda and psychological warfare. He trained in New York and then was stationed in downtown London, where he was put in charge of the Special Events Section of the American Broadcasting Station in Europe. ABSIE, as it was know, went on the air just before D-Day and spent the next two years beaming news and speeches by exiled European leaders to the occupied people of the Continent. Stapp, with his beguiling mix of substance and charm, helped the likes of the Grand Duchess of Luxembourg and King Peter of Yugoslavia deliver messages to their citizens. When the Germans tried to jam it, ABSIE changed channels. When the Germans labeled it the American "Agitation Station," it bolstered the confidence of resistance fighters. It played "Yankee Doodle" every fifteen minutes.

Those who remained at WSM dreamed up new ways to contribute to the war effort. During 1942 the Camel Caravan entertained troops in Panama for several weeks and continued to tour the nation, now by bus. By the time it wrapped that December, the troupe had traveled more than 75,000 miles, covered thirty-two states, and done 175 shows in sixty-eight camps, hospitals, air fields, and bases. Though some twenty-two WSM staffers gave time to the Caravan, its shows were never broadcast over WSM. At the same time, Grand Ole Opry tent shows (there were two traveling units) played free for servicemen at regional bases. Francis Craig's group also played regional military bases, for a time with perhaps his most remarkable vocal duo: Snooky Lanson and Kitty Kallen, just before she went to New York and became a network star.

WSM fed segments directly to the *Army Hour,* a sort of *Stars and Stripes* of the air developed by Ed Kirby. The show could be heard in the States over NBC on Sunday afternoons and globally over the Army's shortwave facilities, tying the many theaters of war together and boosting morale through the most immediate medium available. WSM's features for the show included an interview with an old country couple who had seven sons in the armed forces, exercises involving the building and demolition of a pontoon bridge, and broadcasts from an airborne B-24 bomber.

Numerous shows were aimed at bolstering recruiting efforts, including live broadcasts of young men swearing induction oaths from the steps of the War Memorial Auditorium, one block from National Life. When Nashville's Vultee aircraft company converted to making A-35 Vengeance dive bombers and P-38 Lightning attack planes, WSM interviewed its women working for the first time in pants and coveralls on assembly lines. Downtown, the Nashville Bridge Company converted to building mine sweepers and sub attack boats, whose launches were signaled on WSM with the crack of champagne bottles on steel. Oil and gas barges didn't merit a formal christening, but listeners heard them rumble down their iron chutes and splash mightily into the river. At night, the station rebroadcast BBC and other world news broadcasts, received by shortwave.

Nowhere in Nashville could one feel the impact of the war more poignantly than at Union Station, where huge deployments turned the platforms into scenes of mass departures, kisses, hugs, and tears. The WSM staff orchestra set up at Union Station about four times a week to play for departing troops. Harry Stone observed that "before the band began, these partings were more like boys being led to an execution chamber." But "a morgue was changed into a festive occasion as it should be by WSM."

WSM also sent engineers, writers, producers, and announcers for an NBC Blue Network show called *This Is War.* It helped recruiting effort for the all-female corps the WAVES, sold at least $150,000 worth of "Grand Ole Opry Bonds," and contributed to the rubber salvage drive. Stone personally steered his boat on the Cumberland to Carthage and salvaged two tons of usable scrap. And Dinah Shore, now a top-tier singing star to civilians at home and troops overseas, returned to Nashville to stage a major war-bond rally at the Ryman. WSM furnished a thirty-three-piece orchestra, four singers, writers, promotions, publicity, and production for the two-hour show. Seats ranged from $100 to $500, and the gala raised $650,000 altogether, though it was not broadcast.

Sometimes, WSM's service to the service took the form of day-to-day generosity and resourcefulness. One afternoon in the fall of 1943, the Smyrna Army Air Base Band spilled out of the fifth-floor elevator, frantic and late. They'd driven as fast as they safely could down the pike from Murfreesboro to make a 3:45 live broadcast. An alarmed receptionist guided them into the nearest empty studio, where they unloaded their instruments and began collecting themselves and warming up. It was about 3:40. Dean Upson, former member of the Vagabonds and now the station's commercial manager, heard this down the hall and investigated. The apoplectic conductor told them they were on in three minutes and no one had told them what to do. Upson, perplexed, told him they didn't have a band scheduled for 3:45. The band leader took stock and realized they were at the wrong radio station. They were supposed to be at WSIX, four blocks away. Upson placed a quick call to Jack Wolever, program director at WSIX, who was himself in a fit, wondering how he would fill the next fifteen minutes of dead air. We'll wire you the performance, Upson said. Stand by. With two minutes to spare, WSM engineers set up the feed and WSIX listeners heard the Smyrna Army Air Base Band as scheduled.

WSM's war effort was judged above and beyond the call of duty by industry watcher *Variety* magazine, which cited the station in 1942 for "contributions to military and civilian understanding" and in 1943 for "noteworthy network originations." The publication noted that WSM's service was part of an overall commitment to live entertainment that was raising the profile of its home city. "WSM made its large house band available for USO canteens (and) saw its pride, the Grand Ole Opry, grow to coast-to-coast proportions," the trade paper announced. "WSM produces and presents more commercial and sustaining NBC shows than any other operation in the United States outside of New York, Chicago and Hollywood. Nashville was never known as a show town before WSM. Radio did that for Nashville, via WSM."

Edwin Wilson Craig, insurance executive and newly minted broadcaster, in 1925. (Les Leverett Collection)

George D. Hay, the "Solemn Old Judge," was WSM's first anchoring personality and program director. The Grand Ole Opry was his invention, but it had Edwin Craig's blessing. (Les Leverett Collection)

The National Life and Accident Insurance Company headquarters, circa 1945. WSM occupied the building's fifth floor from 1925–66. Studio C was added when the eleven-story addition to the right was built in 1934. (Les Leverett Collection)

Jack DeWitt as chief engineer of WSM in about 1936. (Grand Ole Opry Archives)

WSM's Studio A in its earliest years. The drapes on the walls were thought to provide good acoustics. (National Archives)

Deford Bailey was the only African American to emerge as a star from WSM's cast of artists, and the only Grand Ole Opry artist who did not dress in hillbilly costumes. (Les Leverett Collection)

Band leader Francis Craig played WSM's opening night and was still there two decades later when his record "Near You" became Nashville's first million-seller. Band "mascot" Pee Wee Marquette went on to become emcee at Birdland in New York. (Les Leverett Collection)

WSM's tower was the tallest in North America when it was built in 1932. Though the transmitting equipment that feeds it has changed many times since then, the tower is still used by WSM today. (Craig Family Collection)

Opposite: By the mid-1930s, WSM had assembled a top-flight announcing staff. From right: Harry Stone, Ott Devine, Jack Harris, David Stone, Tom Stewart, and David Cobb, who would coin the term "Music City USA" for Nashville in 1950. (Grand Ole Opry Archives)

Harry Stone, far right, with Jack Harris, Jack DeWitt and Aaron Shelton (squatting) during a broadcast from onboard the Pan American passenger train. (Grand Ole Opry Archives)

The daily broadcast of the Pan American passenger train, depicted in this postcard, became one of WSM's most popular features during the 1930s. (Grand Ole Opry Archives)

Opposite: Longtime WSM newsman Jud Collins on one of his first assignments—covering war games in Tennessee during the early years of World War II. (Grand Ole Opry Archives)

Minnie Pearl and Pee Wee King (with accordion) perform as part of a special Prince Albert Grand Ole Opry broadcast from the pleasure boat *Idlewild* in June 1946. The on-location show was part of a weekend junket for national magazine writers and editors. (Grand Ole Opry Archives)

Jack Stapp, WSM's ambitious program director during the 1940s and 1950s, with Harry Stone, longtime general manager. (Grand Ole Opry Archives)

Snooky Lanson and Dinah Shore, two of the biggest vocal stars to come out of WSM, singing together with Beasley Smith conducting. (Grand Ole Opry Archives)

Jim Denny working the room at a 1950s DJ convention, about the time he was named *Billboard* magazine's "Country & Western Man of the Year." (Grand Ole Opry Archives)

Grant Turner spun records in Texas before becoming WSM's greatest Grand Ole Opry announcer and a favorite country DJ. He started on D-Day and died after an Opry broadcast in 1991. (Les Leverett Collection)

Sunday Down South, here being produced in Studio C, was typical of the many ambitious live programs produced and syndicated by WSM. (Grand Ole Opry Archives)

Owen Bradley at the keyboard backing up singer Buddy Hall in the 1950s, not long before Bradley would leave WSM to start his own studio. (Grand Ole Opry Archives)

Irving Waugh was a reporter and news announcer before becoming advertising manager, then WSM, Inc., president. He is credited with building Opryland USA in the early 1970s. (Grand Ole Opry Archives)

Ralph Emery, seated, broadcast a hugely influential overnight show from WSM in the 1960s and 1970s. In the studio with him are artists Loretta Lynn and Marty Robbins and WSM leader Bud Wendell. (Grand Ole Opry Archives)

The Waking Crew during the 1960s. Singer Teddy Bart is standing at center, while announcer and host Dave Overton is to the far right. The band was the last live ensemble to play a daily show in American radio when it was disbanded by the station in the 1980s. (Grand Ole Opry Archives)

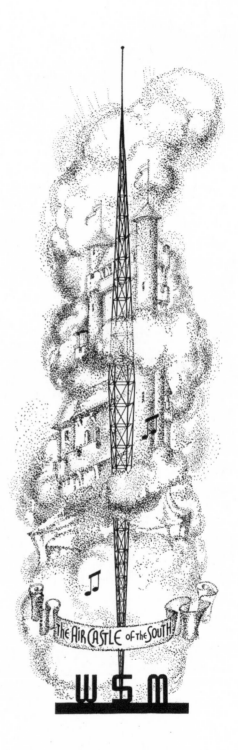

In 1935 National Life marketer
Ed Kirby nicknamed WSM the
"Air Castle of the South." This
fanciful illustration ran in the
company's *Shield* newsletter.

SEVEN ⚡ *One of Our Boys Shoots the Moon*

By 1943 troops nearly outnumbered civilians in greater Nashville, and the city was frequently overrun with soldiers in training or in transit. They filled the hotels, the bars, the theaters, and the streets. Sometimes, when space simply ran out, they slept in parks or on the steps of the post office on Broadway. Many of them loved the Grand Ole Opry, and olive uniforms became as common in War Memorial Auditorium as dresses and overalls. The only problem was they were punishing the governor's beautiful theater, and Harry Stone had to answer for it. "By now I had developed a sort of sixth sense and I felt it coming," he wrote. "I believe it set country music back ten years when I listened to this committee spell out all the reasons why we should not only be put out, but put in jail. But it sure was a nice place."

His next target—his only target—was the big, Gothic, red-brick tabernacle just off Broadway. "I had a heavy heart that day when I set out to see Mrs. Naff, then manager of the Ryman Auditorium," Stone said. "I knew if she turned me down, we had no other place to go."

Lula Naff, then over sixty-five years old, had run the Ryman like the Carnegie Hall of the South for four decades, and approaching her was no small matter. Even in the 1940s, the Ryman was among the most venerated and symbolic public spaces in Nashville, having been an ecumenical church and an eclectic concert hall in the heart of downtown. Its origins make for one of the most repeated stories in the city's history.

One evening in 1885, riverboat magnate Tom Ryman found salvation in the words of a tent evangelist named Sam Jones. He promised Jones that he'd build him a grand tabernacle, and fourteen years of fund-raising and construction later, he delivered. Jones named the building the Ryman Auditorium while preaching at Ryman's funeral. In the years that followed, the hall rang like the inside of a grand piano, first with fire and brimstone, then with choirs and hymns. Symphonies and opera companies followed, as did vocal recitals, ballet dancers, theatrical spectacles, political rallies, fiddlers, and banjo pickers. The building seemed to have been mortared with music and designed with performance in mind.

Stone seems to have made his case, and perhaps after years of depression and war, Naff was glad to land a regular Saturday night show with such a large following. The fifty-two-week lease, at $100 per week, was more rent than National Life had ever paid. But with 3,500 seats, the venerable hall let more than a thousand additional patrons see the Opry each Saturday night. And still, lines more than a block long began to form outside the theater for every show. WSM improved the house with a radio control room, rudimentary dressing rooms, a public address system, and new lighting. It hired a crew of off-duty police and firemen for security, plus ticket sellers, stage hands, and electricians. Jim Denny's concession business expanded. And the Grand Ole Opry had found a comfortable home—a little bit secular, a little bit sacred. Some golden ages really do begin on a date certain. June 5, 1943, launched the Ryman Opry.

That fall, Jack Stapp and Harry Stone pulled off a coup by doubling the number of NBC stations carrying the Prince Albert Opry, from 66 to 129. The price for this success was that the network portion grew more regimented. The Esty advertising agency, which handled the Prince Albert account, sent a man down to sit in on "rehearsals," which puzzled the Opry artists, since they knew not of rehearsals. "You mean you don't rehearse a network radio show?" the Esty man asked in the presence of Minnie Pearl. "You should have seen the look on that man's face," she related. "He was horrified. He went straight to the WSM officials." Roy Acuff was assigned to mollify him. "'I'll tell you how we handle it,' he said. 'We have a fiddle chaser. If we run short, we just let the fiddler play 'til time's up. If we run long, we don't use the fiddler.'

"Well, this guy just went to pieces," Minnie continued. "'You *will* have a rehearsal,' he ordered.'" This caused all sorts of problems. The Saturday morning meetings meddled with the touring operations, severely limiting the options for playing the prior Friday night. Then there was the added burden of a playback on Monday afternoon. The regulars would meet at WSM and listen to a transcription of the previous Saturday night show. The Esty people would listen to a duplicate recording in New York, call Nashville, and offer critiques. They offered Minnie help with writing her routines, which had largely been written by her sister, Virginia. Often what they came up with was awkward, she recalled. "We went for chuckles; they went for belly laughs," she observed. "And sometimes their gags didn't mean much to country folks." Minnie did appreciate one Esty agency suggestion—that she crank up her "Howdy" from a demure country girl greeting to the blaring "HowDEEE!" that became her signature walk-on line.

From a self-interested point of view, the war years could scarcely have been better for the Opry and for WSM, for the global effort that was the war forced young populations and international populations together in a way that couldn't help but spread culture and music. Historian Bill Malone wrote that country music "had taken great strides toward national acceptance during the 1930s but was still basically regional at the end of the decade; it would become a national phenomenon during the war." Jack Stapp observed it directly. "The war is when the change started," he said. "Every Saturday night I'd go over to Fort Jackson, South Carolina, to produce a country show, and after the show I'd walk around the camp and no matter where I went I'd never leave the Opry. The Opry was on every radio in every barracks and there wasn't any way these kids from New York and New Jersey could get away from it. It had to rub off on 'em."

Had it not been for a shortage of shellac, a then-essential ingredient in record making, country music might have grown even faster. But wartime rationing and scarcity affected everyone. WSM withdrew its pending application for 500,000 watts of power, calling it "the patriotic thing to do, considering the amount of vitally needed materials that would have to be used in the station's construction." Opry musicians struggled to keep their shows on the road. "We schemed every way imaginable to get gasoline ration stamps," remembered Minnie. "And our retreads had been retreaded so many times the original rubber began to rot from the rim out. On one 500-mile trip into Nashville we had thirteen flat tires."

National Life Shield Men had to give up their promotional sewing kits, when needles became precious. Aaron Shelton, inspired in part by Governor Cooper's weekly addresses over WSM, grew a victory garden. But few sacrifices were as poignant as the downsizing of the annual company picnic. In the 1920s, National Life had rented a paddle wheel steamboat that carried hundreds of employees far up the Cumberland River, where they disembarked in a shady park for a long afternoon of three-legged races, lounging, and feasting. In the 1930s, busses had taken the Home Office family to Dunbar Cave, a cozy resort spot with vast swimming pools and a natural amphitheater under a large outcrop of rock. During the war, the busses and the gas were unaffordable, so the picnic was held inside the Home Office itself. Employees from C. A. Craig to the white clerical staff (African American porters, cooks, and janitors were offered a segregated event) played bingo for war stamps, contested each other in table tennis and darts, and danced until after dark to Francis Craig's orchestra.

"In 1942," Owen Bradley remembered, "Beasley Smith whetted our appetites and got us into thinking about writing songs." Smith, the easygoing WSM veteran conductor/arranger, had proven success was possible when his first widely known composition, a train song called "Tennessee Central Number Nine," was recorded by Roy Acuff. Inspired, Smith attempted a publishing company in partnership with Owen Bradley and a short, brusque WSM piano player named Marvin Hughes.

"We had a song we had written, called 'Night Train to Memphis' that Beasley more or less instigated," Bradley said. "Marvin had a terrific little song, called 'Deliver Me to Tennessee.' It was recorded by Gene Krupa, Woody Herman, and a few others. I made some contribution by writing a couple of themes." When Hughes and Bradley left for the war, Smith remained at the station and the little company, BMO Music, didn't last long, failing in its bid to corner the market in "Tennessee" songs. But another publisher born in the WSM studios did thrive.

Fred Rose had arrived at WSM in 1933 as a staff pianist with a solid background as performer and songwriter. He had known the Vagabonds in Chicago, and they'd helped him arrange an audition with Harry Stone at a time when Rose badly needed work. His first show, *Freddie Rose's Song Shop,* ran weekday afternoons for fifteen minutes before the evening news, paying about five dollars per spot.

Coming up the hard way as a saloon singer in St. Louis and Chicago, Rose had endured the shady early days of music publishing, where often the only way to make songs pay was to share credit with a vocalist or an orchestra leader, or sell the copyright itself for a paltry one-time payment. But by the late 1920s, he was hobnobbing with the city's top bandleaders, playing on the radio, and recording for Brunswick. Moreover, he was a prosperous member of the hard-to-crack ASCAP songwriting fraternity. Unfortunately, he also had developed a bad alcohol habit that contributed to the dissolution of his first marriage and to his getting fired from a good radio job. Then the Depression nearly ate him alive. There wasn't decent work in Chicago or New York, so he chased a tip about WSM in Nashville, driving South with two other radio performers in May 1933.

At WSM Rose found he'd begun to influence country music without ever having cared a bit about it; the Delmore Brothers, he learned, performed one of his songs. In turn, the country music culture at WSM influenced Rose. Biographer John Rumble wrote that "the Vagabonds' business acumen provided Rose with an excellent example not only of how a pop-to-country transition could be made, but also of how country music could be marketed." His show, however, was pure pop. Rose's playing was called, soft, easy, and unusually relaxed. "Rose's overall approach was informal, and he often 'conversed' with the audience as his melodies flowed in the background," Rumble wrote. "Listeners could telephone requests to the station. Some sources believe that he actually composed songs on the air according to titles suggested by the callers." Rose suffered from horrible eyesight and even with glasses could see neither sheet music nor the clock on the wall, sometimes forcing engineers to cut away from him in the middle of a song when his time expired.

After a year or two, Fred Rose left Nashville, first for New York, where he discovered Christian Science, quit drinking, and further developed his publishing relationships. After he returned to Nashville in mid-1936, Jack Shook, the versatile guitarist who led the Opry's Missouri Mountaineers and played with the Dixie Dons, offered Rose some inroads in Hollywood with cowboy pictures. Artist manager Joe Frank provided his steady mentorship as well. Between 1938 and 1942, Rose traveled back and forth frequently to Hollywood. His main work there was writing songs for Gene Autry and other top singing cowboys like Roy Rogers and Ray Whitley. His classics would include "Be Honest with Me" and "Roly Poly."

So by the time Roy Acuff approached Fred Rose about starting a publishing company, Rose was already steeped in the complexities of the music business, with ties to New York, Chicago, and Hollywood. The deal was consummated in 1942, after Rose had moved back to Nashville for good with his wife Lorene. Acuff was looking for a long-term financial investment, according to Rumble. "It was partly Acuff's growing awareness of song property that made him seek out Rose, whom he admired not only as a creative writer, but also as a veteran who would know the worth of songs and how to protect them far better than he." Moreover Acuff was wealthy and more than able to offer $25,000 for the beginnings of the company. As it turned out, a mere $2,500 would be sufficient, and that came in the form of a loan from BMI. The firm took out an ad in *Billboard* promising "folk tunes and popular hits" from Nashville, and it quickly delivered with popular songs for Bob Wills and Acuff himself. The partners brought in Fred's son Wesley Rose as an executive in December 1945, then added a full-time promotion man early in 1946.

And yet Rose's contributions to Nashville's burgeoning music scene went deeper than playing, writing, or business. "Rose believed that songwriters were the foundation of the music industry and that one of his primary duties as publisher was to assist them creatively and commercially," Rumble concluded. "He thrived in the roles of editor, teacher, and mentor, and he pursued them actively and consciously." It wouldn't be long before he struck up just such a relationship with a lanky, difficult singer songwriter from Alabama who would change the music's history.

W47NV operated like a quiet little brother to WSM-AM. Though it is said to have only run one commercial spot in its decade of life, Edwin Craig was very much behind the station as an outlet for classical music. Even if only a handful of Nashville music fans had FM radios at the time, DeWitt said, W47NV "got [Craig] out of the criticism from his Belle Meade friends for the Grand Ole Opry, and it had a big effect on him." After Tom Stewart left for the war, Marjorie Cooney, who was still doing her Ann Ford news broadcasts on 650 AM WSM, took over as the FM station's general manager. It was a hands-on job that included spinning and announcing records. Cal Young was one of her few employees, a fresh-from-high-school Nashville native and Air Corps cadet stationed in Smyrna. He was desperate to get into radio and badgered Jack Stapp for months for a job as an announcer. He had no experience whatsoever, so Stapp politely turned him away time after time. But eventually Stapp needed a warm body to staff the FM station and decided to give Young a chance.

"I'd do anything I could. I couldn't do it very well, but I just stumbled through it," Young recalled. He spun RCA Red Seal classical albums and big, sixteen-inch transcription discs that came from companies aimed at the musically cultivated market. Cooney mothered him. She advised him that he really should read *Time* and *Newsweek* each week to keep up with current events.

And when he elicited complaints from a bunch of old ladies for playing hot swing music during a show dedicated to a religious school over in Sewanee, Tennessee, she laughed it off. "I've never known a person I think I liked and admired more than Marjorie," Young said late in life. And many others who knew her, including Minnie Pearl, felt the same way.

The FM control room was a closet-sized annex of the AM master control, and sometimes Louie Buck and Vito Pellettieri and some of the other announcers would turn Young's lights off without warning. "They were looking over at the Andrew Jackson Hotel because they thought they saw somebody nude over there," said Young, recalling what was actually a fairly common form of juvenile fifth-floor recreation. "It was about two blocks so they didn't see much of anything."

For Young, just being at WSM was something special. He says the place reminded him of New York, in its look, expectations, and professionalism. But this ardor led to an accident. "I wanted my picture made with a WSM microphone," he said. "So I borrowed one from one of the engineers." The engineer told him to be careful with it, and he said he would be. He got the coveted picture made at a local studio and put the microphone back. "What I didn't tell them back then was, I was going down those steps—must have been twenty steps as you went down to the street—I dropped the damn microphone and man, it rolled down about ten of those steps. I didn't say anything about it. I was scared to death. I don't know if the mic worked after that or not—I doubt it."

In August 1943 seventy-five-year-old C. A. Craig surprised his quarterly board meeting by announcing he was stepping down as chairman of National Life. Runcie Clements took his place, opening up the company's presidency. Edwin Craig had no serious competitors for the position, making him the first president who wasn't part of the original founding group. But if one generation of leadership was giving way to the next, nothing in Edwin Craig's character or style foretold change. Craig lived ensconced in the symbols and comforts of the Old South, working long days but always doting on his wife and three children when he returned at night to their Belle Meade mansion. His benevolent paternalism translated from home to a close-knit National Life culture at work. Nearly every former National Life or WSM employee will eventually use the word "family" to describe the company's climate, and they agree that it started at the top, with the man many of them referred to as Mr. Edwin. WSM trombonist and National Life house photographer Beverly LeCroy said that Craig "was more like a father with 1,700 kids. He loved us."

Neil Craig admired his father's innate sense of diplomacy. "He loved people. People loved him," the younger Craig said. "And he could get down on their level. Or he could go talk to the president of NBC and get on his level too. He was the best I ever saw. He always, first and last, was a people person." And more than a mere glad-hander, the elder Craig threw himself into service: vice chair of the city's Red Cross chapter, member of the Vanderbilt Hospital board of managers, steward of West End Methodist Church, a Mason, and a Shriner. During the war, he volunteered to serve on the local draft board, a dreadful job that nobody wanted. His daughter remembered Craig fielding phone calls from distraught mothers who begged him not to take their boys.

Craig hated to fly. Train rides framed his frequent business travel. He'd go to Los Angeles by way of New Orleans, where he'd stop in the ACME Oyster Bar to drink Sazerac cocktails and sing songs with the old men at the bar. He knew the porters and oyster shuckers by name, and they knew him. After changing trains, he'd ride west in a Pullman car, savoring the rhythm of the rails and reading Louis L'Amour and Zane Grey novels. If he could manage it, he'd steer his travel around a chance to be outdoors with a rod or a gun. He spent many a night in a duck blind with Grand Ole Opry artists and hillbilly pickers. He befriended hunting and fishing guides throughout the South, especially rural Louisiana, whose Cajun people he adored. One guide, "one of the toughest guys you ever saw," according to Neil, named his son Edwin Craig Hall.

At the same time, Craig was as respected and effective as any of Nashville's elite. "Ed Craig was the most outgoing business executive I ever saw," said John Seigenthaler, long-time editor of the *Tennessean*. "He was dynamic. Bill Weaver [Craig's successor as president] was close, but he was close because he'd seen the master operate." Irving Waugh, in a 1978 interview, said Edwin Craig's stature, combined with his fervent belief in country music, was critical to the Opry in withstanding numerous assaults in the 1930s and 1940s. "I feel that, at the time, he was the only person of substance in the whole United States supporting country music," said Waugh with trademark extravagance. "When I say a person of substance, I mean a person of wealth, social position, a person whose personal tastes included classical music. He was a man of catholic tastes. He had a great belief and faith in country music and he wanted it on this radio station."

Craig's other great musical passion—one that bolstered his close relationship with Jack DeWitt—was the opera. When he was in college, Edwin volunteered to be an extra in performances at the Ryman, including dressing up in Egyptian garb to be in the chorus of *Aida*. And from his twenties on, he and his wife Elizabeth traveled to New York every year for the opening of the Metropolitan Opera's season.

Jud Collins liked to tell a story of a time when he saw into Craig's character. One afternoon, an engineer who was tied up spinning records (one of their duties before disc jockeys took over the task) asked Collins to call the NBC control room in New York to resolve a problem with an upcoming feed. But long distance calls were big deals then, and the operators in National Life had to know you had authorization. Collins, ever so young and uncertain, felt stumped:

> I tried Stone and Stapp. Couldn't find them on a Sunday afternoon. Finally I just called Mr. Craig. He said, "Well Jud, is this in the best interest of WSM?"
>
> "Yes sir."
>
> "You tell the operator I've authorized this. One more thing. You can have my authority to do anything you want and spend any amount of money at any time if it's in the best interest of WSM."
>
> I was sort of flabbergasted. I said, "Well, Mr. Craig, thank you. That's very nice."
>
> He said, "Jud, one more thing."
>
> There was a pause.
>
> "Just be damn sure you're right."

As WSM staff peeled away to join the war effort, jobs opened up. One to take advantage was a thirty-two-year-old Texan with flinty eyes softened by a baby face. The Opry had not been part of Jesse Granderson Turner's boyhood. He was a pop music fan who became aware of the Opry's mystique after an early job in Sherman, Texas, where he began spinning country 78s as an early disc jockey. Eventually, he found himself working in Knoxville as "Tex" Turner, where he was involved with the *Mid-Day Merry-Go-Round*, a popular East Tennessee radio barn dance. A fellow announcer there named Ernie Keller moved to WSM and then helped Turner get a job interview with Ott Devine reading commercials and news. He was hired on the spot, though Devine suggested he adopt the more dignified "Grant," and urged him to stay for that night's Grand Ole Opry.

Grant Turner remembered being introduced to "Judge" George Hay that night but not by whom. The Judge was delighted to meet him and asked if he would please sit on a bench beside the stage, watch the show, and form some comments for afterward. They hit it off. Grant Turner's first day of work was June 6, 1944, a day of indescribable anticipation and concern. The station was on war footing, everyone riveted by the NBC and BBC feeds about the Allied invasion of Normandy. Long before they ever saw pictures in *Life* magazine or on the newsreels, and even before the newspapers could catch up, Nashville, like the rest of America, experienced the emotional whipsaw that was D-Day on the radio.

Hay mentored Turner into a major-league announcer, teaching him how to enunciate, leading by example. "He never did a broadcast without a glass of water at his side," Turner recalled about Hay. "He then had a number of vocal limbering-up exercises he did, as an opera singer, going the full range of the scale . . . mi mi mi, la la la and so on." Turner watched Hay audition people, studying the care with which he listened, his enthusiasm for something fine, and his polite demurrals when he told lesser artists the roster was full and he wanted to have them keep practicing. Hay took Turner on the three-block walk to Frank Varallo's on Church Street for three-way chili, an essential Nashville plate dinner of spaghetti topped with tamales and beef and bean chili. Hay also introduced Turner to golf, driving him (terribly) out West End Avenue, miles into the Belle Meade hunt club countryside, to the course at Percy Warner Park. Hay teed up a ball and whanged it with gusto and an edge of un-Judge-like aggression. "You know before I take that swing, I think of a certain person I despise," Hay said. Turner could tell Hay had someone very clearly in mind. "I think of him, and then I hit this ball like I would like to hit him." Turner also remembered coming off the golf course at the end of a day with the Solemn Old Judge when another golfer told them the radio was reporting sad news: President Roosevelt was dead.

In mid-1945, NBC discontinued its long-running *Farm and Home Hour,* a feed and seed program aimed at farmers and farm wives. For WSM, pledged to serve rural audiences, that left a vast hole in its schedule. The station had broadcast daily farm market reports since 1929 and built on that in the 1930s with weekly farm and homemaker shows produced from the Knoxville campus of the University of Tennessee. On the strength of such potent segments as "Home Grown Fruits for Amateurs" and "Bug Bombing with DDT," WSM's agricultural programming earned *Variety* magazine's "Farm Service Station of the Year" award in 1938. The station added *Homemaker's Chat* on Saturday mornings, and by the 1940s, University of Tennessee president James Haskins figured WSM's farm shows were reaching a million listeners. Moreover, the Knoxville-based shows evolved into a more elaborate educational program called *Campus of the Air*, with lectures and poetry readings alongside the farm news. It reached a statewide network of eight other radio stations.

WSM knew the NBC feature was coming to a close and tried to come up with a replacement. Several months of looking for the right farm director proved fruitless. Then all of a sudden, they found their man thanks to a wrong number. Rotund and jovial John McDonald, a dairy farmer with a University of Tennessee agriculture degree, had just quit a vocational agricultural job in Ashland City, a few miles down the Cumberland River. He was in Nashville at the Hermitage Hotel, where a state agricultural official he knew gave him some job tips. "I dialed WSM by mistake," McDonald told the *Tennessean* in 1980. "I had their number in my pocket. I had been thinking about calling them. I asked Harry Stone if the station needed someone who knew something about agriculture. He said he had been looking for someone like that for six months."

As part of his audition, Stone took McDonald to visit with a National Life employee named Charlie Luker, a former farmer, who gave the young man a nod for authenticity. McDonald also spoke with Edwin Craig that day, before officially being offered the job. On his first day of work, he came in with a big hunk of hair cut out where, the day before, he'd needed stitches after an accident with a fishing lure. In McDonald's first on-air interview, the president of the American Farm Bureau said American agriculture was "going to hell in a damn hand basket," then yammered on well past the show's cut-off time. "I knew I was fired," the host said. But it didn't work out that way. Instead, the show born that day—*Noontime Neighbors*—ran for twenty-seven years.

McDonald knew his audience as well as any of the WSM announcers. "Farm people are hard to reach at best. They're hard-headed," he told a group of radio people in 1950. "I can say that because I am one. I grew up a farmer and my Dad was a farmer." He rewrote wire copy of farm reports because he could tell the people who'd written them "haven't ploughed." He used simple language but was careful not to get "too corny." At a station whose other announcers took diction seriously, he said "Missippi" and "y'all" and never acted as anything other than a good ol' boy who'd had a few strokes of luck. He knew the minutiae of cattle breeds, fertilizers, hybrids, and veterinary medicine. He knew that one confused the 4-H club and the Future Farmers of America (FFA) only at one's own peril. He knew that women made 85 percent of the purchasing decisions in the farm home, that they love recipes (if they're "home tested"), and that it was important to have plenty of mimeographed copies ready to mail out if you mentioned one on the air. He even knew how to draw out the often hidden wit of agricultural extension workers or Farmers Home Administration bureaucrats in on-air interviews.

Noontime Neighbors mingled country and pop more aggressively than perhaps any WSM show so far. Owen Bradley led a twenty-six-piece orchestra, often in support of the station's best pop singers. A rock-solid country band called the Musical Millers was arranged by a long-time WSM musician and producer named Milton Estes. Once the show had been kicked off by announcer Louie Buck, Estes essentially anchored the broadcast, introducing McDonald, who sat at a desk with an enormous dinner bell.

Set up in Studio C every day at 12:30, *Noontime Neighbors* drew a live audience of office workers with bag lunches who came from National Life and the state buildings next door. McDonald also frequently took the show on the road, capturing interviews with farmers in their fields on a wire recorder and reporting from Mule Day or the Crimson Clover Festival. Remarkably, though Neighbors could have milked a major sponsorship from agribusiness, it remained a sustaining (ad-free) show for many years. In its early years, it cost WSM $750 per week in talent, production, and travel. But it was one of the first things WSM officials would mention when called on to defend their community service and their clear channel status in Washington hearings.

Irving Waugh felt left out of the war. With his sailing background, he was gung ho to fight on PT boats, but the Navy turned him down based on his academic record. He was now a full-timer at WSM, sharing news and sports duties in the wake of Jack Harris's departure. Married and with a young child, he considered avoiding service altogether. "But as the war moved deep into '42 I became more and more restless, thinking this is the biggest story of my life and I'm not playing any part in it," Waugh remembered. He investigated enlisting in the Marines, but there was no assurance that after boot camp he could get assigned to the combat correspondent division he wanted. Harry Stone countered with a better idea. The War Department wanted several clear channel radio stations to contribute correspondents to the civilian press corps. Waugh loved the idea, but his draft board in Salem, Virginia, wouldn't clear it, saving him, it seemed, to be called up to fight. After more than a year of limbo, Waugh traveled to Salem and confronted them: draft me or let me go overseas with a microphone. They relented, and at last, in late 1944, Waugh began a long journey to and around the Pacific theater.

His first stop was Manila, where he found Jack Harris, by now the chief radio press liaison for General Douglas MacArthur. Harris got Waugh oriented and helped him get an on-the-fly network promotion. NBC paid him $50 for two-minute stories. He was made a stringer under Merle "Red" Muller, a famous *Time* magazine writer who'd been recruited by the network.

"If there was something important going on, he took the broadcast," Waugh said. "If it was a damn dull day, he'd say, 'Irving, you've got the broadcast.' And then I'd say to myself, 'What am I going to do? What's happening? Nothing is happening.' And I'd have to luck into something." He reported from New Guinea about four Nashville soldiers who'd been in combat almost continuously since 1942. He attended press conferences where MacArthur held forth and spouted off the most remarkable strategic information, only to have Army censors keep it out of the reports. He visited the USS *Iowa* because it was a near duplicate of the *Missouri*, the ship that was to play host to the Japanese surrender.

In March 1945 Waugh broadcast a dispatch about the Japanese surrender of Manila, a city badly damaged after the battle for U.S. occupation. He visited the hastily refurbished apartment building where the Emperor's delegation had just stayed the night during its humiliating mission. With his buttoned-up accent ringing through the long-distance, shortwave signal, Waugh reported: "*The building formerly had been a four-story apartment, but the fourth floor had been burned out, and the roof was wholly gone—the concrete flooring of the upper story serving as a roof for the three floors below.*" Not only did he speak in elegant, compound sentences, he found many telling details. He described the woven mats hung in the blasted-out windows and the urban war-torn wasteland outside. The young GIs taking care of the housing had just waxed the entrance hall floor, he said. "*Two of the Japanese slipped on the polished surface, and one went down on his knees.*"

The most remarkable of Waugh's reports came from Japanese soil, just hours after the first U.S. forces landed there following the nation's post-Hiroshima and Nagasaki surrender. The long-planned and long-feared invasion of Japan, expected at one point to cost 100,000 Allied lives, transpired bloodlessly, and radio reporters were lined up to report the news that the Yanks were landing by the thousands at Atsugi, south of Tokyo. Waugh was among the reporters who followed them in, only to learn that the airplane carrying the radio pool's shortwave transmitter had crashed, leaving them no simple way to get their stories to the United States. They were told they could write hundred-word summaries that would be flown out and transmitted by wire to San Francisco. But for a story this big, that seemed unacceptable.

Improbably, Jack Harris came to the rescue. The former WSM newsman was responsible for helping reporters, like Waugh and others, gather and report news from the front, subject to military censorship. That day on the busy, noisy Atsugi airfield, Harris ran and shouted at Waugh to tell his boss, Red Muller, that there was a B-17 bomber on the field with a shortwave radio, which the media could use to reach the United States, by way of Guam.

"To hell with Muller," Waugh thought. He retrieved the story he'd already submitted to the military censor for the newswire and ran down the airfield to find the bomber himself. Once inside the plane, he found two reporters, including CBS's senior reporter Bill Dunn, waiting for the Guam connection to come through on the radio. Suddenly, a colonel appeared, telling the reporters to "get your asses out of the plane" and back to the wire office. Dunn and the other correspondent were furious and lit out to find Jack Harris and his boss, General Diller, to complain.

"I didn't know what to do, so I just sat there," said Waugh. And before five minutes had gone by, the radio crackled to life: "Go ahead CBS," the voice on the other end said.

"Not available," Waugh replied tersely.

"Go ahead Mutual."

"Not available."

"Go ahead NBC."

And so he did, breaking in over the NBC network at about 9:20 p.m. New York time. He interrupted a program called *Kay Kaiser's College of Musical Knowledge* to report that the Americans were on the ground and facing no resistance.

"So I'm reading my copy," recalled Waugh of the moment he became the first American correspondent to report from occupied Japan. "And as I'm doing the broadcast, I became aware that [CBS's] Bill Dunn had become so angry that he charged off and left his copy. So I pulled Dunn's copy over, and he was a better writer than I was. So now I'm integrating Dunn's copy into my copy. I'd been at it long enough I knew I could do that. That was my big moment. I had to think later that was only possible because I wasn't important enough to go tell General Diller off."

Days later, on September 2, 1945, Waugh found himself on board the *Mis-*

souri, docked in Tokyo Bay, a civilian among thousands of sailors and officers who covered every horizontal surface of the giant ship like snow. Waugh stood on the higher of two massive gun turrets, looking down at the deck where delegates were being assembled in rows behind the dark desk where the papers were to be signed. In the midst of it all—again—was Jack Harris, stage-managing the surrender ceremony on the flight deck.

"Harris lined up Lord Louis Mountbatten, for example, the head of the British Empire column," Waugh recalled. "He was lining them all up: the French, the British, the Dutch, Canadians, the Australians. If [generals] were two-stars, Harris waved them out. Only the fives, fours, threes. And he was a lieutenant colonel! So I'm watching that with a big grin."

Besides bemusement, Waugh and all aboard knew a kind of exalted joy that would soon be shared by the entire Western World. They witnessed the foreign minister of Japan, in his top hat and tails, surrender after a fight that would long ago have broken any other nation. The Japanese had endured the firebombing of all their key cities and seen two metropolises erupt in nuclear infernos. The terror had been complete and unprecedented, and now it was over. Back in Nashville, jubilant throngs filled the streets. Military parades coursed up Union Street, and National Life clerks hung out the windows, waving and crying and cheering without any reason to stop.

Jack DeWitt was as pleased as anyone about the war's end, but he was stuck at the Evans Signal Laboratory, living in a rented house with several other officers, and in a funk. Elise wouldn't leave Washington. She said it was because she didn't want to take Jack Jr. out of school, but in fact their marriage was on the rocks. DeWitt's life on the coast of New Jersey was dull. There was little to do at night and one decent restaurant. Jack had no hope of accumulating enough points for discharge until the spring of 1946.

Orders came just after Japan's surrender to develop methods for detecting and tracking long-range missiles, one of the most fearsome new weapons developed in the war. One of DeWitt's projects in the latter half of the war had involved field radar that could track incoming mortar fire and deduce its point of origin, so he was qualified for the assignment. With no flying rockets to detect off the shore of New Jersey, DeWitt thought he could adapt his orders to an experiment that had tantalized him for years. In 1939, he and George Reynolds had tried to shoot a radar signal at the moon from a specially built antenna on the WSM tower grounds, but they found they had far too little power to produce a detectable echo. Now, Jack asked himself, what if we used the moon as a stand-in for a missile? It was a fast-moving body in the sky. And such an exercise could address some critical questions, chiefly: would radio waves cross the reflective ionosphere, travel through space, and return to the earth? The effort, dubbed the Diana Project, after the goddess of the moon, got the green light.

Over five months, DeWitt and a team of four men, all between the ages of thirty-one and thirty-six (Jack was thirty-nine), retrofitted a radar that had done service at Pearl Harbor, doubling its sending antennas. Their base was a twenty-foot by fifty-foot shack on a promontory out in the Atlantic ocean, with marshes of pine and scrub oak behind them. Towering over them was a one-hundred-foot tall antenna that resembled a giant, upended barbecue grill.

DeWitt wasn't in the lab when the detector finally worked. At almost exactly noon on January 10, 1946, when the moon was suspended over the ocean like a scoop of ice cream in the blue sky, an oscilloscope began to wiggle exactly 2.4 seconds after the regular sending pulses. At 186,000 miles per second, that's just how long they'd calculated the signal would take to travel there and back. Civilian scientist Herbert Kauffman proclaimed, "That's it!" And the team went to fetch DeWitt.

The Signal Corps' commander, General Van Deusen, after seeing a separate demonstration, made plans to personally announce the news at a meeting of the Institute of Radio Engineers meeting in New York on January 24. DeWitt sat at the back of the room, waiting for the general to follow the "exceedingly dull" president of Bell Labs. At the same moment Van Deusen took the podium, a newsboy came in the room with an evening paper, whose banner headline read "Army Contacts the Moon." The next day, DeWitt was a celebrity, his picture and news splashed across front pages around the country, including the top of the *Washington Post*. Most stories noted DeWitt's peacetime career in Nashville at radio station WSM. Editorial cartoonists depicted moon men and moon creatures being disturbed by lightning bolts. *Broadcasting* magazine boasted fraternally: "One of Our Boys Shoots the Moon." *The New Yorker*'s lead "Talk of the Town" item riffed on the accomplishment as "man's first tiny venture into the cold, appalling hole of interstellar space."

Observers could only speculate on the ultimate scientific value of the effort. DeWitt told reporters that it proved we could track and communicate with spacecraft, when and if such craft were launched out of Earth's atmosphere. But what really resonated about the story was its optimism and its universally shared sense of wonder, the mingling of a very new science and a very old symbol. The world was anticipating peace, prosperity, and new frontiers of scientific discovery, including space and its mysteries. If they could see that bright future in a full moon, so much the better.

DeWitt's own sense of the future was equally unbounded, and it did not appear that he'd be heading back to Nashville. In February, when reporters were still seeking him out for more detailed feature stories on the moon-radar experiments, he was given the Legion of Merit Medal and a citation "for the conception and development of a radar set which accurately located hostile mortars by their fire and directed counter mortar fire." (He called this his greatest achievement, as it saved lives.) He was being courted by a major engineering consulting firm in Washington, and the radio industry was preparing for a massive set of hearings on the merits of high-powered, clear channel broadcasting. DeWitt even bought a house in Falls Church, Virginia.

Then Edwin Craig called and asked him to lunch in New York. He had two important pieces of news. First, National Life was going to carve out WSM as a subsidiary called WSM, Inc., encompassing the radio station, the Grand Ole Opry, and the Artist Service Bureau. Craig's other news was that he wanted DeWitt to again return from New Jersey to run things—to be president of WSM, Inc. It was a hell of a thing to ask. DeWitt weighed his prospects in Washington against whatever might be blossoming in Nashville. WSM, alive with network productions and national talent, was recognized as one of the best radio stations in the nation, and there was talk of starting a television station, which would be a huge engineering challenge. Not incidentally, it was also now quite clear that his marriage was heading toward divorce. Perhaps it was big-fish-small-pond time again. He looked homeward, to a web of friends and family, to a broadcaster on the make, to a strange brew of Southern bluebloods and hillbillies, to the warm support of Mr. Craig, and he accepted the job.

EIGHT ⚡ *It Helped Everybody in the Long Run*

Harry Stone felt betrayed. Over nearly twenty years he'd managed WSM from a part-time local station to a national powerhouse with a signature show. Just one year before he'd been named vice president and general manager of WSM. And then, without warning, old man Craig made Jack DeWitt his boss, at a much higher salary. It was but one reason that by 1947, Stone looked weary, with deep creases in his cheeks and forehead and gray streaks in his hair. He oversaw a ten-person staff of his own plus sixteen in production and a small army of sometimes unpredictable musicians. A micromanager, Stone tended to get involved to a fault with every foible of a complicated organization. "You had to clear everything with Harry," Irving Waugh remembered. "You couldn't get a ticket to the Opry for your Mother without getting it from Harry."

Stone was taking the Opry in important and profitable directions, but he found himself in regular battles with Mr. Craig and Judge Hay. He favored amplification. They opposed it. He supported Pee Wee King's flashy wardrobe and his hard-swinging country music. They didn't. They seemed to want the show stuck in 1935, with old-time string bands and hillbilly clothes forever. By the end of the war, and especially after DeWitt's appointment, Stone's relationship with Craig lapsed into overt hostility. "Harry was belligerent," Waugh said. "Harry treated Edwin Craig as almost an equal. They were closer to the same age. Harry thought nothing of sticking his face right in Edwin Craig's and arguing with him." For DeWitt, it was a fairly simple situation. "[Harry] didn't like Edwin Craig, and of course I did," he said. "He referred to Edwin Craig as 'that son of a bitch.'"

DeWitt wasn't perfectly qualified for the job, truth be told. He was an engineer by training and temperament, and while he'd been an officer in the disciplined Army Signal Corps, he had little rapport with the carnivalesque Opry cast and no experience with programming, promotion, or ad sales. Harry Stone was the more complete broadcaster, many thought, and certainly the more proven radio station boss. "That son of a bitch was tough as nails," said W. D. Kilpatrick, a record sales representative and future Opry boss. "But he was the best combination radio station manager and Opry manager there ever was."

As good as he was, Stone couldn't keep a rein on Jim Denny, whose sideline concessions business had grown into something substantial. Stone resented watching Denny's employees roaming the aisles of the Ryman Auditorium selling popcorn and souvenirs, the profits all bound for Denny's pockets. Denny was, however, too close to the Opry artists and too smart with a dollar to be ignored or dismissed, so despite some misgivings, Stone had recommended in 1946 that Denny be the first full-time head of the Artist Service Bureau, in charge of Opry stars' live appearances and tours.

For thirteen years, Denny had worked for National Life by day and the Opry the rest of the time. With his promotion, WSM raised his pay by a third and moved him to a fifth-floor office with an assistant, where he figured out the booking business. "Nobody knew as little about it as I did," Denny wrote to his children many years later. "I had no idea what prices I should get for the acts, but it didn't take long to find out." One of his tutors was Mary Claire Jackson (later Rhodes), an assistant to some of the WSM announcers. Writer Albert Cunniff observed that "WSM had treated the Artist Service Bureau in a haphazard fashion in previous years, delegating responsibility for its operation to several people, each of whom had other jobs at the station as well." Denny made the whole operation run better almost immediately. Opry artists found themselves playing arenas, fairs, and auditoriums, instead of schoolhouses.

Denny struck exclusive regional deals with show promoters, the men who put up the money and the posters, who rented the halls and put on the shows. Those on his good side found Denny to be businesslike, honest, and attentive to details like hotels, publicity, and travel. He made handshake deals and he lived up to them. At the WSM offices, meanwhile, he inspired a sort of awe. He wore a diamond horseshoe ring and dressed in impeccable pinstripe suits.

His voice, on the selective occasions when he spoke, commanded attention. He started quietly copromoting some of the shows the Opry stars were playing, sharing in the overhead and taking a cut of the profits personally. He began driving Cadillacs—a new one each year—and sometimes he'd park them in Jack DeWitt's space behind Seventh and Union to rile him. Perhaps the only chink in the armor of his appearance was his toupee, which sometimes appeared ready to scamper off his head.

Jim Denny's new influence was built on his control of the Opry brand. Artists had to pay WSM's Artist Service Bureau 15 percent of their earnings to play under the Opry banner, and it was worth it. Having "Grand Ole Opry" on a show poster in Manchester, Tennessee, or Auburn, Alabama, was such a potent draw that WSM started watching out for unauthorized use of the Opry name. One of DeWitt's early acts as WSM president was to trademark the Grand Ole Opry name, which, to his surprise, had never been done. At a 1947 clear channel hearing, Stone called the show "a national institution" with a reach "far beyond our original plans." That September a cast of Opry stars, including Ernest Tubb and Minnie Pearl, played two nearly full-house shows at Carnegie Hall in New York. Next came Constitution Hall in Washington, D.C., as well as appearances in Germany and Austria. This once humble show, along with its sponsors, its parent company, and its artists, was climbing rapidly to the pinnacle of the country music business.

Most importantly, the Opry was proving to be bigger than any one performer. Roy Acuff left the show for a time in 1946 to pursue personal appearances out West. But Red Foley, a star of various Midwestern radio barn dances, stepped easily into the anchoring role on the Prince Albert Opry feed to NBC. He was more urbane than rustic and he quickly became one of the best-known singers of folk and hillbilly music in America. His full name was Clyde Julian Foley, and he learned music from his father and his friends who hung around dad's general store in Blue Lick, Kentucky. He went on to take voice lessons and study music at college, making him one of the only Opry artists ever to do so. He didn't finish school; Chicago's WLS recruited him in 1931, and he grew popular on the *National Barn Dance.* Then he started his own radio show, *The Renfro Valley Barn Dance,* over WLW in Cincinnati, moving later to Louisville's WHAS. He signed with Decca in 1941 and recorded hits like "Old Shep." His rise to the top slot on the Opry's best-known segment heralded popularity for a new type of singer, one who came from and understood country music but who could croon with the mainstream mellifluousness of a Bing Crosby or a Frank Sinatra. Foley is also spoken of as one of the most entertaining and engaging men ever to step on a Nashville stage.

More than a celebrity factory, the Opry had also become one of the most exciting musical laboratories in postwar America. Bluegrass was largely invented over WSM microphones, recorded by WSM personnel, and promoted through WSM branding. It would grow into one of America's most important forms of roots music, a self-sustaining and evolving subculture and a significant business niche. Today bluegrass enjoys concert hall stages, festivals, and fine arts coverage, in large part because WSM backed it for sixty years.

Bill Monroe was a strapping and coldly serious mandolinist from Rosine, Kentucky, who'd already achieved near stardom as part of a long-running duo with his brother Charlie. But starting in the 1940s, he achieved something much greater. Working with a complex amalgam of rich musical influences, including blues, swing, jazz, gospel and old-time fiddle music, Monroe fused a new alloy of country music so distinct it earned its own name and legacy.

The name came from Monroe's band, which in turn was named after his home state. Monroe led many iterations of his Blue Grass Boys beginning in 1938, and once he became an Opry member in the fall of 1939, he grew to near Acuffian stature. And at the end of 1945, he found the personnel that truly completed his vision: banjo player Earl Scruggs, singer/guitarist Lester Flatt, fiddler Chubby Wise, and bass player Cedric Rainwater. This legendary quintet would play together for scarcely more than two years before Flatt and Scruggs peeled away to form their own world-renowned band. But over the coming decades, Monroe continued to graduate expert musicians from his band, populating the bluegrass landscape. His tastes strongly influenced what was and wasn't bluegrass, including its acoustic instrumentation, its bone-chilling harmonies, its instrumental flair, and its bluesy heart. He would earn the title "Father of Bluegrass," and his sound and songwriting had so much drive, passion, and bite that he would become the earliest WSM/Opry musician to be inducted into the Rock and Roll Hall of Fame. To Harry Stone, Jack DeWitt, and Edwin Craig, of course, he was but one of many talented performers on a show that was making their radio station known across the nation and the world.

With the war behind them and a huge new market for country music opening up, WSM officials began to pitch the Grand Ole Opry to new constituencies.

Some of its postwar promotional efforts were more organized than the Opry's staging. Perhaps the most ambitious, planned by Harry Stone and Jack Harris in tandem with the Esty advertising agency, brought a group of national newspaper and magazine writers to Nashville for a June weekend junket in 1946. Harris, who was only recently back from the war in his new assistant manager role, arranged elaborate hospitality, anchored at a suite of rooms at the Hermitage Hotel.

"You are to have a bar in operation in the main suite, which we will use as headquarters for the group," Harris wrote to hotel manager Bill Caldwell. Guests were to be told if they wanted anything, to pick up a hotel phone and ask for "George." "Your phone operators will be completely filled in, so that all such calls for George from our party rooms will immediately be plugged in at a special desk where one of the Georges will be in attendance." The Georges weren't to accept tips. The rooms were waiting with fruit, flowers, a carton of Camels, and a can of Prince Albert cigarette tobacco.

The station prepared talking points about each of the visiting writers and editors. Every WSM staffer who would have contact with the delegation was to know some basics about them as individuals. Jack Cluett, radio editor for *Woman's Day*, was a wealthy former gag writer who "likes to drink a lot." Jim Felton, radio editor for *Time*, came from California, swam, played tennis, and had just bought a new house. Ruth Champenois of *The Woman*, Florence Somers of *Redbook*, and Betty Parsons of *McCall's* were all close friends. Clyde Carley, associate editor of *True*, was related to Acuff and came as a ready-made fan of the Grand Ole Opry. And Carley Wheelright, associate editor of *Parade*, was "unmarried" and "handsome."

Harris marshaled his forces with the same precision and perhaps more humor than he had on the deck of the USS *Missouri*. "While the wine will flow like a Grand Ole Opry ballad, the staff of WSM will have to be on its toes every minute to assure success of one of the most important promotional ventures we have ever undertaken," he wrote in a memo to the staff. "Our mission is to show them the Grand Ole Opry, particularly the Prince Albert broadcast from the [riverboat] *Idlewild*. It is further to give them the type of Southern hospitality they have probably heard about, but never really seen and felt before."

On Friday at about 6:00 p.m., a plane chartered by the Esty agency landed at the airport, where Harris and Stone met the media. Two busses and a station wagon, escorted by motorcycles, carried the reporters to the Hermitage Hotel, where they were greeted warmly by Stapp, Louie Buck, and another announcer named Winston Dustin. After settling in, they were delivered to the Noel Estate, a venerable Nashville property, where they were met in the backyard by most of the senior WSM staff, including George Hay. Former Vagabond singer turned ad-man Dean Upson presided over the bar. Open-pit Tennessee barbecue was served alfresco. *Noontime Neighbors* host John McDonald had been put in charge of spraying the yard for chiggers.

The rest of the weekend unfolded with a similar attention to detail and alcohol. A bar was open at 8:00 a.m. at the hotel the next morning. Lunch was served with mint juleps at the Belle Meade Country Club. The guests were offered their choice of afternoon fun: golf, swimming, tennis, horseback riding, a visit to a Tennessee Walking Horse farm, or a tour of the Hermitage (Andrew Jackson's home, from which the hotel had taken its name) and the Parthenon. That night, the entire group watched the opening of the Grand Ole Opry at the Ryman and got tours of its cramped backstage. WSM staffers were under instructions that "the Opry story is good enough as it is—Do not try to embellish!" Then everyone was driven to a dock where they boarded the *Idlewild*, a steam pleasure boat that visited Nashville for a few weeks each year for moonlight dance cruises. On board, the Opry's Prince Albert portion ran smoothly from 9:30 to 10:00, with Red Foley, Minnie Pearl, the Oak Ride Quartet, and comedy from the Duke of Paducah. The show was beamed by shortwave to a receiver on a bank of the Cumberland River and then relayed to WSM, where it was simultaneously broadcast and piped to the NBC network. Listeners on over 130 stations nationwide heard the show, enhanced by the sounds of the paddle wheel, the boat's bell, and a calliope.

Sunday featured a fish fry at Marrowbone Lake. Fishing gear and boats were provided, and Louie Buck offered a prize for the largest fish caught. A jukebox played Grand Ole Opry artists. And after a long afternoon, and another stop at the hotel, the writers were delivered back to their plane. They took home souvenir boxes with fresh farm butter and slices of Tennessee ham in dry ice, plus a bottle of Jack Daniel's Tennessee whiskey.

The weekend was a smash. The *Banner* called it "the largest group of magazine and newspaper syndicate writers and editors ever attracted to this city for a single event." Grant Turner remembered reams of good press in its wake. But only a few weeks later, Jack Harris decided that Nashville had become too parochial for him. "I realized I'd made a mistake," he said in 1993. The war, he said, had been "a broadening experience, but most of the people had not left and they were very satisfied to do what they had been doing for a long time." Nashville, he said, was an "old Southern town" where the prevailing attitude was: "If it was good enough for my granddaddy, it's good enough for me . . . I found out that you can't go home. I had changed too much, and home hadn't changed that much, and I just wasn't happy."

Harris found his new life through powerful friends he'd made in England. Oveta Culp Hobby had organized the Women's Army Corps and steered it to a vital place in the war effort. Her husband, William P. Hobby, was a former governor of Texas who owned the *Houston Post*. The couple also owned radio station KPRC in Houston; in early 1947, Harris accepted their invitation to run it.

In the WSM master control room, where the on-duty staff usually gathered when they were not working or playing table tennis, the announcers and engineers frequently talked about the music industry, and there was plenty to discuss as the war came to a conclusion. Big bands were getting smaller. Small record labels were getting bigger. Modern jazz and R & B were dethroning swing as the nation's hippest music. Independent labels sold fifty million records in 1946 alone, partly through aggressive promotion to a growing number of small radio stations, which couldn't afford transcribed, syndicated programming. Country music was thriving nationwide, especially in California, where so many southern refugees had migrated during the Dust Bowl. But if Nashville had a chance of competing for some of the burgeoning country music business, it would have to develop into a place with more for an aspiring hillbilly singer to do than simply audition for the Opry.

One of the station's newer announcers, Jim Bulleit could see that Nashville wasn't ready for the music business in 1945. A WSM wartime recruit from small town Indiana, Bulleit had been a miner, a cowboy, and a sideshow performer before he went into radio. In Montgomery, Alabama; Twin Falls, Idaho; and Griffin, Georgia, he multitasked his way through announcing, sales, and program production. Historian Martin Hawkins, who has documented Nashville's embryonic music business, says when Bulleit auditioned at WLAC, he was told he was overqualified and was referred to WSM. (At the same time, a young aspiring DJ named Sam Phillips was shunted in the opposite direction and found gainful employment at WLAC before moving to Memphis, founding Sun Records, and changing the world.) In any event, Bulleit clearly recalls the date he started at WSM, the second anniversary of Pearl Harbor, December 7, 1943. Before long, he was announcing on the Opry, hosting a Francis Craig segment, and running the Artist Service Bureau. He was acutely aware that he was the only talent booker in Nashville, and that the city still lacked recording studios and music publishers, save for Acuff-Rose. "[Bulleit] expounded at great length about the pent-up demand for records that would become evident when the war was over," recalled Aaron Shelton. "His ambition was to start a record company."

Two years later, he did just that, leaving WSM to launch the Bullet Recording and Transcription Company. Its first trade ad in *Billboard* at the end of April 1946 announced: "Hillbilly records from the home of the Grand Ole Opry." And its first release spoke volumes about where Nashville was headed. "Wave to Me, My Lady" by Brad Brady and his Tennesseans had "Zeb's Mountain Boogie" on the flip side. Brad Brady was none other than Owen Bradley, deftly seasoning his swinging big band style with just a touch of hillbilly ruckus, and to everyone's surprise, the "throwaway" B-side became a jukebox hit. Though it was only distributed in Nashville and Birmingham, "Zeb's Mountain Boogie" sold out several pressings. It marked a small victory for the scarcely born Nashville record business, largely because the songs had been recorded in town, at an off-hours studio at WSM. At the time, that was the only option, but that was about to change too.

Bulleit's foray into record making and selling offered an irresistible invitation to WSM's technical staff to offer recording services. Engineers Aaron Shelton, George Reynolds, and Carl Jenkins had been watching for years as Opry stars made records in New York, Chicago, or Hollywood. It was, wrote Shelton, "always expensive and not too satisfactory from an artistic standpoint . . . Many . . . were unable to relax and perform to the best of their ability when surrounded by an almost foreign environment and personnel, most of whom were unsympathetic and unappreciative of their talent." Shelton imagined he and his colleagues could do a better job on their home turf.

WSM had certainly been a recording studio before. Pee Wee King, Owen Bradley, and Eddy Arnold had used Studio B to cut syndicated shows during the war, and in December 1944, Arnold cut his signature hit "Cattle Call" for Victor at WSM, a session many peg as the first in Nashville for a major label release. Thus a full-service recording studio, especially one owned and operated by the men who engineered the Opry stars' sound over the airwaves each week, seemed a smart bet. Reynolds was, in Shelton's appraisal, a "superb audio engineer" who also had a grasp of business basics. Jenkins had solid background in studio installation, wiring, and fabrication. And Shelton himself was long familiar with the disc-cutting machines, for he'd been recording commercials and syndicated shows for WSM since 1939. He knew audio circuits, but he also felt equipped to relate to the talent. He liked country music and the people who made it, and he knew about the balance of sounds that made an effective record.

In late 1945 or early 1946, the trio pooled its resources and got an extra $1,000 loan from Third National Bank. They didn't leave their WSM jobs; this would be an off-hours moonlighting operation. DeWitt said he didn't care as long as it didn't interfere with their WSM work. Without a contract or a ceremony, they formed Castle Recording Company, a name pulled straight from WSM's slogan, with a castle-in-the-clouds logo. The team's first investment was a belt-driven master cutting lathe that etched a mono track into a spinning acetate disc (tape-recording was years away). There wasn't room for it at WSM, so they installed the bulky machine in the station's old broadcast house on Fifteenth Avenue, producing a less-than-ideal situation in which the mixed signal traveled through phone lines to the transmitter building before being recorded. Engineers had to place a call to find out if they'd gotten a good take. "Through our close association with WSM, we were allowed to rent at a nominal fee the use of one of their studios at hours when the station had no need," recalled Shelton. This "was recognized by all concerned as only a temporary stop-gap arrangement while we scouted around." Even in temporary quarters, Castle Recording made an impact, especially on December 11, 1946, a day that heralded Nashville's postwar music revolution.

Hank Williams, much to Fred Rose's relief, was sober when he arrived at National Life that winter's morning. Rose had arranged for a band from the Opry to back his new discovery—a volatile, brilliant, and raw-boned country singer from Alabama whom he'd agreed to produce for the small Sterling Records label in New York. One of those side musicians, Vic Willis, remembered Williams as pathetically skinny and overworn for twenty-three years old. They rehearsed that morning and had lunch at the Clarkston Hotel coffee shop, where Hank turned down a waitress's offer of a beer. Then they cut four songs, including Williams's first commercial single, a bouncy gospel number that asked, "Can't you hear the blessed savior calling you?" Its B-side was the secular heartbreak song "Never Again." The record did well enough to justify a follow-up session in February, when they cut Hank's "Pan American," the song inspired by the WSM railroad broadcast. They convened again in April, and August, and November, recording four sides per day, including country landmarks "I Saw the Light," "Honky Tonk Blues," "Honky Tonkin'," and "I Can't Get You off of My Mind." All, not by accident, were published by Acuff-Rose.

Even if Hank wasn't prepossessing, Castle's engineers knew they were hearing somebody remarkable as they coaxed his voice and guitar onto disc. Shelton recalled that the whole crew thought this singer was "almost hypnotic in his effect on an audience, even the limited few in the control room." They joined Rose in lobbying to get Hank on the Grand Ole Opry. The campaign ultimately took two years and the personal intervention of Jim Denny, because Stone and DeWitt knew full well of Williams's binge drinking, which could unpredictably wreak havoc among his associates, family, and fellow musicians. But at least the boys at Castle knew they had made their first important records.

A record made by no means guaranteed a record sold, especially in country music, where the sector of the music business we now call "retail"—record merchants—lacked shape in the 1940s. One who stepped into the breach was Opry star Ernest Tubb. The Texan used to say that the secret to his blockbuster success wasn't that his voice was very good but that its sheer ordinariness made guys all across America think they could surely sing as well. He was an ordinary-looking man too, with large ears, a crooked grin, and an Adam's apple almost as large as his capacious nose. But he had an inimitable style, fountains of charisma, and a relaxed swinging baritone that gave songs like "Thanks a Lot" and "Waltz across Texas" an irresistible friendliness. By 1947 Tubb was not only one of the most successful Opry stars, he was about to become the next one to use his relationship with WSM to launch an outside business that would help country music as much as it helped him.

Ernest Tubb Records, a mail-order record store and shop front downtown on Commerce Street, filled a void. Postwar record dealers, if they carried hillbilly records at all, kept them segregated from the pop and classical titles. Like other country singers of the day, Tubb got sore when he was approached by fans in cities and towns around the nation telling him they loved him on radio but couldn't find his records anywhere. When Tubb first came to Nashville in 1943, only Hermitage Music Company, a jukebox operator, dealt in country records—selling off its used platters at cut rates. By 1946 a handful of stores sold records, emphasizing pop music.

Tubb had already enjoyed a strong war-years run on WSM's early morning shows. By 1947 he starred in a pre-Opry show from the WSM studios sponsored by Carter's Chicks, a company that mail-ordered live baby chickens by the millions. Once finished, he'd go to the Ryman to play his 11:00 to 11:15 p.m.

Opry segment, which he sponsored to sell his songbooks. Then, beginning in early 1947, he'd head back to the WSM studios for his *Midnite Jamboree,* where his own Texas Troubadours would share the mic with guest Opry artists like Red Foley, Johnny and Jack, and Bill Monroe. Tubb biographer Ronnie Pugh wrote that Tubb's midnight broadcast "became the centerpoint of three shows that visiting acts like Johnny Bond, Jimmy Wakely, Margaret Whiting, or Floyd Tillman worked—the Prince Albert Grand Ole Opry at 9:30 [NBC's portion], the 'Midnite Jamboree,' and the next day's 'Sunday Down South' broadcast." If Tubb couldn't be in town, David Cobb spun records from the Ryman Auditorium for a holdover Opry audience.

When Tubb's store held its grand opening in May 1947, WSM was there, with microphones and its now ubiquitous remote truck. Cobb, who hosted all of Tubb's radio shows, was there, as were Harry Stone and Dollie Dearman, who had been dating since the war. Dollie, though she didn't care for country music, was close friends with Minnie Pearl and was hired on as one of the first clerks at Tubb's shop. The gala went out live on a Saturday afternoon before the Opry, and before long the shop was the home of the *Midnite Jamboree* as well. Post-Opry crowds migrated a block to the small store and crowded in between the record bins. Some milled outside where it was cooler and listened to the music and talk over loudspeakers. Millions more heard it for decades over WSM.

The store's record business took off more slowly, not for lack of demand but because of the sheer fragility of 78-rpm records. The Tubb family remembered that as many as six in ten of the records mailed out in flat cardboard boxes arrived broken. Tubb and his partners agreed to absorb those losses and simply send out another copy. Since mail orders accounted for 70 percent of Tubb's business, breakage was a key reason the store lost $10,000 per year for its first five years. Relief came in the very late 1940s, when Columbia introduced its 33-rpm "microgroove" LP and RCA produced the small, 45-rpm single. For a year, these new formats battled for dominance, before the industry called a truce and began building phonographs that could accommodate all three speeds. Happily for Tubb, the new records were harder to break.

Tubb's only other obstacle was a certain mistrust among other artists. Some initially thought he was serving only himself, though history records that he was exposing and marketing country music as a whole. "I spent a lot of money advertising records and I think that within six months they all saw that I was creating a bigger demand for records by advertising over the Grand Ole Opry," Tubb said. "It helped everybody in the long run."

Though he was not yet fifty years old, veteran orchestra leader Francis Craig settled into semiretirement around the end of the war, playing his last NBC broadcast in early May 1947. Later that summer he took on the dual role of music librarian and disc jockey, something by then widespread in radio but new at the conservative WSM. One of Craig's duties was to screen new records that came into the station, to see if they were suitable for airplay on the Air Castle of the South. In most cases, he placed little white labels on either side of the 78s and wrote "F.C. O.K." Suggestive lyrics earned "Do Not Play," and sometimes he took a yellow crayon or even a pen knife and made an X across the disc. Meanwhile, Craig's weekday, late-morning DJ show *Featuring Francis Craig* tried to cultivate the same ambience that better-known big band leaders like Paul Whiteman and Tommy Dorsey offered in their new record shows on the networks. He spun records by WSM alums like James Melton and Dinah Shore, and a WSM press release from that summer said that Craig "will do live interviews with music stars betwixt recordings."

Francis Craig also continued to write music, and one day in 1946 he called his daughter and her friend to the living room to hear a tune he'd written the night before. It was a lilting, lightweight number with a little slip-note, half-step rise as a musical hook. It had no lyrics, but those soon followed when Craig met Kermit Goell, a boisterous New Yorker who'd come to town to pitch songs, at the Hermitage Grill Room. Craig played his new tune and urged Goell to write some lyrics, which he did on a menu. Its title: "Near You."

In January of 1947, Craig, who had never had an especially successful recording career, was looking for a swan song. He collaborated with Jim Bulleit on a session in WSM's Studio C. Bulleit's chief purpose was to record Craig's longtime theme song "Red Rose." Shelton engineered the session, mixing the orchestra through three overhead microphones to a single track. Owen Bradley, who is sometimes remembered as the producer of the session, was there early in the evening, but had to leave for a 9:30 live engagement at the Andrew Jackson. The band also cut "Sometimes I Wonder" and "Hot Biscuits" and concluded by trying to think of a song that would make a good B-side for "Red Rose." After playing through several, Craig and Bulleit agreed on "Near You." They rehearsed a few times and recorded it in one take.

"Red Rose" was released in March and hyped with all the resourcefulness a tiny label like Bullet could muster. Over downtown, airplanes dropped roses that could be exchanged for a free record. But local jukebox play didn't translate into brisk sales, and Craig rationalized that all he'd really been shooting for all along was a disc for posterity and for his girls. It's not as if a twenty-year-old song was going to storm the charts anyway.

But then one of those quirky music business things happened, the kind that can only be explained by chaos theory, where little actions produce large consequences. Cal Young, the DJ who dropped the WSM microphone down the National Life stairs, was now twenty-five and spinning records for WKEU, a tiny station based at a hotel in Griffin, Georgia. He remembered: "I came home one weekend and 'Red Rose' had just come out, so I went down and bought it and didn't pay any attention to the other side of it." It was unusual for a DJ to wander into Ernie's Record Mart to purchase records he could easily get free, but Young had grown up in the Francis Craig era and was curious. He took it back to Georgia. "And down there we'd play anything," he said. "So it got flipped over right away." After just a few spins of "Near You," a local record shop called asking where they could get some copies. I got it in Nashville, Young said. It's on Bullet. Call your distributor. And apparently they did. "They sold the hell out of 'em," Young said. "It really did catch on there."

Bulleit and his wife were driving to South Carolina in the early summer for a vacation and they were surprised how often they were hearing "Near You" on the radio. Author Robert Ikard recounted that "as soon as they reached the beach, Bulleit received a frantic phone call from his staff to get back home and take care of a business problem he had never encountered, an overwhelming demand for one of his products." In June, they sold 80,000 copies, then 200,000 in July, then 400,000 in August. By October, he was 600,000 units behind, and some in his network of far-flung record pressing plants were giving him fits by shipping more copies than they reported and keeping the profits. But even in a cutthroat industry, Bullet rode "Near You" to remarkable heights.

"What I was really proud of was that we were the first little record company, or independent as we were called, to ever not let the majors catch us on a sale," said Bulleit, in reference to the major labels' practice of rushing out "cover" versions of regional hits. Versions of "Near You" came from the Andrews Sisters, Alvino Ray, Frankie Laine, and Victor Lombardo, "but we outsold them," Bulleit said. "Near You" hit #1 on *Billboard*'s "Honor Roll of Hits" on September 27 and didn't let go for seventeen weeks, an all-time record. Frank Sinatra hammed up the song on radio's *Your Hit Parade*. *Billboard* called the record's success a "freak happening." And Nashville celebrated its latest native son to enjoy big-time (pop music) success. "Everywhere you go,

'Near You' is either sung, played, or fried in deep fat,' said an announcer at a gala Ryman Auditorium concert for Francis Craig, where WSM musicians presented Hawaiian, country, and operatic versions of the song.

Castle Recording, which now had Hank Williams and a #1 pop record to its credit, couldn't remain in WSM's studios, so Aaron Shelton and company set out looking for a room large enough to hold a hillbilly band and "possibly smaller pop orchestras." They looked nearby, so WSM engineers could slip over for lunch-hour sessions. They settled on a former dining room on the second floor of the Tulane Hotel, a gone-to-seed brick block popular with musicians and traveling salesmen. The would-be studio had dusty oak panel walls, high ceilings, and supporting columns that roughly divided the room into two sections. The accoutrements—the ceiling fans and chandeliers—were long gone, and half the room was piled with disused furniture. The hotel needed the storage, so the engineers built a partition wall and then subdivided the remaining space into a studio, a control room with an eight-foot-long window at chair height, and a small room for the master lathes.

"The windows in the control room and cutting room facing Eighth Avenue presented quite a problem," Shelton related. "The noise from the heavy duty trucks pulling up the hill from Church Street to Union Street was particularly annoying, and the late afternoon sun beaming through these windows caused a heat problem in both these technical areas." Those were closed with insulation and sheetrock. In spare hours, they cleaned the paneling and painted the walls. They placed sound baffles around the room, installed a U-shaped vocal booth, and assembled their own monitors for studio playback, designed after the large Altec-Lansing horn speakers used in movie houses. WSM, then upgrading equipment, sold the team a Steinway studio grand piano, a Hammond organ with a revolving speaker cabinet, and a small celesta. The Castle crew poured nearly all of their first-year earnings back into the studio, upgrading to an eight-channel mixing console designed by George Reynolds, which allowed setting up multiple mics for almost any size group. After a year, they had both a Scully master cutting lathe (state of the art for the time) and a new prize, a model 200 Ampex tape recorder.

Castle's shakedown session tracked a short commercial jingle for a jewelry store owned by Harold Shyer, with Snooky Lanson on vocals. "Snooky apparently was not too keen to be doing a strictly local commercial jingle, but he was too professional to indicate this to Mr. Shyer," wrote Shelton. "Snooky decided to quote a price that seemed very high ($500, I believe) for such a small amount of work. Harold Shyer accepted Snooky's price without hesitation. And so, with Owen Bradley as his accompanist, Snooky gave the highly reverberant new Castle studios this inconspicuous inception." The tag line of the commercial stuck in their brains for years: "If Harold says it's so, it's so."

Irving Waugh shifted from the microphone to the business side of WSM almost as soon as he returned from the Pacific. He sold commercial time for about a year, and in early 1948 he was made commercial manager. On the surface, the job couldn't have been easier. WSM was backlogged with quality national and regional sponsors. They needed caretaking, but Waugh scarcely had to go drum up new business. When local concerns inquired about advertising, Waugh would usually refer them on to WLAC or another local station. Most sponsorships were for half-hour or quarter-hour blocks, and even the rare thirty-second spots were sold to national accounts, like Bulova Watches. Commercials of that sort ran occasionally at the top or bottom of the hour, never more than one in a row.

Moreover, time sales wasn't the numbers-driven science it would become. Although rudimentary radio ratings research had been available since the early 1930s, WSM didn't acquire any until 1948, when Waugh looked at studies by the Broadcast Measurement Bureau. What he saw surprised him—an audience of about ten million people, broken down by age and by county, most of whom identified country music as the main reason they tuned in at least weekly. But in general, "we sold on coverage, power, prestige," said Waugh. "We had very little demographic information, and didn't bother to seek it. We had success stories, like [long-time bluegrass sponsor] Martha White Flour in Nashville."

The environment allowed Waugh to be more than just the sales manager, because, as he said, "DeWitt didn't manage the station. He knew, of course, engineering, but I ran sales and programming, and in effect, I kept peace between Denny and Stapp, who didn't care for each other particularly, because Denny thought of himself gradually taking over—which he was." Still, the developing synergies between Denny's Artist Service Bureau, the Opry itself, and the nascent Nashville music business gave Waugh, with his ties to national advertising accounts, influence over the ways WSM could advance the country music agenda. His first triumph in this regard followed negotiations that produced a Friday-night edition of the Grand Ole Opry.

The story begins with "Colonel" Tom Parker, who would become familiar to many as manager of Elvis Presley. The imposing Parker had come from Florida, where he'd been a dogcatcher and show promoter, but now he was in Nashville, haunting the WSM studios and carving out his place in the music business. After a long courtship, he landed Eddy Arnold as a management client. Arnold was a newly minted star, and Parker thought it was time for Arnold to get off the Opry with its meager fees and into his own starring role, preferably on WSM itself. Parker got Ralston Purina, the feed and meal maker, to sponsor a half-hour syndicated show starring Arnold, and then he tried to sell it to WSM for the half hour before the Opry. This required a negotiation between the Gardner Agency, representing Ralston Purina, and Waugh, responsible for all ad revenue on WSM. And Waugh had several demands.

First, WSM wouldn't air a prerecorded show on Saturday night after years of taking pride in live local programming. The Gardner Agency indicated that it could take the show to WLAC, which had already offered a slot on Friday night. Waugh didn't want to see that happen, so he told the Gardner representative that WSM would take drastic steps to protect its identity as *the* country music station in Nashville. "I told him that if he went on the other station on Friday night, we would put a live country music show against him, and in front of him, and behind him . . . I said, 'I hate to say this, because it sounds as though I'm threatening you, but this means that much to our company.'" The Gardner man countered: Eddy Arnold would host a live show on Friday night on WSM, but WSM would have to follow through on Waugh's "threat." To keep Arnold from sounding like a hillbilly in a sea of pop music, WSM would add new live country music shows before and after the Arnold show. Waugh took that deal, but quickly found out he had displeased Edwin Craig.

"Mr. Edwin kept me upstairs for three and a half hours one day about it," Waugh told Opry historian Jack Hurst. "He said that this was too much exposure, that having (a country show on Friday night) would damage the Opry. He wanted me to take the Friday night show off, but he wouldn't order me to take it off. I told him that this was in keeping with what he had always told us to do: to try to make friends for the parent company, deliver the biggest audience we could deliver and if possible to make a dollar. I said, 'This will do all of those things.'" Craig pressed his case but wouldn't order the change. Waugh said, "We stayed up there until it was time for him to go to dinner—he had a party or something at home—and he never asked about it again."

Historians have dated the resulting show, the *Friday Night Frolic*, to 1948 or 1949, but radio schedules in the *Tennessean* don't show a full slate of hillbilly talent on WSM's Friday nights until 1952. Eddy Arnold's "new" show (without country music before or after it) was hailed in an advertisement in early October 1950. By November, country standout George Morgan has a half hour after Arnold. It seems likely that because of Craig's reluctance, the *Friday Night Frolics* coalesced gradually in the early 1950s, rather than the common perception that a full-fledged Studio C show was designed in the late 1940s.

Neil Craig agrees that his father was needlessly pessimistic about the public's appetite for country. On family vacations Edwin would spin through the radio, hearing country come out of every Podunk town in the South, and it bothered him. That had to be bad for the Opry, he'd say. But the Opry seemed impregnable. It generated $600,000 per year in ad revenue, and that much again through the Artist Service Bureau. WSM was sitting on a "gold mine," according to a late 1949 article in *Variety* magazine. It employed 230 people, 200 of them talent. And after a decade of silence on the promotional front, company newspaper *Our Shield* at last touted the value of the Grand Ole Opry to the National Life sales force. With the Opry about to celebrate its twenty-fourth birthday, the company newsletter noted the show's "potential value to Shield Men is greater today than ever before." One article suggested a sales pitch: "Good Morning, Mrs. Thrifty, my name is Will Shield. I just dropped by to ask you if you folks ever listen to the Grand Ole Opry."

The Opry's successes did not incline Jack Stapp to back off of his drive for good, live, broad-based radio programs during the rest of the week. He urged remotes whenever possible, feeding NBC from multiple Nashville locations on New Year's Eve, for example, or broadcasting locally from country clubs, fairs, and political events. Chiefly, though, Stapp's WSM was defined by its excellent music. A show fed to NBC featured Owen Bradley's orchestra fronted by a striking new female singer from Rome, Georgia, named Dolores Watson. She'd impressed Ott Devine and Owen Bradley and would go on to win one of Arthur Godfrey's prestigious talent competitions.

About the same time, Stapp also singled out Anita Kerr, a versatile keyboard player and singer working at another local station, to assemble a vocal chorus that could work all sorts of shows, from pop to hillbilly. She was barely twenty, but WSM musician Jack Gregory had recommended her as an exceptional talent who could read, write, and arrange. The long-running vocal group the Dixie Dons reportedly felt nudged aside by the new Anita Kerr Singers, but perhaps like the orchestra when he first arrived, Stapp wanted his own ensemble. Kerr was born into an Italian family that owned a grocery store in Memphis, and she began performing on WREC there. After marrying, she moved to Nashville.

Stapp told her he needed much more than just another singer. "I said you've got to rehearse and make arrangements, the whole damn thing," Stapp recounted later. It seemed to take her very little trouble to do just that, however. She and her fellow singers started working regularly on *Sunday Down South,* by then a signature show sponsored by the Lion Oil Company.

One of the Anita Kerr singers, Dottie Dillard, who had been with WSM since about 1947, got to step forward herself on *Appointment with Music,* another NBC feed that debuted as a summer replacement for the Jimmy Durante Show in mid-1948. She and Snooky Lanson shared duties, with Owen Bradley conducting. Early 1949 saw WSM's local children's show *Wormwood Forest,* written by Tom Tichenor and directed by Marjorie Cooney, become a network feed as well, after two years of being heard only over WSM's signal. Most triumphantly, Snooky Lanson landed his own Saturday-afternoon network show about the same time, bolstering his profile. Not two years later, he announced he'd landed a five-year contract to be a featured male vocalist on *Your Hit Parade,* the first big pop music countdown show, which was moving from radio to TV over NBC. It was a coveted slot, one previously held by a young Frank Sinatra. Lanson and his wife and two children moved to Connecticut so abruptly that he had to cancel a Friday appearance at the Sulphur Dell ball park prior to the Junior League All-Star Game. His small-time gigs were over.

Bullet Records' success extended far beyond Francis Craig and became part of something much bigger in Nashville. Indeed, for a label that really put its faith in R & B, hillbilly, and gospel music, "Near You" was atypically oriented to pop audiences. Bullet released the first-ever sides by B. B. King of Memphis in 1949 and records by the Big Three Trio out of Chicago, featuring a young Willie Dixon. Though Jim Bulleit sold his interest in the label to a business partner in 1949, the label enjoyed success with boogie-woogie piano player Cecil Gant, gospel group the Fairfield Four, and country records by Zeb Turner, Leon Payne, Autry Inman, and a young guitar hotshot named Chester ("Chet") Atkins. A Bullet employee helped launch Tennessee Records, which had its own recording studio and introduced blues and gospel singer Christine Kittrell, while boosting the career of noted songwriter and producer Ted Jarrett.

Other independent labels followed, lending depth and breadth to the city's record business. In 1947 and 1948, Owen Bradley made a brief go of two labels, a country/gospel imprint called World and a pop enterprise called Select. His partners were Dottie Dillard, the singer, and Hank Fort, a female song and jingle writer married to one of the National Life Forts. Newcomer label Republic would soon issue Snooky Lanson, pop/country pianist and Opry figure Del Wood, and the sugary Pat Boone, a local lad on the make. Randy Wood, owner of a hugely successful mail-order record shop in Gallatin, entered the record business in 1950, forming Dot, the only Nashville-born independent to grow into a national powerhouse.

All the while, Nashville's night clubs thrummed with creamy swing, elaborate floor shows, and fervent jazz and R & B. During this little-known golden age of Nashville, a huge array of stars, regional comers, and local strivers played live at places like the Skyway on Murfreesboro Road, the Del Morocco and the Revillot in the black mercantile district of Jefferson Street, and at the Carousel and the Gaslight in a downtown row called Printer's Alley. The scene encompassed black and white (though rarely did the twain meet), and as far as the nightclub scene went, there was scarcely any country music at all. Richard Frank Jr., who grew up dancing to Francis Craig and Owen Bradley and later became a powerful country music attorney, said, "In the forties and early or mid fifties, jazz, blues, and race music were as important in Nashville as country music. And it was their lack of cohesion and organization and focus that caused them to stay where they were while country music expanded and became a major force internationally." But that consolidation, that star-making conformation, had yet to take place.

This was the highly charged atmosphere in which David Cobb, by then one of WSM's signature announcers, coined a phrase that helped define Nashville's new identity. Cobb, a left-of-center man in a right-of-center environment, stood out on the fifth floor of Seventh and Union. Colleagues remembered him as a beatnik, a bohemian. Some said he'd came back from WWII with an earring. His publicity photo from the late 1940s showed him posed, stern and sensual, with a cigarette cocked near his chin, his pencil-thin moustache and glossy wave of hair suggesting a Hollywood leading man.

In early 1950 Cobb was billboarding *The Red Foley Show*—a sustaining half hour fed to NBC in the mornings with Owen Bradley, the Jordanaires, and guitar wonder Grady Martin. Cobb's role was to set up the show at the top of the half hour before handing over emcee duties to Foley. "One morning," Cobb told the CMF's John Rumble, "for no good reason, I changed my introduction a bit. I don't know where it came from: '*From Music City USA, Nashville, Tennessee, the National Broadcasting Company brings you the Red Foley Show!*'" After the show, Cobb was called to Jack Stapp's office. He thought he might be in trouble. "I thought, what did I do wrong today?" An excited Stapp barked,

"Where did you ever get that idea? That's the greatest thing I ever heard!" And he encouraged Cobb to keep using "Music City" on the air.

It didn't take long for the tagline to reach common parlance. That summer, the tiny Dixie Jamboree label issued a 78 by Dick Stratton and the Nite Owls declaring that "They used to call it Nashville, but I'm here to say / That now they call it Music City USA." That fall, Dinah Shore, in a twenty-fifth anniversary message of congratulations to the station, toasted her hometown with the phrase. "A lot of us now in New York and Hollywood know that WSM [she seems to have meant to say Nashville] has really become known as Music City, U.S.A." By 1951 there was a WSM-TV show called *Music City USA*. And over the next decade, the M section of the phone book gradually filled up with Music City "This" and Music City "That," from Music City Tavern to Music City Mobile Homes. If there was a downside for Cobb, it was that henceforth, Stapp thought of him as the guy who could name anything, and he'd excitedly call when he had a new show in the works. Cobb said, "He thought I could just pull them out of the air."

Two more hit records of 1950—both country/pop hybrids about Tennessee that bore the stamp of Fred Rose and WSM—fulfilled the promise of "Near You" and Cobb's Music City moniker. One was Red Foley's smash "Chattanooga Shoe Shine Boy." The other was Patti Page's thirteen-week #1 hit, "Tennessee Waltz," written by Pee Wee King and Redd Stewart.

Jack Stapp and Harry Stone were credited with "Shoe Shine Boy," but Stapp was always clear that he hadn't written it, just shared in the moment that led to the idea. "I was with Harry in the office one Saturday morning after the Opry rehearsal. I was sitting in his office. Everybody had started writing songs around here. Clifford [the ubiquitous WSM porter] was giving me a shoe shine. And the network was on. The band was playing a jazzy type tune, and Clifford was keeping rhythm to it. One of us said that's an idea for a song. Let's have Fred Rose write a song about a shoeshine boy." Rose set some new lyrics to an old tune called "The Dogtown Strut" and called it "Boogie Woogie Shoeshine Boy." Red Foley said he'd cut it as a B-side but that since he'd had luck with songs with Tennessee titles, he'd record it as "Chattanooga ["Chattanoogie" in some versions] Shoe Shine Boy." Recorded at Castle and published by Acuff-Rose, the song exploded.

"Tennessee Waltz" was written in a car one night in 1946. King and Stewart were driving back to Nashville from Texarkana, listening to WSM. When they heard Bill Monroe's "Kentucky Waltz" on the air, Stewart got a notion to write, if not an answer song, then an analogous song with Tennessee in the hook. King took over the driving so Stewart could write on a kitchen matchbox cover, setting lyrics to a King instrumental called "No Name Waltz." The next day they showed it to Fred Rose, their publisher, who liked it but who made the kind of subtle change he was famous for—Instead of a bridge beginning "O, the Tennessee Waltz; O, the Tennessee Waltz," he wrote, "I remember the night and the Tennessee Waltz." The song was recorded by many artists, black and white, country and pop. The most explosive version, Patti Page's, and sold six million copies. Cover versions appeared from Guy Lombardo, Sammy Kaye, Les Paul and Mary Ford, Jo Stafford, Anita O'Day, and Spike Jones. The song even became a hit in Japan with Japanese lyrics. Tennessee governor Gordon Browning sang it to great acclaim on the Opry stage.

Country music was freer than ever to cross borders of geography and style, and WSM had the talent and the resources to take the music anywhere. In the late 1940s, for example, the station put together a transcribed program about the history of country music, not for local broadcast, but for distribution to the BBC. Announcer Ernie Keller narrated and engaged in dialogue with Judge Hay, plus Opry stars Dave Macon, Roy Acuff, Bradley Kincaid, and others, about the journey of British Isles folk songs across the Atlantic to the American South. This remarkable audio not only offered a firsthand account of country music's origins by some of its most important pioneers, it demonstrated WSM's commitment to the genre and its diverse legacy. It's easy to love country music on its face, they seemed to be saying, but one always loves it more when one knows its story. WSM's leaders, especially Hay and Stone, were bold enough to claim country music as an American birthright, a potent indigenous voice of the people, as well as a viable commercial market. Likewise, much of the nation, in its extraordinary journey from depression and world war to peace and prosperity, had embraced country music as a new vessel of expression and chronicle of experience. A business that could influence new markets and new audiences had finally begun to organize in Nashville, almost exclusively through the people and facilities of WSM. With television on the way, this increasingly savvy Southern broadcaster had access to an entirely new medium that would spread and shape the music for the next half century.

NINE ⚡ *The Balance of Power Has Shifted*

Americans lived with the *idea* of television, the bewitching vision of it, for decades before the TVs themselves arrived like an army of flying saucers in department stores across the nation. Even before WSM radio went on the air, popular-science magazines showed people gathered around color television sets, and in 1928 Charles Jenkins, an inventor in Wheaton, Maryland, was issued the first TV broadcast license in the United States. In 1930 Jenkins broadcast the first television commercial, and the BBC began regular TV transmissions, even though there were scarcely any television receivers to pick them up. Philo Farnsworth and Vladimir Zworkin surpassed Jenkins's mechanical model, developing the electronic television that became the global standard. In the mid-1930s the introduction of coaxial cable, which could carry phone and television signals, began to shape how TV would spread. AT&T began building a network to distribute programming across most of the nation, but not—at least for some crucial early years—in the South.

None of this was lost on Jack DeWitt, who very much wanted to expand into television. He saw to it that WSM was the first Nashville broadcaster to obtain a television license in the summer of 1948. Edwin Craig had taken Harry Stone and George Reynolds to a citywide meeting of broadcasters to talk about television as early as October of 1944, but as the war wound down, it was unclear how fast or even whether National Life would pursue

TV. Craig was skeptical. He'd seen a milky, eight-inch picture in New York, and he wondered aloud to colleagues how that could amount to anything. He asked DeWitt and Stone to write up a study of the pros and cons of going into TV. "It was pretty bad," remembered DeWitt. "It was an awful lot of money to take on."

Television would require new studios, built from scratch, with sets, lights, backdrops, props, wardrobe, makeup, and other things one didn't need for even the most elaborate radio shows. At minimum, they'd have to develop and write shows covering news and public affairs, kids' interest, cooking, and fashion, and they'd have to figure out the infrastructure for taking cameras out on remote shoots. Moreover, WSM's existing advertising base was national and regional. They scarcely even sold local spots, so how would they make money? Above all, Craig knew that unlike his radio signal, which blanketed more than half the United States, a TV station would scarcely reach the borders of Davidson County. That wasn't going to sell any more insurance.

But RCA/NBC was pressing its many radio affiliates to get into television. Irving Waugh attended a lavish meeting at Princeton in about 1948 where "General" David Sarnoff offered a glimmering vision of the future, where television would lead and radios would take on new roles in people's lives. (To prove it, he produced the first portable transistor radio Waugh had ever seen.) Edwin Craig would have heard firsthand from his old friend Niles Trammell, now president of NBC, about television's bright future. The hometown press was working Craig over as well. In a June 8, 1948, editorial called "Time to Catch Up," the *Tennessean* accused all of Nashville's radio broadcasters with foot-dragging on TV, especially WSM. "The public has every right to expect television this year from WSM—both because of its history as a vigorous and enterprising pioneer in radio as well as because of the clear-channel privileges it has enjoyed so long and profitably." Nashville, it concluded "wants television and wants it this year."

National Life tentatively promised to have a television station up and running in 1949, but didn't come close. That May, a *Tennessean* story noted that "Nashville, a conspicuous blind spot on the television map of the United States, must wait another year—perhaps longer—before this amazing new baby of science opens its eyes in Middle Tennessee." The story charged local broadcasters, WSM excepted, with getting a late start in applying to the FCC. By then, Memphis had an independent station. So did 40 percent of the country, including Louisville, Oklahoma City, Richmond, and many others cities of comparable size. "We're not stalling," DeWitt told the newspapers.

Eddie Jones, the *Nashville Banner*'s first television columnist and long-time chamber of commerce executive director, said DeWitt and Irving Waugh were the prime movers behind TV at WSM. "You had two guys who were not Craigs who were from different directions saying, you know, we are a broadcast leader and this is the next life of broadcasting, and we ought to jump in there and get going with it. Jack desperately wanted to build a new station and buy the big tubes. And they had plenty of money, so why not?" Most compelling, the rapidly filling television broadcast spectrum led to a temporary FCC freeze on new stations after September 30, 1950. If WSM could make it on the air by then, they'd have a local monopoly for up to three years in the new medium. Even so, Craig resisted until the last minute. "I remember so well that he had his back to the windows of the boardroom," said Waugh. "He turned around in his chair and looked out the window and he finally said, 'We pioneered broadcasting in Nashville. I guess we owe it to the community. Go ahead and build the damn thing.'"

"The magnitude of the job . . . began to sink in," wrote Aaron Shelton. The station bought two RCA TV cameras; based on the two they'd purchased, engineers started constructing two more from parts. After much wrangling with the city and the Civil Aeronautics Board, they selected a site for their 500-foot transmitter tower, almost exactly where the original WSM radio transmitter had been near Ward-Belmont. They rigged up a remote unit—a retired bread truck outfitted with monitors, switchers, power supplies, camera cables, tripods, lighting, and a microwave transmitter to send signals back to the studio. Working with a consulting firm, they ordered and installed a film chain, film projectors, slide projectors, monitors, lights, follow spots, and a massive audio/video patch board.

The single greatest obstacle to getting a TV station up and running in Nashville had nothing to do with WSM's will or FCC policy. The problem was access to network programs. AT&T's growing national network of coaxial cable feeding programming from New York didn't come any closer than Louisville. Other southern stations were going on the air using a primordial video recording format called kinescopes, which the networks mailed to Atlanta, Birmingham, or Houston for delayed broadcast. That wouldn't do; Craig's one edict was that WSM-TV go on air with live network programming. But 175 miles of hill country separated them from the trunk line of American television. Jack's audacious solution harnessed microwaves—high frequency radio signals that beam like a spotlight from point to point. DeWitt wanted to tap the AT&T network line in Louisville and shoot it, by microwave, to WSM for rebroadcast over their TV tower. If they could have done it in one hop, nobody would have thought twice. But because of the curvature of the earth, the system would need five hilltop relay stations. Each would have a receiving dish listening to its counterpart up the chain and a sending dish aiming down toward Nashville.

DeWitt and a new Vanderbilt graduate named Lucien Rawls poured over topographical maps of the land between Nashville and Louisville. After a lot of study, they found their target sites. Somebody looked up every property owner and contacted them. Why did they lease their hilltops for huge iron towers, two radio dishes, a brick building, new power lines, and a whole list of uncertainties about lightning, fires, and electricity? Because John McDonald, host of *Noontime Neighbors* and friend to every rural soul, personally visited with each owner about it. WSM's ambassador of agrarianism was, reportedly, five-for-five in his mission to secure use of the properties, stretching from Holsclaw Hill, south of Louisville, to Gallatin, Tennessee.

The launch point—the roof of the Louisville *Courier-Journal* newspaper building—also had its roots in the station's legacy of good will. "The owners— the Binghams—still had a feeling of obligation to WSM for the services we had rendered them during the great flood," Aaron Shelton observed about a debt that was by then more than twelve years old. Thus did WSM begin building the longest privately owned TV relay facility in the United States, a temporary jigger job with a price tag of a half-million dollars.

Despite Craig's misgivings about the overexposure of country music, Stapp and Waugh had no reservations when sponsors, artists, and country music fans began to find common interest in WSM radio's early morning time slots, manifested by a boomlet of fifteen-minute hillbilly shows. The Vagabonds and Pee Wee King had filled some of the first a.m. country segments in the 1930s. Later, Roy Acuff and the Delmore Brothers took the trouble to get to National Life's fifth floor at or before sunrise to play mere fifteen-minute blocks of time. Ernest Tubb was a staple at dawn in the 1940s, sponsored by R.C. Cola. By 1950, the early morning hours had become a miniature Grand Ole Opry, with emerging stars like Little Jimmy Dickens and Cowboy Copas on the air between 5:30 and 7:30, waking up the farmers and hawking sponsors' wares. Announcers like Grant Turner, David Cobb, and Louie Buck, despite their long hours and many duties, would come in early to turn the station on and project some of their famous personality between musical numbers. The shows attracted key advertisers, who paid hungry musicians and who stuck with country music for years to come.

"If you were in town, you were required to do the early morning shows," said country and bluegrass veteran Mac Wiseman. At the time, Wiseman played with Bill Monroe's band and boarded at the Tulane Hotel. He woke up and, at dawn, walked up the hill with his guitar in all kinds of weather to take the elevator to the fifth floor. "Quite often, I was the only Bluegrass Boy there," he said. "(Fiddler) Chubby Wise and Bill and those guys were sleepy. So I'd go on the air for fifteen minutes with me and the guitar and get some mileage out of that." He has called those spots his personal springboard to the Opry itself.

Sometimes, sponsors worked with artists like Wiseman on a "per inquiry" or P.I. basis, which paid a commission linked to the number of people who called in about the product in question. "You had to be able to pitch—baby chicks, ladies hose, and all that jazz—on a percentage basis," he said, recalling the economics of morning country radio. "If you couldn't sell, you didn't eat!" Like scores of country singers of the late 1940s, he'd been working P.I.'s for years, selling songbooks over small Virginia radio stations. "Consequently, I was right at home doing it by myself on WSM," he said. "And man, think about the coverage I was getting . . . I still contend that [the early morning is] the most saleable time with radio. Because those ladies are up getting their husbands off to work and the kids off to school. And they can do their chores and get breakfast and still not miss anything on the radio."

Another star of the 1950s who remembered the mileage he got out of the early WSM slots was Carl Smith. Three days a week he played with a band at 6:15 a.m. "But the other three mornings a week are when I really got my education," he said. "It was 5:15 in the morning on Tuesday, Thursday, and Saturday. And on Sunday morning I did a fifteen minute hymn show. Just me and my guitar. No band. They wouldn't let me have one picker. An announcer put me on and I don't know where he went, but there was nobody else there. It was me in the studio with an open mic, and if I had to cough, I had to cough. But it was the greatest education, because I learned how to talk to people and how to think. Because in radio, you've got to visualize them people out there listening."

In the loose and caffeine-addled atmosphere of WSM, with Opry announcers, pickers, and artists milling about trying to crack each other up, some of country music's golden era stars made some of their most unaffected and upbeat music. One exceptional series starred Hank Williams, then at the height of his career, on a regular show sponsored by Mother's Best Flour. These fifteen-minute tours-de-force married salesmanship and musicianship, and were delivered with the ease of a bunch of guys hanging around a clubhouse. Hank and Louie Buck swapped twangy talk, read scripted pitches without sounding like they were reading, and talked their way casually into songs. Williams sang his own familiar material, gospel standards, and covers he never recorded anywhere else. He sold Mother's Best cornmeal nearly as earnestly and effectively as he sold a song. Typically, the show's first ad was aimed at the farm wife and her need for perfect cornbread. The latter was all about the farmer, with talk of antibiotic feed supplement to help chicks grow "more bigger." And somehow, there was time for one of Hank's sidemen, like Don Helms on steel or Jerry Rivers on fiddle, to shine on a solo instrumental. The boys weren't always rock solid on the chord changes, but it never threw them. Riding over bumps was just part of the road.

The September deadline pressed on everyone at the new WSM-TV, especially the engineers. The microwave link was touchy, working one day and failing the next. The audio had a tendency to arrive with spikes of static, and the only good solution became to lease a land wire from AT&T to bring down the sound in a separate feed from Louisville. Worst of all, the Nashville Bridge Company, contracted to build the five-hundred-foot tower that would hold the huge, eight-thousand-pound antenna, had been stymied by bad weather. They told DeWitt they couldn't finish until October at the earliest. As a stopgap, they hastily built a one-hundred-foot guy-wired tower with a simpler antenna, in hopes of reaching what was approaching ten thousand local TV sets. Anticipation was keen. When WSM-TV started transmitting its test pattern, a fixed image of an Indian head, people excitedly called the station reporting reception. Some people just left the test pattern on.

The cameras worked; it was time to take the promotional operation on the road. The jiggers took the new remote unit truck and set up racks of heavy, hot-running gear in mid-July at Harvey's Department Store. The prominent downtown merchant had already committed to sponsoring WSM-TV's opening broadcast and was selling televisions as fast as it could. WSM entertainers stood on a stage above a display of handbags and played to two television cameras across a crowded aisle, while the image played on TVs on the showroom floor. On August 13 the setup moved to a 300-foot tent at the Tennessee State Fair, with Opry artists, Snooky Lanson, Beasley Smith, Dottie Dillard, and Jud

Collins on site. The Carter Family, a reconstituted mother-and-daughters version of the most important early group in country music, performed with their new guitarist, Chet Atkins. The *Tennessean* ran a sixty-four-page supplement heralding the coming of television, and *Sunday Down South* was simulcast on radio and the closed-circuit television display. Fairgoers were able to stream past a camera positioned so they could see themselves on a TV screen for the first time, prompting giggles and gasps.

DeWitt wanted a month between the final installation of the microwave relay and the station's on-air date. He got three days. He and everybody in the station knew they weren't really ready, but the deadline was inflexible. "We gathered early that morning at our new TV studios and prepared to do our best," wrote Shelton. Louisville was still flickering in and out. DeWitt—president of WSM—took off his jacket and went to work with pliers, wire cutter, and solder. The audio-patch amplifier was flaky; Shelton and company made a last-minute reroute to bypass it entirely. When 1:10 rolled around, the engineers were soaked with sweat and very unhappy. The entertainers took their places, trying to look as cool as possible under vicious lights. Owen Bradley was at the organ, his brother Harold, in a sportcoat and bow tie, ready with his arch-top guitar. Ott Devine was the first to speak, welcoming viewers to WSM-TV and plugging Harvey's Department Store. Dottie Dillard sang a number. Two other women offered household hints and modeled clothes. As Dillard prepared to sing her closing number, the camera pulled in close, and a housefly landed on her nose. Shelton remembered it vividly. "Dottie, being the professional that she was and having a keen sense of humor, slowly crossed her eyes and looking down her nose, observed this intruder for at least two seconds and then calmly began her song."

Viewers called in from across the city reporting that even with the temporary transmitter, they were receiving the station clearly. But the segue to the afternoon's highlight show foretold of trouble to come. The Notre Dame versus North Carolina football game from South Bend was supposed to be coming down the relay, but all that came through were "streaks, tears, glitches and occasional vertical rolls" as Shelton put it. In at least one local tavern, groans of disappointment went up when a "Network Trouble" sign was placed on an easel in the WSM-TV studio. It didn't look like the signal would be fixed for some time, so somebody called Opry singer Little Jimmy Dickens, who rushed to the station and found himself singing country music on television with fifteen minutes' notice. About an hour later, the network fixed the problem (for it was not WSM's fault in the final analysis) and the second half of the game came through fine. A few days later, just as WSM radio had done twenty-five years prior, WSM-TV broadcast game one of the World Series, a triumph. But when the downlink failed the following day, rubbing out a game-winning Joe DiMaggio homer, DeWitt had to go on the air and apologize.

A few days later, NBC president Niles Trammell came down from New York to help his old friend Edwin Craig celebrate the anniversary of WSM and the inauguration of WSM-TV. Though the station had the luxury of picking its programming from any of the three networks on normal nights, station programmers carefully hewed to only NBC and local shows during Trammel's visit, save for the World Series. On October 8, WSM and WSM-TV simulcast an hour-long dedication program that included veterans George Hay, Francis Craig, Beasley Smith, and Joseph MacPherson, with narration by Jud Collins and Ernie Keller. Edwin Craig praised the "staff of fine young men, who have worked tirelessly through many sleepless nights to iron out the difficulties inherent in this new operation, and whose encouragement has been your sympathy and understanding."

The *Nashville Banner* had the same competitive misgivings about television that it had a quarter century before about radio. Eddie Jones, a feature writer for the newspaper before WSM-TV went on the air, remembered that once again Jimmy Stahlman and his deputies debated just ignoring the TV story and eschewing TV program listings, so as not to feed their advertising competition. But one day Jones's boss, Charlie Moss, the executive editor, called Jones, admitting the paper had better take some notice of TV. He asked Jones to start a column.

"I wrote two or three a week," Jones said. "But I didn't have a TV set! I'd go down to Harvey's into the TV department and watch the shows. I'd been doing this about a month. And Charlie called me one day and said, 'Eddie, that column's looking pretty good. How do you like TV?' I said, 'Well Mr. Moss what I see is pretty good.' He said, 'What do you mean, what you see?' I said well, 'I don't have a set.' He said, 'Goddamn! How are you writing all this shit?'" Jones replied: "Well, they send out news releases, and I go down to Harvey's and watch the shows. Do you think the paper might help me get a set?"

He thought a minute and said, "I'll go half with you."

DeWitt heard complaints for months from viewers and the newspapers about the inconstant network downlink, but gradually it began to work more reliably. He had a team of engineers tending to the five towers round the clock as the winter of 1950 came on. At the end of January, DeWitt decided a field trip would be a good idea—an inspection tour to fine-tune each site. He took Aaron Shelton and link supervisor Andy Sutton in the company's Plymouth station wagon, driving to Kentucky on a cold but otherwise ordinary day. As they reached the hilltop nearest Louisville, a dusting turned to heavy snow. The link looked good, and they headed south, while the roads grew ever slushier.

When they arrived at Elizabethtown just before 7:00 p.m., two inches of snow lay on the dirt road to the tower and on the radio dishes themselves. The radomes, the plastic hoods covering the sensitive receiver at the focal point of each dish, were covered with ice. The team swept out the dishes, cracked off the ice, filled out some logbooks, and drove on. Bonnieville, Kentucky, proved harder to reach. The dirt road up the hill dropped down in a hollow, and the car rammed up against snowbanks that piled up and stopped them cold. It was dark but for their headlights, and they were in abjectly lonely country, where moonshiners could be watching for, or shooting at, suspected revenuers. DeWitt personally knew of a still on one of these mountains. But breaking free was the only option. "We would back up about twenty or thirty feet and bang into the piled up snow with as much momentum as possible and bulldoze our way forward another ten to twenty feet," Shelton said. Jack abandoned the wheel and got out to walk, telling Aaron and Andy to stay put. They kept bulldozing and eventually arrived at the top of the hill ten minutes behind DeWitt. The station's engineer had gone home, but the signal looked good. It was 2:00 a.m. when Andy went outside to sweep out the dishes, and when he returned, he had to confess that he'd cracked one of the radomes while deicing it. It was fixed with a thermos bottle coffee cup, which served duty for two weeks before its retirement.

The station wagon had calcified into a dented hulk, frozen in second gear. DeWitt had to swing around without using reverse and rumble back down the hill. By the time they approached Bowling Green at daybreak, one tire chain was missing and the rest beat like loose tank treads on the icy road. At a service station just north of the city, a mechanic gouged them on a new set of snow chains. Then in town, an auto dealer fixed the transmission while the three ate breakfast. Two stops later, the team arrived at Rock Bridge near Gallatin, one microwave hop from WSM-TV's antenna in Nashville. DeWitt checked in for the first time with the station, and an engineer told him they'd been without primary power for fourteen hours and were not expecting any for another day. Nashville had been assaulted by the most devastating blizzard in a century, a storm that stretched from Texas to Maine and claimed hundreds of lives. In Nashville, trees ripped apart under the weight of thick coatings of ice, and by the morning of February 1, the *Tennessean* reported that the city looked "as if the area had been under artillery fire." Roofs collapsed into homes and businesses. Stray power lines spat fire in the snow, making huge clouds of steam. A water main burst at Second and Broadway, turning the hub of downtown into an ice pond. Most of the city was without power for days, but using back-up generators, WSM-TV only lost four hours of air time.

Gradually, television became more routine for the WSM crew. Shelton remembers the station's first live remote broadcast the following spring—a two-camera pickup of a stock car race from an East Nashville race track. The light was poor, and it rained, but the cameras worked anyway. Harvey's continued to be WSM-TV's leading sponsor, and the station would cut to a camera in the store several times a day. A large crew produced a lunchtime variety show for women, with Dave Overton at a downtown hotel, featuring a small orchestra, singers, audience interviews, and Overton's ad-libbing prowess.

But no televised event stirred as much excitement as the finals of the South-eastern Conference basketball tournament on March 3, 1951. When Vanderbilt upset Kentucky, the top-ranked team in the country, coached by the legendary Adolph Rupp, it was the most surprising and glorious moment in the city's athletic history. "Students pounded on tables in Nashville restaurants, toured the city with automobile horns blaring, danced jigs in dormitory hallways and some tumbled out of their rooms into the rain," reported the *Tennessean*. Thousands had seen the victory live on WSM-TV, by feed from Louisville. DeWitt remembered it as the galvanizing event that made Nashville a TV town and WSM-TV profitable. Despite the costs and despite the technical troubles, being a monopoly in the hottest new medium in the world put the station in the black in six months.

The Artist Service Bureau under Jim Denny handled the touring schedules of about one hundred Opry artists by 1950, but it was much more than a booking agency, said Frances Williams Preston, then the station's vivacious receptionist. "It was the Artist *Service* Bureau," she explained. "They would get involved in everything to do with the artists. When an artist signed on to the Grand Ole Opry, they just took his career over, and they were a part of his family. I mean, they got him out of jail, they put him in hospitals, they put him in rehabilitation places. They helped pay for the new baby coming along. You know, everything they could do to keep that artist's life, trying to make it a normal life, they would try to do." Denny also helped connect cash-loaded Opry artists with good local bankers, and he began booking them beyond concert venues, at personal appearances and on commercial spots. He scouted jingle work for non-Opry artists like Owen Bradley, hooking him up with United Biscuit Company and Happy Family Baking Powder for a percentage of the fee.

Harry Stone had tried and failed to swing side deals with Opry acts, where Denny was succeeding, further annoying Stone. Stone tried to collaborate with Denny on a popcorn concession, but that ended in bitter feelings, and on March 14, 1950, Stone wrote to Denny to say that the time had come for WSM to supervise the concessions at the Ryman Auditorium. "For this supervision, I believe you agree that WSM is entitled to a commission," he asserted. By this time, Ryman concessions were grossing $20,000 annually and personally netting Denny $6,000, which was roughly equal to his WSM salary.

By summer the strain of working at odds with DeWitt and competing with Denny for influence over the Opry proved too much for Stone. He announced his retirement in July, citing poor health. Country star Eddy Arnold came to the aid of his friend, paying Stone's moving expenses when he shipped out to manage a television station in Phoenix, Arizona. He'd been with WSM for twenty-two years and at the core of its decision making for twenty-one. He was inextricably linked to the Opry's achievements, because for all his crabbiness and guile, he was widely remembered as somebody who genuinely loved country music and wanted to see it play the best forums. He could have put the Grand Ole Opry in a gymnasium, but he talked his way into two of the finest concert halls in the South. His barn dance, because it was as much his as it ever was George Hay's, had earned its way to Carnegie Hall and the capitals of Europe, despite the ambivalence of its own hometown. He left Nashville feeling abused and underappreciated, and he probably thought he'd never come back.

With Stone on his way out, Denny moved to consolidate his power. In a long letter to station executives, he made his case that in addition to running the touring operation, he should be Opry manager. "I would like to have an Artist Service Bureau that would have complete charge of all of the bookings and managers of acts as well as the acts themselves," Denny wrote. He urged that the new position answer directly to the president and that the audition process not be "brushed off as it is at the present time." Mostly he emphasized that the show was "haphazardly handled" and a success "in spite of all of us connected with it and not because of any of us." His sober conclusion: "Without a doubt, we have the hillbilly program of the nation but we are coasting on our laurels instead of trying to improve the program."

Denny's letter worked. He was promoted a new general manager position at the Opry in January 1951, reporting to DeWitt. Programming and personnel at the Opry remained Stapp's purview, but Denny was in charge of everything else related to Opry talent including booking and management. Almost immediately, however, DeWitt and Denny crossed swords. In March the president asserted control over Opry concessions, buying the equipment and stock of what was now a fairly elaborate and lucrative business. Albert Cunniff wrote that "Denny was not happy with the settlement." He felt "railroaded by the station, which ignored" his prior permissions. Denny "pointed out to DeWitt that other halls around the country leased concession rights to concessionaires, not the incoming shows. Nevertheless, WSM moved in." It would not be the last of their battles.

In the wake of Acuff-Rose's successes with "Tennessee Waltz" and "Shoe Shine Boy," it became abundantly clear that controlling the copyrights of hit songs was the likeliest path to wealth in the music industry. Jack Stapp, as head of WSM's musical productions, had watched for years as song publishers came from New York, making the rounds of the office and the Opry stars, trying to get their companies' songs recorded and broadcast. Once on record or in a repertoire, a song could earn royalties indefinitely. Publishing was largely a relationship business, and there were few people better at that than Stapp, so when he and his old war-era buddy Lou Cowan of CBS in New York started talking over the idea of starting a music-publishing company, it seemed like an obviously good idea. Cowan, a power player responsible for TV game shows like *The $64,000 Question,* offered an initial investment. BMI president Bob Burton, another good friend of Jack's, advanced the company an additional $2,000. Cowan and Stapp forged the deal at a 1951 dinner in New York, while Cowan's wife Polly absentmindedly drew a picture of a tree on her menu. It gave a name to Stapp's new side job, song scouting and song plugging in Nashville for Tree Publishing Company.

Back home, Stapp looked for help, somebody in the music community who could listen out for new songs and songwriters. He turned to the pool of pickers who congregated in WSM's lounge and at the Clarkston Hotel coffee shop next door. First he tapped steel guitar genius Jerry Byrd, but it soon became clear that Byrd's mind was entirely on his session work. Then in 1953, Stapp's eye fell on Buddy Killen, a young bass player who often spent the night at National Life so he'd be earliest in the pool, trying to pick up seven-dollar sideman slots on the country morning shows. Killen had come to town playing with the Jamup & Honey minstrel act and spent some miserable months on the road with some hillbilly bands. He very much did not want to get back in a bone-jarring touring car. About that time, however, Killen became aware that several WSM announcers aspired to be songwriters. They asked Killen, a respectable singer, to make demo tapes for them that they could give to Tree. Stapp, they told him, was prepared to pay ten dollars per night for the sessions.

The studio time came from a new source. Owen Bradley and his brother Harold, the guitar player, had recording fever. They'd already opened two facilities in Nashville when they set about modifying a house in the Belmont neighborhood into a studio for both sound and film. "It was called 'Bradley's Film and Recording Studio,'" remembers Owen's son Jerry Bradley, himself a major music executive. "They had a lot of film equipment. They would make country music films, commercials, industrial movies, and they did some things with Minnie Pearl." Owen hired a WSM engineer named Mort Thomasson to help wire the place, and while he worked out bugs in the system, sometimes in all-night marathons, Buddy Killen stood with his guitar before a microphone, singing songs that WSM announcers hoped might make them rich.

Stapp dropped by during one of these lonely sessions. He was friendly and asked Killen about himself. Killen, young and earnest and very much aware of Stapp's influence at the Grand Ole Opry, was on his best behavior. They seemed to have a rapport. One day Stapp called Killen and asked him to go meet with and record a new singer working the Andrew Jackson Hotel. "She's written some songs," Stapp said. "Would you mind getting with her?"

"I don't know anything about that," Killen shyly protested.

"Ah, you'll do fine," Stapp replied, with what Killen would learn was uncharacteristic nonchalance.

"So I went down and got with her and listened to her songs and took her out to the studio and put them down. They were gospel songs. So I called him and told him what I'd done. And he thanked me. And a couple hours later, he called me at home and he said, could you come down to my office? I said, sure. I didn't know what the deal was. And I go down and we talked about the weather and everything. And he says, 'How would you like to go and work for Tree?'

"I said, 'Mr. Stapp I don't know anything about publishing.'

"He said, 'I don't either. We'll learn together.'"

People loved Jack Stapp, even if he was a bit high-strung. The engineers enjoyed needling him. Once, during a ventriloquist act on *Sunday Down South,* one of them feigned alarm and told Jack he'd just realized that the dummy didn't have a microphone in front of him. Stapp, choosing worrying over thinking, fretted aloud that they needed to get a mic in there! And yet for all of his perfectionist ways in the movement of talent and the timing of shows, his colleagues said he never cracked whips. His style resembled Owen Bradley's—relaxed but focused, candid but respectful. Frances Williams Preston, the one-time WSM receptionist, called him flamboyant and said he was fond of Cadillacs. His influence lay in his connections. "Well he knew everybody," said longtime Nashville radio station owner Bill Barry. "Not just here in town. He knew everybody in Hollywood, New York, Chicago. He'd pick up the phone and talk to 'em."

Killen quickly found out that Stapp lacked the organizational prowess that is sometimes found wanting in creative types. The modest archive of Tree Publishing—some lead sheets and some audio tapes—was stuffed inelegantly in the drawer of a WSM desk belonging to Stapp's secretary. It looked to Killen like somebody else's taxes, and he more or less ignored the mess as well. Instead, he got Stapp to spring for a $50 reel-to-reel tape recorder so that he could trot around town, meeting with prospective writers and harvesting their songs. He had no office but his car and the WSM house phones.

When Jim Denny followed Stapp's lead and got into the publishing business himself in 1953, he was, as in all things, more disciplined about it. He formed Cedarwood Publishing in partnership with Opry star Webb Pierce; each staked $200. He took an office next door to National Life with a full-time "girl Friday" and a staff writer. The latter, Danny Dill, was an Opry act who would later write the famous country lament "Long Black Veil." The administrative assistant was Dollie Dearman, Camel Caravan dancer, Ernest Tubb's record shop clerk, Ryman concessionaire, and now, as if in final rebuke to Harry Stone, Denny's girlfriend. The whole operation was an audacious move that added to his leverage over the careers of Opry artists and that further antagonized DeWitt.

Cedarwood struck gold first, when Webb Pierce massaged "Slowly," a yearning honky-tonk lament, into a huge hit. Not only a landmark for sonic innovation—the first pedal steel guitar solos of a steel-saturated era—it earned *Cash Box*'s title of "Best Country Record of the Year" in 1954. Tree would have to wait for its first smash until 1956, when Elvis Presley recorded "Heartbreak Hotel" by Thomas Durden and Mae Boren Axton of Nashville. That same year, Cowan sold his interest in Tree to Stapp, who cut Killen in for 30 percent and his secretary Joyce Bush in for 10 percent. The gesture was thanks for years of perseverance and low pay—sweat-equity investments in the future of Music City.

Hank Williams, the most famous and famously troubled country singer in the world, more than once called up Edwin Craig at home during dinner hour—from the Madison, Tennessee, sanitarium. "His wife had had him locked up," said Craig's daughter Elizabeth Proctor. "He'd been drunk for some days. And he'd get permission and call Daddy from the jail. And the houseman, serving those dinners to the whole family at the long table, would come in and say, 'Mr. Craig, it's that *man*.'" And Daddy would get up and go to the phone, and he'd say, 'Now you just calm down, now. Miss Audrey is going to let you out. But just calm down and be quiet. And as soon as you get over this drinking, Miss Audrey is going to let you out.' Then he'd come back to the table. And he said, 'You know what? He's going to write a million-dollar record while he's in jail. This is when he writes best.'"

WSM had finally made Williams an Opry member in 1949, but his drinking became one of the touchiest problems for WSM management. They couldn't easily jettison their most dynamic and well-loved act, a man who was revolutionizing country music before their eyes. And his problems beyond his drinking, including devastating back pain and a wife who could be a first-class harpy, had a way, some said, of earning him even more sympathy than scorn. Yet his unpolished side was an abrasion in the mostly civilized world of National Life's signature show. His no-shows and his mean streaks were particularly offensive to Jack DeWitt, who was ready to be done with Mr. Williams.

The second week of August 1952, Denny and Carl Smith visited Hank at his apartment, where he was living without his ex-wife, his child, or his new fiancée. His longtime friend and virtual manager Denny offered the ultimatum. Management already wants you fired, he said. If you don't make your next Opry appearance on August 9, you're gone. And sure enough, Hank no-showed. Denny had to deliver the final blow by phone. Hank responded by going on a bender.

Ernest Tubb ran into Edwin Craig in the National Life parking lot just after the episode.

"What do you think Ernest?" Craig said.

"Well, I hate it, but I saw the tears in Jim's eyes, and I know it was the hardest thing he ever had to do," Tubb replied. "He told me he was going to try and get Hank to straighten up."

Craig replied: "I'm sure Jim means well, but it may work the other way. It may kill him."

The Opry firing didn't kill Hank; he killed himself over the next six months. He expired in a touring car some time on New Year's Eve as 1952 gave way to 1953; Denny was a pallbearer at the most grievous funeral in country music history.

In the very late 1940s, Aaron Shelton joined an entourage traveling with Eddy Arnold as he cut some sides at RCA's busy studio in Chicago. Shelton was able to look over the facilities of what amounted to Castle's chief competitor, since the proliferation of Nashville studios was still a few years away. "After spending the entire day at RCA studios, I was convinced that we were doing a better job in some respects," he said. He had reason to be proud. Castle's sound was coming to dominate the country charts. According to Shelton's records, Castle made half of 1952's thirty top-sellers on *Billboard*'s country and western chart, including landmarks like Hank Williams's "Jambalaya," Kitty Wells's groundbreaking "It Wasn't God Who Made Honky Tonk Angels," and Webb Pierce's "Back Street Affair." Hank made Castle his base for nearly all of his recording career, rolling out "Your Cheating Heart," "Kaw-Liga," and many other timeless works.

All this work kept WSM engineers over at the Tulane Hotel for more hours than they should have been. (Edwin Craig began to notice and talked it over with DeWitt, who said it hadn't caused him any problems so far.) Castle cut for Cincinnati's King Records, including Cowboy Copas and Moon Mullican. Dot Records magnate Randy Wood asked Shelton to produce some sessions in the 1950s, including Mac Wiseman, pianist Johnny Maddox, and Cajun country artist Jimmy C. Newman. Castle hosted a session with pop star Rosemary Clooney, who monopolized the control room phone for phone calls to her new beau Jose Ferrer in London. The Andrews Sisters of "Boogie Woogie Bugle Boy" fame cut a duet with Red Foley. Georgia Gibbs brought New York attitude and salty language to her sessions. The Castle engineers felt their way into the new era of multitrack recording and overdubbing, the art of layering new parts over prerecorded tracks. They fooled around with novel effects like echo or reverb, primitive though they were.

Fooling around was really what the jiggers did best. Keeping the machinery running at WSM was by now way past routine, and their attempts to relieve boredom ran the gamut from trying to crack up on-air announcers through the control room glass to outright pranks. Buddy Killen remembered a time when the engineers helped announcers David Cobb and Ernie Keller try to undo the buttoned-up announcer Tom Hanserd. "[Tom] was so intense. He just really wanted to do a good job, and every little thing bothered him. So one time they put someone else in another studio doing the news, and Tom thought he was doing the news. So they put him 'on the air' and he starts reading. And the microphone says, 'Tom stop spittin' on me!' [They had secreted a tiny speaker under the grill of the microphone and were talking from the control room.] Well, he just kept reading. And it said again, 'I said, dammit stop spittin' on me!' He just went into spastic disorder." About the same time, when DeWitt was about to marry the woman with whom he'd spend the rest of his life, the engineers, in keeping with their penchant for diagramming complex solutions, posted a chart on the wall depicting how the couple might spend their wedding night.

But in the studio, the fun mingled with a studied professionalism. Castle proved a worthy base for the first wave of major-label record men who came to Nashville trying to expand and develop the hillbilly record business. Outsiders all, they shaped the studio system for generations to come. "Uncle Art" Satherley, an Englishman with precise diction and perfectly pleated suits, represented the majestic Columbia Records. He made records by Bill Monroe, Red Foley, and George Morgan. Paul Cohen of Decca Records exuded contagious enthusiasm on his regular two-to-three-week stays in Nashville, and, of course, the Castle men were all comfortable around his part-time assistant, WSM's moonlighting Owen Bradley. Among their sessions: Ernest Tubb, Kitty Wells, and Webb Pierce. From Capitol, Ken Nelson and Lee Gillette steered sessions. Nelson oversaw the work of Hank Thompson, Faron Young, Sonny James, and the Louvin Brothers, while Gillette engaged Castle to cut pop records, like Ray Anthony's "Marshmallow World" and "Stardust." Aaron Shelton also fondly remembered Don Law, another Englishman who followed behind his mentor Satherley at Columbia. Law, who worked with Jimmy Dickens, Carl Smith, and Lefty Frizzell, among others, was "a rather conservative person with a subdued, dry sense of humor, a large amount of musical knowledge, and a well-controlled taste for good Canadian whiskey," Shelton wrote. "Don had an iron-clad rule—well at least a tin-foil-clad rule—that he would not take a drink until after the recording of the third tune of a session. But he once told me, after looking around to be sure that no one else heard, that he might occasionally record the third tune first."

Castle also fostered the first cadre of top Nashville session musicians who would come to be known as the A Team. Many, like piano player Marvin Hughes and guitarist Jack Shook, were WSM veterans. Farris Coursey, a drummer from *Sunday Down South* and many other WSM shows, kept time with sticks, or in the case of "Chattanoogie Shoe-Shine Boy" with a snapping rag. Owen Bradley's production duties for Decca opened the door for another piano player, Floyd Cramer, to add his signature slip-note style to records. Grady Martin, a guitarist from Little Jimmy Dickens's Country Boys band, brought a virtuosic versatility to the studio. A new crop of daring, fleet-fingered fiddlers was epitomized by Tommy Jackson, best remembered for his fire-breathing take on the "Orange Blossom Special." As sliding steel guitar became a hallmark of honky-tonk music, Ohio-born Jerry Byrd became nearly as much a fixture at Castle as the piano and piano bench. Here's where the camaraderie and informal collaboration of the Nashville studio was born. These were mostly southern men who talked to one another the way southern men talk, with wit and a gift for narrative, irreverent but respectful, and always serious about the music.

Conventional wisdom held that television would be the death of radio, and although the obituary was premature, the adjustments were hard. The radio networks hemorrhaged sponsorships and had to cut rates and talent budgets. Hundreds of stations parted ways with the networks and turned to local businesses, which boosted their radio advertising 400 percent between 1946 and 1958. Transistors made radios smaller and more portable. They became standard in automobiles, and the formula of gathering around the radio for scheduled shows gave way to the personal, on-the-go, all-the-time-companion model we know today.

These changes threatened country radio barn dances everywhere, not to mention WSM's very approach to programming. Craig and DeWitt ended their ten-year experiment with FM broadcasting in March of 1951, ostensibly due to a shortage of electronic gear stemming from the Korean War effort. But on the AM side, the company recommitted WSM to the live-radio ethic, with the Grand Ole Opry as a cultural and commercial showpiece. Waugh took out full-page ads in *Variety, Time,* and *Fortune* magazines, brazenly asserting WSM radio's strength and vitality, urging that sponsors not "bury them alive." Two years later, WSM applied to *Variety* for its showmanship award with a highly produced audio pitch—a set of four fifteen-minute transcription discs—targeted by name to the magazine's editor, George Rosen. Over a swelling orchestral theme reminiscent of the score of *Gone With the Wind*, an announcer asked rhetorically, "Mr. Rosen, did we do what we said?" Did we not, he queried, live up to our promise of the 1951 *Variety* advertisement to expand, rather than cut, live programming? The presentation sampled Dolores Watson's sparkling vocals from a show called *Tin Pan Valley* as "the kind of thing people said we wouldn't be doing in 1953." Further, the station bragged that "music is a big business in Nashville, and WSM has made it so." It cited articles from magazines like *Nation's Business, Collier's Weekly* and the *New York Times* magazine noting that "the balance of power has shifted" from New York and Hollywood in the entertainment business. In a bit of aural theater, the announcer asked Mr. Rosen to walk over to "Joe" at his adding machine, who tallied up 904 live network feeds in 1953 alone. And they could claim that not only did the Opry play to "the biggest studio audience in the world" for a radio show, but that it boasted an incredible sixty-six performers who had released at least one hit record in the prior year. The pitch paid off. *Variety* named WSM the best all-around radio station in the United States.

TEN   *Jack, We Got a Real Problem*

"*Howdy you'nses! This is your bald-headed, hand-spanked, corn-fed, gravy-sopping, snaggle-toothed, cross-eyed old country boy, Eddie Hill, telling you he crochiates your cards and letters and is a hawg about you!*"

In coat and tie, surrounded by records, he sat before an open microphone and a pair of industrial-weight turntables in a small studio on the fifth floor of the National Life building on a winter's night in 1952. Wide-eyed and wired with enthusiasm, "Smilin'" Eddie Hill sounded like nothing that had ever been broadcast from the Air Castle of the South. He was a thirty-year-old hillbilly singer, instrumentalist, and humorist from Benton, Tennessee, "just several ax-handles, five wagon greasin's and a few cucumber vines from Nashville," as he put it. And although he came off as a nut, he was a powerful man, a disc jockey whose nightly show was a 50,000-watt bully pulpit for country music made in Music City.

"To me he was the most powerful DJ at that time in the business," said Opry star Mac Wiseman. "Several times, [when] I'd record at Castle Studios, we'd run off an acetate dub, and I'd hotfoot it right up the hill with that acetate, and within two or three hours of singing into that microphone, Eddie had it on the air. It was a scoop for him. My advantage was that the other radio stations monitored Eddie all the time because they knew he got the scoops. I'd get it on Eddie's show while it was still sizzling, because I knew how many other disc jockeys were waiting with baited breath for a new release."

By the early 1950s there were indeed hundreds of country DJs around the nation, as live radio gave way to the more economical format of a personality spinning records. Conservative WSM, habitually resistant to anything but live or network radio, came slowly to the new era. Nashville's WMAK and WKDA had prominent country DJ shows by the end of 1948. And WSM did give some of its stars like Francis Craig and Snooky Lanson short pop-record shows as early as 1947. But not until the early 1950s did WSM come to grips with the reality that DJs were displacing barn dances like the Grand Ole Opry as the key star-makers in what *Billboard* magazine was now calling "country and western" music. Many in management and most of the station's employees moonlighting in music publishing and record production had a strong interest in making sure that WSM's cadre of artists were well promoted to these far-flung taste-makers. Much of WSM's tumultuous 1950s was shaped by the steps it took to court and leverage the influence of this new army of country music evangelists.

One exemplar, a rail-thin twentysomething named Tom Perryman, could be found barking over his microphone in Gladewater, Texas. He had been raised on a farm near the oil fields of East Texas, where his late father had been a field geologist. In 1943 he badly injured his back in a rough school yard game, and as part of a difficult recovery, he endured spinal fusion surgery, among the first ever done in Dallas. "After that surgery I was in plaster casts from my knees to my neck for about three or four months and laid up at the hospital and then later in a hospital bed out at the farmhouse," he recalled. To endure the staggering boredom and discomfort (he once let his cat in his bed, and fleas got in his body cast), he listened to the radio, the Grand Ole Opry included, via NBC. He paid special attention to the announcers—to Louie Buck, David Cobb, and Jud Collins—and tried to imitate their commanding, resonant tones. He remembers it as learning to "illustrate with his voice."

After a brief stint in the Navy, where he received basic radio training, Perryman worked as a operator/announcer/disc jockey at KEBE in Tyler, where his first country record show was billed as the "KEBE CO-ral." Next came the Gladewater job, where he launched the "Hillbilly Hit Parade." At the same time, he began arranging live shows in the area, signing up talent from the artist service bureau of the *Louisiana Hayride,* an influential radio barn dance located just a few miles away in Shreveport, Louisiana. Perryman's first show as a promoter drew a big crowd in Jacksonville, Texas, to see Hank Williams, Johnnie & Jack, Kitty Wells, and Slim Whitman in 1948. He also touted, on the air and at live shows, local strivers like future superstar Jim Reeves. And in this he was not alone. A generation of DJs throughout the South and Midwest promoted artists and live shows as a natural extension of their roles as personalities and taste-makers in their local communities. "[We] were just star-struck egomaniacs," he says, half joking. "Let's face it, the disc jockey in these markets was as much of a star as the artist was. Because they were there every day." This manifold life they led—as DJ, interviewer, talent developer, and show promoter—was a vital part of the growth of country music in the postwar years.

One of the few people in Nashville who knew what Tom Perryman and his small-town colleagues were up to was Murray Nash, employee of the now thriving Acuff-Rose publishing company. Formerly a talent scout for RCA and Mercury Records, Nash was, by 1952, promoting records featuring Acuff-Rose songs directly to DJs. Consequently, at a time before there were full-time country "format" radio stations, Nash compiled a nearly complete list of disc jockeys playing country music shows on general-purpose radio stations around the nation.

How that list became the genesis of WSM's vibrant and vitally important "Disc Jockey Festival" is a subject of conflicting memory. Nash said that he approached Jim Denny with the DJ list and the idea of inviting the DJs to Nashville in November, ostensibly to celebrate the birthday of the Grand Ole Opry. Denny, Nash said, ruled the idea out as too expensive and complicated. Nash said he also got turned down by Jack Stapp and then public relations director Bill McDaniel. So Nash took on the invitations himself, asking only that WSM provide letterhead and postage. Wesley Rose confirmed that Acuff-Rose printed the invitations and stuffed the envelopes, while WSM ran them through its postal meter.

McDaniel took credit for the idea in a 1960s *Billboard* retrospective. "Although we were well aware of the importance of the disc jockeys in the promotion of the 'Opry,' we had never really gone out of our way to encourage their effect on the music," he recalled. "We had recently learned that we could obtain a fairly reliable list of the nation's disc jockeys so the idea was conceived to entertain them at the party in Nashville on the night of the anniversary performance of the Grand Ole Opry."

Still others say it was Bill McDaniel's new assistant Harrianne Moore. In her version, she overheard Murray Nash and McDaniel talking aimlessly about the list and volunteered the idea. "I said to Bill McDaniel, 'Look, you've got a list of all the country music disc jockeys. So why not invite them to a celebration of the Grand Ole Opry's birthday?'" she said in 2004. She couldn't recall what Nash was doing at WSM with the DJ list, but she was quite confident in her story. Moreover, publisher Buddy Killen backs her up, and Irving Waugh publicly applauded her for her idea at a banquet in 1970.

In any event, 672 invitations went out with scarcely two weeks' notice. Many jocks, like Perryman, sent word back that they'd have loved to come but there was no time to arrange travel and coverage of their shifts. Those who did arrive on November 22, 1952, were given entrée to the ballroom at the Andrew Jackson Hotel. Irving Waugh remembered a quiet gathering of fewer than one hundred people, including a few wives who'd come along. Waugh consulted with Jack Stapp, who ran back to Seventh and Union to round up a bunch of National Life secretaries to come over to mingle and liven things up. Waugh led the applause when the Solemn Old Judge cut the Opry birthday cake, and stars like Jimmy Dickens, Minnie Pearl, Red Foley, Ray Price, and Cowboy Copas glad-handed DJs from twenty states. By the time the day was over, the DJs had met dozens of Opry stars, walked the halls and studios of WSM, seen the mysterious city of Nashville for the first time, and met one another. A fraternity was in the making, one born of enthusiasm and a burgeoning marketplace. They went back to their stations and talked on the air about what a time they'd had in Music City.

WSM followed up with a newsletter that spotlighted record releases and live appearances by Opry artists, plus news items and talking points for DJs across the country. It emphasized the closeness of the Opry family with news of babies born or folks in the hospital. "What a disk jockey needs most is interesting information upon which to base his patter in introducing records," the station said in publicity material prepared in all likelihood for *Variety* magazine. "We decided that furnishing such material was a good way to get more of the records made by our artists played on other stations." WSM staff intervened on behalf of DJs who were having trouble getting new records from record companies, and they arranged drop-in visits by Opry stars at radio studios around the country. It built relationships with DJs in Europe and Japan. Which all means that by the mid-1950s, WSM and the Opry's Artist Service Bureau were acting like the promotions arm of a large record company, engaging in multipronged assaults on the hearts and minds of DJs around the country and the world.

When management approved a second convention for November 1953, the public relations department officially named the event the Disc Jockey Festival, while it remained informally known as the Opry birthday party. This time, Tom Perryman did come and found that more than four hundred others had done so too. He met dozens of DJs who were promoting country music on record, live in their studios, and in gymnasiums, auditoriums, Elks Lodges, and churches around the country. He found that a variety of industry players were fleshing out the November weekend into a sprawling, exhausting good time. Record companies and music publishers sponsored hospitality suites and receptions. *Country Song Roundup* magazine threw a party. Acuff-Rose hosted a banquet on Saturday before the Opry. Ebullient Opry artist Jumpin' Bill Carlisle lived up to his nickname by jumping up on a table and performing spontaneously, giving birth to a tradition of showcases. The gathering merited coverage in *Billboard* magazine.

Also that year, the performing rights organization BMI gave its first-ever awards for Nashville songwriters. The idea came from another young woman working ostensibly in a support capacity, WSM receptionist Frances Williams. "I went to Bob Burton, who ran BMI, and I said, 'I think that you should have an award for your songwriters,'" she related. "He liked the idea, but the only time not filled in by a lunch or dinner was Friday breakfast. He said, 'Nobody will come out to hear songwriters or see songwriters at seven thirty.'" Williams replied, "The songwriters will come. You open the door, they will be there." And sure enough, Nashville's first great modern songwriters, including a number of prominent stars who wrote for Acuff-Rose or Hill and Range, came to assert their own place in a blossoming industry. A house band, with Owen Bradley, Harold Bradley, and Chet Atkins played the songs that had earned the most radio airplay over the past year. "I knew some songwriters, and I knew how sensitive they were, and how they were never rewarded," Frances Williams Preston said in 2004. "And I saw all the stars get all the big awards, and this little guy sits here, and he wrote it, and gets no recognition." Not many years later, Preston was asked to set up and run BMI's southern regional office in Nashville, setting her on a path that she would take to the top of BMI and the music industry nationally. All because she naturally took to heart what would become a Nashville credo: "It all begins with a song."

Yet another WSM tradition had been born by the second DJ convention—a Friday night show celebrating platter spinners from across the nation, *Mr. DeeJay USA*. Another Jack Stapp inspiration, Mr. DeeJay invited one DJ each week to travel to Nashville, stay at the Hermitage or Andrew Jackson, and go to dinner with star announcer Grant Turner. Then the DJ got to host his own show on WSM from 10:30 to midnight, after the *Friday Night Frolics*, spinning records and interviewing artists who stuck around after the Studio C show ended. Launched May 16, 1953, Mr. DeeJay featured jocks from stations large and small. Major-market hotshots were recognized, and small-town jocks got to feel like king for a day. Being invited to be Mr. DeeJay during the DJ convention was a particular honor, and that's what happened to Tom Perryman in November 1954. He did his segment live from the lobby of the Andrew Jackson Hotel. "If you got to come up here and be the guest of WSM and the Opry and meet and hobnob with all of these people whose records you'd been playing, you were part of 'em," Perryman remembered. "It was the greatest thing that could happen to a small town disc jockey."

The times were marked, Perryman said, by fellowship and a spirit that welcomed newcomers and cherished established stars. Out in the country, artists could drop in radio stations, visit with the air personalities, and play a few songs, just by showing up. In Nashville, the camaraderie played out in more formal ways than merely the dice and card games in the halls and the impromptu performances in the smoke-filled hotel suites. The DJs got organized. The earliest attempts at corralling far-flung jocks into an association foundered, but on November 21, 1953, the Country Music Disc Jockeys Association (CMDJA) was born, with about one hundred charter members. Its published objective: "to further a greater and more widespread public acceptance of country music through the betterment of country music disc jockey programs." Perryman was on the board. Nelson King of WCKY in Cincinnati was named president. None of the officers were from Nashville, though WSM disc jockeys Eddie Hill and Joe Allison signed on as members. A statement issued that fall made it clear that despite its origins at WSM's convention, "WSM is in no way responsible for the formation of the organization."

If WSM was late in coming with DJ shows, it had only to look locally for a model of how to do them right. WLAC had joined the 50,000-watt clear channel club in 1942, some years after being launched, then sold, by National Life's hometown competitor, Life & Casualty. Despite a robust presence in Nashville life, WLAC never managed to become the promotional goldmine WSM had for National Life. Suffering from the Depression, Life & Casualty sold WLAC to its general manager, J. Truman Ward, soon after Ward became president of the National Association of Broadcasters in 1934. In the 1940s, the station carried the CBS lineup in Nashville, including stars like George Burns,

Eddie Cantor, and Lum & Abner. It maintained a staff orchestra that regularly played the network, produced live drama, and hosted scores of hillbilly artists (including some WSM performers looking for extra work).

After World War II, WLAC took an unexpected turn. By adopting record shows and by setting a remarkable group of disc jockeys free to explore music without prejudice, WLAC became the voice of the Other Music City—the rhythm & blues ferment happening in clubs along Jefferson Street—the black yin to WSM's white yang over Nashville's clear channel, nation-reaching airwaves.

Although black music was heard over WLAC as early as 1939, it wasn't associated with specific air personalities until Gene Nobles discovered a new audience in 1946. At the suggestion of some students from one of Nashville's black universities, Nobles experimented with boogie-woogie, blues, and jazz on his nighttime record show, to great public response. He played Louis Armstrong, Pearl Bailey, Billie Holiday, and Fats Waller, said his studio engineer Bill Rainey in 2001. "We began to get notes and letters from people requesting that kind of music. He realized he had a pretty good thing going there." Historian Martin Hawkins wrote that by the time Bill "Hoss" Allen joined the air staff in 1949, "most of the evening hours were given over to black music. Station owner Ward found that he had carved out a niche for himself. 'We realized there was no other station covering the South playing R & B late at night like that,' he said in 1975." A third jock, John Richbourg, known on air as John R., had been on staff since 1942, but when he got in the swing of WLAC's new R & B sound in his late-night shift, he was able to offer vital early exposure to artists like Otis Redding, Marvin Gaye, and Little Richard. He knew and supported many of the musicians; Ella Fitzgerald sang at his funeral.

Speaking in chilled-out, soulful voices that many listeners mistook as black, Allen, Richbourg, and Nobles tapped a world of music that had been right under southern culture's collectively upturned noses for decades. Music from "race" and "sepia" lines of the major labels, along with vital artists on independents like Chess, Atlantic, and Savoy, exploded to a $25-million business by 1955, thanks to stations like WLAC spinning the sounds that were coalescing into rock and roll. Locally, WLAC's DJs drew from and promoted a thriving new Nashville record economy, with labels like Bullet, Republic, Tennessee, Excello, and Dot. Hawkins observed that "while the majors [labels] saw Nashville solely in terms of country music, the independent labels bridged the two solitudes of black and white music. In other words, they reflected the Nashville music scene as it really was."

WLAC's white DJs saw with musical, commercial, and perhaps even moral clarity something that eluded WSM's patrician owners and many of its country-loving partisans. WLAC's audience, which included Elvis, Johnny Cash, Jerry Lee Lewis, and many other white rockers with country roots, grasped it too. Rhythm and blues was country music's sibling. Both were forged from folk and gospel influences, some overlapping, some distinct to racial experience. Country's "ancient tones" (to borrow a Bill Monroe expression) traced an Anglo-Saxon thread to England, Scotland, and Ireland; R & B was animated by the joy, discipline, and abandon of the African drum circle, albeit tempered by generations of enslavement and discrimination. Yet both spoke to and for common people and their most profound, most universal concerns. Both offered a bridge to the other, for anyone wise enough to follow their ears across.

Unfortunately, even as the historic and dichotomous contrasts of Nashville's two 50,000 watters inspired some great American musicians to integrate white country and black R & B, WSM replied with little but cultural and economic myopia. Rock and roll was, for WSM, a genre non grata when it barreled out of Memphis in 1954. Ralph Emery, the legendary WSM DJ of the 1960s, explained the station's conservatism as more than prudishness, but a kind of loyalty to its original audiences. "There was more profit in rock than country in the waning 1950s. The WSM listenership was down and could have been improved by playing rock & roll," he said in his autobiography. "But [management] was more concerned about keeping its initial, pre-Depression families of listeners." Thus when urban renewal efforts and the Capitol Hill Redevelopment Project bulldozed the slums behind the National Life building, including several important black nightspots, and when National Life at last installed air conditioning in 1953 (one year after the hottest summer on record) and employees had to be reminded to keep their windows closed at all times, it marked an unwitting metaphor for the insularity of WSM in the coming decade.

The station nurtured its new pop singers like Buddy Hall, Dottie Dillard, and Dolores Watson, cultivating a sweet and genteel sound that could, depending on the song and the mood, be serene and moving or insufferably cloying. Hall was the station's replacement for Snooky Lanson after he left for *Your Hit Parade*. A former Arthur Godfrey "Talent Scout" singer and a Perry Como fan, Hall was one of thirty-eight singers who auditioned for Jack Stapp and Owen Bradley on a recruiting trip to New York. Dillard, a member of the Anita Kerr singers, excelled at playful lyrics and perfect diction. She could be heard on many of the station's routine variety shows, such as *Sing for Your Supper,* sponsored by "carefully cup tested" American Ace Coffee. There, backed by Owen Bradley's orchestra, her take on songbook standards was supple and charming.

Dolores Watson's voice evoked more of a satiny, candle-lit ambience. She arrived in the late 1940s after winning a talent contest in her hometown of Rome, Georgia. Initially, Bradley hired her to sing with his dance band at the Plantation Club on Murfreesboro Road. But soon, she had her own shows on WSM. One early delight was *Dreamtime,* where her singing, backed only by Chet Atkins's gentlemanly guitar, proved airy and transcendent. For that matter, Atkins, then blossoming into Nashville's premiere guitarist and producer, was a regular presence on WSM in the 1950s. None of his shows was remembered more fondly by music aficionados than *Two Guitars,* an unrehearsed exploration of the crossroads of country, pop, and jazz with the legendary steel guitarist Jerry Byrd.

WSM missed its most obvious chance to bless and benefit from the unarranged marriage of country and R & B when Elvis Presley played the Grand Ole Opry on October 2, 1954, just three months after recording "That's All Right" and "Blue Moon of Kentucky" at Sun Records in Memphis. That most famous of all early rock and roll recording sessions spoke to the fusion Elvis was creating. The latter song came from the pen of Bill Monroe, a certified Opry star and father of bluegrass music. The former was an R & B song by Arthur "Big Boy" Crudup. And perhaps the melding of those styles with pop crooning and hillbilly music would have played better with the Opry audience and staff had Elvis merely looked more like the new breed of emerging country smoothies, say Jim Reeves or Sonny James. Presley couldn't have been more polite or deferential on that night at the Ryman, and he was well received over at Ernest Tubb's *Midnite Jamboree,* but his pink shoes and his gyrating hips left the Opry crowd cold, whereas they'd gone crazy for Hank Williams, who shook his knees but did not swivel his pelvis.

When Elvis came to Nashville for the following year's DJ convention, both *Cashbox* and *Billboard* had picked him as the most promising new country and western artist on the horizon. Frances Williams signed him in at the registration desk. "I'll never forget that, because he had on mascara, and he had on blue rhinestone cufflinks. And no man ever wore blue rhinestone cufflinks or mascara," she said. Jack Stapp told folks they'd better take notice of Elvis, because he was going to be huge. Nevertheless, WSM let him get away. Elvis would spend much of the next two years building his career down in Shreveport on the stage of the Opry's chief competitor, the *Louisiana Hayride.* Tom Perryman booked him enthusiastically in East Texas starting in 1954. But WSM officials and Nashville's new country entrepreneurs spent much of the mid-1950s upset that Elvis and his ilk were destroying the market for country music by drawing off young people. Perhaps the truth is that WSM's roots in the segregated South blinded its leaders to an opportunity disguised as a musical rapprochement of black and white. Elvis, who would wind up being enshrined in the Country Music Hall of Fame in 1998, had deep roots in country and a preternatural love of black music. But the Opry establishment, for all its virtues, couldn't see that far in 1954.

The drama in Nashville began to attract the attention of the music trade press. With recording, publishing, radio, and touring, Nashville now had the pieces in place to begin shaping the music business. *Billboard* and *Cashbox* began to cover the city with regular stringers. The most famous of those early reporters was a tiny man from Knoxville with a Popeye face, a cigar typically wagging from his teeth, and a tour de force talent for "doubletalk" that could seduce, beguile, embarrass, and delight even the least gullible sorts. Charlie Lamb's story reads like a John Irving novel: his mother was a trapeze artist, his father a circus entrepreneur, animal trainer, ventriloquist, and magician. Despite a peripatetic childhood, he got as far in school as some prelaw undergraduate work at the University of Tennessee, and during World War II he became an undercover cop for the Army Air Corps, though he weighed in at about 105 pounds. He got married in Mississippi while stationed there, then moved to Knoxville, where he became a copy boy and then a reporter for the *Knoxville Journal*. Like a hummingbird hopping from flower to flower, it was on to radio and concert booking. WROL had an artist service bureau for the pickers and singers it employed. Among them were two future Nashville star acts, the bluegrass duo Flatt & Scruggs and the tough and handsome Carl Smith. Lamb promoted shows for both, riding around Knoxville in a car with his pal Buddy Killen, barking about the night's bill over electric megaphones on the car roof.

Somehow, when *Cashbox* magazine decided it needed a Nashville "rep" around 1951, Charlie was the right man at the right time. "Rep" implied both reporter *and* representative, capable of simultaneously gathering news and selling ads to the very people he was soliciting for stories. (What we would now call a conflict of interest was in that day regarded as getting by in new industry on a shoestring.) With three children to support and pittance pay,

Lamb commuted for a time before he moved, eschewing hotels and sometimes writing his column by the side of the road on a manual typewriter. "Often I would shave in a cold creek at Crossville, before coming to Nashville," he told Nashville writer Walt Trott. "Finally, I had to have some place where people could contact me, so I paid a parking attendant next to the Ryman twenty-five cents a day to answer the phone there and say 'Charlie Lamb Agency.' I gave it out as my telephone number."

One of the first things Charlie Lamb did in Nashville was visit Jim Denny, boss of the Opry. Frances Williams directed him toward Denny's office. Next he knew, Lamb was talking to a man more than twice his size, confidently stating his business: "To tell him I was in town and that I was writing columns and so forth and I was covering the Grand Ole Opry and I would like to have some kind of freedom of entrée with him and with the different people here." The Opry was getting sporadic coverage from various newspapers, but Lamb told Denny he was ready to take on the Opry entertainment matrix as a full-time beat.

After that, Lamb virtually lived at WSM. "In gathering my news, I would go to the fifth floor at lunch time for the dinner bell show [*Noontime Neighbors*]. And all the artists were there that weren't on the road. They picked their mail up there," he said. He went back for the *Friday Night Frolics* and never missed an Opry. "I was just living and working and breathing Grand Ole Opry. I made tight friendships with all the officers and executives of the station, because I saw to it that every one of them ended up one way or the other in my column." That column gave Lamb the springboard he needed to launch his own *Country Music Reporter* in 1956, the first music business periodical published in Nashville.

Charlie Lamb, if he didn't sense it immediately, found out that Frances Williams was no mere receptionist. She was a bright, observant, and poised young woman with a college degree and a kernel of certainty that the one option she was being offered by her situation in life—teaching school—wasn't sufficient. Pressed by her father to get a summer job, she reluctantly agreed to be a "messenger girl," delivering mail at National Life. "In the radio station there was always activity and there was always music, and there were stars. So they got their mail pretty often," she recalled. "And the Death Claims Division is probably still looking for their mail, because I just wasn't too interested in those other areas of an insurance company." One day, she noticed that the WSM receptionist was pregnant; at

National Life, Shield Babies may have been celebrated in the newsletter, but they marked the end of a Shield Girl's career. Williams knew this. She approached Jim Denny about the job. "So he called, and the human resources manager said, 'You can have her. She's not worth a damn.' So anyway, I got my job as receptionist at WSM."

Today, Frances Williams Preston remembers WSM being *green*. "Green vinyl floors, a round green and gray desk. Very institutional looking," she said. And as busy as a bus station. One observer from the day likened WSM's lobby to Times Square on election night, another to New York's Radio City. Song pluggers came in from New York to meet with Stapp or the orchestra leaders. Colonel Tom Parker and other manager/promoters squatted in the lobby doing business—sometimes in competition with Denny's artist bureau—over WSM's free phones. Scores of musicians passed by with their cases, coats, and hats. Opry stars came in to check their mail. And there were disc jockeys and announcers, engineers, delivery men, and dozens of public figures large and small, who came to do brief talks about anything from the doings of the Ladies Hermitage Association to running for Senate. "We had politicians coming in, because we were a clear channel station, and they had free time," Preston said. "So that meant that a politician doing an interview or a program on WSM could be heard all over the United States."

With Denny down the hall running the Artist Service Bureau, a good bit of the traffic through her lobby consisted of trusted band members, family members, and managers hauling road receipts. "I can remember Bill Monroe's girl Bessie, Big Bessie, they called her," said Preston. "She'd bring—it looked like a valise, a large bag, a purse like thing—full of cash. And they would sit there in that office on the fifth floor and count out thousands and thousands of dollars, when they were paying their fees to the Artist Bureau."

Besides greeting visitors, Williams's chief duty was to answer fan mail—requests for pictures, bizarre testimonials of idol worship, and dead earnest suggestions of how characters on the soap operas should handle their problems. But she was restless and looked for other things to do. Marjorie Cooney, who was still doing her Ann Ford news broadcast, took a liking to the much younger Frances and encouraged her natural self-starter qualities. "Nudge, nudge, nudge," she'd say when a good idea came up, and Williams was usually more than game to bring it to fruition. She drove large parts of the DJ convention logistics. She developed, scripted, and hosted a fashion show for WSM-TV. When she was elected "Miss Fire Prevention" for the annual safety parade cosponsored by WSM and WLAC, she pushed the predictable role into new territory by jumping off a tall fire engine ladder into a rescue net. And she did color commentary for WSM-TV's coverage of the Iroquois Steeplechase, a cross-country horse race and high-society social held in a large park south of the city. WSM had covered them all on radio and took on the ambitious job of putting the event on television. Williams cruised the upper-crust crowd in their Old South regalia and tried her best to coax answers out of Belle Meade matrons, who largely froze in the presence of the WSM-TV cameras.

Williams didn't know she was preparing herself to be one of Nashville's first female business executives and eventually the corporate CEO of BMI worldwide. "There were so few things for women to do," she said from behind a desk at Nashville's BMI office in 2004. "I knew I didn't want to type. I knew I didn't want to be a secretary. And it probably was the best thing I ever did, because if I'd learned to type, I might still be sitting somewhere behind a desk with a computer now." The vast desktop was, indeed, computer free.

It was just a matter of time before Jim Denny's aggressive mix of booking, management, and publishing got him in trouble with WSM artists and management. When Jack DeWitt began to suspect that the Artist Service Bureau chief was booking shows on the side, he audited Denny's books in the summer of 1953 but found nothing amiss. But Ernest Tubb fell out with Denny. And so did Roy Acuff, who asked for a meeting with DeWitt in early 1955 to complain that Denny was giving the best shows to his cronies and leaving others the crumbs. Denny replied that Acuff himself wanted special treatment. Acuff, wrote Albert Cunniff, called "secret meetings with the Opry talent to air his complaints about Denny and to try to have Denny taken down a notch—or dismissed." Others have said that Acuff and Denny were in a struggle to be the top power player at the Opry.

When Opry stars began to generate hit after hit from songs published by Denny's company, Cedarwood, it really raised eyebrows. Buddy Killen, looking back in 2004, said Jim Denny was "the epitome of abuse . . . Cedarwood had become pretty hot [by 1955]. Jim was getting songs recorded by all the stars. And it became pretty apparent that he was utilizing his position to get that done. He was getting a lot of complaints from the artists, because everybody was looking to [WSM] to book all the Grand Ole Opry acts. And he was playing favorites." W. D. Kilpatrick, D to his friends, one of the earliest Nashville country record sales reps and talent scouts, said Denny simply held the best hand in Nashville in those days and he played it aggressively. "Good dates were that hard to come by," he said. "If you controlled the booking, then you controlled who recorded what."

At the time, Denny's defenders outnumbered his detractors. His camp included enormous stars of the day, like Carl Smith, Jimmy Dickens, and the irreproachable Minnie Pearl. When DeWitt asked every Opry member to put his or her candid thoughts about Jim Denny in writing, he "apparently received little or no bad reports," according to Cunniff's account. And in the wider world of country music, Denny just got more and more popular. In May of 1955, *Billboard* named him second runner up in its "Country and Western Man of the Year" poll, after Fred Rose, who had just died the previous December, and Steve Sholes, the producer making RCA into a major label powerhouse.

This meant little to DeWitt, who resented Denny's persona and his obviously large income. Though Denny was in the midst of a year in which his staff would arrange more than 2,500 personal appearances by Opry artists, historians agree he was booking shows on the side, making private money off the Opry brand. This was foremost in DeWitt's mind when he sent a memo to the entire WSM staff on August 2, 1955:

> "Over a period of many years various members of the WSM staff have engaged in outside business activities, some of which have not conflicted in any way with their principal job at WSM. There have been and are other businesses which conflict directly and others which may be considered to conflict by people on the outside with whom we do business. The Board of Directors of WSM, Incorporated has considered this problem very carefully and has come to the firm conclusion that it will be necessary to review all of these businesses, and in some cases require that they be terminated in the interest of harmony within our organization, and the company's present and future business relations with clients, talent, and others.

DeWitt insisted that staffers disclose, by that Friday, any outside business activities. "Failure to list businesses in full, even though the interest may be minor, or failure to receive permission to engage in new businesses in the future, will be considered a very serious matter."

The most immediate consequence of the memo was the end of the Castle studio. For years, DeWitt's attitude had been one of indulgence toward his fellow engineers, even while Edwin Craig made his displeasure over the arrangement clear. But the Castle group was somewhat ready to pack it in anyway. George Reynolds (a close friend of DeWitt who was appalled by Jim Denny) was by now vice president and technical director of WSM, Inc. Carl Jenkins was studio supervisor of WSM radio, and Shelton was chief engineer of WSM-TV, a huge job, especially on the eve of color television. Each man had more than twenty years with the company and retirement benefits beginning to build up. They ranged in age from forty-four to forty-eight, and Reynolds had already had a heart attack. Moreover, the Tulane Hotel, Castle's headquarters, was slated for demolition in a year. So, Shelton said, "we opted for the security and permanence that WSM Inc. seemed to offer."

Denny replied to DeWitt on August 4 with a memo listing Cedarwood and his newer Driftwood publishing companies. Denny disclosed that he owned principal stock in both but asserted that they were run "completely independent of my services." He followed up with a twelve-point letter, which he read in person to the WSM board. He noted that he'd been stripped of the concession business he had built, that he'd endured a clean audit of his books, and that he'd been besieged by accusations from Roy Acuff. He said he'd asked for the meeting because he'd heard from a reliable non-WSM source that people in the industry were being approached inquiring whether they might want Denny's job. Some on the board must have squirmed, because the rumor had merit. DeWitt had already inquired after Murray Nash, musicians-union chief George Cooper, and record man D Kilpatrick.

The coup didn't happen overnight, however. ("Everything up there took forever," said Killen.) While the behind-the-scenes power struggle played out, the Opry rocketed along. In October WSM announced the first ever network television exposure of the Opry, a thirteen-episode, monthly series over 130 ABC stations, sponsored by Ralston Purina. That November's DJ convention was the largest and weirdest yet, a thirtieth birthday for the Opry that featured a visit from Elvis and a famous Hank Snow publicity stunt. A live elephant paraded in front of the Andrew Jackson Hotel, wearing a banner that said "Hank Snow Never Forgets—Thanks DeeJays." Meanwhile, Denny just forged ahead at his usual breakneck pace. In March of 1956, *Billboard* named him "Country and Western Man of the Year."

But the long knives were out. Some time in early 1956, DeWitt consulted with the National Life board, which agreed that Denny needed to operate artist booking for WSM, Inc., and not for himself. "He'll have to come to toe with the establishment," is how DeWitt summed up its position. DeWitt told historian John Rumble: "We knew what was going on and we winked at it for a long time and finally (Denny) became so obstreperous that something had to be done about it. I had a real zoo going on there." DeWitt's remarks to a third interviewer suggest how DeWitt saw Denny's ultimate aims: "His main objective was to take over the Grand Ole Opry. That's what he wanted to do.

It finally got to the point where he thought he had enough strength to take it over. I don't think he thought he could force me out, but he would liked to have done it."

So on September 24, 1956, DeWitt called Denny to his office and told him the board wanted him to stay and that they'd virtually double his salary if he did, but in exchange, he'd have to divest his publishing sideline and devote all of his time and efforts to WSM. Denny said if that's the case, you'll have to fire me. It seems DeWitt did so.

Journalist Charlie Lamb says that he had warned Denny that his many conflicting interests could get him in trouble. He also says he was there in Denny's office the day of the denouement. Denny got called away to the eleventh floor, and when he came back, his eyes were glistening. He looked out the window at War Memorial Building. "They gave me the ax," Denny said.

The banner headline of the third issue of Charlie Lamb's *Country Music Reporter* read: "JIM DENNY EXITS OPRY." The story said that Denny had been "separated from all connections with the station in a surprise move by the station's management." Denny told the paper that the separation had little to do with his ownership of Cedarwood. "It is strictly a personal matter between DeWitt and myself in which DeWitt feels that no employee of the station should be better off financially than himself." Denny went on to say that he intended to pursue the rest of his career in country music, and he asked people to "stop by and say hello" at his new offices on Seventh Avenue North, just a block from National Life.

The same story reported that D Kilpatrick would be the new Opry manager. In a telegram to Opry talent, DeWitt wrote, "We have felt for some time that it would be advisable to have one person to whom all matters pertaining to the Grand Ole Opry would be referred, and we feel that Mr. Kilpatrick is well qualified to handle this position." As for Lamb, the story put his paper on the map. "I scooped *Billboard* and *Cashbox*," he said. He flew with a stack of papers to New York and handed them out personally at the Brill Building.

Denny was handling twenty-seven acts with over one hundred performers when he left WSM. Now those artists had a wrenching choice to make. Opry singer Martha Carson and her manager/husband hosted a secret meeting where Denny explained what had happened to about fifty people, including some of the biggest names in country music. He told them about his new Jim Denny Artist Bureau, which stood ready to continue on as their booking agent without interruption. The artists had to ask themselves what the Opry really meant to them and why they should remain loyal. Many saw DeWitt as imperious and uncommunicative, and his frequent mass communiqués by letter had only hardened an impression of a man with an impersonal touch. Moreover, Denny was lining up the biggest package tour in country music history, remarkable for its number of artists, its free tickets, and its sponsor, Philip Morris, arch competitor of Opry sponsor R. J. Reynolds.

"The artists all seemed to be on Jim's side," Carson said. "We had all heard that DeWitt had threatened to fire any Opry act he caught doing business with Denny, but we decided to go with Jim anyway." The mutiny included Carl Smith and Webb Pierce, who were partners in Cedarwood publishing, and some hot newcomers, including Jim Reeves, Jean Shepard, Kitty Wells, George Jones, June Carter, and Faron Young. In a telegram to DeWitt, they and their managers collectively said Denny "will represent our acts and ourselves for all phases of radio and television, both local and network."

Irving Waugh was furious. "We lost a hell of a lot of people," he recalled. "It wasn't necessary." Waugh thought Denny had been railroaded and was more than ready to turn his acidic scorn on DeWitt and new Opry manager Kilpatrick. At their first meeting at the cabin workshop behind DeWitt's home, "I was ugly with Kilpatrick," Waugh admitted. The encounter pretty much sealed how those two men felt about each other forever. Kilpatrick observed years later that whenever he was in Waugh's presence, "he looked like he was always smelling something just a little off-color."

Kilpatrick had been in town six years when he got the top Opry job. He was well liked and had produced some solid records for Mercury. But not everybody understood the choice of an A & R (artists and repertoire) man with no booking or management experience to helm the Opry and its Artist Service Bureau. Kilpatrick's chief concern was the age of the artists, especially after so many current stars had departed. "They were as old as Methuselah," he remembered. He set about recruiting new blood, and before his brief tenure was over, he would sign tall Missourian Porter Wagoner, Cajun-influenced Rusty and Doug Kershaw, Wilma Lee & Stoney Cooper, and future rock and roll heroes the Everly Brothers.

Kilpatrick also tried to reassure the shaken Opry artists with a plan to "increase the attendance at your personal appearances by more attractively and comprehensively plugging your dates." At its core was an overnight record show promoting the Opry. WSM had inaugurated overnight record shows in 1955 or 1956 with *Music All Night,* hosted alternately by Eddie Hill and another beloved country DJ, T. Tommy Cutrer. That show had been spurred in part by a new Cold War mandate that kept clear channel stations on around the clock for civil defense purposes and likely by WLAC's longstanding success in the overnight slot. But where Hill and Cutrer played a broad array of country music, Kilpatrick built his show around Opry artists. With DJ Cutrer's blessing (he was tired of the grueling shift), Kilpatrick hired Tom Perryman from Texas for the overnight slot.

Lamb's newspaper ran a story and a photo of Perryman. He had horn-rim-topped glasses perched on his forehead, a face creased by the Texas sun, and a plaid western-cut suit. He gabbed into a WSM microphone, his hand raised as if in emphasis about a particularly good record. Perryman held a contest to name the show, promising a "lifetime gold-plated admission ticket to the Grand Ole Opry" for the winning entry. And *Opry Star Spotlight,* a show that would become a WSM institution, began in the fall of 1956. "Because of WSM's dominance in the country music field," the story said, Perryman "expects to hear from lumbermen in Oregon, truck drivers in Texas, waiters in all-night restaurants in Florida and stay-up-late housewives from coast to coast." On his opening night, October 6, many celebrities and well-wishers "dropped by to wish him luck."

It seemed as if the tempests might be over. Program director Jack Stapp had quietly opted to separate from Tree Publishing and remain at WSM. *Life* magazine ran a big spread about country music and the Opry that he had worked hard to pitch. The first big event of WSM's new year was the latest hoopla homecoming by Dinah Shore. She was greeted as she got off the airplane at Berry Field by the state's first lady. She addressed the state legislature, then wafted through Nashville smiling, glad-handing, and declaring the visit "the most memorable occasion I've ever known." That night, her regular NBC variety show was telecast from the Ryman, where she appeared with Acuff in "Dinah's version of a Tennessee Barn Dance."

Trouble loomed, however, at WSM's most ambitious new project, a state-of-the-art television tower. While WSIX and WLAC had launched Channels 8 and 5 respectively in 1953 and 1954, WSM-TV, or "King Four" as it billed itself, remained the city's undisputed ratings leader, with Jud Collins as the city's most trusted newsman. So the decision to build a new transmitter in early 1957 looked like a good investment in staying number one. The site was a 670-foot hilltop in a residential neighborhood. The tower, a 1,262-foot megalith by the same Blaw-Knox company that had built the old WSM-AM tower, was to be the third highest in the country. It consisted of a triangular tube held up by guy cables at 300-foot intervals. The steel was a new alloy so special that Blaw-Knox was preparing a trade magazine ad featuring WSM's new TV tower. Jack DeWitt had told the city two years prior, "The tower we propose is a very heavy and strong tower which has safety factors far beyond anything ever built in the South."

In early February the new television studio building was complete, and a team of engineers was wiring the place up, with George Reynolds in charge. A General Electric tower engineer had come to town from Syracuse to oversee the hoisting of the actual TV transmitter to the top of the tower. On the afternoon of the fourth, four steel workers were working on the mast. Jack DeWitt and Aaron Shelton were downtown working on a new device in the WSM shop. Jack's brother Ward, whose construction company was in charge of the new TV studio building, was driving into town from the east, and he reached a point on the highway where he was used to seeing the tower—except this time, it wasn't there. At the same time, George Reynolds Jr., the engineer's son, was downtown in his office at International Printing, where he could see the TV tower, a slash on a hill in the middle distance, going up from his window. He noticed it, turned to answer a question from a colleague, turned back, and the tower was missing from the landscape. Viewers of WSM-TV's late-afternoon soap opera *Modern Romance* heard a bizarre audio malfunction. An alarmed, disembodied voice said over the broadcast, "Oh my God! Send help! The tower has just fallen down!"

Reynolds recalled that it took ten seconds for what had happened to register in his mind. "I missed it coming down," he said.

Reynolds's father had been walking under one of the guy lines when he heard an explosion and the sound of shearing metal. He and Carl Jenkins dived in a ditch and covered their heads as hundreds of tons of steel and cable slammed to the earth. Eyewitnesses said the top of the structure flew apart and showered to the ground, while about half of the tower toppled over. All four steel workers—Ray Maxwell, 27, George Presler, 33, Robert Lee Kirshner, 30, and Donald Ward Kinnan, 25—were killed. One victim landed on the roof of the broadcast building. Three trucks and a car were crushed. A dog was beheaded. Though none of the many houses nearby took a direct hit, a quiet residential neighborhood reeled at the shocking sight of morgue wagons, twisted iron, and fallen shrapnel in backyards. Blaw-Knox canceled its advertisement in the nick of time.

"To this very day, none of us closely connected to this tragedy knows exactly what went wrong," wrote Aaron Shelton in the 1980s. But some had their suspicions. George Reynolds Jr. said his father believed the tension was allowed to get radically out of balance among the three sets of guy wires and that when one became slack, the other two pulled the structure apart and then to the ground. DeWitt at least knew WSM wasn't responsible for the tower at the time of the collapse; Blaw-Knox and GE still owned it, with plans to formally turn it over to DeWitt when he was satisfied the job was done right. Still, though he was able to build a new tower of the same design on a more remote hill, DeWitt couldn't help but be haunted by the gravest engineering failure he'd ever been a party to.

Things continued to topple at the Opry as well. In late February, Webb Pierce, who'd quit the show and then come back, lashed out at the Opry in an ugly final parting. Kilpatrick announced to the newspapers that Pierce had been let go over "unwillingness to conform with long established rules and regulations." Pierce said he'd resigned, over WSM's 5 percent cut of every show he and other Opry stars played. "I do not feel they are entitled to charge us for being on the station," he said. "They call it an 'artists' fee for services,' but if I've ever gotten any services from them I'd like to know what they were!" Pierce also objected to the station using his picture and name in a National Life sales brochure. "I told Mr. Kilpatrick today that WSM should pay me for the use of my name if I have to pay them for the use of the Grand Ole Opry name," he said.

Though hard to imagine, WSM suffered even more trouble from one of its loyalists. In the predawn hours of May 27, 1957, a Monday, DeWitt was wakened by the phone. He heard station news director Bill Williams say, "Jack, we got a real problem." Williams explained that Ernest Tubb was in jail, arrested for firing a handgun in the National Life lobby. The trouble had started the previous week in Meridian, Mississippi, where annually for five years, Tubb, Hank Snow, and a slate of Opry stars had staged the Jimmie Rodgers Memorial Day Celebration, with a ticketed concert and a WSM remote broadcast from the Singing Brakeman's hometown. That year, Denny routed his free Philip Morris Country Music Show into Meridian on the same weekend, drawing away crowds Tubb and Snow had worked for years to build up. The artists were furious and remained so for many years. But Tubb, who began something of a bender that weekend, took a notion of revenge right away. According to

Tubb biographer Ronnie Pugh's meticulously researched account, Tubb woke Denny with a phone call and berated him. Denny proposed a mano-a-mano confrontation on the steps of National Life. Then he rolled over and went back to sleep, while the inebriated Tubb drove downtown in his blue Cadillac, wearing house slippers and armed with a .357 Magnum. When he arrived in the lobby, Bill Williams and announcer David Cobb were on their way in for the morning shift.

A security guard known as Mr. Lawrence confronted the singer, "Ernest, you can't have that gun in here."

"The hell I can't," Tubb replied.

Mr. Lawrence invited more trouble: "Well, you sure can't fire it."

And with the words, "Like hell I won't," Tubb aimed more or less away from everyone and fired a round into the woodwork above the elevator.

An engineer upstairs called the police, who took Tubb to the drunk tank, with Williams in tow. Opry historian Jack Hurst wrote: "While Williams waited for him to complete the mandatory three hours incarceration for public drunkenness, Tubb bought cigarettes for the other inmates and sang to and with them." The *Banner* reported that Tubb was released on bond at 9:00 a.m. and that at 10:00 a.m. he failed to appear for trial and automatically forfeited $60 in cash bonds. Harianne Moore, by then WSM's PR director, told the *Tennessean* that the shooting incident "had nothing to do with the station. It was more or less a private matter with Ernest."

The Tubb incident was the most outlandish fallout from the Denny affair, but not the last. Stapp was growing ever more aware of the fortune he could be making in publishing. Waugh had been upset by DeWitt's ultimatum, fearing (correctly) that chasing off Denny would weaken WSM's standing in the booming country music business. Moreover, he thought that DeWitt hadn't followed the board's instructions to give Denny the choice of divestiture or resignation, so tensions remained high at the station into the summer of 1957.

"We continued to battle inside for several months," Waugh said. "I then decided that I would leave and go to WSIX to run the radio/television station." DeWitt took this news poorly, blowing up at Waugh with all of his pent-up frustration over this recalcitrant, unmanageable broadcasting company. "Get the hell off the property!" he bellowed at Waugh. And another odd thing happened, Waugh said. "Stapp disappeared. I didn't know where he was. I think he later told me he was in Cincinnati. And I think he was gone nearly four weeks." Buddy Killen, Stapp's business partner, remembered it slightly differently. "He took a week off. He checked into the hospital—if I remember correctly, Baptist," said Killen with a laugh. "He didn't want them to know where he was while he made a decision about what to do. Jack had the strangest ways of doing things sometimes. It was amazing. I knew where he was, and he and I stayed in touch. But he didn't want them to be able to get to him, 'cause he was actually *working* on going to work for WKDA."

Waugh continues the story: "When I left and Stapp disappeared, DeWitt felt that the departure of both of us jeopardized possibly his position—that it looked like there was a major problem with reasonably important people in the organization. He contacted me to see if I could help him find Stapp, not to fire him but I think to try to get him to come back. I was gone only two to three days to WSIX. Mr. Craig came back to town [and] was kind enough to want me to come back. I really was not happy going to WSIX. If I'd have had an ownership position I would have felt differently. I came back, and when I did, Stapp came into the station with a written resignation, put it on DeWitt's desk, and left."

When Stapp's departure was announced on June 11, DeWitt was cordial. "Much of the success of our programming during [the last eighteen years] can be attributed to Jack Stapp," he said in the *Banner*. Lamb wrote at the time: "Affable, imperturbable, ready to work long hours whether at his desk or in rehearsal, Stapp's friends say he has lifted both the office of program manager and the programs which he directed to new highs in acceptance." And apparently, there really were no very hard feelings, for Stapp continued to produce the Prince Albert Opry for NBC. Chiefly though, he became general manager of WKDA, a fledgling rock and roll station, and returned as a partner in Tree. Ott Devine replaced Stapp as WSM program director.

At the same time, DeWitt made the most sweeping reorganization of his tenure, splitting WSM into two divisions. Bob Cooper, sales manager since 1955, and Waugh were named general managers of radio and television respectively. It marked the first time the radio station had a general manager since Harry Stone, and the demarcation of power was probably long overdue. Each broadcaster had grown rather vast. Radio included nine departments, 250 announcers, musicians, disk jockeys, news writers, copywriters, engineers, traffic, and clerical personnel. Its assets, said the *Country Music Reporter*, included "an eight-man news department, a widely recognized farm department, and one of the South's most active sports departments." TV had nearly one hundred employees on the producing, writing, and technical side, with access to a talent pool of over two hundred people, many of whom worked both stations. Waugh also hired two men who would leave major marks on WSM's televised future:

sales manager Tom Griscom and executive producer Elmer Alley, formerly of WSM radio.

Even so, stability remained elusive. Jimmy Dickens quit the Opry within a week of Ott Devine's promotion to be on Denny's Philip Morris show. In August, six-year veteran DJ Eddie Hill signed with the Jim Denny agency. The father of seven cited, in all frankness, "opportunities that will mean more to me financially." He sent his "sincere regret" to Bob Cooper. Perhaps toughest of all, R. J. Reynolds ended its sponsorship of the Prince Albert Opry after almost twenty continuous years. Harry Stone, whose drive and faith and friends at the Esty agency had kept the relationship strong for the first ten years, was of course long gone. People weren't rolling their own cigarettes as much any-more either, which Kilpatrick said was undermining demand for Prince Albert itself. Probably most important, NBC was simply going out of the live radio business. When The Prince Albert Opry wrapped on NBC on December 28, 1957, it marked the last of the radio network's live musical shows, making it one good candidate for the last gasp of the golden age of radio. Cold comfort that was to the artists and the station losing a coveted national platform. For Kilpatrick, it was a blow to his pride. "It broke my heart," he said in 2004. "I damn near cried."

As the 1957 DJ festival got rolling, twenty-four-year-old Ralph Emery couldn't help but notice that people were treating him better than he'd ever been treated in his life. Artists were approaching *him*, and other DJs acted subtly deferential. He'd been to two of these confabs before, but this was his first as an employee of WSM. Few people in the room had climbed so far. Emery grew up poor in tiny McEwen, Tennessee. In his autobiography, he called his father a drunk and his stepfather "a bum." But his mother was a devotee of WSM, and she noticed Ralph's delight in the station enough to note in his baby book that the Air Castle of the South was his favorite. He idolized Grant Turner, Louie Buck, and David Cobb. So after a difficult and introverted childhood, Emery found a job with a tiny radio station in Paris, Tennessee, which led to a better job at Nashville's WNAH. In radio he saw a career where he could be somebody and overcome a long-standing "inferiority complex." Emery studied under WLAC DJ John Richbourg at the Tennessee School of Broadcasting, where he learned to read wire copy and worked to rid his voice of its hillbilly twang.

Eventually, he landed a job at WSIX, one of Nashville's big three radio sta-tions, for $75 a week. There, Emery discovered his penchant for long, on-air interviews. A frequent visitor was newcomer Marty Robbins, a Jimmy Dickens discovery from Phoenix. "Marty would visit my show, and when the microphone was turned off, he shouted and waved his fist at the window facing WSM," Emery remembered. "'Those sons of bitches won't play my records!' he'd yell. He was especially angry at WSM's Eddie Hill." Emery did a stint at WMAK, the city's new rock and roll station. But he was fired there after a short time for warning a fellow DJ that *he* was going to be fired.

Out of work, Emery applied for the only open job in town—one that seemed out of reach. WSM's overnight slot was open again, and because he auditioned against announcers who didn't know how to spin records and talk at the same time, Emery got the job. Like so many others, he was happy to take a pay cut to go to WSM. "Every day in the studio on the bulletin board they posted your assignments," he said in 2000. "Just to see my name alongside all of those names, who as far as I was concerned were almost immortal in broadcasting, they'd been doing it for so long. And here at the end of the day was 'Emery, 10 p.m. to 5 a.m.' That was a real kick."

Morale surged at the 1957 and 1958 DJ conventions. Country music seemed back on track. Columbia Records's Mitch Miller, arguably the most powerful A & R man in the world, told the gathering, now two thousand strong, that country risked losing its soul by chasing crossover dreams. "Country writers noticed that the pop singers were taking their stuff and making hits," he said. "So they started writing their stuff for the pop singers instead of from the heart or guts, like they had been. Well you can guess what happened then. Country music lost its appeal. But the writer . . . went back to the simple, honest, straight-from-the-heart writing, and now country music is stronger than ever."

Tom Perryman remembers that around that time, disc jockeys actually started to go to seminars during WSM's confab. The two big issues he remembered were the transition from 78-rpm records to the new, lighter, harder-to-break 45s, and a musical trend being embraced by producers Chet Atkins and Owen Bradley—lush, orchestrated background vocals. The Anita Kerr Singers and the Jordanaires, an all-male counterpart, were working all the time, bringing a pop gloss to country recording sessions by the likes of Jim Reeves, Ferlin Husky, and Patsy Cline. "We had some dyed-in-the-wool traditionalist disc jockeys who, if it had [background] voices on it, then they wouldn't play it," Perryman said. "Jim Reeves was one of the very first who did that. When they took fiddle and steel out and put voices and arrangements, *God . . .* But some of us liked it." Lovers of traditional country music aren't famous for their adaptability to new musical trends, but they learned to live with, and eventually embrace, this so-called Nashville Sound. Pop-sensitive and TV-friendly, it ushered in a blockbuster era in the life of Music City.

The Country Music Disc Jockey Association, however, wasn't faring so well. After four years, the group lacked mission and money. In something of a desperation play, the CMDJA arranged a fund-raising show in Miami, tied to a record merchants' convention. D Kilpatrick and Wesley Rose helped line up talent, but the show barely covered its expenses, and at a meeting the next day, the DJs were desperate. That's when prominent Washington-area show promoter Connie B. Gay made what Kilpatrick called a "hellfire and brimstone" speech, to the effect that country music needed an industry-wide trade association, not a DJs-only support group. Such an organization could coordinate the interests of artists, managers, publishers, record companies, and radio stations, through an evenly parceled out board of directors. With that, the disbanding of the CMDJA was set in motion, and its remaining $1,250 was offered toward the launch of the Country Music Association (CMA).

The CMA's first organizational meeting at the 1958 DJ convention empowered Kilpatrick to hire a secretary for the fledgling trade association. An associate of Jack Stapp suggested her friend Jo Walker for the job. Walker only took it because she knew and respected Gay and Rose and because she was restless. "I knew nothing about country music," she said. "In fact I'd never been to the Grand Ole Opry." It scarcely mattered. Walker's role was to assist a hand-picked executive director—in other words, a man.

In WSM's Studio C, on November 20, 1958, a CMA board of directors was selected. When Ernest Tubb suggested recruiting Harry Stone as the first executive director, all other candidates were dropped. Everyone, it seemed, wanted Stone back in a managerial role again, and when asked, he agreed to move from New Orleans, where he was managing a television station, to take the job.

"I always thought he was a perfect person for that position," Walker (now Jo Walker-Meador) said in 2004. "Harry was homesick, I think, and anxious to come back to Nashville." Unfortunately, the nascent CMA had no budget and no plan for revenue, an oversight that caught Stone off guard. "Harry thought that the big record companies were already putting money into CMA," said Walker. "[In fact] the board was looking to Harry to find ways to raise funds to support the association. It was sort of a general misunderstanding there. We had no money. My salary was practically nothing. So Harry just stayed ten months." All wasn't lost for Stone. His many friends in the country music business made some introductions and helped him land a job with the Tennessee Electric Cooperative Association, which he kept until he died in 1968.

Jo Walker, however, stepped up and patiently built an organization that sponsored industry-wide awards and marshaled demographic data for the nation's advertising agencies. It lobbied radio stations to adopt an all-country format; a great many of them did. The CMA could count only eighty-one full-time country stations in America in 1961. By the time Jo Walker-Meador retired in 1991, there were more than 2,100.

Jack DeWitt, an engineer accustomed to control and finely machined moving parts, must have wondered whether he'd done the right things for WSM during the turbulent 1950s. The upheavals couldn't have been entirely his doing, he would have rationalized. He didn't condone guns going off in lobbies and off-the-books shenanigans. But had he sold the Opry out, dethroned it prematurely? Or had he steered the soberest possible course through a personality crisis and an inevitable bubble burst?

The best answer to this question lies in what happened to country music in Nashville as a result of DeWitt's most courageous decision—to ban moonlighting and live with the consequences. WSM's short-term loss was Nashville's boon. When Stapp and Denny were forced to leave WSM, their businesses achieved a legitimacy and autonomy they had not enjoyed before. Cedarwood, Driftwood, and Tree joined Acuff-Rose to further flesh out the skeleton of Nashville's new music business. Their rivalry fueled profits, which hired new writers and inspired further competitors to get into the business. Their cooperation, both in the context of the CMA and the day-to-day sharing of ideas and even songs, described a new community that was about to seduce a large part of the music and business culture out in the United States.

When Castle studio closed in 1955, it had a similar effect on recording. New studios began to meet the demand that Castle had fostered and served. The most important, indeed the seminal Music Row business, was Owen Bradley's studio at 804 Sixteenth Avenue. In about 1955, Owen and brother Harold knocked the first floor out of a house to create a high-ceilinged audio study. About a year later, they had a soon-to-be-famous Quonset hut erected on the same property for sound and film. Bradley got away with his own, less-disruptive moonlighting until producing for Decca became more lucrative and all consuming than his WSM work. In May of 1958 he officially resigned after eighteen years with the station and made Bradley Studios the local headquarters of the thriving Decca Records. He was replaced at WSM by Marvin Hughes, a dapper little man who played nine instruments and whose résumé included Dot Records, the Nashville Symphony, and the direction of the old National Life company chorus.

One year later, in May 1959, D Kilpatrick, who had never really settled into a groove with the Opry or WSM's top management, was replaced by WSM program director and veteran announcer Ott Devine. Some thought Devine too reserved for Opry management, but he got off to a good start by calling an industry-wide meeting that included WSM officials, artists, managers, publishers, Harry Stone, and even Jim Denny. It cleared the air. It lasted three hours, and afterward, Ernest Tubb called it "the greatest thing that has ever happened." Devine also updated the Opry stage and modernized its sound, allowing drums (actually a single snare drum) for the first time.

A certain understanding had been achieved. Although WSM would never again dominate the country music business, that had never been its objective. Denny's perhaps-too-free enterprise bolstered the whole community and capitalized on the World War II country music boom just when that was necessary. DeWitt's decision to ban moonlighting ended an unhealthy near-monopoly at the core of country music in Nashville, creating conditions for real competition and growth. The decade about to dawn would be Music City's biggest ever, and that would be good news for National Life, the Opry, and WSM, just as it would be for Music Row.

Most conversations at the 1959 convention were about how and why country music was on the make again, with radio stations converting over now in significant numbers, and spectacular songs like Harlan Howard's "Heartaches by the Number" emerging as exemplars of a new creative ferment in Nashville. The BMI Awards moved uptown, from a hotel breakfast to a banquet at the Belle Meade Country Club. Pop singers looked to Nashville for material more than ever, and country singers took determined aim at the pop charts. A growing cadre of brilliant studio pickers and players had time to simply sit and invent and spark each other on creatively, because that's what musicians do when they're fed and sheltered.

An observation made by Charlie Lamb a couple years before in his newspaper proved more valid than ever. Music buyers, he'd written, were leaping genres without prejudice, looking for anything that moved them. "It is a recognition that the categories have merged, that one category today is borrowing successfully from the other; that like so many different rivers converging, they are all finding the welcoming sea."

ELEVEN ⚡ *A Code and a Concern*

Bob Cooper wanted the world to know that the 1960 DJ convention was on the level. The general manager of WSM radio knew that Congress was investigating record and radio ethics and that rock DJs like Alan Freed were being pilloried on a national stage. Besides outright payola (money in exchange for airplay of specific records), the government had accused record labels of financing junkets by DJs to music conventions. To avoid guilt by association, Cooper invited two leading congressional payola investigators to Nashville that November. He disclosed that WSM had spent about $16,000 from its publicity budget on the 1959 convention. WSM dropped its long-standing cocktail party in favor of a breakfast (only to have several record labels gladly step in and spring for bars and hospitality suites). Most conspicuously, WSM dropped "Disk Jockey" from the event's official name, dubbing it the Country Music Festival. And in general, while there was another record crowd, the weekend was more subdued, with less boozy, brazen behavior and more seminars.

"On the level" aptly described Bob Cooper's management style as well. D Kilpatrick called him the best all-around radio man he ever knew. Stocky and solid, Cooper sported a Johnny Unitas haircut and Army style horn-rimmed glasses that helped him only so much with his terrible eyesight. He favored bow ties and plaid or seersucker sportcoats, and he ran WSM with a steady tiller and low-key persuasion. He'd come out of an advertising agency background, and even then he had a way of breaking down ideas about what couldn't be done. Or as one colleague said, he could sell you something without your knowing you were being sold.

Hank Fort, the songwriter, remembered a call from Cooper with some work.

"Mr. Shyer wants a jingle," he said. Harold Shyer was a venerable local jeweler on Church Street. "He wants his full name in there once, and he wants his name mentioned three times. And he wants you to put in there about how many watches [he has], Bulova watches, Longines watches and Elgin watches, because they are his specialties."

"Yes sir," Fort said.

"Get their slogan in: 'If Harold says it's so, it's so.'"

"Yes sir."

"Oh, by the way, he wants you to put in there that he has Keepsake diamond rings, because that's his *big* specialty."

"Okay, Bob."

"Oh, by the way, he has silverware as well as jewelry."

This all had to come in well under a minute, but that's what Fort was being paid $186 to do, so she put all that on a pad and sat at her piano until she had it. Snooky Lanson sang the resulting jingle, which ran for fifteen years.

In the 1960s Cooper was still quietly getting results. He swung another Carnegie Hall appearance for the Opry in November of 1961, a benefit for the New York Musicians Aid Society that sold out and drew warm reviews. He developed a Grand Ole Opry syndicated program, placing the show on some 350 radio stations, the most ever. And with the University of Tennessee, he worked out a distance learning program with complete college courses on music and Tennessee history that ran on WSM in the early morning and earned college credit for participating listeners.

Out at Channel 4, however, Irving Waugh was bored. "Nothing was happening," he remembered in 2004. "I had the television station, Bob Cooper has the radio station. I don't like the setup, but that's the way it's going. De-Witt and I can barely tolerate each other." Waugh's secretary Margaret Parker remembers him pacing like a caged cat during those years. "He would come out to my desk sometimes and literally hit the top of my typewriter pretty hard and say, 'Margaret, it's *dull* around here; let's make something happen.' So he often *made* things happen." There was, for example, the time he tried to get new National Life President Bill Weaver (Edwin Craig's son-in-law) to buy a professional football team. He got as far as a golf game with NFL commissioner

Pete Rozelle, but his dream sank when Rozelle told him only individuals and not corporations could own teams. What Waugh really wanted was for WSM to buy other broadcasters. They were cheap, he thought, and it would be so much more interesting to have a chain of television stations rather than just one. But ultimately, while DeWitt was in charge, and keeping him at a distance, Waugh was frustrated. "I [couldn't] get to first base," Waugh said. "DeWitt wasn't interested in doing anything."

Jack DeWitt actually had plenty on his mind, but his projects must have looked rather remote to some of his colleagues. In 1960, for example, he got a grant from the National Science Foundation to "investigate the possibility of using television techniques with telescopes," a project that led to an associate faculty position at Vanderbilt University's Arthur Dyer Observatory; a research trip to Flagstaff, Arizona; and the presentation of a paper at the Imperial College in London. But DeWitt's hobbies weren't entirely self-indulgent; many directly helped WSM grow as a broadcaster. His astronomical work, for one thing, introduced him to the new world of transistors. These miniature, literally cool devices replaced hot, fragile vacuum tubes and ushered in the electronic and computer revolution. DeWitt used them to develop a patented new amplifier that was deployed at his TV station and that sold briskly on the market. Though he was shot down once again in applying for 750,000 watts of power in the fall of 1962, DeWitt earned one of his highest career accolades when the National Association of Broadcasters gave him its Engineering Achievement Award in early 1964. As if to add a flourish to that accomplishment, he set off that summer on one of his signature engineering jags, a perfect marriage of science and station publicity.

For DeWitt, satellites combined his passion for astronomy with his knowledge about radio communications. In 1957 he'd stood with George Reynolds at Reynolds's place on Kentucky Lake, had watched Sputnik go overhead, and had said, "See that? That's our future right there." Now, seven years later, he learned from some of the jiggers talking on a break that WLAC-TV, Channel 5, had announced it would soon be featuring the first-ever weather photos from space, via NASA's new Nimbus One satellite. The engineers from WSM-TV and WLAC were friendly competitors who frequently shared gear and ideas in the field in ways that made both better broadcasters. But DeWitt had no intention of getting beaten on this front.

"Hell, we're the space station!" he said. "Do we want to give those guys a run for their money?"

George Reynolds, Aaron Shelton's best man and oldest friend, had died of a heart attack the previous fall, and George Jr. was now a bright engineer on staff. DeWitt drew up a circuit diagram and handed it to him. "Build this for me," he said. Then, in the workshop, DeWitt and his engineers built, from scratch, a ten-foot high radio receiving dish, on a pivoting mount, with a large helical twist of copper tubing coiling out the front. Though it looked like a prop from a bad science fiction film, it was mounted on the roof, tied to Reynolds's circuit board, an old FM police receiver, an amplifier, and a regular reel-to-reel tape recorder. Ten days after DeWitt's having the idea, on the morning of August 29, a hillbilly picker, part-time preacher, and station hired hand named Blythe Poteet swept the huge antenna across the sky, according to timing and coordinates supplied by DeWitt. Out of the amplifier and on to the tape came a series of beeps. The beeps, played back through an oscilloscope, painted—one line at a time—a picture unlike any of them had ever seen: the white pinwheel of a hurricane bearing down on the Carolina coast from 575 miles up. They mated that with a transparency map of the eastern United States and interrupted the morning cartoons to show their work. They beat Channel 5 by two weeks and, indeed, everybody else virtually anywhere. While other TV stations waited for special gear to translate the Nimbus data, WSM-TV had broadcast some of the first weather satellite pictures in U.S. commercial television using shop surplus.

Jack DeWitt's ingenuity was by then an accepted fact of life in Nashville. He was as prominent as any member of the Belle Meade establishment, albeit in his niche of local "genius." When the Swan Ball became the city's premiere society event of the year in the mid-1960s, Jack attended in formal white tie and tails, along with the Craigs and the other National Life board families. A lot of people did, and still do, view DeWitt with a sense of awe. But in his world and his time, he *was* different—different from his Old South peer group and different from the hillbillies. DeWitt seemed to have wished he could mix better with the country music crowd ("real hickories" he called them, attempting affection), but when he tried, it came tinged with incomprehension. He'd go to the Opry when he had to, sometimes out of sheer guilt. He once said, "I wanted to show them that I had a great interest in the Grand Ole Opry, which I didn't at all."

One of DeWitt's hidden strengths, however, was his attentiveness as a mentor, and in the early 1960s, nobody could have known that he was grooming a future leader of WSM who would rank with Edwin Craig and Harry Stone in vision and character. E. W. "Bud" Wendell was a second-generation National Life Shield Man from Ohio who'd been transferred to the Home Office after spending the 1950s distinguishing himself in the field. His role was general troubleshooter, a man who for many years was sent out by train, car, or airplane to handle crises in the sales force. One day in about 1962, Wendell was summoned from the cafeteria to the office of Robert Musto, the executive who oversaw National Life's entire sales force. Musto, who was there with DeWitt, said, "There's an opening over at WSM, and we think that you'd fill that opening very well, and we'd like you to consider transferring over to WSM." Wendell then asked a question that made him laugh years later. "Mr. Musto, I've come a long way now. I'm at the Home Office. Is there any room for advancement over at WSM?"

"Well," he said, "Certainly there's room for advancement. I don't ever expect to be president of National Life and you should never expect to be president of WSM, but I'm sure there's room for advancement."

The future president of WSM said, "I'll take it."

By many accounts, the move was Edwin Craig's way of supplementing DeWitt's managerial shortcomings while retaining his strengths in the role of engineer/president. "Later on I was told that the decision was more Mr. Craig's decision than Mr. DeWitt's or Mr. Musto. He had felt that WSM was getting a little too far out," Wendell recalled with bemusement, "and maybe a little too liberal, and that he thought that maybe somebody born, bred, and raised in the insurance side could bring a little of that over to WSM." None of that set DeWitt against Wendell. Quite the opposite. Once Wendell got up to speed on the issues of the broadcasting business, he was given responsibility for a mid-1960s foray into the beginnings of cable television. But more important, DeWitt passed on the soul and spirit of what he and Craig had been trying to do since 1925. Wendell said, "He took me under his wing and really tried to impress me with the traditions of WSM, and of the good it can do, and that this is really a public service, not a high profit business. I mean, he felt that way."

Despite its diminished influence over country music at large, WSM could—and did—take a major share of credit for sowing (broadcasting, if you will) the seeds of an industry that was growing, literally in rows, on Sixteenth and Seventeenth Avenues. A 1960 promotional brochure counted ninety-five BMI publishers, sixty-five ASCAP publishers, two hundred full-time songwriters, 750 union musicians, and fifteen recording studios. WSM was, it said, "the station that built a city—Music City USA." By the end of 1962, music added $40 million to the local economy, and Nashville was the second busiest recording center in the United States, after New York. "Record Row," later called "Music Row," a quasi-campus of converted houses and storefronts, began attracting tourists. Bill Denny, Jim's son, remembers working at Cedarwood and looking up from his desk to see families with their hands cupped to their eyes, trying to peer in his ground-floor plate glass windows.

At the end of the decade, Paul Hemphill—a freelancing former *Atlanta Journal* writer and son of a Tennessee-born coal miner, railroader, and trucker— wrote *The Nashville Sound,* arguably the first great work of modern journalism about the city's music scene. His book counted forty studios, 1,500 union musicians, a similar number of songwriters, twenty-nine talent agencies, seven record pressing plants, four hundred music publishers, fifty-three record companies, and seven trade newspapers. He noted the BMI and ASCAP buildings standing at the end of Music Row "like twin Statues of Liberty." The new Country Music Hall of Fame had gone up in 1967, virtually between them. The Row itself looked like "a montage of for sale signs, old houses done up with false fronts to look like office buildings, leggy secretaries swishing down the sidewalks, dusty Cadillacs parked close to the buildings as though they were stray dogs hiding under houses in the mid-August heat, Johnny Cash sneaking into a studio back door with his shades on . . ." Push-button phones, sixteen-track recording studios, Glen Campbell, and Charley Pride were hot. Owen Bradley and Chet Atkins presided as producer-kings (kindly ones to be sure), who guided the Nashville Sound to massive success. Chiefly, everybody seemed intent on making sure that whatever else they did, they had a good time. As Pride's producer "Cowboy" Jack Clement has said, "We're in the fun business. If we're not having fun, we're not doing it right."

Musical crossroads were being paved in Nashville as fast as the intersections of its burgeoning suburbs. The range of influences at work in town sprawled nearly as wide as the roots of music and American culture itself, including the deeply rooted yet commercial folk songs of Bob Dylan, the whirlwind of Elvis, and R & B artists like Ruth Brown and Clyde McPhatter. They, and scores of other musical pied pipers, came to Nashville seeking the studios, the producers, the pickers, and the vibe. Country music reached new plateaus of conventional popularity—playing the *Today Show* and other milestones of normalcy—while accommodating strong new ingredients. The folk music craze blossomed into a bona fide national musical movement that bolstered and deepened country. Many of the artists WSM had helped launch, especially the bluegrassers like Bill Monroe, Mac Wiseman, and Flatt & Scruggs, found their careers unexpectedly revived by the ardor of college students, including a counterculture that would have given Edwin Craig heartburn. Perhaps most extraordinary, Nashville also became a destination for a Shakespearian cavalcade of writers who emigrated as if in thrall with what songwriter/publisher Fred Rose had quietly birthed—a place where an elegantly written song for ordinary people was worth something. That list is long indeed, but it included no less than Harlan Howard, Roger Miller, Felice and Boudleaux Bryant, and Kris Kristofferson.

All this helped country music's standing in the Nashville power structure only a little. Bill Denny said the conflict between Belle Meade and Music Row persisted. "The business community was happy to sell you a car, but they didn't want their daughter to marry your son if you were in the music industry," he said. "I think the real breakthrough was the banking industry. They were really the first business, other than the broadcasters, to kind of recognize the value and the substance and the business acumen within the industry. For a long time, if you said you were in the music business, you couldn't get a telephone. You had to make a big cash deposit and keep ahead of your bill."

Tennessean editor John Seigenthaler said the Opry remained a source of embarrassment for many: "Almost everybody in those days went to church downtown. On Sunday morning, people from the West End went down to Fifth and Broadway and turned left. And they saw the mess that the Opry had left there the night before. And much of that mess was on the street. And people were mad as hell about it. There came a time when National Life paid to have that street cleaned overnight, so there was not that problem. Country music was looked down on. It was more an eyesore, more an oddity than a complement to the community."

Edwin Craig came to rely on popular performers, like Minnie Pearl and Roy Acuff, to help mollify civic disdain for the Opry, but with a cultural cold war on his hands and a massive insurance company to run, the last thing he wanted was trouble with his radio station's non-Opry fare. He took a personal interest when things strayed from the polite and the acceptable. When DJ Larry Munson spun the breathy, sexy Julie London, Craig chewed him out personally. "Get that crotch music off my radio station!" he hollered over the phone. Once, in the predawn hours, Grant Turner played a Little Jimmy Dickens novelty record called "Just a Bowl of Butter Beans," sung to the tune of the old hymn "Just a Closer Walk with Thee." Ralph Emery has related that "at that particular moment in time, the president of the Methodist publishing company was up early, shaving, to catch a plane. He heard 'Just a Bowl of Butter Beans' and thought it was sacrilegious. He was appalled. He called his good friend E. W. Craig. It was like the Army chain of command. It just came down all day, level to level to level, until it got to Grant, and I don't think we saw that Jimmy Dickens record ever again."

Most of the time in the 1960s, you'd have heard Perry Como or Pat Boone records, the safest of the safe, on WSM. But beneath the sleek patina of its daytime pop shows and buttoned-up, businesslike newscasts, the radio station retained qualities of the zoo that had cost DeWitt sleep. *Noontime Neighbors* was crossing into its third decade, with John McDonald, now a sort of baron of all things agricultural, still ringing the dinner bell before every show. He walked with a cane, weighed more than three hundred pounds, and always dressed in natty suits. A virtually ungovernable department unto himself, he sold his own show's sponsorships and a lot more besides. "I was in a little glass cubicle, and right across from me was John. So I would talk to him every day," said longtime Opry house manager Jerry Strobel. "He was always on the phone trading something. Buying and selling. Whether it be a tractor, a Cadillac, or whatever." Strobel once went along with McDonald when he toured the Frosty Morn meat packing plant, got treated like a country star by his loyal sponsor, and drove his big car home with the trunk full of free steak.

"It was nothing we didn't tease him about," said Frances Williams Preston. "John always had an angle . . . But the farmers believed in him and what he said and the news that he passed on." Indeed, he was a tireless broadcaster who did a 5:30 a.m. and noon farm report into the early 1980s. *Noontime Neighbors* ran for twenty-six years. And for decades, he had the respect and admiration of nearly everyone of consequence in the farming business. When he celebrated his twenty-fifth anniversary with WSM, the secretary of agriculture came from Washington for the gala dinner.

In the 1960s, McDonald made the transition to WSM-TV with enthusiasm, if not always with grace. WSM producer Elmer Alley directed McDonald's Sunday show, and "dreaded it all week." One day McDonald came on the set with a piglet. "And he was cradling this pig much as you'd cradle a baby," Alley recalled. "And he had a pill half the size of a golf ball. And he was going to show you 'how to give a *peel* to a *peeg*.' So he put that pill in the pig's mouth and he rammed it with that ram-rod he had, and the pig urinated. And the stream went right up in front of his face and all over the floor and all over John. And I didn't have anywhere to go, so I faded to black. And as I was fading to black, John was saying, "Somebody throw a tow sack over that wet spot, will ye?""

Musically, *Noontime Neighbors* could swing from pop chanteuses Dolores Watson or Dottie Dillard to country stars like Ernest Tubb or Red Foley, but one wouldn't have heard any country music on the *Waking Crew,* a live, weekday morning free-for-all that became a WSM signature. It ran for thirty years, through the 1960s, the 1970s, and even well into the 1980s, eventually outlasting every other non-network live radio ensemble in the nation. It grew out of a show Jack Stapp launched in 1951 called *Eight O'clock Time,* with Beasley Smith conducting a fairly traditional musical variety hour. By the 1960s, host Dave Overton had transformed the *Waking Crew* into a daily event that was more a band with a show than a show with a band. "They told us, 'You guys are going to have to talk,' remembered Beverly LeCroy, a trombonist who played the entire thirty-odd-year run of the show. "I never talked much back then. I said, 'Like what?' They said, 'Just talk.'" By 1969, Overton was paying homage to LeCroy as a "radio personality" whose impromptu stories on air had included "being attacked by 347 ducks in Centennial Park [and] comic interpretations of a department store detective, a bank robber, and a shoe salesman."

Nonmusical regulars on the *Waking Crew* included a Vanderbilt linguistics professor named Maxwell Lancaster, known on the air as Dr. Philologue, who did a daily riff on the derivation of words. An elderly Nashville woman named Mrs. Fannie Earhart made herself a fixture, attending the show almost every day for a dozen years. Overton would visit with her and then have her read out of the paper some item she'd found amusing. Most remarkable may have been longtime WSM newsman Bill Williams. One of his signatures was to relate, not read, the news. Teddy Bart, who sang on the *Waking Crew* for years, said, "Bill would write his script, then take the script and write lead notes for himself, throw away the script, and bring in the notes and ad lib the news. He was always accurate. And it was amazing. It sounded like he was talking to you." Williams was most famous, however, for his weather reports—delivered every day in rhyming verse.

The show lost its studio audience when WSM moved from the National Life building to the Knob Road studios, where TV and radio cohabitated after 1966. The building was cinder-block sterile, but piano player Joe Layne says the show's personality loosened up on the hill. "When we got up there, it took on a new blend for some reason or other. Maybe it was too stuffy down there [at Seventh and Union]. The whole thing evolved into something that will never happen again in a lifetime. I was kind of the bad boy of the group. I'd come up with pretty weird things."

One Monday, Overton asked Layne a simple enough on-air question: "How was your weekend?"

"Dave, I'm a new person."

"Really what happened?"

"I've started a new church—the Power in the Blood Church."

Overton went along with it. "Really?"

"Yeah, and we've got a theme song." Layne got the band to swing into a few bars of the old gospel standard, "There Is Power in the Blood."

"Where are you meeting?" Overton asked.

"Well, there's a phone booth downtown on Third Avenue."

At that point, everyone laughed and sort of moved on.

"That week I started getting *donations*," Layne remembered. "Well when the first donation came in it was cool. But when we got five, six, seven, eight, then I got called on the carpet. And I really got reamed, big time [by] Irving Waugh—a sweet guy, still is. I had to get back on the air and tell 'em we were only kidding about the church. And I had to try to send the money back!"

The Waking Crew band was also directed by trumpet player and arranger Bill McElhiney, a WSM veteran who played jazz at night and extensive pop studio work on the side. The band had thirteen pieces until the mid-1960s, when it was slimmed to ten. It still had three saxes, two trombones, Jack Shook on guitar, and a full rhythm section. George Cooper, by then the most ancient of the ancients and still in charge of the musicians' union, played bass. Two or more vocalists were always on hand, including at times Dottie Dillard, Dolores Watson, Carolyn Darden, Kay Golden, Marty Brown, and Teddy Bart. Bart, who played many roles at WSM in the 1960s, said Overton anchored the show brilliantly. "An extraordinary talent," he said. "He had a Bert Parks type of quality to him. An entertainer and yet a broadcaster. A lilt in the voice. Jovial. The name Dave Overton was a household word."

Bart had his own run-ins with the stodgy propriety of WSM on Nashville's first free-form radio talk show—a legendary afternoon slice of chaos pairing Bart with salty sportscaster and DJ Larry Munson. A piano-bar singer from Johnstown, Pennsylvania, Bart grew up wishing he were Arthur Godfrey. He'd never given Nashville a second thought before he landed there for a two-week engagement in the late 1950s, a few years out of high school. His base, the Voodoo Lounge, was in Printer's Alley, Nashville's block-long excuse for a red-light district, not five blocks from National Life. It had a burlesque club, the Gas Light, the Voodoo, and the Carousel. Bart noticed musicians from town making their way to the Carousel late every night after their own gigs.

Some went to sit in with the remarkable house band, guitarist Hank Garland and his quartet. Most were there to have a few drinks, listen to jazz, and clear their heads of the work-for-hire music they'd made all day. Beegie Adair, a newcomer from Kentucky, played piano behind Garland on those late-night gigs. She remembered Waking Crew trumpeter Carl Garvin sitting in and playing like Chet Baker, as well as Louis Nunley of the Anita Kerr Singers offering swinging standards on the microphone.

"Nashville's musical aura started to take hold of me," Bart said. He met and wrote songs with Beasley Smith, by then enjoying the semiretirement of mulling over lyrical minutiae and fielding calls from Dinah Shore or Kitty Kallen saying hello or needing to consult on something musical. Smith recommended Bart for a job at WSM, and when he got one, Bart found himself overjoyed and underdressed. He was astonished to see a radio station where everyone still wore suits and ties. He flopped as a disc jockey, never getting a handle on the whole changing-records-while-talking thing, but loving the talk itself. And everybody liked the good-natured Yankee, so they figured out what to do with him. There was a piano in the studio, and he'd sit there and play to liven up Don Russell's record shows. The hosts would kibitz, in a safe little coffee klatch. Then Bart got a new partner.

Larry Munson was one of WSM's legendary sportscasters, a gravel-voiced tough guy who brought Vanderbilt basketball to 650 AM for the first time, back before the university even had a proper gymnasium. He'd been formally trained in the radio art of reenacting football, baseball, and basketball over the air, complete with sound effects, from crowd noise to thunder in the distance. For years, he multitasked at WSM, calling games, spinning records, and filming, in the field, a fishing show that ran for years on WSM-TV. He was the only DJ at WSM to play real jazz fans' jazz—Count Basie, Nat Cole, and Duke Ellington—and this caused chin rubbing and knitted brows up the chain of command. It took an unexpected and timely award from the Women's Advertising Council for the "best music in town" to get management off his back.

A new early-1960s show called *This Is WSM* was conceived to run from 1:00 to 5:00 on weekday afternoons. Initially, scripted discourses on public affairs and civic doings mingled with easy listening pop. Each announcer hosted a two-hour segment, including David Cobb, now heading into his fourth decade of broadcasting. Perhaps thinking that they both liked jazz, Bob Cooper chose Larry Munson's two hours as the new showcase for piano-playing Teddy Bart. It was a hotter combination than he ever guessed.

"From day one, Larry and I hit it off just like Martin and Lewis," Bart said. "There was a chemistry. He and I, about three days into this, discarded the script and just ad libbed. Ott [Devine] used to get terribly upset because we'd disregard the script. But we did our own thing."

"The piano was turned to face me," said Munson. "I was only about fifteen feet from him. And I had turntables on both sides of me. Bart was supposed to be just sort of sitting there diddling on the piano while we talked in between songs. That was the conception of the show. But the trouble was with the two of us we couldn't look at each other without falling over on the floor laughing, because semi-consciously we were getting very close to a dangerous line."

Bart sometimes lined up guests, including, one day, the newly crowned Miss Ohio on a postpageant goodwill tour. "She walks in that room and she looks like $900 million," Munson remembered with a mixture of awe and regret. "She sits down in that chair. We had an album playing, and Bart blushed the moment she came in because . . . you didn't see people like that very often. She sits right across from me. I'm looking at Bart and I'm trying not to laugh, because she is absolutely gorgeous. And when the record ends, Teddy introduces her, but he's almost laughing, because he knows that I'm thinking something. And before I can say anything to get us in trouble, he says to her, 'How is your diphthong?'"

A diphthong is a vocal segue from one vowel sound to another that classical singers, like the unfortunate Miss Ohio, study, but that's not what it sounded like to anyone in the room or on the air. Munson continued, "I died right there. I couldn't talk. She flushed a thousand shades of red. And Bart has crashed down on the piano. He got to laughing so hard he couldn't play. I've never forgotten that particular incident. That girl was embarrassed right out of her shoes."

One day, after a somewhat risqué interview with Eddy Arnold, the country star said, "You guys know they're never going to let you continue this, don't you?" Munson looked quizzical. Arnold said, "This is too good. The National Life people are never going to let you continue this." But Bart and Munson felt that Cooper backed them up. "He was aware that WSM was probably a little straight laced," Munson said. "He was in favor of the thing in the afternoon. It was more or less his idea to take a shot at it and see what happened." When Munson left after about two years, Bart went on to host his own interview show, a more serious afternoon of talk that brought in heavy-hitting and controversial guests. By constantly pushing Cooper's indulgence to the limit with on-the-fringe guests, from the Ku Klux Klan to Students for a Democratic Society, Bart added vividness and context to WSM's news coverage of the tumultuous 1960s.

No WSM personality of the era came close to having the national impact of Ralph Emery. Between 1960 and 1972, Emery was an emperor of the night, commanding the fifty clear channel kilowatts with a low-key but almost evangelical dedication to country music. Third-shift workers, restless students, twenty-four-hour cafes, truck drivers, and others turned their imaginations over to Emery, both his wide-ranging choice of music and his casual, rambling interviews. Other DJs listened to Emery, as they had Eddie Hill before him, and shaped their own shows based on what was working for Ralph.

The nightly routine captured beautifully the stylistic dichotomy of WSM. From 7:00 to 10:00 p.m. David Cobb played classical music for his loyal, cultured listeners. The veteran announcer had a way with album liner notes, reading them so conversationally that his audience thought he was talking expertly off the top of his head. He drank espresso in the studio before anybody else had ever heard of such a thing. He grew his hair long and, by virtue of his longevity and night-time shift, he got away with wearing cowboy boots and jeans to work. He'd settled into a life on a farm in Franklin, and one night, Emery came in to find Cobb patiently skinning a snake he'd killed that afternoon on his property, while a classical album spun in the background.

After a news break, those of Cobb's civilized listeners who kept their radios on heard Emery's theme song crackle and cackle out of the speakers: Flatt & Scruggs playing "Shuckin' the Corn." "I'd work from 10:00 p.m. to midnight," reminisced Emery. "Then we had a Bible tape—a paid religious spot—*The World Tomorrow*. We'd roll the Bible tape, which was a nice break for me. And at 12:30 when that was over, the engineer was gone till five in the morning. I was alone. I look back on that and wonder what they were thinking. There were no commercials. There was no prep work [or instructions] except to play records. And they gave me a blank log and a handful of public service announcements. And they didn't say to read them. It just said if you read any of these, write down what time you read them. That was it. To turn a twenty-four-year-old kid loose on a 50,000-watt radio station that would reach forty states, Canada, and the Caribbean . . . as I look back, I think that's wild."

Emery's one mandate came straight from the name of the show Tom Perryman had helped institutionalize—*Opry Star Spotlight*. Each night would emphasize a different Opry member. Emery would go down the cast list alphabetically to avoid the appearance of favoritism, playing a disproportionate amount of that night's artist and perhaps even having him or her sit in on the show. Over time, he found he had to complement Opry artists with hotter newcomers, who might have looked forward to guest spots on the Opry, but who had no plans to become regular members. "My argument was, 'I've got to play hit records,'" Emery said. "Now fortunately the Opry had a pretty good roster, [including] Marty Robbins and Jim Reeves. But I said we've got a lot of people who haven't had any hits for years. If I sandwich Ernest Tubb between Buck Owens and George Jones, I'm okay. But [listeners have] got to know if they tune in they're going to hear hit music. We went around and around with that a lot."

That independence meant that before long, Emery began to have a measurable effect on careers. He doesn't contest the widely held impression that he broke Buck Owens around 1960, when he became wildly enthusiastic about the West Coast singer's twangy "Under Your Spell Again," which reached the top five. When he received Owens's "My Heart Skips a Beat," which went #1 in 1964, Emery helped make a minor hit of the B-side, a Bakersfield classic called "Together Again."

Whereas he'd initially tried to keep himself awake with coffee in the dark empty studio, Emery perked up the show with guests—artists from the famous to the obscure who came by to take advantage of Emery's open-door policy. The most regular, Marty Robbins, the Western-influenced artist behind the smash hit "El Paso," didn't like to sleep at night, so he hung out regularly with Emery, sometimes talking on the air, sometimes lurking and conversing with the DJ only during records and commercials. Over the months and years, every country music artist of consequence spent hours with Ralph, talking away the night. Conway Twitty visited as he was trying to cross from rock and roll to country in about 1963. One night Merle Haggard, Crystal Gayle, Loretta Lynn, the Wilburn Brothers, and six others packed into a smoke-filled studio to talk and sing. Guests frequently dropped by after a night of drinking at Tootsie's Orchid Lounge, across the Ryman Alley from the Opry. "Many nights I marked the closing of Tootsie's by the arrivals of guests to my show," Emery remembered.

In 1963 Emery took on additional duties for WSM-TV. Program director Elmer Alley was looking for an early morning show leading into NBC's *Today* show. Channel 5 had Eddie Hill on in that slot, while Channel 4 was running college courses for credit at 6:00 a.m. So Alley invited Emery to host *Opry Almanac*, the first show produced in expansive new WSM-TV studios built on

Knob Road, west of downtown. Emery's very first television guest could have been no more sublime—a young Loretta Lynn who sang with only her own guitar as accompaniment. The show took about a year to became a hit, before it became an institution, attracting at its peak two-thirds of the television viewers in Nashville with a mix of wake-up talk, guests, and Opry star performances, prerecorded to video and dropped in. (Emery eventually convinced Irving Waugh to spring for a live band on the show.) Initially, Emery sat in a little faux-kitchen set wearing a red checked shirt ("I looked like a Purina box," he remembered). What his viewers probably didn't appreciate is that Emery had been up all night, doing his radio show from 10:00 p.m. until 5:00 a.m. He'd nap forty-five minutes on the lumpy commissary couch, then smile through his fog at the television camera.

The fatigue led to the low point of Emery's career. One morning, about five minutes before air time, he complained to one of the show's band members that he was so tired he wasn't sure how he was going to make it. The picker produced a little yellow pill that jerked Emery to life like pushing a starter button on an inboard motor. For some years after that, Emery was unhappily hooked, as were many of the long-toiling musicians of the era. A local physician known as Dr. Snap wrote amphetamine prescriptions for songwriters on multiday writing sprees or bus drivers keeping the country tours moving. The most popular were "Old Yellers." Emery remembered a favorite gag in which someone would press a yellow thumbtack in the floorboards next to the Opry mic, then watch in amusement as musicians walking by tried to pick it up.

Emery was already on an emotional skid. His marriage to Opry star Skeeter Davis was failing, and as his depression deepened, he asked to be let off of the all-night show. That break lasted about a year, and it prompted another inspired move by Bob Cooper. Tex Ritter was a veteran country music star who, in 1964, moved from California to Nashville to become a member of the Opry. Cooper thought Ritter's sweet and salty personality would work on *Opry Star Spotlight,* so he proposed that Grant Turner and Ritter work together on the difficult shift. It worked for a time, but Turner's wife grew impatient with her husband's awful hours. By that time, Emery had steadied himself and was ready to come back. Cooper wanted Ritter to stay on.

"My first thought was I don't think it will work. I'd always been solo and I've never worked with another on-air personality," Emery said. But Ritter had been a boyhood hero of his, so he gave it a try, and the chemistry worked beautifully. Emery was inquisitive, impudent. Ritter was gentle and loving with a deep, gravelly, rolling-thunder voice. Sometimes he would doze off quietly in the wee hours, and Emery would just press on. Ritter "became a father figure to me," Emery said. "We became big buddies. That was a fun time in my life." The duo lasted about two years. Emery continued on, eventually getting his bad habits under control and reviving the spirit of the early *Opry Star Spotlight*.

The talk was peerless. One night, Emery sat up late with Opry star Jim Ed Brown in the creaky chair opposite. An Arkansan, and a walking subwoofer like Ritter, he spoke in a low, velvet voice of how Elvis had rattled their world nearly twenty years before. He and Emery spoke of rockabilly music, of DJ Tom Perryman, and the great Hubert Long, the showman of Shreveport. Brown mentioned casually that, as a matter of fact, Elvis was in town recording, a name-drop that was sure to create a mini traffic jam on Music Row the next day. Emery punctuated the conversation by spinning a record: Chet Atkins and Jerry Reed making webs of lacy country counterpoint on a Merle Travis guitar tune called "Cannonball Rag." The years rolled by, full of nights like this, guest after guest and star after star. Listeners grew closer to their favorite artists and heard the history of country music told in questions, answers, and stories. There was simply no end to the stories.

WSM maintained the essential qualities that distinguished it as a standard-setting AM broadcaster. Its large news department won the prestigious Radio Television News Directors Award in the early 1960s, and it kept a close watch on community doings. An actress and former foreign service official named Barbara Moore, WSM's "Witness for Women," appeared on a number of entertainment and public affairs programs. She became one of the station's defining personalities in the 1960s and early 1970s. Bob Loflin and Hal Durham were important and versatile announcers, disc jockeys, interviewers, and personalities of the era. Teddy Bart summed up the station's ethic nicely:

> Profit was not a motive. It was a concern and an interest, but it was not the overriding motive. Nobody paid that much attention to ratings. It was almost as if there was an implicit understanding among the management of what the character and culture would be without it being written down or expressed. You knew when you crossed the line, but you almost knew implicitly that you were on a higher level than another station. It must be like playing for the Yankees. It was the tradition of those who had gone before you, the stories that you constantly heard in the hall. And you just knew. And no matter who was elevated to management seemed to absorb that special energy of

knowing that it was special to be there. So the vision was almost inspired rather than dictated.

Profit mattered little because by 1963, National Life was one of the largest insurance companies in the country, and the radio station and the Opry amounted to a fraction of the firm's income. But the parent company, so staid for so long, was about to go through the most dramatic and fitful changes of its life, with huge implications for the Grand Ole Opry and the broadcaster that built it.

For one thing, National Life had run out of room at the old Home Office. The company had purchased and occupied every property on its block, but still it was straining with 1,700 Nashville employees in six buildings. National Life had been eyeing new property outside of Davidson county since the 1950s, but a complicated negotiation with the city over taxes ultimately encouraged National Life to stay downtown. In late 1965, president Dan Brooks announced that the prestigious architects Skidmore Owings and Merrill would design new corporate headquarters—a white, thirty-one-story, stone and glass monolith on the same block as the old building. It was to be the tallest building in the Southeast at the time and (by design) one floor higher than the 1957 Life & Casualty building five blocks away.

Studio C had already been reclaimed by the insurance company in 1965, when National Life announced WSM would move. *The Friday Night Frolics*, now almost as coveted a ticket as the Opry itself, moved to the Ryman as the *Friday Night Opry*. The Waking Crew moved to the Grill Room at the Hermitage Hotel for many months. In April of 1966 National Life finally moved the radio station out entirely into a new addition at the TV studio on Knob Hill, clearing 13,000 square feet at Seventh and Union. It was an abrupt and costly uprooting. Photographer Les Leverett remembers talking to Ott Devine's secretary in the program director's outer office about a pushcart full of 78-rpm records that seemed destined for the dumpster. The secretary said they were throwing those away, so both of them began salvaging records. Suddenly Ott Devine appeared and bellowed, "Leave those things alone!"

"Now I knew somebody was going to put 'em on the elevator, take 'em down to the basement of the National Life building and dump 'em," Leverett continued. "So after work that day I went down there, and sure enough, it was sitting back there behind the elevator. All by itself. And I salvaged some more." Along with stacks of old records by everyone from Opry stars to Duke Ellington and Tommy Dorsey, the station threw away stacks of transcription discs with years of WSM air checks and syndicated shows. Another casualty was the music library—handwritten scores by Beasley Smith, Francis Craig, and Owen Bradley bound with string, tucked into walls of cubby holes. "I spent Saturdays for months throwing away sheet music," said a rueful Ruth White, a music librarian and Opry ticket office worker in the mid-1960s. "It was disastrous to be honest with you." She remembers one collection of very old 78-rpm records by the likes of Uncle Dave Macon that had, for some reason, been kept in a safe so forgotten that a locksmith had to be hired to crack it. This time capsule wasn't investigated. It was tossed. Even with the first Country Music Hall of Fame and Museum being built at the end of Music Row as a repository for such items, National Life's attitude toward its WSM archives appears to have been one of a stressed-out matriarch sick of looking at clutter, too tired to remember sentimental attachments, and all too ready to dispose of the old before moving into the new.

Not long after the move, WSM got new leadership as well. Jack DeWitt surprised Irving Waugh and everyone else when he announced he was taking early retirement in the spring of 1968. Edwin Craig didn't want him to go, but DeWitt felt he had no choice. His new adversary within the company was Bill Weaver, son-in-law of Edwin Craig, longtime financial executive and heir apparent to the presidency of the company. Six-foot-five and brash, sometimes to the point of abrasiveness, Weaver unfortunately rubbed DeWitt the wrong way. Irving Waugh stood up to Weaver's sometimes overbearing personality ("He loved to needle people," Waugh explained) but DeWitt's milder manners weren't up for any more intracorporate jockeying.

"Well, I got headaches from it. I really did," he told an interviewer. "I got stressful headaches from it. I'll never forget going to my doctor about it, and he said I can give you some medicine. It helped me. He said you've really got to get out of the business you're in, or you've got to retire."

DeWitt told the newspapers he was planning to devote more time to designing and developing electronic equipment and to astronomy, though he remained on the WSM board. Edwin Craig said of his old comrade, "We could not have built WSM Radio and Television into the major voices they are without his pioneering engineering creativity." George Reynolds Jr., who'd grown up in the thrall of DeWitt's accomplishments and whose father did most of the president's shop work, spoke for the dozens of engineers who'd kept the broadcaster broadcasting for so many decades. "Jack was a hands on guy. And he was a wonderful person," he said. "He was an engineer first. The station was run by engineers until Dad died and Jack left. And the engineers wouldn't think anything in the world about going to the shop and building something." The *Nashville Banner* concurred and gracefully sidestepped some of the managerial drift at WSM in its editorial tribute to DeWitt by observing that he "is first of all a scientist" and predicting that the world hadn't heard the last from Nashville's renaissance man. Jack held at least four patents by this point and continued to work at night in his cabin workshop. Friends remember that his curiosity never failed him: he would take backlogs of scientific journals out on his boat, read them and, one by one, toss them into Kentucky Lake.

In sad punctuation to the changes at his company and his broadcasting stations, Edwin Craig died in June of 1969. He was hailed as a "giant" of the insurance industry and a radio pioneer, not merely for starting a powerful station but for guiding broadcasting policy through the Clear Channel Broadcasting Service and the National Association of Broadcasters. He was seventy-six years old and a paragon of business ethics and civic dynamism. He'd served on numerous boards, including Vanderbilt Hospital and the Chamber of Commerce. His résumé went on and on. "He embodied a code and a concern which are becoming all too rare these days," said National Life chairman Dan Brooks. "He had untold thousands of friends at all levels in this company who looked up to him for special kind of inspiration and humanity."

For DeWitt, Craig's death was a profound passage. He told an interviewer in 1995: "Edwin Craig never let me down. If I had to name two or three people that have had a great influence on my life, he would be one of them. He was always a kind man. Not always agreeable, but he always trusted me." He called him Mr. Craig, never Edwin, until the end. And late in his life he gave Craig a gift—an armillary sphere sundial—a band of copper oriented along the path of the traveling sun with an arrow through the middle pointing always at the North Star. It sits in the garden of the Craig estate on Belle Meade Boulevard to this day.

TWELVE *The Whole Complex Is a Studio*

Jack DeWitt's retirement and Craig's death coincided with the most radical changes yet for National Life. Chairman Dan Brooks and president Bill Weaver had both climbed to prominence through the company's investment division, managing the billions of dollars in accumulated reserves insurers have to carry. Now they were as powerful as any businessmen in the state of Tennessee. That, combined with the trend of the day toward corporate diversification, made the company more interested than ever in new lines of business. In 1968, National Life merged with Third National Bank, under the name NLT, for National Life Third. A few years later, banking and insurance combinations were outlawed by the federal government, but even after divestiture of the bank, according to business historian Bill Carey, "the insurance company kept the name NLT and most of the conglomerate philosophy that led to its formation." After a few years, NLT owned a real estate firm, a computer services company, and WSM, Inc. "Each," said the NLT annual report, "is a synergistic development of expertise gained in the parent firm."

Irving Waugh, DeWitt's successor as president of WSM, quickly proved that he believed in synergy too, as well as rapid forward motion. In charge at last of radio, Channel 4, and the Grand Ole Opry, his pent up energy and ideas were unleashed in a torrent of new initiatives. Some had been set in motion by Weaver even before DeWitt left, perhaps another cause of the friction between the men. In June of 1967, *Billboard* magazine reported that WSM was looking to get into music publishing and the record business. That fall, the company acquired an FM station and took it to the air one year later, entering what was by then a crowded local market. At a time when FM was at last overtaking AM as the nation's preferred form of radio, WSM-FM was the midstate's strongest signal, with 100,000 watts, playing adult contemporary music like Montovani, Roger Williams, and Doris Day. David Cobb spun classical, and Hal Durham hosted "sophisticated jazz."

When Waugh began to sift through his own priorities, the first thing he focused on was the Opry. "It had been neglected," he said. "It needed much stronger management. I felt that it had become a backwater in the music arena." Ott Devine, for all his years of service and his authoritative broadcasting voice, was drinking too much, and his relations with the artists had deteriorated. Wendell said he often wasn't even there, sending his secretary in his stead. "He was in charge of some sixty acts, and he got so he would chew people out for no reason," said Ralph Emery. "He finally alienated so many people at the Opry that Irving Waugh had to step him down." That said, Devine was hardly alone in his struggles with alcohol. Drinking contributed to the premature end of general manager Bob Cooper's career and probably his life as well. In truth, booze was nearly as grave and persistent a problem over the decades for WSM's staff as it was for the country music community. Harry Stone, Jack Stapp, and Ralph Emery struggled with the bottle as surely as, though not as famously as, Johnny Cash or any number of other country stars that could be named. There don't seem to be cases of the fatally toxic dependence of a Hank Williams or a Keith Whitley among the WSM crew, but as in so many families, men of great accomplishment buckled under all kinds of temptations, some of them private, some of them spilling into the arena of work and trust and effectiveness. And as with other families, support was offered even when mistakes had been made and feelings had been hurt.

Waugh's choice to replace Devine with Bud Wendell was surprising too, given Wendell's status as DeWitt's protégé. Almost as soon as he'd been named president, Waugh called Wendell to his office and told him, "I'm going to make you manager of the Grand Ole Opry—*now.*"

Wendell wasn't happy. "Irving, we've not had the greatest relationship and if you think this is the way to get rid of me, maybe you're right," he said. "But by God, I'll go down there and run that Opry. You're sending me down there because you think I'm going to fail and that's your way to get rid of me!"

"So that's the kind of relationship we had," Wendell said in 2004. "We laughed about it a lot afterwards, because he always said, 'I knew you better than you knew yourself, and I knew what you'd do down there.'"

Wendell's first Saturday night could scarcely have produced a stranger circumstance, for the city had been placed under a curfew by Mayor Beverly Briley. Two days before, on April 4, 1968, Martin Luther King Jr. had been assassinated just two hundred miles west in Memphis. Wendell called the mayor personally and said, "I'm sure you mean everything except the Grand Ole Opry. We've got three or four thousand people coming to town." The reply: "It *includes* the Grand Ole Opry. You will not do the show." National Guardsmen had been deployed in the city to quell sporadic violence, though Nashville experienced nothing on the scale of the nation's biggest cities, which were burning. That ominous weekend marked the first instance in a generation that the Opry had been preempted by anything, a signal of tempestuous times that, in Nashville, included important lunch counter demonstrations and other significant chapters of the Civil Rights Movement. These dramas played out just down the street from WSM's headquarters and just outside the Ryman's stained glass windows. But WSM's news department gave civil rights demonstrations as little play as possible. Wendell put up mesh over the Ryman windows for the first time, for fear of flying bricks or flaming projectiles. He was, after all, a second-generation insurance man.

Inside the hall, as Waugh had hoped, Wendell brought his troubleshooter's experience to the show. "I wanted him to meet and mingle in the current music community, to get to know people, to breathe more life into the Opry, and he did," Waugh said later. More life meant new blood. Most members of the Opry, Wendell recalled, were like Marty Robbins, at least in their forties. The show's old-time heartbeat came from a dwindling cadre of 1930s-era Opry fiddle and string band pickers who still played every week. But those performers didn't need to tour and follow up on their hit singles. For those who did, Wendell liberalized the prevailing performance requirement for Opry members, from twenty-six weeks per year to twenty. Even Wendell had to admit that the lost income of playing Saturday nights in Nashville had grown, even as the Opry was less essential to any artist's career. Most important, said Ralph Emery, Wendell brought the human touch back to the Opry backstage. "He bought watches that said 'Grand Ole Opry' for all the men and pins for the ladies. And he really began to give them a lot of fatherly love," he said. The message: "'We love you, we want you to stay here. We're proud of you.' And he smoothed out everything. They came to love and respect Bud. He was actually the perfect guy to do that."

Waugh's other great concern was the Opry House itself. The Ryman had taken hundreds of nights of punishment in its almost thirty years of service. People call the building the "Mother Church of Country Music," but National Life Executives began thinking of it as the mother of all firetraps. Summer temperatures inside reportedly topped 120 degrees. Some of the pews were literally held up with Coke crates and patrons were complaining of long splinters that tore clothing and flesh alike. "It scared the hell out of National Life," said Wendell. "Scared the hell out of us that were down there. I read every now and then [that] the artists were just up in arms that we were going to leave the Ryman Auditorium. And hell, every one of them just couldn't wait to get out of [there] and have parking and dressing rooms."

By this point, the Ryman actually belonged to WSM. Weaver and DeWitt had negotiated its purchase from its board of directors in 1963 for $208,000. But even before then, WSM officials had been exploring new homes for the Opry, including a 6,000-seat coliseum at the state fairgrounds. Now the matter was urgent. Renovation of the Ryman appeared painfully expensive and not very practical given the goal of growing the audience. How, where, and when to find a new Grand Ole Opry House was Waugh's concern. The answer began to jell, he said, during a visit to Houston for a golf outing set up by—of all people—WSM's news pioneer Jack Harris, by then a Houston broadcasting power. On that trip was Judge Roy Hofheinz, a big thinker and doer after Waugh's own heart, who had recently steered the $42 million Astrodome into improbable existence. Waugh saw the massive stadium—a huge, air-conditioned pleasure dome—with its adjacent complex of hotels and a theme park, and became intrigued. "I began to think if the Castle was Disney's centerpiece on the West Coast and the Astrodome was Judge Hofheinz's centerpiece for the complex that he'd constructed, then the Opry House could be a centerpiece." But of what? For inspiration and refinement, he turned, as he often did in those days, to Elmer Alley.

A WSM veteran from the sound effects days of radio, Alley had, since the early 1950s, directed programming on WSM-TV. He'd made the jump far more reluctantly than many of his generation. "I didn't want any part of [television]," Alley said in 2004. "I loved radio. [But] all of a sudden the live shows dried up, and it became sitting in a control room and being there for station breaks and playing announcements and playing records. It was just totally boring. So then I had an opportunity to go out there as a director and was scared to death. They more or less just set me down with the cameras and told me to do a show, which I promptly fouled up by getting cameras in the wrong position. I really did have to start over as a rank amateur. I've never liked it as well as radio."

But Waugh knew how creative Alley was. In fact, he'd once talked him back to WSM-TV with an unusually rich offer after Alley left WSM for a time to continue in radio. Alley had made a morning ratings smash with his recruitment of Ralph Emery. He'd given Jud Collins a platform to become Nashville's Walter Cronkite, both via the evening news and the long-running Nashville civic staple, the *Noon Show*. And he'd outdone Channel 5 in the afternoon with an American Bandstand–style dance show called the *Five O'clock Hop*.

Alley had also programmed or produced a slate of Saturday afternoon country music television in the late 1960s and early 1970s that, over WSM-TV or over the many other stations that aired them via syndication, inspired a new generation of musicians. At 4:00 p.m. came Ernest Tubb's lanky Texas-meets-Nashville persona. Then, in half-hour blocks, there followed a parade of musically focused, live-performance shows that covered nearly every style of country music: the corny but venerable Stoneman Family, the entrepreneurial and ambitious Wilburn Brothers, the stylish Porter Wagoner, and, at 6:00 p.m., bluegrass stars Flatt & Scruggs, still sponsored by Martha White Flour after so many years. And those were just the hosts. Including guest appearances, nearly every country artist of consequence performed on WSM-TV in the afternoons in the 1960s, just as they had over radio in the 1930s and 1940s. A generation that grew up learning country through its ears gave way to one steeped in imagery of hay bales, barn dances, suits with string ties, gingham dresses, rhinestones, and rube comics.

Sometimes it seemed that Alley and Waugh relished taking different sides of an issue. "He and I would get into hellacious arguments," Alley remembered. They had facing offices, and their verbal jousts could be heard down the hall and through the walls. "I love Irving," said Alley in a common paradoxical impression of Waugh. "He knew I'd do anything in the world for him. I liked him because he would challenge you. He wouldn't tell you what to do. He'd stop by my office, just stick his head in the door and say, '*Surprise me, lad!*' And he meant it."

Alley recalls that in that spirit he presented Waugh a memo outlining the vision of Opryland USA, well before Waugh went to Houston. The plan, Alley summarized, was to "go out and find a typical piece of Tennessee countryside along the river and design a park which would reflect different types of country music." The new Opry House and a small motel would complete the entertainment complex. Waugh, in any event, took this plan to the NLT board, which, in good corporate fashion, demanded a feasibility study. President Bill Weaver was a stickler for return on investment. "Put a pencil to that," he'd say. The study, by a West Coast firm, came back pessimistic. But Waugh more or less ignored the findings and promised Weaver a return he could live with. Because what Waugh knew and trusted in was a statistic gleaned from exit polls of Opry crowds—that the *average* Opry fan traveled over six hundred miles, usually by car, to see the show. How could a theme park—by then a hot form of American family entertainment—fail to be something those tourists would visit during the weekend? Waugh's gamble—Opryland USA—was formally announced in late September 1969. Waugh called it "a logical and creative extension of a growing institution." Dan Brooks promised a park "of great beauty" without "the garish, honky-tonk commercialism that has sprung up around some of the other amusement areas around the nation."

Brooks's remark was a veiled reference to downtown Nashville and the surroundings of the Ryman Auditorium. Tootsie's Orchid Lounge may have incubated Nashville legends and inebriated the stars as the Opry's cross-alley entertainers' lounge, but Lower Broadway generally had become a magnet for cheap souvenir vendors, strip bars, and general seediness. The question remained: what to do with the Ryman? And with the same blind spot for history that led to the dumping of the WSM music collection, National Life's top brass produced an idea so bad that it actually helped make Nashville, in a roundabout way, a more proud and progressive city. On March 20, 1971, Dan Brooks announced that the Mother Church of Country Music, approaching its one-hundredth anniversary, would be torn down and the bricks used to build a commemorative "Little Church at Opryland." "The Opry House is a grand old lady, and we do not intend to let her come to an ignoble end," said a completely sincere Brooks. A board of advisors on the design and placement of the chapel was named, including Brooks, Waugh, Roy Acuff, Ernest Tubb, Bill Monroe, two local ministers, and the Reverend Billy Graham.

By happenstance, the Ryman had earned a wider national profile just two years before, when it housed the Johnny Cash Show, an ABC series taped between 1969 and 1971. Cash was easily the most popular figure in country music at the time, and perhaps its first star since Hank Williams to truly obliterate boundaries of genre or culture. The show, while not produced by WSM, Inc., was shot on what was essentially a National Life–owned sound stage. That exposure probably helped the Nashville historic community, which, alarmed and motivated, protested National Life's plans for the city's most venerated concert and assembly hall. The company paused and retreated to an outside consultant, which backed its client's assumption: the Ryman was beyond repair. "It would be unprofessional for me as a theatrical designer . . . to recommend the preservation or the reconstruction of the Ryman," wrote hired New York authority Jo Mielziner. Immediately, Benjamin H. Caldwell, president of the Tennessee Historic Sites Federation, protested, calling the report "incomplete" and "superficial." City council hearings, letters to the editor, and even a visit from an interested Nixon administration followed. According to a landmark piece of Nashville reportage by Garrison Keillor for the *New Yorker* in 1974, which covered the history of the Opry and the imminent move to its new modern home, the Ryman's heritage was sold locally more on the basis of its architectural significance and the Carusos and Paderewskis who had performed there than its status as country music's holiest shrine. Another authoritative voice entered the fray at its testiest point. *New York Times* architecture critic Ada Louise Huxtable dedicated a long Sunday column to Nashville's "landmark." National Life's plans, she wrote, were rooted in "a mixture of architectural ignorance and astute business venality." They would mean "abandonment of a neighborhood that needs help and speeding the death of downtown." Good urban design, she wrote, would use the Ryman as a centerpiece of downtown redevelopment. As for the proposed Little Church, she offered "first prize for the pious misuse of a landmark."

National Life argued, with some justification, that it couldn't afford to build Opryland, an Opry house, a hotel, and renovate the Ryman too. It couldn't make Opryland work by doing it halfway, and it didn't want to build a competing attraction in a depressed downtown for weekend nights. So when the Grand Ole Opry moved, amid bittersweet tears and family togetherness, to its new showplace in the spring of 1974, the company put the Ryman in mothballs, opening it only for dollar tours, served by its tour bus division.

Elmer Alley, in keeping with Irving Waugh's commands, saw to it that the ceremonies surrounding the new Opry House were *different*. Ribbon cuttings and golden shovels were forbidden. When ground was broken, Brother Oswald, Acuff's dobro player of an astonishing thirty years, tilled the soil with a mule and plow, while the press took pictures. When the Opry staged its first-ever show from the new building—a modern concrete and timber abstraction of a church—Alley turned to Acuff himself. Vintage film of a young Roy Acuff and the Smoky Mountain Boys performing "Wabash Cannonball" was projected on a large scrim at the front of the stage. After a verse and chorus, Acuff and the Opry cast were revealed from behind with a heart-stopping swell of the stage lights and a smooth segue from taped to live performance. A crisp new red-barn backdrop hovered behind the musicians. Guests and family sat on pews at the back of the stage, facing the audience. Musicians were still visible milling in the backstage wings. "People just gasped," Alley said in 2004. "I heard about it for years."

The other indelible memory from the Opry's move was President Nixon's visit to the show, less than a half year before his humiliating resignation. Protestors picketed him near the Opry House grounds. Jerry Strobel, Opry house manager, remembers struggling to find a photograph for the Opry program of Nixon smiling. When Nixon arrived, he was in fact jovial, famously singing "Wild Irish Rose" for his wife Pat (it was her birthday) and letting Acuff teach him how to spin a yo-yo. It was the first time a president of the United States had ever visited the Opry, and others—especially Republicans—seemed to make a point of it in the following years.

By this time, Opryland USA, essentially in the Opry House's front yard, was two years old and already deemed by the *Banner* "a whopping success in which the entire Nashville community takes pride." It had been carved and landscaped out of a stretch of woodland along the Cumberland about two miles upriver from downtown, accessible only by car, along a new highway named for Mayor Beverly Briley. It had indeed come out quite green and leafy. Four thousand trees had been transplanted by huge truck-mounted tree spades. Villages had been built with plazas and gazebos in a colonial Americana vein. Water flowed through much of the park. Two fully operational antique steam locomotives chugged around the perimeter. A hand-carved gondola ride that had spent years in Copenhagen's Tivoli Gardens was reassembled from five thousand pieces. There were dancing chickens and goats.

Waugh, who had lost plenty of sleep in the final months, wondering if anybody would actually come to his colossal gamble of a theme park, was delighted to discover that the parking lot was too small. The planned motel had been upgraded to a four-hundred-room hotel with convention facilities. The Opry House had been tricked out with the latest television and sound gear, and it was ready for use.

Waugh had even managed to launch another Nashville country music institution in the run-up to the opening of Opryland's first season in the spring of 1972. Fans had been coming to Nashville for years trying to be near the Country Music Festival. Although nobody resented the fans' interest, they were becoming a nuisance at what was, ostensibly, a professional convention. Waugh, meanwhile, needed a galvanizing event to kick off the first season of

Opryland. So he proposed a country music festival to be cosponsored by the record labels, WSM, and the CMA. He called it Fan Fair, another Elmer Alley suggestion. The CMA was wary, but ultimately agreed to be a partner after Waugh guaranteed WSM would cover any losses, which proved briefly necessary. Fan Fair's first year at the downtown Memorial Auditorium, a new domed arena, was less than a success (despite a staggering lineup), chiefly because it was held in mid-April, before schools let out. A shift to June and, eventually, to the easier-to-manage state fairgrounds, made Fan Fair a profitable and popular event that the CMA manages to this day as the CMA Music Festival.

By 1974 most of the world had a mental picture of Nashville, however skewed. Robert Altman's film *Nashville,* which portrayed Music City USA as a gothic enclave for redneck prima donnas and me-generation hippies, didn't help the city's self-image. Indeed, it made a lot of the city's old-liners angry. On the other hand, only a handful of in-the-know music devotees knew of the Nashville portrayed in a much more intimate and realistic film of the period, *Heartworn Highways.* Home movies and interviews with songwriters Guy Clark, Townes Van Zandt, and their soon-to-be-famous brethren, offered Nashville as a new Left Bank for young writers of a sung American poetry.

Somewhere between the incisive parody and the bohemian documentary, a populist, family-friendly picture of Music City came radiating out of National Life, now fully in the come-to-Nashville business. Irving Waugh made Bud Wendell head of Opryland, as well as the Opry, and pushed ahead at last with NLT's oft-delayed plans to build the Opryland Hotel. Wendell and Waugh wanted one thousand rooms. Bill Weaver gave them six hundred but acceded to their wishes to build extensive convention space. By the time the hotel opened in November 1977, it had prebooked $15 million worth of business. Just three years later NLT announced $40 million in expansions to both the rooms and meeting/exhibit space. Wendell's choice to run the hotel, an L. A. veteran named Jack Vaughan, proved a dynamo, presiding over one of the largest and most successful hotel launches in history.

"He created the convention business in Nashville, Tennessee," said Wendell. "And it worked beautifully for us, because conventions typically don't meet in the summertime when you've got a park open. So you got all these people coming to fill those rooms. Conventions typically don't meet on Friday, Saturday. They usually come in Sunday. So now we've got the Grand Ole Opry fifty-two weeks a year to plug those in on the weekends. We've got the park in the summertime and conventions to fill the rest of it out. And it was just a wonderful, wonderful formula. It just worked like a charm."

Arguably the lynchpin of this synergistic boom off Briley Parkway was the maturation, under Wendell, of Opryland USA into a venue for live musical entertainment. Theme parks were everywhere in the 1970s and 1980s. All had shows, but none could match Opryland's commitment to talent discovery and development. Other parks set performances to at least some taped backing. But Opryland used live ensembles as exclusively as NBC had in 1930s radio. "In the summers in those years we worked more union musicians in that one park than any one thing on the planet," said Lloyd Wells, Opryland's music director between 1974 and 1997. "We had something like 160 full-time union musicians working out there—double shifts." And that's not counting the singers and dancers. Wells and a staff of six flew around the country every winter, visiting scores of colleges and city auditoriums to audition between three thousand and five thousand singers and musicians for perhaps three hundred parts in Opryland shows. Young performers coveted the jobs for their training, their camaraderie, and as a springboard to larger things. Some early cast members went on to *A Chorus Line,* Las Vegas's *Follies Berger,* and television's *Happy Days.* Actor Jerry Dixon called Opryland "the College of How To Get To Broadway" in a 1993 *Banner* story. "After you do those four shows a day, outside in ninety-degree weather and ninety-percent humidity, you can do anything," he said. By then, Opryland could claim among its alumni movie actors Mary Elizabeth Mastrantonio, Jim Varney, Cynthia Rhodes, and Broadway performers Jodi Benson, Michael Blevins, Stephen Flaherty, and Reese Holland. Musicians Marty Roe, Dan Truman, and Jimmy Olander reconfigured their group for Music Row and became the hit band Diamond Rio. Country band Little Texas also jelled at Opryland, and two members of Restless Heart met there. Solo artists with Opryland work experience include gospel star Steven Curtis Chapman, country songwriters Dean Dillon and Skip Ewing, and glitzy singer Lorrie Morgan. Conductor Ted Taylor went on to the Chicago Lyric Opera and the New York City Opera.

The park's signature show was a retrospective of early popular songs called *I Hear America Singing,* staged with elaborate *My Fair Lady*-style costuming. It was one big medley, a smoothed-over musical product geared to the tourist trade, but it and others like it offered dozens of musicians good day-job money, along with time getting better at their craft and profession, if not always their art. Another medley-based show traced the history of country music from the 1920s to the present day. Meanwhile, indoor and outdoor stages featured Dixieland jazz, bluegrass, modern pop/rock, and frequent spot shows by Grand Ole Opry stars, all coordinated in one-hour blocks designed to channel visitors from one venue to another past souvenir stores and eateries. There were rides, though nothing that would break any height or speed records. The more distinctive impression was of a hotbed of singers, dancers, accompanists, choreographers, and squads of assistants. There were constant vocal rehearsals and cleanup rehearsals in the morning before the show started. Said Wells: "It was like a factory."

The park's entertainment ambitions were supplemented by another division within WSM, Inc. Launched in 1974, Opryland Productions acted as an independent television company to exploit the Opry House's television soundstage, which at the time was said to be the largest in the world. Besides jumping into the bustling world of syndicated country shows with *Dolly, Marty Robbins' Spotlight, That Nashville Music,* and *Porter Wagoner,* Opryland Productions filmed *Dance in America* on the Opry House stage for public television. The division branched into sports, awards shows, and myriad specials. Late 1970s productions included Lucille Ball in *Lucy Comes to Nashville* with Mel Tillis, Barbara Mandrell, and others; Glenn Campbell's *Back to Basics;* and the syndicated *Pop Goes the Country* with the likes of Ronnie Milsap, Tammy Wynette, Eddie Rabbitt, and Charley Pride.

For Nashville musicians like pianist Beegie Adair, the jazz aficionado from Printer's Alley, the combination of WSM's radio and television shows, Opryland Productions, and the theme park made Nashville an ideal place to live and work. "There were a lot of people like me," she said in 2004. "A typical day would be to get up, do the *Waking Crew,* race home and have a shower, eat some lunch, go back and do the *Noon Show,* and play for completely different kinds of singers. Then I might go do the Ralph Emery show (when it moved to cable television in the evenings). Sometimes it would be all country. One day it was Robert Wagner who wanted to play all Count Basie tunes. Then maybe [I'd] go work in a club and play jazz or cocktail music, or go play a private party, or go do a record session. That's what kept me going financially."

For newcomers to Music City, the park and the productions often meant a first job, something to rely on while building a network. "For entertainers who came to town, it was just a safe, fairly stable training ground for people to transition from life in college or life in high school to the music business—a kind of system and program that I don't know exists anywhere (today)," said Don Cook, who played bass in an Opryland country band his first summer in

Nashville. Cook, who went on to produce platinum-selling albums for Brooks & Dunn and others, added that "I continued to work there for three years and met people who would go on to be friends and colleagues in the music business down the line. It was an invaluable place for just getting a lot of on-stage experience in a really concentrated period of time."

Opryland Productions even sent out mobile units. Over the years they filmed a Christmas special in Disney World, followed the Pope in the Dominican Republic, interviewed Jimmy Carter at his Plains, Georgia, home, and won an Emmy for contributions to coverage of the 1976 Summer Olympics in Montreal. The park and hotel themselves became favored locations for television. Mike Douglas taped his show beside the swimming pool. Crystal Gayle and Ray Stevens offered specials from the Stagedoor Lounge inside the hotel. "The whole complex is a studio," wrote Caleb Pirtle in a 1979 history of the park. "It was made that way."

The man who made it that way was David Hall, a one-time janitor at WSM-TV who studied audio/video engineering and launched a long, lucrative career under WSM's umbrella. He'd wired Opryland and the Opry House before moving into management. In 1977 he was named Opryland Productions General Manager. By 1981 Hall was claiming Nashville's arrival as a television town. "Traditionally, the film and TV industry was localized on the East and West Coasts. Now, Nashville is the Third Coast," he told the *Banner*. (Hall claimed to have coined the term, which would define this era of Nashville's entertainment history, and no one has convincingly contradicted him.) Already, Hall had overseen productions for the new Home Box Office and Showtime networks, plus a Ralph Emery talk/variety series called *Nashville Alive*, being readied for Ted Turner's cable network in Atlanta. And he was in on the planning of something much bigger.

WSM's ambitions in the ascent of cable began in the mid-1960s, when Bud Wendell built a cluster of local networks around Middle Tennessee at the behest of Jack DeWitt. "This country is going to go wired," Wendell remembered DeWitt saying. "It's going to be cabled. We need to explore this." Wendell made the rounds of the early cable television expos, card table affairs in small hotels, where speculators learned how to lay claim to and run local franchises. Known then as Community Antenna Television, all the systems could do, in the absence of dedicated cable television networks, was offer a wired version of broadcast channels that couldn't reach outlying markets. WSM, through a quiet and uncharacteristic joint venture with its insurance competitor Life & Casualty, formed Middle Tennessee CATV, delivering Nashville's TV stations to towns like Cookeville and Tullahoma.

"Our real goal," said Wendell, "was to get experience, because by then we all thought someday cable television is going to come to Nashville, Tennessee. We are then the logical people to get the franchise. We're home folks." That vision was stymied when a new federal law barred owners of local broadcast TV stations from also owning cable franchises. But more than ten years later, when Wendell was president and CEO of WSM and all it surveyed, Opryland Productions was successful enough that he and his management team began contemplating getting back into the cable business, not as a distributor but as a network. "I remember telling [the NLT executive committee] basically that we thought we had all the pieces to create a network, that it was going to be a long pull, it was going to take a lot of money, but that we were early in the game, and if we were successful, as we thought we could be, the sky was the limit," Wendell said. The conservative NLT board likely would have passed on the idea in normal times, but Wendell's plan coincided with unprecedented business struggles.

By the late 1970s, some said NLT had become overstaffed and complacent, relying on industrial insurance as its largest source of income, even as the product itself appeared to be fading into history. What had been a reasonable deal for low-income people now appeared to more and more like exploitation, and in 1979, *60 Minutes* ran an exposé that focused on National Life and said as much. The company's stock declined, and although NLT never lost money, profits in 1980 dipped for the first time in ten years. With analysts calling its stock undervalued and its huge pool of assets undermanaged, the company looked increasingly vulnerable to a corporate takeover. The most likely acquirer, American General Corporation of Houston, hovered over National Life for more than a decade.

American General did acquire Life & Casualty in 1967, plus at least two other insurers in the meantime. In the early 1970s, American General began buying National Life stock until, by 1978, it owned 5 percent of the company, sparking speculation that it was about to pounce for control. In a defensive move, National Life acquired Great Southern, another Houston insurance company, in a deal designed to make themselves too big to swallow. It didn't work. Nashville business historian Bill Carey wrote that "by 1979, NLT was under siege" with suitors that included American General, Charter Oil, and the Seagram Company. That's when NLT Chairman Rusty Wagner declared at a board meeting that unless NLT made a bold move to bolster the company's stock price ("hit a home run" is how Wendell remembers him saying it) they'd likely be acquired. So Wendell put the cable network back on the table, and the board gave it the green light—at least a $60 million gambit in an emerging medium that would take at least five years to return profits, if it ever did.

The new direction wouldn't come without sacrifice. In the fall of 1981, WSM-TV was sold to Gillett Broadcasting of Wausau, Wisconsin. The first sale of a WSM media property in history, shocking because it was so remote to the corporation's culture, was a calculated move to raise funds—about $40 million as it turned out—toward the $60 million launch of The Nashville Network (TNN). Most employees who didn't stay with Channel 4 (now WSMV) moved over to the TNN side, notably Elmer Alley, whose job was to build the new network's programs, with David Hall running the show as general manager. The would-be network set up in a suite of trailers behind the Grand Ole Opry House. WSM radio, an ever smaller piece of a growing media company, moved to a new home near the Opryland Hotel, a one-story colonial that looked a bit like the old Brentwood transmitter house, whose elegant 1932 tower was still very much in use.

Bold though it may have been, The Nashville Network wasn't enough to mollify all of the company's old family shareholders. "National Life was a pretty paternalistic company," said Ridley Wills. "And some members of the third generation, my generation, who didn't work at National Life, wanted to maximize their profits and thought it ought to be putting out more dividends. That often happens to third generations; they want their money. None of us who were up there wanted to sell it." According to Wills, his family and the Craigs fought to hold on while members of the Fort and Tyne families paved the way for corporate suitors. In the spring of 1982 American General formally bid for National Life. National Life made a counteroffer, which the larger company fought in court.

Margaret Ann Robinson, Edwin Craig's daughter, remembers a time of "grieving and fighting" over a company that had become far more than a livelihood for her siblings. It was a literal extension of the family, run by uncles, cousins, and in-laws—the very focal point of their social and ethical universe. It was hard enough to watch the old Home Office at Seventh and Union—literally in the shadow of the new NLT tower—crumble under the wrecking ball in 1981. When National Life finally lost its fight to remain independent in July 1982, it was like losing a patriarch. "I did not know who I was or what I was without the National Life behind me," Robinson said in 2004. "It's still very tender." The

Craigs' Belle Meade relatives kept mum about the whole difficult affair, in stoic southern fashion. "I didn't say anything, because it was kind of like somebody had died," said Donia Craig Dickerson, Francis Craig's daughter. "I remember being purposely quiet about it. I wasn't going to discuss it . . . I just thought it was the end of a beautiful era, the end of a beautiful story."

The story was far from over for hundreds of TNN, WSM, and Opry employees who were still working in a fog of suspense. What would become of them in the hands of an out-of-state insurance giant? It became clear to Wendell almost immediately that all of the former National Life's entertainment properties would be sold yet again, in whole or as parts. So amid the throes of getting TNN up and running, a new round of corporate courtship began. "We're running absolutely full speed—hiring people every day, turning cameras on, doing deals with Westinghouse for distribution," said Carl Kornmeyer, then a National Life financial analyst. "We are going literally twenty-hour days, seven days a week. And then the tire kickers start. People are coming in deciding whether they want to buy this stuff. They want to see everything." On the list of leading suitors: Anheuser-Busch of St. Louis, Marriott, U.S. Tobacco, and the New York investors Kohlberg, Kravis, and Roberts. In the mix as well was a sentimental favorite, a consortium of investors that included Neil Craig (ready to commit the family fortune), Ridley Wills II, and a prominent local business-man named Bronson Ingram. When the bidding got too rich, the old National Life families had to drop out, while Ingram remained interested as a long-shot bidder. What happened next could hardly have been stranger. Neil Craig's home phone rang. It was Minnie Pearl, with a way out of the whole mess.

Minnie Pearl, now nearing seventy years old, wore many more hats than her famous straw sun blocker with the $1.98 price tag. She was a devoted wife to Henry Cannon, a pilot and owner of a charter air company that delivered Opry stars all over the United States; a dedicated board member for numerous Nashville charities and civic organizations; an international persona; and a down-to-earth Nashville neighbor. Margaret Ann Robinson was one of many who thought of her as Sarah Cannon and who regarded her as the essential ambassador between cultural Nashville and country music Nashville. "She was always invited to be on the list and to be on the board of everything that came along," Robinson said. "She was constantly trying to get the artists—the country music people like herself—and the city of Nashville together. And she died trying. She never quit trying. If you wanted to reach fund-raising for the Symphony, you got Sarah to come to your ball. And Sarah would get up three tables and pay for everybody that you can think of." Eddie Jones, the *Banner* TV columnist who didn't have a TV, freely admits he used Miss Minnie "unmercifully" when he became chief of the chamber of commerce between 1967 and 1987. "If we had an industrial development prospect or a site relocation thing and had some reason to believe the decision-makers had a country music interest, we'd bring Minnie into dinner, and she'd regale them. She'd say, 'Hey, you fellas need to come on down here. We do this all the *time.*' She was a great salesperson."

She lived in a large house next door to the Governor's Mansion in the Forest Hills neighborhood, and she was a familiar sight on Belle Meade Country Club courts in her crisp tennis whites. Pianist Beegie Adair remembered being one of hundreds if not thousands of Nashvillians in and out of the music business who exchanged sincere hellos and visited with her in the grocery store. Pearl had even survived a public scandal in the late 1960s—an extraordinary comedy of errors involving the downfall of an eccentric would-be governor and a fried chicken franchise with her name on it. But Minnie endured and deepened into a southern player for the ages. She and Roy Acuff, the power-broker of the Opry as long as he was alive, became close friends and allies. When Bill Weaver needed to settle something down at the Orpy, he'd call Roy and Minnie to come have lunch in his office and talk it over. They'd work quiet solutions and pave the way for new ideas in the always-guarded Opry cast. "I don't know how Bill would have managed WSM with all else he was trying to manage if he hadn't had Roy and Minnie," said Weaver's widow, Elizabeth Proctor. And "if you couldn't go through the Craig/Weaver/Robinson power structure and you wanted to get something done," Eddie Jones said, "the smart thing to do was to take Minnie to coffee and say, how can we make this work? She had great credibility with her peers. If she came and said something was a good idea, we've got to get behind this, you had it whooped."

For thirty or more years, as the Opry's signature comedienne, Minnie Pearl became a favorite guest on the *Tonight Show, The Carol Burnett Show,* and *The Jonathan Winters Show.* The producer of the latter, Sam Lovullo, tapped her to join a new country comedy and music show called *Hee Haw* in 1969. Hillbilly to its core, *Hee Haw* became the most popular country television show of all time, a hit in syndication all through the 1970s and 1980s. With Minnie as one anchoring cast member, the show revived a number of careers and introduced new ones. Grandpa Jones, a veteran singer, banjo player, and songwriter, was a throwback to Uncle Dave Macon. Buck Owens and Roy Clark, a dazzling singer and picker respectively, anchored the show musically, while the buxom "Hee Haw Honeys" burst out of their Lil' Abner getups.

The show's owner, Oklahoma City publishing and media executive Ed Gaylord, sincerely loved country music. A much older fellow, he and wife Thelma used to come to Nashville to hang out on the set when the show was being taped in thirteen-week runs at the Opry House. The Gaylords knew Minnie Pearl well, and she and Lovullo helped introduce Ed Gaylord to Bud Wendell. The two men struck up an easy, trusting relationship. Thus, when Gaylord's self-named company bought Opryland, the hotel, and all of the related radio and cable properties in 1983, the locus of corporate control may have left Nashville, but to everyone's relief, the locus of decision making did not.

"Ed Gaylord invested in Bud Wendell," explained Kornmeyer. "He didn't spend any time telling Bud Wendell, 'here's what you ought to do.' He bought into Bud Wendell as much as he bought into Opryland USA, Inc." His only mandate: "Keep doing what you're doing." That included TNN, which went on the air just three months before the sale of Opryland was finalized. It also included a pet project of Wendell's that had been churning for some time—a paddle wheel showboat that would offer tourists and conventioneers one more experience during their lengthening stays, as well as a floating homage to the Nashville of one hundred years before.

There had been, after all, a happy ending, a white knight who was happy to let the company continue along as it had been. Veterans of the Opry and WSM say they felt no real shifts, with Wendell at the helm before, during, and after the transition. "Of all the people that tried to buy Opryland—if it couldn't be us, Ed Gaylord was our first choice," said Margaret Ann Robinson. "Ed Gaylord understood country music and the country musician. And we knew as long as he was the buyer, for his lifetime, it would all be all right."

The Nashville Network went live at 8:00 p.m. Tennessee time on March 7, 1983, with Ralph Emery hosting a "coast to coast party." It began with an hour-long musical salute from the Opry House with Roy Acuff balancing a fiddle and bow on his chin (a trademark move) and Patti Page in a sequined gown. Tammy Wynette appeared by satellite from Chicago, Bill Monroe and Emmylou Harris from the set of *Austin City Limits,* and Tanya Tucker and Hoyt Axton from the Palomino Club in Los Angeles. Opry star Bill Anderson said optimistically, "Years from now, people will remember March 7, 1983, just like they do the day the Grand Ole Opry went on. A hundred years from now they'll be talking about us."

Emery anchored the network with a Johnny Carson–style talk show that focused on country artists without being limited to them. Over the years, he interviewed Lily Tomlin, Jay Leno, Jimmy Stewart, Robert Duvall, President George H. W. Bush, Barbara Eden, Wayne Newton, and Tommy Lasorda, among many others. His country-star guests included the ascendant and the transcendent: Reba McEntire, Merle Haggard, George Strait, Johnny Cash, Willie Nelson, Ronnie Milsap, Dolly Parton, and on and on. In 1986 *Cable Guide* magazine named Emery the most popular personality on cable television. He is widely seen as instrumental in launching the careers of Randy Travis and Lorrie Morgan, and he gave Oklahoman Garth Brooks some of his earliest national face time. The show wasn't without controversy on Music Row. Some executives thought TNN overexposed country stars, robbing them of their mystique. And often the record labels counseled their artists to stay away from Emery's lengthy, unpredictable, and sometimes aggressive interviews. Media coaches in town actually role-played Emery in exercises designed to prepare artists for what they regarded as the toughest interview they'd ever have.

With eighteen hours initially and eventually twenty-four hours to fill, just about every kind of Nashville music and entertainment style and outlet was put on TNN in its early days. Beegie Adair got to play jazz from the Maxwell House Hotel with saxophonist Dennis Solee. Johnny Rodriguez played his Tex-Mex country from Nashville's Cannery. The call went out for "hot country dancers" trained in "all facets of dance, including jazz, ballet, adagio and clogging" for a show called *Dancin' U.S.A.* Teddy Bart, by then a news anchorman on Channel 2, was tapped for a midday, thirty-minute interview show with musicians. The Riders in the Sky, a Nashville-born cowboy revival band with Grammy Awards in its future, were hired to host *Tumbleweed Theater*, a Western movie showcase. And some familiar country artists stepped into some odd new roles, no more so than singer/songwriter Bill Anderson hosting a game show about country music trivia. A broadcast of Willie Nelson's all-day Farm Aid concert from Champaign, Illinois, in the fall of 1985 put TNN on the map nationally.

In its early years, TNN was by turns quaint, brilliant, slick, brassy, and cheesy, but by the late 1980s, the network had helped make Opryland USA (now the blanket corporate name for Gaylord's country music empire) Tennessee's largest private employer with 3,227 permanent employees and $350 million in gross revenue annually. Opryland drew 65,000 people on most Saturdays and more than two million visitors a year. The hotel kept its 1,891 rooms mostly full.

By 1987 Hall could call TNN "the hottest thing in cable television." It would be the first profitable year for the network, the first of many. Most of its shows were either produced in-house or by TNN crew working with freelance producers like Jim Owens. By the end of the 1980s it was the seventh-largest cable network in the United States and the most watched, curiously, in Canada. TNN reached forty-nine million households and it featured the Opry for thirty minutes weekly, to strong ratings. It had earned its way onto cable TV in Manhattan, bolstering the image of country on Madison Avenue. The network's diverse live music lineup included concert specials by Johnny Cash, George Jones, Bill Monroe, Don Williams, and many others.

In 1991 Gaylord acquired Country Music Television (CMT), a fledgling video channel in the model of MTV. CMT and TNN were managed separately, under David Hall's direction. At the same time, country music accelerated out of a mid-1980s lull, shattering all prior records for sales and radio success. With a neotraditional pendulum swing usually attributed to Ricky Skaggs and Randy Travis, the vaunted "Class of '89" graduated superstars and class acts like Clint Black, Brooks & Dunn, Dwight Yoakam, and Alan Jackson, a one-time employee of the TNN mailroom. In 1991 the career of Garth Brooks surged toward megastardom, moving the bar for what constituted major label success in the country music format up several feet, for better or worse.

Gaylord's country-TV networks pushed and benefited from that growth. Hall is clear which came first in his mind. "Country music took off in the nineties *because* we controlled both TNN and CMT," he said. "We were *the* driving force in country music. Where else does a brand like country have two networks pounding out twenty-four-hours a day, seven days a week, what the music is about. We drove that acceleration because we used TNN and the live shows to build the personality, and we used CMT to sell the music."

Never had so many Nashville musicians worked so steadily. The offices of the cable networks, the production company, the park, and the hotel were all within walking distance of one another in a growing complex of theaters. Roy Acuff moved into a house adjacent to this new Music City microcosm, turning the Opryland complex into his backyard. One longtime employee likened the operation at its height to the back lot of Twentieth Century Fox, with its constant flow of musicians, technicians, and stars. Usually remembered as the apex of tourism in Nashville, 1990s Opryland also had an incalculable effect on the musicians who made up the real fabric of Music City.

Then in 1994 Wendell spearheaded a project that crystallized WSM's legacy in modern Nashville, while bolstering the city itself. The Ryman Auditorium, notwithstanding a badly needed cosmetic upgrade in 1989, had largely languished for twenty years, home to tours and a handful of movie shoots and special concerts that couldn't accommodate balcony guests for safety reasons. At last, Gaylord invested $9 million to renovate the venue top to bottom. The pews were scraped of gum and restored. A new foyer reoriented the box office side from Fifth Avenue to Fourth Avenue and made space for the building's first ever HVAC system. A proscenium wall was built for the first time, with multiple floors back stage making room for up-to-date dressing rooms and all-new broadcast technology. Museum cases around the back of the hall showcased the pre- and post-Opry history of the 110-year-old building.

And that was far from all. Gaylord launched another thousand-room expansion of Opryland Hotel. Workers were so scarce, Gaylord recruited hotel workers from Puerto Rico and bought a 150-room motel on Murfreesboro Road to house them. Gaylord built new corporate headquarters on Briley Parkway and introduced a new Nashville On Stage live music series. It opened the Wildhorse Saloon, a new country dance club, on Second Avenue, and promoted it with a daily show on TNN. Its investments that year totaled $200 million. "There's no indication that the company has hit a ceiling on growth," wrote Mary Hance in the *Banner*. Or on imagination. The next summer, the U.S. kayaking championships were held on the fabricated Class III rapids of Opryland's Grizzly River Rampage as part of a run-up to the Atlanta Olympics of 1996.

Just about anything seemed possible. Gaylord Entertainment had taken the WSM legacy of investing in entertainment and built it to international stature, using the newest forms of mass media. But this magic kingdom, so long in the making, so fruitful for its home city, was in a more precarious position than any of its visitors or its thousands of employees could have imagined. By the early 2000s Opryland USA and TNN would not exist. Gaylord, under new leadership, would change direction and make major decisions that would mystify investors and the local community alike. And in the turbulence, WSM, the country music station of the century and the accidental architect of Music City, would be taken to the brink of extinction.

Epilogue

SIGNAL FADE

For his stewardship of the Grand Ole Opry and the growth of TNN and CMT, E. W. "Bud" Wendell was inducted into the Country Music Hall of Fame in 1998, just one year after his retirement as Gaylord's CEO. He was remembered by former employees and Opry artists as a warm, effective leader whose philosophy about the WSM/Opry complex strongly resembled its original leader Edwin Craig. Almost from the day Wendell left, Gaylord became a more controversial and troubled company.

Wendell was, for example, surprised and mystified by one of the first decisions made by his successor, former Gaylord CFO Terry London. The board had approved a deal to tear down Opryland USA and replace it with a large shopping mall called Opry Mills. The rationale was that park attendance had slipped below the critical two million mark in the middle 1990s, and that even with massive capital investment, it would be hard to compete with year-round, technology-heavy amusement parks in Florida and California. It was estimated that the "destination" mall would attract millions more people per year to the doorstep of the Opry House and the Opryland Hotel.

It didn't work out that way. Business writer Bill Carey called Opryland's closure "a crushing blow" for Nashville tourism. City officials, newspapers, and citizens were irate at Gaylord from the first announcement. "The emotional attachment from the community was not weighed heavily enough," then

PR director Tom Adkinson explained in retrospect. "That presented a real burden to us. We were constantly on the defensive from the time the decision was made." Even Gaylord now concedes Opry Mills was a bad idea. "It's clear that the closing of the park negatively affected the number of tourists that visited Nashville in the summer," Gaylord spokesman Greg Rossiter told the *Tennessean* in 2004. "The current management team has found no compelling reasons why the decision to close the park was taken in the first place."

An even bigger loss for Nashville's entertainment portfolio came as an unintended consequence of Wendell's last major business decision. In 1997 Gaylord sold cable properties TNN and CMT to Westinghouse, TNN's long-time minority owner and marketing partner. Wendell and the board understood and expected that TNN would remain a Nashville-based network, but with significantly greater leverage in the marketplace and greater access to investment capital. Unfortunately, relying on historic relationships proved naïve in the consolidating new media economy. In rapid succession, CBS bought Westinghouse, which was in turn acquired by media giant Viacom, owner of MTV. With little notice, TNN's Nashville offices and production operations were dismantled and the network was ultimately reinvented as Spike TV, which targets a young male demographic with action movies, extreme fighting, and bikini-clad models.

Many of the newly out-of-work engineers, stage hands, editors, and trained television crews might have been absorbed into a newly invigorated Opryland Productions. But Terry London's Gaylord was emphasizing new investment in hotels and resorts, and the company got out of the TV business almost entirely. "He shut down the production facilities. Just shut 'em down," Wendell said of London. "Got rid of everybody. Just like he shut the park down. He had a totally different vision. I never could figure out what it was he wanted to accomplish."

Gaylord suffered other setbacks, notably a digital entertainment division that lost tens of millions before laying off eighty-five people and shutting down. The company acquired two Christian music World Wide Web portal/retail sites and sold them less than two years later. It purchased a profitable Nashville startup called Songs.com, one of the first online marketing and retail sites for independent musicians, and killed it in one year. It launched a fan site called MusicCountry.com, which also died with the bursting of the first dot-com bubble. Gaylord also spent millions trying to launch a country record label with a well-paid Music Row veteran at its head. It signed only one artist and never released an album before being shuttered. London resigned in July 2000.

In a few years, Gaylord had retreated from being a national player in entertainment production and dismantled many of the synergistic businesses that kept the Grand Ole Opry vibrant. Not only did this put WSM and the Opry in a more tenuous position, it affected all of Nashville. Lloyd Wells, the Opryland music director, said hundreds of Nashville musicians were "making a fair, decent living [at the Opryland complex]. And when that thing closed, I can just see them all scattering. Because the town can't support them. There was not enough work. So they had to go somewhere else. God knows where they all went. The economic impact on the musicians and performers was real bad."

Tom Adkinson, Gaylord's former PR director, agreed that Gaylord's retreat from show business hurt the soul of Music City. "It absolutely had an effect on the city's personality. It made a difference in that creative community," he said. "I have a friend at church who is a violinist. She earned a good wage playing in one of the big shows at Opryland every year. I'm sure that was the secondary income in her household, but it was significant. Over the course of time, the park would take an eleven-member band and make it nine, or have smaller shows. I remember her observing to me [that] there's not many places where a violinist can make any money. That's one aspect of the company that wasn't hidden, but it wasn't ever understood or stated."

Not in the modern era anyway. But as late as 1966, WSM regarded its role as employer of creative people as important, prestigious, and even commercially sound. In a self-written and forgivably self-congratulatory article in a *Tennessean* supplement spotlighting Country Music Week and the DJ convention, WSM offered a statement of purpose as clear as anything it ever committed to paper. "The body and soul of music is, of course, the musician," it said. "In Nashville he has prospered, whereas in other regions of the country—lacking a patron—he has sought a more financially sound if less satisfying form of work." With this article, WSM accepted a mantle it had worn unconsciously for years—that of a "patron" of music. "Through the long, lean years, music still originated from these studios and halls," WSM said. Even in that relative lull of the mid-1960s, well after the boom in live radio had subsided and before TNN or Opryland were even contemplated, WSM reported that it was paying out the equivalent of 1,400 recording sessions per year to union musicians. Some members of the Opry staff band had been making their living for decades entirely from being part of WSM's cadre of musicians, highlighting "the key, almost singular role the Opry and WSM have played in the survival of a music industry in Nashville."

With the demise of TNN and Opryland, this supporting piece of Music City's substructure was gone, and little has come along to replace it. Teddy Bart, the singer/pianist/interviewer, speaks for a lot of people when he blames Gaylord's new leadership for the decline. To his mind, 1997 marked the end of a line of visionary producers who sought to develop mass entertainment that was popular because it was good, not engineered to be popular—George Hay, Harry Stone, Beasley Smith, Jack Stapp, Owen Bradley, Irving Waugh, Elmer Alley, and Bud Wendell. "Those people were *impresarios*," Bart said, relishing the word as much as the idea. "As contrasted with the bean counters that run the [entertainment] business today. They were *showmen*. Each one with an innate sense of knowing talent, audience, the various components to putting on a show. These were the Ziegfelds of our time. Today when you go to someone with a concept, it's: 'Is it [targeted to the] 18–25 [demographic]? Let's test it.' These people didn't need focus groups. They *were* the focus groups. There was a compass inside which directed where the audience was and how to get there . . . I just cannot tell you the respect I have for that era."

Amid the turmoil at Gaylord, WSM-AM hummed along, under the radar as it were, with classic country music spun by expert DJs during the week and the Grand Ole Opry every Friday, Saturday, and Tuesday night, broadcasting over the same diamond-shaped radio tower Jack DeWitt and Edwin Craig had erected in 1932. The station had struggled for an identity during the 1980s and early 1990s, veering from what one program director called a "comfortable old shoe" personality to stunt- and contest-driven attempts to woo a radio public that had largely moved on to FM for music. Indeed, for years during the Wendell administration, WSM-AM was allowed to compete with its higher-fidelity, stereo sibling WSM-FM, while playing a too-similar format of country music.

By its seventieth-fifth anniversary in October 2000, however, WSM sounded like nothing else on the dial in Nashville or in the United States. Under operations manager Kyle Cantrell, who had grown up on WSM and who studied its history, the AM signal was reasserting itself as a taste-maker and talent developer in traditional country music. Whereas the nation's two thousand commercial country FM radio stations relied on short, similar playlists of contemporary pop country, WSM adopted the slogan "Too Country and Proud of It," and played records from the 1940s to the current day across many subgenres of traditional country music, including honky-tonk, Western swing, folk, and bluegrass. It played songs from the Grammy-winning, old-time country soundtrack of "O Brother, Where Art Thou?" when hit-driven FM country wouldn't. It sent its DJs out to live, old-time country music events and it revived *Opry Star Spotlight*, bringing in guests who talked and performed live deep into the night.

"We needed to make an impact," Kyle Cantrell summarized in 2004. "This station needed to be bigger than the local market. An AM radio station playing music is never going to compete on a local ratings level. So what we needed to do was go out and make the station bigger than life so it's not about local ratings. This was my rationale: it's not about how many people listen so much as it is the impact of the station in a bigger sense. WSM needed to once again become the dog that wags the tail. It needs to be the station that people, if they're involved with country music, have to be involved with."

One of the signature voices of WSM at the time was Eddie Stubbs, a DJ and bluegrass fiddle player whose passion for and expertise about country music history has few equals in the nation, let alone in Nashville. He parlayed his wide respect for and among traditional country music stars into thorough on-air interviews and career retrospectives. "Everybody was on fire," Stubbs said of the years between 1999 and 2001. "This place was not just a job. It was our life. It was a part of our soul. When you're into something so deep and it means so much to you it goes beyond a fan base. It turns into a love, and it turns into passion. I know for a fact that it was that way for me, and it was for Kyle Cantrell."

But Cantrell's experiment in reinventing WSM came to a sudden halt on August 15, 2001, just a few months into the tenure of new Gaylord CEO Colin Reed, an Englishman who came from the Las Vegas hotel and casino industry. The new administration had taken a top-to-bottom look at the units of the company and decided that the classic-country WSM wasn't contributing to the bottom line. In a meeting that Cantrell will never forget, WSM's general manager told him that in about a month, the AM country station he loved so much was going to be converted to a news-sports-talk format.

Once the plans leaked to the news media, Nashville rallied to WSM's defense. Country star Vince Gill said he was willing to call in seventeen years of favors from Gaylord to keep WSM country. Young torchbearer Brad Paisley and one of his mentors, Bill Anderson, asked for and got a meeting to lobby CEO Reed. The January 2002 protest rally outside the studios earned coverage in the *New York Times* and on National Public Radio (NPR), while an Internet petition, ultimately with more than nine thousand signatures, proved that WSM, through its Webcasting presence, had fans all over the world. After two weeks of suspense and agitation, Reed called a press conference at the Ryman Auditorium to say that WSM would in fact remain country. "The last two to three weeks were very helpful to me in seeing the potential" of WSM's classic country format, Reed said. "I knew it was there. I just didn't know how big it was, and I think it's big."

Even so, WSM operated with smaller budgets and less autonomy. Kyle Cantrell and six other station veterans were let go in early 2003. In March of that year, WSM-FM was sold to radio company Cumulus Media, while WSM-AM had its ad sales department moved by contract to Cumulus. That led to another round of layoffs at WSM-AM, leaving a small, demoralized staff. In 2004, WSM's offices were moved out of their freestanding building at the edge of the Opryland Hotel complex and into a basement of the Opry administration building, while its studio moved to what had been a remote broadcasting booth in the Opryland Hotel itself. For the first time in more than seventy years, the phones at WSM-AM were answered by a recording, not a person.

What will, or should, become of WSM and the Grand Ole Opry in the twenty-first century? Can these intimately intertwined properties thrive in a publicly traded company chiefly focused on the hotel and hospitality business? Gaylord certainly has made a shining example of one venerable institution profitably reinventing itself, and that's the Ryman Auditorium, which plays host to all kinds of concerts from country to classical to rock. Under the management of concert promoter Pam Matthews, the first woman to run the Ryman since Lula Naff, it was twice named the nation's finest concert venue by the prestigious *Pollstar* magazine in the 2000s. It is possible to imagine WSM, with sufficient investment, as a kind of audio equivalent of the renovated Ryman. In a time when traditional country music fans are giving up on Top 40 commercial country radio, WSM with its international Web presence might be positioned as the on-air, online authority on country music worldwide.

Others have proposed that WSM, the Ryman, and the Opry be spun off as a nonprofit institution, a living museum and a showcase for American roots music past, present, and future—not unlike the very marketable (and Opry-inspired) Prairie Home Companion. Under this scenario, all the inter-related historic WSM properties would be run by owners whose loyalties weren't divided and whose expertise wasn't stretched thin. Besides, one might argue also that after all it's been through and all it has accomplished, demanding that WSM live or die by the media economy's new rules feels a bit like asking your grandmother to work at Burger King to make ends meet. How we rescue seniors from economic indignity and American cultural icons from economic obsolescence are questions policy makers, communities, and academies should discuss at length. How WSM might fulfill its destiny in a technologically dynamic time is a question Gaylord and Nashville could do much more to answer together.

As for Nashville, it will always be Music City, but without a major entertainment investment engine at its core, the coming years will test its ability to remain vital and relevant to the larger music economy. The music business is changing radically, and radical change has never been in Nashville's character. The city's best hope may be a new generation of entrepreneurs smart enough to reinvent artist development by marrying talent, technology, and creative sponsorship (insurance companies? self-rising flour? roll-your-own tobacco?). Nashville's music and entertainment companies could do worse than take cues from the first wave of Music Row pioneers, the ones who learned the art of the deal at WSM. Some of the old ways of doing business—sharing scarce resources, outrageous marketing, brazen moonlighting, modest expectations, handshake deals, and even frequent parties—have been forgotten in the rush toward efficiency, size, domination, public offerings, and the like. Many music-business professionals crave a return to basics, where music and the delight it brings can be reasserted as the core commodity. What George Hay once said of the Opry could easily apply to Nashville's musical heart: "It is as fundamental as sunshine and rain, snow and wind and the light of the moon peeping through the trees. Some folks like it and some dislike it very much, but it'll be there long after you and I have passed out of this picture for the next one."

It will be whatever we who cherish it make of it.

Notes

Introduction

WSM's central role in building Nashville is asserted in Brown, Les, "WSM Stretched 'Opry' a Country Mile, Catapulted Nashville as C&W Centre," *Variety,* Oct. 29, 1969. The Peter Taylor quote about Nashville comes from the novel *A Summons To Memphis.* Historical facts about Nashville come from Doyle.

Chapter 1: On the Very Air We Breathe

Jack DeWitt's interaction with Ward-Belmont School was recorded in the *Ward-Belmont Hyphen,* Apr. 1, 1920, and Apr. 21, 1922, Belmont University library, Nashville. DeWitt's biographical details are drawn from an interview with Chuck McDonald and an unpublished autobiography, both in the collection of Gaylord Entertainment; a DeWitt family diary; and a Country Music Foundation (CMF) oral history interview with John Rumble, July 1986. Early radio history comes from Barnouw and Douglas. The origins of National Life are covered in Stamper; the origins of WSM and opening night are covered in the *Tennessean,* the *Nashville Banner,* and *Broadcast News,* Nov. 12, 1932.

ALSO CITED:

DeWitt, John H., Jr., "Early Radio Broadcasting in Middle Tennessee." *Tennessee Historical Quarterly.* Spring 1972.

Johnson, Dixon, "Let Jack Alone." *The Nashville Tennessean Magazine,* May 12, 1946.

Davis, Louise Littleton, "From Chicken House to the Moon." *Nashville Tennessean Magazine,* June 2, 1963.

"WSM, at Nashville, 'We Shield Millions.'" *Radio Digest,* Nov. 7, 1925.

The Shield: Mar. 11, 1924; Apr. 28, 1925; Aug. 11, 1925; Sept. 22, 1925; Sept. 29, 1925; Oct. 6, 1925; Oct. 20, 1925.
Nashville Banner: Oct. 4–6, 1925.

Author interviews: Ward DeWitt, Elizabeth Proctor, Neil Craig, Margaret Ann Robinson.
CMF oral history with David Stone.

Chapter 2: The Ears Are Eyes

The baseball anecdote comes largely from the *Banner,* Oct. 5, 1925. Jack Keefe's biography comes from his obituaries in the *Banner* and *Tennessean* on Oct. 15, 1954. Early programming and personality details are drawn from *The Shield,* which was renamed *Our Shield* in 1926. Many early WSM performers and shows are described in the Nov. 12, 1932, issue of *Broadcast News.* Edwin Craig's struggles with interference come from correspondence in WSM station files at the National Archives. Station budget figures come from WSM testimony before the Federal Radio Commission (FRC), Docket No. 887, Sept. 1930. The riverfront story is from Shelton's memoir. The chapter also relies on Wolfe's *Good Natured Riot* for the origins of the Opry, and Ikard's *Near You* on Francis Craig, as well as Jack Hurst's *Nashville's Grand Ole Opry,* Morton and Wolfe's *DeFord Bailey,* Hawkins and Escott's *Shot in the Dark,* Foust's *Big Voices of the Air,* and Peterson's *Creating Country Music.*

ALSO CITED:

Davis, Louise, "He Raised a Rookus." *Nashville Tennessean Magazine,* Aug. 17, 1952.
Garvey, Daniel E, "Secretary Hoover and the Quest for Broadcast Regulation." *Journalism History* 3:3. Autumn 1976.
"WSM's Fourth Birthday." *Radio Digest,* Oct. 1929.

The Shield or *Our Shield:* Sept. 22, 1925; Oct. 27, 1925; Nov. 24, 1925; Jan. 19, 1926; Mar. 16, 1926; May 25, 1926; June 15, 1926; Oct. 5, 1926; Oct. 12, 1926; Nov. 2, 1926; Dec. 7, 1926; Jan. 4, 1927; Jan. 3, 1928; Jan. 11, 1927; Feb. 21, 1928; Mar. 20, 1928; Mar. 27, 1928; Apr. 14, 1928; June 19, 1928; July 3, 1928; Nov. 8, 1928.

Author interviews: Donia Craig Dickerson, Elizabeth Proctor.
CMF oral histories: David Stone, Vito Pellettieri.

Chapter 3: A Pleasing Spectacle

The international fan mail to WSM was recorded in a little-known National Life publication for policyholders called *Shielded Homes* (fourth quarter 1931) from the collection of Leroy Troy. The full-power hearings and related documents come from the archives of the FRC, National Archives, Docket No. 887. Details of George Hay's wage garnishing of DeFord Bailey can be found in Morton and Wolfe, p. 84. Francis Craig and Beasley Smith details come from Ikard and from Broome and Tucker's *The Other Music City,* plus a *Nashville Banner* story ("Smith to Conduct 25-Piece Jubilee Orchestra," March 21, 1951). Minnie Pearl's story comes from her autobiography. Alton Delmore's observation of the tower comes from his autobiography. Day-to-day details of the station and programs come from *Our Shield*, the *Tennessean* and the *Banner*.

ALSO CITED:

"Nine Stations Given Maximum Power." *Broadcasting*, Oct. 15, 1931.
"WABC Half-Wave Antenna Promising." *Broadcasting*, Oct. 15, 1931.

Broadcast News: Mar. 19, 1932; Apr. 30, 1932; June 4, 1932; July 9, 1932; July 23, 1932;
Our Shield: Feb. 5, 1929; Oct. 30, 1928; Jan. 20, 1931; May 10, 1932; May 17, 1932; May 24, 1932; May 31, 1932; June 7, 1932; July 19, 1932; Aug. 2, 1932; June 21, 1932; Aug. 9, 1932 (source of the "steeplechase" metaphor); Oct. 4, 1932; Nov. 8, 1932; Nov. 22, 1932.

Author interviews: Donia Craig Dickerson, Neil Craig, Ridley Wills II, Watt Hairston, Marjorie Cooney.

Chapter 4: Air Castle of the South

The scene with the *Pan American* is reconstructed from detailed accounts of the broadcast included in Aaron Shelton's memoir, plus several articles ("Did You Ever See a Locomotive Dress-Rehearse?" *Shielded Homes*, third quarter 1935; Harris, Jack, "Radio Broadcast Revels in Romance of the Rails," *Radio Varieties*, May 1940.) The Depression in Nashville is covered in volume two of Doyle's *Nashville Since the 1920s*. The internal National Life correspondence comes from the collection of Ridley Wills II. Ed Kirby's papers at the Library of American Broadcasting (LAB) include several biographical sketches. Also see *Broadcasting* ("How Radio Is Selling Life Insurance," Feb. 1, 1935, and "We Pay Our Respects to Edward Montague Kirby," Feb. 1, 1937.) The "early training guide" is in the Library of Congress (*A Guide Book to Ordinary Production for Old and New Shield Men*, National Life, 1932). The Stone story about Jehovah's Witnesses is from Ed Kirby's written recollections for a "Radio Pioneers" archive, dated Feb. 15, 1952, at the LAB. Harry Stone's memories come from "Looking Back," a first-person account published in *Country Music Who's Who*, year unknown. The Opry's progress comes from Wolfe, Hay, and an *Our Shield* story from Nov. 2, 1936, plus Vito Pelletieri's oral history at the CMF. The *Tennessean* editorial praising the Opry was published July 3, 1935. Jim Denny's biography comes largely from Cunniff's *Journal of Country Music* series, cited in the bibliography. Minnie Pearl's autobiography is referenced. Jack Harris material comes from an oral history by Joseph Ryan at KPRC-TV, Channel 2, Houston, Aug. 16, 1993, collected at LAB, as well as *Shielded Homes*, fourth quarter 1934. Snooky Lanson's story comes from Ikard and the *Tennessean* (York, Max, "Snooky Still Has a Song," May 23, 1976). Dinah Shore's details come from Cassiday. Facts about WSM's involvement with the Fisk Jubilee Singers comes from Harry Stone's FCC testimony, 1947, at Vanderbilt University.

George Hay's experience with news wire services comes from Grant Turner's "Grant's Corner" script, March 26, 1987, Gaylord collection.

ALSO CITED:

Our Shield: Apr. 4, 1933; Apr. 18, 1933; Apr. 25, 1933; Jan. 1, 1934; Jan. 8, 1934; Jan. 22, 1934; Feb. 5, 1934; Feb. 12, 1934; Mar. 5, 1934; Mar. 26, 1934; Apr. 2, 1934; Aug. 27, 1934; Oct. 8, 1934; Dec. 10, 1934; Mar. 4, 1935; Aug. 12, 1935; Oct. 28, 1935; Dec. 2, 1935; Jan. 20, 1936; Feb. 3, 1936.

Author interviews: Majorie Kirby, Neil Craig, Les Leverett, Charles Wolfe, Ridley Wills II.
CMF oral histories: Irving Waugh, Jack DeWitt, Vito Pellettieri, David Stone.

Chapter 5: We Must Serve These People Tonight

Details about the National Life building come from the *Home Office Shield,* a company publication (November 1935), as well as Stamper. The news operation is documented in *Shielded Homes* (third quarter 1937). Remote broadcasts come from Shelton and the *Home Office Shield* (April 1938). Details of the flood are found in oral histories by Jack DeWitt (CMF) and Jack Harris, as well as written memoirs by Shelton and Ed Kirby, plus *Our Shield* (Feb. 1, 1937, and Mar. 1, 1937). Also essential is Harry Stone's FCC testimony, 1947, where the teletype transcript was recorded. Regional context came from the *Banner.* Clear channel information comes from Foust and *Broadcasting.* The facsimile experiments are drawn from *Rural Radio* and WSM's FCC license renewal application, June 1939, National Archives. The birth of Broadcast Music Incorporated (BMI) is well covered in Malone, Sanjeck, and Sanjeck, and the CMF book edited by Kingsbury, *Country: The Music and the Musicians.*

ALSO CITED:

Fuqua, Tom, "Radio Weather Forecast as 'Stormy' for Next Five Years." *Tennessean,* July 8, 1934.
"WSM Opens Short-Wave Station." *Rural Radio,* May 1939.

Author interviews: Beverly LeCroy, Marjorie Cooney, Marjorie Kirby, Bill Barry.

Chapter 6: Guts and Brass

A bit of Jack Harris's *Gone with the Wind* coverage can be heard at the *Lost and Found Sound* archives (www.npr.org/programs/lnfsound/stories/001124.wsm.html), and scenes from Atlanta come from Worthy, Larry, "Gone with the Wind Atlanta Premiere," *About North Georgia* (http://ngeorgia.com/feature/gwtwpremiere.html). Background on Jack Stapp comes from the *Atlanta Constitution* (Mar. 13, 1932, and May 29, 1932), the *Sunday American* (Mar. 25, 1934), a WSM bio from the Gaylord archives, and Stapp's two oral history interviews at the CMF (Aug. 8, 1972, and May 14, 1974). Show dates and times are confirmed by ten years of WSM program guides prepared for advertisers, on file in Vanderbilt University's special collections. The *Nashville Times* celebrated WSM on Oct. 15, 1939, and the Opry on Jan. 18, 1940. Owen Bradley material comes from a long interview with Otto Bash and Edward Morris in the *Nashville Musician,* Aug./Sept., 1988, as well as Robert K. Oermann's "In Memory of Owen Bradley" in the *Journal of Country Music,* Broome and Tucker, and Hawkins and Escott. Pietro Brescia was profiled in the *Nashville Times,* Dec. 24, 1939. Episodes of *Mr. Smith Goes to Town* and *Riverboat Revels* was included in Cantrell's *WSM Remembers* radio program, and scripts for *Revels* are on file at Vanderbilt. World War II staff departures and field reporting are documented in Shelton. Jack Harris's oral history informs WSM's news coverage of the war, along with the Harris and Kirby book, *Star-Spangled Radio.* Wartime service is covered in Harry Stone's 1947 FCC testimony, the Rinks dissertation, the DeWitt autobiography, the Shelton memoir, and the WSM application for a *Variety* magazine award, at Vanderbilt special collections.

ALSO CITED:

Harris, Jack, "1939 at WSM in Retrospect." *Shielded Homes,* second quarter, 1940.
Sparks, Jim. "An Interview with Owen Bradley." *Advantage Magazine,* Oct. 1984.
"Band Goes to Wrong Station but Fast Work Puts It on Air." *Banner,* Nov. 27, 1943.

Author interviews: Jud Collins, Ridley Wills, Bill Denny, Irving Waugh.
CMF oral histories: Jack Stapp, Irving Waugh.

Chapter 7: One of Our Boys Shoots the Moon

The section on the Opry's moves references Sherman's history of Union Station, Eiland's history of the Ryman, and Stone's *Who's Who* article. Minnie Pearl's anecdotes come from her autobiography. John Rumble's dissertation is the basis for biographical facts about Fred Rose. Country music history comes from Malone and the *Encyclopedia of Country Music.* Stapp's remark about the music spreading comes from Hemphill. Grant Turner disclosed many biographical details in his "Grant's Corner" commentary scripts, Gaylord files. The origins of *Noontime Neighbors* and John McDonald come from Rinks, Stone's FCC testimony, the *Tennessean* (York, Max, "First Broadcast Almost Ended Career," Oct. 5, 1980.), and a speech by McDonald to BMI ("Building and Holding a Rural Audience," June 25, 1951), on file at LAB. Particulars of DeWitt's moon radar experiment can be found in *Broadcasting,* Jan. 28, 1946; the *Washington Post,* Jan. 27, 1946; the *Philadelphia Inquirer,* Jan. 27, 1946; the *Kansas City Times,* Mar. 18, 1946; DeWitt's autobiography; and "Project Diana" at *www.infoage.org/diana.html.*

ALSO CITED:

"WSM Voluntary Transfer Asked of FCC Follows Pattern of WOW Transaction," *Broadcasting.* Feb. 12, 1945.

Author interviews: Cal Young, Beverly Le Croy, Jud Collins, Neil Craig, Irving Waugh.

Chapter 8: It Helped Everybody in the Long Run

Thoughts on Harry Stone come from the Cherry *R&R* interview with Irving Waugh, Jack DeWitt's CMF oral history, and Cunniff's Jim Denny articles. The journalists' visit is documented in memos and letters archived at Vanderbilt University. The origins of Bullet Records and Castle Recording are covered in Hawkins and Escott, Shelton, and the articles listed below. Numerous records cleared for airplay by Francis Craig (and a few that weren't) are in the collection of Les Leverett. Craig's success with "Near You" is described in detail in Ikard, as well as in Hawkins and Escott. Jack Stapp's CMF oral history is the basis for the Anita Kerr material. The Hank Williams anecdotes comes from Elizabeth Proctor and Escott. Origins of the *Friday Night Frolic* come from CMF oral histories and author interviews with Irving Waugh. David Cobb tells the "Music City" story in a CMF oral history (1983). According to the U.S. Patent and Trademark Office, the first Grand Ole Opry trademark application was filed Jan. 3, 1949, and granted July 11, 1950.

ALSO CITED:

Flans, Robyn, "The History of Nashville Recording." *Mix,* Mar. 1988.

Rumble, John, "The Emergence of Nashville as a Recording Center." *Journal of Country Music,* Vol. 7, No. 3.

Hawkins, Martin, "Bullet Records: A Shot in the Dark." *Journal of Country Music,* Vol. 8, No. 3.

Pugh, Ronnie, and David McCormick, "The Ernest Tubb Record Shops: A Fifty-Year History." Commemorative booklet, May 3, 1997.

"Snooky Lanson Lands Contract on 'Hit Parade.'" *Tennessean.* Sept. 22, 1950.

Author interviews: W. D. Kilpatrick, Bill Denny, Elizabeth Proctor, Les Leverett, Aaron Shelton, Cal Young, Kyle Cantrell, Dick Frank Jr.

CMF oral histories: Irving Waugh, Jack Stapp.

Chapter 9: The Balance of Power Has Shifted

National Life's development of television is sourced in Shelton, DeWitt's Gaylord oral history, the *Tennessean* (July 30, 1948, and May 1, 1949), author interviews with Irving Waugh, the *Home Office Shield* (Aug. 1950), *Our Shield* (Oct. 16, 1950), and Mikelbank, Peter, "On the Air!" *Nashville!* Magazine, March 1985. WSM's morning country shows deserve much more coverage than they get here. Chief sources were program guides in the *Tennessean* and *Banner,* plus Hawkins and Escott and author interviews with Mac Wiseman and Buddy Killen. Carl Smith's recollections come from a speech he made at the CMF. The Mother's Best Flour show with Hank Williams came from Cantrell's *WSM Remembers.* Williams's demise is taken from Escott. Castle Studio's chart history comes from Shelton.

ALSO CITED:

"Harry Stone Will Resign WSM Job." *Nashville Banner,* July 12, 1950.

Author interviews: Eddie Jones, Mac Wiseman, Buddy Killen, Bill Barry, Frances Williams Preston, Jerry Bradley, Elizabeth Proctor.

Chapter 10: *Jack, We Got a Real Problem*

Eddie Hill's quotes and profile come from Teeter, H. B., "Platters and Palaver," the *Nashville Tennessean Magazine*, Jan. 25, 1953. In addition to sitting for an interview, Tom Perryman provided scrapbooks that were invaluable for impressions of the early DJs and the DJ convention. Accounts of the first DJ convention come from Rector, Lee, "Birthday Celebration Spurs Origin of CMA," *Music City News*, Oct. 1979 (revised by Murray Nash), an Eddie Jones *Banner* column from Nov. 19, 1952, and Ferrell, Liz, "Hey, Mister DeeJay," *Inside WSM*, second quarter 2000. WLAC's DJs are described in Hawkins and Escott and in Havighurst, "Change in the Air," *Tennessean*, Nov. 24, 2001. Charlie Lamb's life story comes from Trott and from an interview with the author. The DeWitt moonlighting memo and Denny narrative is drawn from Cunniff, supplemented by the *Country Music Reporter*, Oct. 6, 1956, and Oct. 20, 1956, from the CMF library. The WSM-TV tower accident comes from interviews, plus the *Banner*, Feb. 5, 1957. Webb Pierce's departure is described in the *Tennessean*, Feb. 20, 1957. Ernest Tubb's firearm story is drawn from Pugh, plus the *Tennessean*, May, 28, 1957. The final national date of the Prince Albert Opry is sourced to Dunning and Shapiro. The CMA's formation is documented in the *Music Reporter* (Nov. 10 and 24, 1958) and the *Encyclopedia of Country Music*. Owen Bradley's departure is reported in the *Tennessean* and *Banner*, both on May 14, 1958. The Charlie Lamb benediction quote is from the *Music Reporter*, May 25, 1957.

ALSO CITED:

"Grand Ole Opry Seen Over 130 TV Stations." *Banner*, Oct. 16, 1955.
"Jim Denny Exits Opry." *Country Music Reporter*, Oct. 6, 1956.
Gillis, F. B., "Grand Ole Opry, WSM a Team." *Country and Western Jamboree*, Dec. 1956.
"Jack Stapp Leaves WSM, Buys Firm." *Banner*, June 11, 1957.
"Ott Devine Picked WSM Program Chief." *Banner*, June 14, 1957
"Jimmy Dickens Leaving Opry for Another Show." *Banner*, June 18, 1957.
"Eddie Hill Resigns from Station WSM." *Banner*, Aug. 12, 1957.
Maples, Bill, "Comeback of Country Music Cheered." *Tennessean*, Nov. 16, 1957.
"WSM Brass and Opry Star Reps in Precedent-Shattering Meeting." *Music Reporter*, May 25, 1959.
Anderson, Pat, "Country Music Rise Is Debated." *Tennessean*, Nov. 13, 1959.

Author interviews: Charlie Lamb, Tom Perryman, Mac Wiseman, Frances Williams Preston, Harrianne Moore Condra, Buddy Killen, W. D. Kilpatrick, George Reynolds, Ward DeWitt Jr., Ralph Emery, Jo Walker Meador, Dolores Watson.
CMF oral histories: Irving Waugh, W. D. Kilpatrick.

Chapter 11: A Code and a Concern

The 1960 DJ festival was described in the *Tennessean,* Sept. 25 and Nov. 5, 1960. The Bob Cooper story comes from a Hank Fort oral history with interviewer Edwin Dunham, Jan. 12, 1966, at LAB. Jack DeWitt's scientific pursuits are described in his autobiography, as is the weather satellite episode, supplemented by the *Home Office Shield,* Oct. 1964, and the *Tennessean,* Aug. 31, 1964. DeWitt's relations with the Opry are discussed in his Gaylord oral history. The 1960 WSM promotional brochure is in the Vanderbilt collection, and statistics about Nashville as a recording center come from "A Big New Sound Blows out of Nashville," *Broadcasting,* Jan. 28, 1963. Ralph Emery's autobiography was supplemented by several interviews with the author. Details of WSM's move can be found in the *Banner,* Aug. 13, 1965, and the *Tennessean,* Nov. 25, 1965.

ALSO CITED:

Author interviews: Cal Young, Irving Waugh, Margaret Parker, George Reynolds Jr., Jack Clement, Larry Munson, Ralph Emery, John Seigenthaler, Elmer Alley, Beverly LeCroy, Joe Layne, Teddy Bart, Les Leverett, Ruth White, Kyle Cantrell, Bud Wendell, Elizabeth Proctor.

Chapter 12: The Whole Complex Is a Studio

Life at WSM in the late 1960s and early 1970s is largely based on author interviews, but details of the Opry's move from the Ryman to the Grand Ole Opry House and the building of Opryland are supplemented by Pirtle and Crawford and by stories in the *Tennessean* (Oct. 14, 1969, Sept. 28, 1969, Mar. 21, 1971, Aug. 8, 1971, Jan. 30, 1972) and the *Banner* (July 9, 1971, Nov. 7, 1972, Nov. 28, 1971, Apr. 15, 1981). Bill Carey's business history of Nashville proved especially helpful in keeping track of the large-scale changes at National Life, and his account of the saga of John Jay Hooker and Minnie Pearl's Fried Chicken is a must-read. Entertainers graduating from Opryland to more show business were covered in the *Banner* on June 6 and June 11, 1993. Opryland TV productions were cataloged from the *Tennessean* Oct. 8, 1978 and Nov. 1, 1979. The Nashville Network (TNN) programming was drawn from *Tennesean* stories on Oct. 17, Nov. 28, and Dec. 19, 1982.

ALSO CITED:

Hall, Alan, "Cable Television May Turn Nashville into 'Third Coast' for Producers." *Banner,* Aug. 30, 1981.
Bailey, Greg, "Nashville Network Profits Cheer Chief." *Banner,* Apr. 24, 1987.
Baxter, Emme Nelson, "Opryland 'City' Booming: CEO." *Tennessean,* Dec. 5, 1989.
McCall, Michael, "Critical Year Awaits TNN: Network Fine-Tunes Lineup." *Banner,* Aug. 28, 1989.
Wood, Tom, "Opryland Rapids Await Olympic Hopefuls," *Tennessean,* Nov. 10, 1994.

Author interviews: Ralph Emery, Bud Wendell, Lloyd Wells, Jerry Strobel, Elmer Alley, Beegie Adair, Don Cook, Margaret Ann Robinson, Donia Craig Dickerson, Alan Nelson.

Epilogue: Signal Fade

Key events in the modern history of Gaylord can be found in Carey and a Gaylord timeline at www.gaylordentertainment.com/AboutUs/7.2_AboutUs.htm, as well as numerous stories in the *Tennessean* and the *City Paper*. The *Tennessean* supplement with the WSM "patron" manifesto appeared Oct. 16, 1966. Gaylord's disavowal of the Opryland closure is in an article by Jeanne Naujeck, Aug. 15, 2004. The George Hay quote is from his Opry history.

ALSO CITED:

Author interviews: Bud Wendell, Tom Adkinson, Paul Schatzkin, Lloyd Wells, Kyle Cantrell, Liz Ferrell, Eddie Stubbs.

Bibliography

Books and Monographs

Acuff, Roy. *Roy Acuff's Nashville: The Life and Good Times of Country Music.* New York: Putnam, 1983.

Barnouw, Erik. *A Tower in Babel: A History of Broadcasting in the United States to 1933.* New York: Oxford University Press, 1966.

"Broadcast Pro-File" of WSM prepared for Middle Tennessee State University. Publisher Unknown. Hollywood.

Broome, P. J., and Clay Tucker. *The Other Music City: The Dance Bands and Jazz Musicians of Nashville 1920–1970.* Nashville: Nashville Assn. of Musicians AFM Local 257.

Carey, Bill. *Fortunes, Fiddles & Fried Chicken: A Nashville Business History.* Franklin, Tenn.: Hillsboro Press, 2000.

Cassiday, Bruce. *Dinah! A Biography.* New York: Franklin Watts, 1979.

Cusic, Don. *Eddy Arnold: I'll Hold You in My Heart.* Nashville: Rutledge Hill Press, 1997.

Delmore, Alton, with Charles K. Wolfe, ed. *The Delmore Brothers: Truth Is Stranger Than Publicity.* Nashville: Country Music Foundation Press, 1995.

DeLong, Thomas. *Radio Stars.* New York: McFarland & Co., 1996.

Douglas, Susan. *Inventing American Broadcasting 1899–1922.* Baltimore: Johns Hopkins University Press, 1987.

Douglas, Susan. *Listening In: Radio and the American Imagination.* New York: Times Books, 1999.

Doyle, Don H. *Nashville in the New South, 1880–1930.* Knoxville: University of Tennessee Press, 1985.

Doyle, Don H. *Nashville Since the 1920s.* Knoxville: University of Tennessee Press, 1985.

Dunning, John. *The Encyclopedia of Old Time Radio.* New York: Oxford University Press, 1998.

Eiland, William U. *Nashville's Mother Church: The History of the Ryman Auditorium.* Nashville: Opryland USA Inc., 1992

Emery, Ralph, with Tom Carter. *Memories: The Autobiography of Ralph Emery.* New York: Macmillan, 1991.

Escott, Colin, with George Merritt and William MacEwen. *Hank Williams: The Biography.* New York: Little, Brown, and Co., 1994.

Fisk Jubilee Singers. *In Bright Mansions.* Liner notes, 2003.

Foust, James C. *Big Voices of the Air: The Battle over Clear Channel Radio.* Ames: Iowa State University Press, 2000.

Fox, Herbert. *Reflections: 25 Nights at the Swan Ball.* Nashville: Swan Ball Book Committee. 1989.

Guralnick, Peter. *Last Train to Memphis: The Rise of Elvis Presley.* Boston: Little, Brown, and Co., 1994.

Hall, Wade. *Hell-Bent for Music: The Life of Pee Wee King.* Lexington: University Press of Kentucky, 1996.

Harper, William. *How You Played the Game: The Life of Grantland Rice.* Columbia: University of Missouri Press, 1999.

Hawkins, Martin, and Colin Escott. *A Shot in the Dark: Country Music on Independent Labels, 1945-1955.* Bear Family CD box set, 1999.

Hay, George D. *A Story of the Grand Ole Opry.* Nashville: privately published, 1945.

Hemphill, Paul. *The Nashville Sound: Bright Lights & Country Music.* New York: Simon & Schuster, 1970.

Herr, Kinkaid. *Louisville & Nashville Railroad 1850-1963.* Louisville: L&N Co., 1964.

Hilmes, Michele. *Radio Voices: American Broadcasting, 1922-1952.* Minneapolis: University of Minnesota Press, 1997.

Hurst, Jack. *Nashville's Grand Ole Opry.* New York: H. N. Abrams, 1975.

Ikard, Robert W. *Near You: Francis Craig, Dean of Southern Maestros.* Franklin, Tenn.: Hillsboro Press, 1999.

Killen, Buddy, with Tom Carter. *By the Seat of My Pants: My Life in Country Music.* New York: Simon & Schuster, 1993.

Kingsbury, Paul, ed., *Country: The Music and the Musicians.* New York: Abbeville Press and Country Music Foundation, 1994.

Kingsbury, Paul, ed., *The Encyclopedia of Country Music.* New York: Oxford University Press, 1998.

Kirby, Ed, and Jack Harris. *Star-Spangled Radio.* Chicago: Ziff-Davis Pub. Co., 1948.

Malone, Bill C. *Country Music USA,* Revised ed. Austin: University of Texas Press, 1985.

Millard, Bob. *Country Music: 70 Years of America's Favorite Music.* New York: HarperCollins, 1993.

Morton, David C. and Charles K. Wolfe, *DeFord Bailey: A Black Star in Early Country Music.* Knoxville: University of Tennessee Press, 1991.

Nash, Alanna. *The Colonel: The Extraordinary Story of Colonel Tom Parker and Elvis Presley.* New York: Simon & Schuster, 2003.

Pearl, Minnie, with Joan Dew. *Minnie Pearl: An Autobiography.* New York: Simon and Schuster, 1980.

Peterson, Richard A. *Creating Country Music: Fabricating Authenticity.* Chicago: University of Chicago Press, 1997.

Pirtle, Caleb III, and Gerald Crawford. *The Grandest Day.* Nashville: Opryland U.S.A., 1979.

Pugh, Ronnie. *Ernest Tubb: The Texas Troubadour.* Durham, N.C.: Duke University Press, 1996.

Rinks, Jerry W. *We Shield Millions: A History of WSM 1925–1950.* Ph.D. diss., University of Tennessee, 1993.

Rumble, John Woodruff. *Fred Rose and the Development of the Nashville Music Industry, 1942–1954.* Ph.D. diss., Vanderbilt University, 1980.

Russell, Fred. *Bury Me in an Old Press Box: Good Times and Life of a Sportswriter.* New York: A.S. Barnes and Co., 1957.

Sanjeck, Russell, and David Sanjeck. *The American Popular Music Business in the 20th Century.* Oxford University Press, 1984.

Schlappi, Elizabeth. *Roy Acuff: The Smoky Mountain Boy.* Gretna, Louisiana: Pelican Publishing Co., 1978.

Shapiro, Mitchell E. *Radio Network Prime Time Programming, 1926–1967.* McFarland & Co., 2002.

Shelton, Aaron. Unpublished autobiography, circa 1990.

Sherman, Joe. *A Thousand Voices: The Story of Nashville's Union Station.* Nashville: Rutledge Hill Press, 1987.

Stamper, Powell. *The National Life Story.* New York: Appleton-Century-Crofts, 1968.

Terkel, Studs. *Hard Times: An Oral History of the Great Depression.* New York: Pantheon Books, 1970.

Trott, Walter. *The Country Music World of Charlie Lamb.* Nashville: Infac Publications, 1986.

Wolfe, Charles. *A Good-Natured Riot: The Birth of the Grand Ole Opry.* Nashville: Country Music Foundation Press and Vanderbilt University Press, 1999.

"WSM Remembers." Radio series produced for WSM by Kyle Cantrell, circa 2000.

Articles

Cherry, Hugh. "The R&R Interview: Irving C. Waugh, Country Music's Evolution in Nashville." *R&R.* Jan. 27, 1978.

"Craig, Giant of Insurance Industry, Dies." *Nashville Tennessean.* June 27, 1969.

Cunniff, Albert. "Muscle Behind the Music: The Life and Times of Jim Denny." *Journal of Country Music.* Vol. 11, nos. 1–3.

Hieronymus, Clara. "Edwin Craig Had an Idea Back in '25." *Tennessean*. Oct. 15, 1967.

Peterson, Richard A. "Single-Industry Firm to Conglomerate Synergistics: Alternative Selling Strategies for Selling Insurance and Country Music." Anthologized in *Growing Metropolis: Aspects of Development in Nashville*. Nashville: Vanderbilt University Press, 1975.

Stone, Harry. "Looking Back." *Country Music Who's Who*. Year unknown.

"We Pay Our Respects to Edwin Wilson Craig." *Broadcasting*. Mar. 15, 1936.

Wolfe, Charles K. "The Air Castle of the South: 75 Years of WSM." *Bluegrass Unlimited*. Dec. 2000.

Wolfe, Charles K. WSM chronology prepared for Beth Thompson, Opryland. Feb. 20, 1994.

Wolfe, Charles, K. "The WSM Story." *Inside WSM*. Fourth quarter 2000.

Archives and Collections

Personal papers of John H. DeWitt Jr.

Collected papers of William D. Jackson. Nashville Public Library.

Nashville Banner archive. Nashville Public Library.

Francis Craig Papers. Special Collections Section, Jean and Alexander Heard Library. Vanderbilt University, Nashville.

WSM Radio & TV file. Special Collections Section, Jean and Alexander Heard Library. Vanderbilt University, Nashville.

Gaylord Entertainment archives, Nashville.

Library of American Broadcasting (LAB). University of Maryland, College Park.

Country Music Foundation (CMF), Nashville.

National Archives. College Park, Maryland.

Index of Song Titles

Subject Index

Denny, Bill, 110, 210

Denny, Jim, 180; and Artist Service Bureau, 168–69, 190–93; and birth of Cedarwood Publishing, 172; and Charlie Lamb, 188, 193; clash with Ernest Tubb, 197–98; concession business, 110, 122, 139; fired from WSM, 193; and Hank Williams, 147, 173–74; and Jack Stapp, 152; launches Jim Denny Artist Bureau, 193–94; and music publishing, 203–4; as Opry general manager, 170; Philip Morris show, 197; struggle with Jack DeWitt, 140, 170, 190–93; ties to Opry, 75, 110; youth and career at National Life, 75

Devine, Ottis (Ott), 80, 106, 129, 216, 221, 225; made WSM program director, 199–200; made Opry manager, 204; on premiere of WSM-TV, 165; on *Riverboat Revels,* 112

DeWitt, John H. "Jack," 12, 26; and astronomy, 56–57, 207; and Bud Wendell, 208–9, 235; and classical music, 3, 98, 128; and the Clear Channel Group, 96–97; early years, 2–7; and employee moonlighting, 174; and FM radio, 98–99; and Hank Williams, 147; and Harry Stone, 69, 138–39; and Irving Waugh, 152; issues antimoonlighting memo, 191; and Jim Denny, 139–40, 170, 190–95; Legion of Merit Medal, 137; made president of WSM, Inc., 137; meets George Patton, 114; Project Diana (moon radar experiment), 136–37; relationship with Edwin Craig, 10, 128, 222–23; retires from WSM, 222–23; and shortwave radio, 97–99; superpower testimony before FRC, 42–43; and television, 159–62, 166–68; and television tower, 196–97; tenure and legacy as WSM president, 203, 208–9; and weather satellite images, 207–8; work at Bell Labs and first marriage, 39–40; World War II service, 118, 135–37; as WSM chief engineer, 53; at WSM opening, 15–16; and WSM studio life, 175; and WSM tower, 54, 57;

DeWitt, Ward, 56, 196

Diamond Rio, 233

Dick Tracy Show, 106

Dickens, Little Jimmy, 162, 165, 175, 181, 191, 200, 211

Dill, Danny, 172

Dillard, Dottie, 108, 111, 155; as 1950s staple 185–86; on *Noontime Neighbors* and *The Waking Crew,* 213–14; on WSM-TV, 164–65

Dillon, Dean, 233

DiMaggio, Joe, 166

Disc Jockey Festival (also Country Music Festival or DJ convention), 180–83, 192, 201–2, 205

disc jockeys, 129–30, 149; in emerging country music, 179–185, 205

Dixianas, The, 80

Dixie Dons, The, 112, 125, 154

Dixie Tabernacle (Fatherland St.), 72–75

Dixon, Willie, 155

Does Crime Pay?, 55

Dolly, 234

Dorsey, Tommy, 149

Dot Records, 156, 174, 184, 204

Douglas, Mike, 235

Dreamtime, 186

Driftwood Publishing, 192

Dr. Philologue. *See* Lancaster, Maxwell

Duke of Paducah, The, 143

Dunn, Richard, 107

Durante, Jimmy, 155

Durden, Thomas, 172

Durham, Hal, 220

Dustin, Winston, 143

Duvall, Robert, 241

Dylan, Bob, 210

Earhart, Fannie, 213

Edison, Thomas, 40

Edwards, George "Honeyboy," 49

Eight O'Clock Time, 213

Eisenhower, Dwight, 114

Ellington, Duke, 215

Ellis, William, 5

Emery, Ralph, 185; hired by WSM, 201; on *Opry Star Spotlight,* 217–20; on television, 218; on TNN, 240–41; youth and radio career, 200–201

Ernie's Record Mart, 150

Estes, Milton, 132

Esty Agency, The, 122, 142, 200

Evans Signal Laboratory, 118

Everly Brothers, The, 194

Ewing, Skip, 233

Excello Records, 184

Exum, Fred "Pop," 27–28

Fairfield Four, The, xv, 155

Fan Fair (CMA Music Festival), 231–32

Farm Aid, 241

Farm and Home Program, 37

Farnsworth, Philo, 159

Featuring Francis Craig, 149

Federal Communications Commission (FCC), 35, 85, 99, 160–61

Federal Radio Commission (FRC), 35, 41, 52, 53

Ferrer, Jose, 174

Fibber McGee & Molly, 86

Ward, J. Truman, 29, 183

Ward, Rebekah Williams, 2

Ward-Belmont School, 1–2, 5, 30, 43, 47, 51–52, 161, 84

War Memorial Auditorium, xv, 28, 43, 89–90, 107, 119

Watson, Dolores, 154, 177, 185–86, 213–14

Waugh, Irving, 69; at DJ convention, 181; and D. Kilpatrick, 194; early career 116–17; and Jack DeWitt, 206; move to ad sales and WSM management, 152; and management crisis of 1957, 198–89; as president of WSM, 224–29; promoting WSM, 176–77; and Ralph Emery, 219; and television, 160, 206; World War II service/news coverage, 132–35

WBAP (Dallas/Fort Worth), 10, 46, 97

WBAW (Nashville), 26–27, 36

WBPA (portable transmitter), 91

WBT (Charlotte), 52, 86

WCBQ (Nashville), 6, 21, 24, 26

WCKY (Cincinnati), 183

WDAA (Nashville), 2, 5

WDAD (Nashville), 24, 25, 27, 28,

WEAF (New York), 4, 29–30, 41

Weaver, Bill, 206, 222, 224, 229, 239

Wednesday Midnighter, The (show), 82

Wells, Kitty, 174, 180, 194

Wells, Lloyd, 233

Wendell, E. W. "Bud": in cable television and TNN, 235–36, 240–43, 244; made Opry manager, 225–26; put in charge of Opryland, 232; takes first job at WSM, 208–9

West, Madge, 55, 60, 66, 76

Westinghouse, 29, 35, 39, 245

WFAA (Dallas/Fort Worth), 97

W4XA (WSM classical shortwave), 98–99

W47NV (WSM classical FM), 99, 126–27

WGN (Chicago), 48, 97

WGST (Atlanta), 105

WHAS (Louisville), 86, 93, 140

Wheeling Jamboree, The, 86

White, George L., 83

White, Lee Roy *Lasses,* 49

Whiteman, Paul, 80, 149

Whiting, Margaret, 148

Whitley, Keith, 225

Whitley, Ray, 125

Whitman, Slim, 180

WHN (New York), 86

Wilburn Brothers, The (Teddy and Doyle), 218, 228

Wildhorse Saloon, The, 243

Wilds, Lee Davis "Honey," 49

Williams, Bill, 197–98, 213

Williams, Don, 242

Williams, Hank, xiv, 63, 151, 163, 180, 186, 225; fired from Opry and death, 173–74; recording at Castle, 146–47

Wills, Bob, 85, 126

Wills, Jesse, 23

Wills, Ridley, 10, 11, 17, 65, 66, 78

Wills, Ridley II, 8, 238

Wilson County Fair, 27, 110

Wise, Chubby, 141, 163

Wiseman, Mac, 163, 174, 178, 210

WJZ (New York), 30, 41

WKDA (Nashville), 179, 199

WKEU (Griffin, GA), 150

WLAC (Nashville), 33, 45, 76, 144, 152; disc jockeys and rhythm and blues, 183–85, 195; hires Irving Waugh, 116; hiring Owen Bradley away from, 111; origins of, 29; and television, 195

WLAC-TV, 207

WLS (Chicago), 9, 15, 86, 97, 140

WLW (Cincinnati), 96

WMAK (Nashville), 179

WMAQ (Chicago), 48

WMC (Memphis), 9, 11, 17, 20, 77

WNOX (Knoxville), 50

WOAN (Lawrenceburg), 11

Wolever, Jack, 120

Wood, Del, 156

Wood, Randy, 156, 174

Work, John, 51, 82

World in Review, The, 76 112

World Series, 18, 166

Wormwood Forest, 155

WREC, (Memphis), 154

WRVA (Richmond), 86

WSB (Atlanta), 10, 12, 97

WSGN (Birmingham), 116

WSIX (Nashville), 120, 195, 198, 200

WSM: "Air Castle of the South" slogan, 83–84; African Americans and, 48–51; announcing staff, 106–7; Artist Service Bureau, 73, 100, 115, 139–40, 144, 152, 154, 168–70, 181, 189; benefits from World War II, 123; call letters, 13; children's shows,19–20, 155; classical music, 98–99; commercial sales, 42, 47, 160; coverage of 1937 flood, 92–95; coverage of World War II, 133–35; and disc jockeys, 178–85; dramatic shows, 55; early morning country music shows, 147; ensemble variety shows, 67; facsimile broadcasting, 97–98; fan mail, 41, 43, 49, 78; farm/rural broadcasting, 130–32; and 50kw, 41–43, 52–53, 59–60; first anniversary,

28–29; first staff orchestra, 38; first studio, 13–14; first transmitter, 12; formation of WSM, Inc., 137; identity as country music station, 153, 158; impact on Nashville music business; 43, 106, 154, 246–47; interference problem, 29, 34–36; live remote broadcasts, 37, 91–95, 119; investment in, 29, 38, 42; management, 47–48; moves out of National Life Home Office, 221–22; moves to near Opryland Hotel, 237; move to 5,000 watts and 650 signal, 36; named Variety radio station of the year, 175–76; National Life vision for, 12–13; and NBC, 30, 37, 44, 48, 53, 60, 73, 80, 82–83, 91, 98, 105, 108, 111, 119, 130, 155, 177; news broadcasting, 76, 112–14, 117; news coverage in the 1960s, 215–17, 220; offices in the 1950s, 189; opening night, 14–17; origins of, 9–12; Pan American broadcasts, 61–65, 91–92; political coverage, 48; power struggle of the 1950s, 190–93; programming in the 1920s, 28; programming in the 1930s, 42, 45–51, 55, 66–68; programming in the 1940s, 154–55; programming in the 1950s, 185–86; promotion and publicity, 141–44, 181; proposed format change in 2002, 247–49; public service in World War II, 113–15, 117–20; pursuit by CBS, 106–7; radio tower/transmitter, 52–54, 56–59, 61; reach of signal, 41; religious broadcasting, 70, 217; and rhythm and blues/rock and roll, 185–86; rural/farm service, 43; shortwave and FM broadcasting, 98–99, 176, 225; sound effects, 81, 111; sponsored shows, 36–37, 54, 152; sports broadcasting, 18–19, 42, 81, 117; stature, 74, 76, 105, 117, 127, 199, 220–21; studio audience, 70–71; Studio C, 70–71, 108, 132, 149, 154, 221; studios, 55–56, 89; "superpower" application (500 kw), 123; syndicated shows, 78; as webcaster, 249; women on, 19–20, 95–96

WSM-FM, xiv, 225, 249

WSM Hollywood Show, The, 80

WSM-TV, 159–62, 164–68, 189–90, 199–200; and country music syndicated shows, 228; and Elmer Alley, 227–28; and John McDonald, 212; and Ralph Emery, 218–19; sale to Gillett Broadcasting, 237; tower construction and disaster, 195–97; and weather satellite premiere, 207–8

WWJ (Detroit), 10

WWVA (Wheeling, WV), 86

Wynette, Tammy, 234, 240

Yoakam, Dwight, 242

Young, Cal, 126–27, 150

Young, Faron, 175, 194

Your Hit Parade, xv, 150, 185

Zworkin, Vladimir, 159

CRAIG HAVIGHURST is an independent writer and producer based in Nashville. A former music critic and business writer for the *Tennessean,* he now reports for public radio and writes for print and television. As a freelancer, Havighurst has contributed to the *Oxford American, Entertainment Weekly,* the *Wall Street Journal, Acoustic Guitar, No Depression,* and numerous other national publications. His short documentary on the history of WSM radio for Nashville Public Television won a regional Emmy Award. In addition, he was the recipient of the 2004 Charlie Lamb Award for Excellence in Country Music Journalism. His production company, String Theory Media, specializes in documentaries about music and musicians.

Music in American Life

"Happy in the Service of the Lord": Afro-American Gospel Quartets in Memphis
    Kip Lornell

Paul Hindemith in the United States   *Luther Noss*

"My Song Is My Weapon": People's Songs, American Communism, and the Politics of
    Culture, 1930–50   *Robbie Lieberman*

Chosen Voices: The Story of the American Cantorate   *Mark Slobin*

Theodore Thomas: America's Conductor and Builder of Orchestras, 1835–1905
    Ezra Schabas

"The Whorehouse Bells Were Ringing" and Other Songs Cowboys Sing   *Guy Logsdon*

Crazeology: The Autobiography of a Chicago Jazzman   *Bud Freeman, as Told to
    Robert Wolf*

Discoursing Sweet Music: Brass Bands and Community Life in Turn-of-the-Century
    Pennsylvania   *Kenneth Kreitner*

Mormonism and Music: A History   *Michael Hicks*

Voices of the Jazz Age: Profiles of Eight Vintage Jazzmen   *Chip Deffaa*

Pickin' on Peachtree: A History of Country Music in Atlanta, Georgia   *Wayne W. Daniel*

Bitter Music: Collected Journals, Essays, Introductions, and Librettos   *Harry Partch;
    edited by Thomas McGeary*

Ethnic Music on Records: A Discography of Ethnic Recordings Produced in the United
    States, 1893 to 1942   *Richard K. Spottswood*

Downhome Blues Lyrics: An Anthology from the Post–World War II Era   *Jeff Todd Titon*

Ellington: The Early Years   *Mark Tucker*

Chicago Soul   *Robert Pruter*

That Half-Barbaric Twang: The Banjo in American Popular Culture   *Karen Linn*

Hot Man: The Life of Art Hodes   *Art Hodes and Chadwick Hansen*

The Erotic Muse: American Bawdy Songs (2d ed.)   *Ed Cray*

Barrio Rhythm: Mexican American Music in Los Angeles   *Steven Loza*

The Creation of Jazz: Music, Race, and Culture in Urban America   *Burton W. Peretti*

Charles Martin Loeffler: A Life Apart in Music   *Ellen Knight*

Club Date Musicians: Playing the New York Party Circuit   *Bruce A. MacLeod*

Opera on the Road: Traveling Opera Troupes in the United States, 1825–60
    Katherine K. Preston

The Stonemans: An Appalachian Family and the Music That Shaped Their Lives
    Ivan M. Tribe

Transforming Tradition: Folk Music Revivals Examined   *Edited by Neil V. Rosenberg*

The Crooked Stovepipe: Athapaskan Fiddle Music and Square Dancing in Northeast Alaska
    and Northwest Canada   *Craig Mishler*

Traveling the High Way Home: Ralph Stanley and the World of Traditional Bluegrass Music
    John Wright

Carl Ruggles: Composer, Painter, and Storyteller   *Marilyn Ziffrin*

Never without a Song: The Years and Songs of Jennie Devlin, 1865–1952
    Katharine D. Newman

The Hank Snow Story   *Hank Snow, with Jack Ownbey and Bob Burris*

The University of Illinois Press
is a founding member of the
Association of American University Presses.

Composed in 11/14 Bulmer
with Smokler display
by Jim Proefrock
at the University of Illinois Press
Designed by Paula Newcomb
Manufactured by Thomson-Shore, Inc.

University of Illinois Press
1325 South Oak Street
Champaign, IL 61820-6903
www.press.uillinois.edu